DUDICK
on
Manufacturing Cost Controls

Thomas S. Dudick

Prentice-Hall, Inc.   Englewood Cliffs, New Jersey

Prentice-Hall International, Inc., *London*
Prentice-Hall of Australia, Pty. Ltd., *Sydney*
Prentice-Hall Canada Inc., *Toronto*
Prentice-Hall of India Private Ltd., *New Delhi*
Prentice-Hall of Japan, Inc., *Tokyo*
Prentice-Hall of Southeast Asia Pte. Ltd., *Singapore*
Whitehall Books, Ltd., *Wellington, New Zealand*
Editora Prentice-Hall do Brasil, Ltda., *Rio de Janeiro*

© 1985 by
Prentice-Hall, Inc.
Englewood Cliffs, N.J.

Library of Congress Cataloging in Publication Data

Dudick, Thomas S.
  Dudick on manufacturing cost controls.

  Includes index.
  1. Cost control. 2. Costs, Industrial.
I. Title. II. Title: Manufacturing cost controls.
TS165.D83 1985   658.1'552   84-15090

ISBN 0-13-220971-3

Printed in the United States of America

The
Author

Thomas S. Dudick is consultant to Ernst & Whinney in cost systems, product costing, pricing, manufacturing cost, and operating controls. He has served as budget director, plant controller, and internal consultant for GTE-Sylvania, Allen B. DuMont Laboratories, and Raytheon Company.

His educational background includes a B.S. degree from New York University and an M.B.A. from Boston University. He has been guest lecturer at Boston University, Loyola College, Harvard Business School, and the China Enterprise Management Association in Peking, China, where he participated in seminars given to key industrial executives from all parts of China.

He is the author of *Cost Controls for Industry* (Prentice-Hall), which has been translated into Portuguese; *Profile for Profitability, How to Improve Profitability Through More Effective Business Planning,* and coauthor of *Inventory Control for the Financial Executive* (all three by John Wiley); and editor-in-chief of the *Handbook for Business Planning and Budgeting for the Executive with Profit Responsibility* (Van Nostrand Reinhold).

To my wife, Ann

Foreword

Effective, systematized cost control measures are critical for any management team intent on increasing profits. At one time, profitability was viewed by many as largely a function of technological advance or product innovation. Those are key factors; however, their bearing on profits depends in large measure on how effectively and economically they are applied. This requires effective cost control and, in turn, accurate cost information. In addition, it is important to select the cost control system best suited to the individual organization's needs and circumstances. Selecting and implementing a suitable cost control system can be challenging.

Companies that refine their methods for controlling the costs of manufacturing their products will be better positioned to improve their profit margin and increase their growth in the marketplace. In this book, the author offers counsel on how that process can be carried out most expeditiously and productively. Especially valuable in this book, then, is a detailed analysis of job costing, process costing, actual costing, direct versus full costing, and standard costing.

How successful the management team is in implementing the system that has been selected depends on how well the team understands and applies modern control methods of product management. To help with success in this area, the book includes a thorough analysis of the interface between computerized cost accounting and inventory management. The need to develop accurate overhead costing rates and a flexible budget formula is clarified.

An extensive background is provided to equip the reader for the next important step in cost control management—the actual costing and pricing of products to increase profits. Of particular value here is the book's analysis of various product costing and pricing methods, and its discussion of external factors and internal strategies which affect costs and prices. In any highly competitive market, proper pricing unquestionably should provide an incentive for response by the customer as well as providing an acceptable return for the manufacturer. In addition, the information contained in a cost control system gives management the tools it needs to investigate the company's overall operating performance.

Next, the author discusses methods for analyzing financial results and reviews in depth the special reporting, coordinating, and controlling techniques for operating a business. Mr. Dudick emphasizes the need for information detailed enough to provide the flexibility to discover problem areas, yet broad enough not to become burdensome and expensive.

The book is addressed to all levels of management who share the responsibility for cost effectiveness and profit planning and administration. The author provides detailed analyses of reliable techniques that have proven successful for other companies, and presents new ideas that can be adopted and tailored to the reader's line of business. Thomas S. Dudick is to be congratulated on his comprehensive treatment of a difficult subject. This volume can be a basic guide and useful reference for anyone interested in refining manufacturing operations and developing effective marketing strategies with a view toward improving profits.

RAY J. GROVES
CHAIRMAN AND CHIEF EXECUTIVE
ERNST & WHINNEY

How This Book Will Multiply Company Profits and Personal Reward

The book presents fresh approaches, tested tools and techniques, growing out of real-world situations experienced in using the appropriate costing system for costing and pricing products as well as maximizing profits and controlling costs.

One need only scan the table of contents to appreciate the practical value of this book. Additionally, the contents can be used to good advantage in conducting in-house training. Divided into the following three sections, this action guide provides answers in three critical areas:

- Cost systems to fit management needs for control
- Costing and pricing products to maximize profits
- Analyzing and reporting financial results

Select case examples, carefully researched from the actual experience of well-known, successful companies (names disguised), buttress and illustrate new solutions to problems step-by-step.

The book covers the following 85 Firing-Line Answers chapter by chapter, adding up to a dynamic, proven program for manufacturing cost control you can adapt to your situation.

85 FIRING-LINE ANSWERS IN THIS BOOK

1. Manufacturing costs can run higher than 80 percent of sales revenues. Factory managers are frequently frustrated because they are inundated with "reams" of reports on direct labor, the smallest of the three elements of manufacturing cost, but receive virtually no information on material usage, the largest of the three. Chapter 1.

2. See a recommended format for an overview report of manufacturing costs that breaks down the three elements and lists the expenses within these elements. Chapter 1; Exhibit 1-3.

3. How a make versus buy decision went sour in the Alcor Division of a large company. Lesson to be learned. Chapter 1.

4. There are only two basic cost systems: job costing and process costing. These can be modified through use of options, but the basics remain the same. Chapter 1; Exhibit 1-5.

5. See Exhibit 1-6 for the key features of the two basic cost systems and their variations. Chapter 1.

The 85 Firing-Line Answers address themselves to questions asked each day by thousands of executives with responsibility for profits. These executives, under constant pressure to produce a good return on investment, are not interested in theory—they need real-world answers to real-world problems. It is the belief of the author that this book fulfills these needs.

Thomas S. Dudick

Contents

SECTION I

Cost Systems to Fit Management
Needs for Control

1

Associating Costs with Manufacturing Processes and Products

Chapter 1 provides nonfinancial executives with an overview of the accounting treatment of the three elements of cost as well as the segments making up each of these three elements. It explains under what conditions certain items, which are treated as overhead in process costing (repetitive production), would be treated as material or as direct labor in job costing. Also shown in this chapter is a diagrammatic flow of production costs through the work-in-process and the finished goods inventories when job costing is used and when process costing is used.

Another purpose of this chapter is to clear up a common misunderstanding of cost system interrelationships. Many are of the impression that there are a number of unique cost systems. Actually, there are two basic cost systems—job costing and process costing—to which different options are applied. This is much like purchasing a basic car with either a manual or automatic shift.

GIVE MANAGEMENT FULL VISIBILITY
OF THE THREE COST ELEMENTS

Although manufacturing cost is the major portion of product cost (see Exhibit 1–1, Breakdown of Total Product Cost), most factory managers are rarely provided with a breakdown of the manufacturing costs in a convenient summary form so they can obtain a proper perspective of the operations for which they are responsible (see Exhibit 1–3, Overview of Manufacturing Costs).

The factory manager is frequently inundated with the mass of detail prepared for direct labor—by far, the smallest of the three elements of factory cost. The reason is that the underlying paperwork used for payroll preparation lends itself readily to classification by employee, by shift, by shop order, by work station, by operation number, by the amount of time required to perform each operation, and the like. The computer is a "natural" for presenting such information in almost every conceivable combination in such massive detail that the users are frequently overwhelmed by the output of such information for the smallest of the three elements.

Material, on the other hand, which frequently accounts for a larger segment of manufacturing cost than direct labor and overhead combined, receives very little detailed analysis that the size of this element warrants. Such an analysis includes details that are usually accumulated in broad figures on cost-accounting worksheets that rarely "see the light of day" once the monthly closing is completed. How greater visibility can be given to material flow through the process (as well as direct labor and overhead) will be illustrated in Chapter 8, Computerized Cost Accounting (Inventory Management Interface). This chapter will illustrate process by process by inventory category how one company accumulates the three elements of cost.

Manufacturing Costs Can Account for More Than 80 Percent of Sales

This can be illustrated by several divisions of a major company that is rank ordered between 100 and 125 in the *Forbes* roster of the United States' biggest corporations. This company has sales exceeding $3 billion (see Table 1–1).

	($000 Omitted)							
	Division A		Division B		Division C		Division D	
Sales	$104,938	100.0%	12,089	100.0%	21,528	100.0%	14,245	100.0%
Manufacturing cost of sales	91,000	86.7	10,588	87.6	18,506	86.0	11,810	82.9
Gross margin	13,938	13.3	1,501	12.4	3,022	14.0	2,435	17.1

TABLE 1–1

A key executive of this company advised that he had asked the corporate controller why it wasn't possible to obtain a breakdown of manufacturing costs but was told that in the interest of simplification the present system merged the three elements as they moved through the cost system. He expressed the hope that the planned program of computerization would provide for the separation of the three elements—a rather vague response.

A review of Polaroid's manufacturing cost of sales for the ten-year period* 1971 through 1980 shows a lower cost of sales to sales percentage than in the preceding example. However, the percentage for Polaroid jumped from 46 percent for 1971–72 to 61 percent for 1979–80. Two years were taken at both ends of the decade to avoid the influence of a single, unusually low or high figure. A breakdown by accounting period in such a situation would show the trend of each of the three elements.

A breakdown into the three elements of the manufacturing cost of production will not, in itself, pinpoint the reason for increased manufacturing costs. It will, however, raise important questions, the answers to which can be highly productive. The following checklist is illustrative of some of the questions that might be asked.

---

*Source: Annual Reports.

CHECKLIST FOR STEPS IN REDUCING
THE THREE ELEMENTS OF COST

MATERIAL

Is the purchasing department obtaining three bids for major items before purchasing?

Are blanket orders issued by the purchasing department to obtain the benefits of volume purchases?

Is the ordering lead time sufficient to assure that shipments are made by the most economical means?

Are production losses and customer returns being reviewed carefully to reduce such losses to a minimum?

Does the engineering department review product design to determine if costs can be reduced by standardization of components or use of substitute material?

DIRECT LABOR

Are the workplaces efficiently laid out?

Is there an efficient routing of work through the various processes?

Are materials and parts at the workplace being replenished regularly to avoid downtime due to "waiting for material"?

Is the tooling issued out of the tool crib always sharp to minimize downtime and production losses?

Are production orders sequenced properly to minimize need for frequent changeovers?

Are automated machines used wherever possible to reduce labor costs?

OVERHEAD

Are preventive maintenance procedures being followed regularly to eliminate expensive breakdowns?

In multiplant companies, are operations such as plating (which requires expensive water treatment facilities) consolidated to reduce high investment in costly facilities?

Are fabricating operations such as metal forming, molding, and die casting, consolidated as much as possible to take advantage of specialization and reduction of investment in equipment?

Are such functions as painting, cleaning, and security contracted out to minimize costs of such services?

BREAKDOWN OF TOTAL PRODUCT COST BY MAJOR CATEGORIES

Exhibit 1–1 illustrates the buildup of total product costs—both manufacturing and nonmanufacturing. This is shown in the four columns identified as A, B, C, and D.

The Three Elements of Manufacturing Cost (Column A)

In medieval times and during the early years of the Industrial Revolution, overhead expenses were small and were not recognized as an element of cost, as were direct labor and material. Direct labor plus material were called *prime cost.* Many companies priced their products by doubling prime cost. This provided for profit and those costs that we now refer to as overhead or indirect costs. As the Industrial Revolution progressed and overhead became larger, it was recognized as the third element of cost. The distinction as to which costs are material, direct labor, or overhead is not always clear-cut for the following reasons.

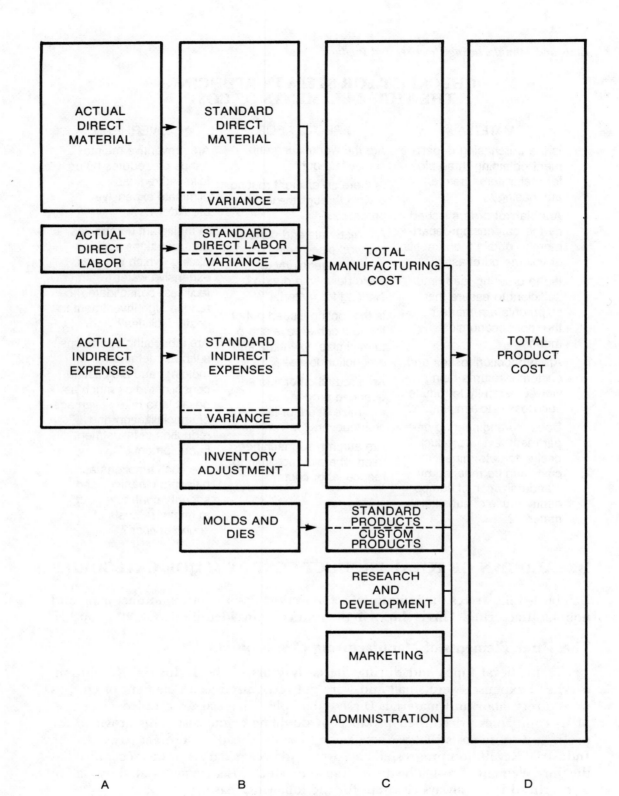

EXHIBIT 1–1:
BREAKDOWN OF TOTAL PRODUCT COST

6

Material. In most cost accounting systems, items of relatively small material cost are considered to be supplies in the overhead category. This is a perfectly acceptable practice for nuts that cost only five cents each, for gasket material that costs only a few cents a sheet, and for welding material whose cost is likewise small. However, when a company that manufactures industrial valves used to control the flow of liquids begins to produce similar valves for use in nuclear plants, the "small" items such as nuts, gasket materials, and welding rods can aggregate as much as $1500 per valve. Obviously, these items must now be reclassified as material and the costs associated directly with the valves on which they are used. If this is not done and the above items are left in overhead, the industrial valves would be overcosted and the nuclear-type valves would be undercosted.

Direct Labor. A similar situation occurs in direct labor. For industrial-type valves, rework costs are relatively minor because sandholes in the casting are not dangerous. However, when the same type of valve is built to nuclear specifications, a substantial amount of rework is required in gouging out the sandholes, welding, grinding, hand dressing, X-raying, heat treating, and inspecting. These costs, rather than being charged to overhead and allocated to both types of valves through an overhead rate, must, as in the case of material, be charged directly to the nuclear valves.

Overhead. The increased use of fully automated machines (including robots), which require no direct labor attention, mandates the use of machine hours as a basis for applying overhead to the product. Surprisingly, a number of financial executives in highly sophisticated companies still use direct labor as a base for application of overhead to products through a single plantwide overhead rate. The obvious result is that products spending little or no time on the fully automated equipment are overcharged, while the others that utilize the equipment are undercharged.

BREAKDOWN OF THE THREE ELEMENTS BY "STANDARD" AND "VARIANCE" (COLUMN B)

Exhibit 1–1 shows each of the three elements of actual cost broken down between the standard (allowable) portion and the variance from standard—the sum of the two being equal to the total actual cost.

Inventory Adjustments. When standard costs are used, the product is usually of a standard type with interchangeable parts that are built to stock. It is therefore likely that inventory adjustments would be required to record valuation adjustments when the standards are changed (usually annually), when losses through obsolescence are incurred, and when differences are found between the book values and the values based on the actual physical units determined by the annual physical inventory.

Mold and Die Costs (Tooling). Tooling used on a customized product being made for a specific customer is usually the property of the customer and is billed with the first run of parts shipped to him. For standard products, tooling becomes part of overhead but it can be applied to the product by two methods:

- The entire amount of tooling cost can be assigned to the department using the tools and charged to the product through the departmental overhead rate.
- When the costs of the individual tools vary quite widely, an amortization cost per unit would be charged to the specific product on which the tool (or tools) are used. The unit cost would be based on the cost of the tool divided by the estimated number of units to be produced.

Total Manufacturing Cost (Column C). This consists of the three elements of manufacturing costs already covered.

Research and Development (Engineering). This category includes research on new products and manufacturing processes, as distinguished from engineering conducted in the factory on existing products and processes.

Marketing. This category includes sales, advertising, promotion, and distribution. These include such items as salaries, occupancy costs, fees to advertising agencies, and office-related expenses.

Administration. Administration covers corporate office expenses such as salaries of officers, office staff, related occupancy costs, and other office expenses. Administration is frequently referred to as "general and administrative."

Total Product Cost

All of the cost categories shown in column C add up to the total product cost shown in column D.

Exhibit 1–1 portrays a medium-size company with several manufacturing plants reporting to a corporate office. An example would be a company making light bulbs of various types. There are three plants—

- Plant 1–A highly automated plant that makes the high volume, popular-size incandescent light bulbs.
- Plant 2–Another incandescent lamp plant making the more specialized types—such as street lights, railroad headlights, and decorative lights.
- Plant 3–A highly automated plant making fluorescent lamps.

These three plants, each headed by a plant manager, report to the corporate office which furnishes such corporate services as research, marketing, finance, legal services, and those other services that are more efficiently performed centrally.

In larger companies with more varied product lines, the manufacturing plants would be grouped into divisions headed by vice-presidents (or division presidents) who report to corporate headquarters. This can be shown in a highly simplified example in which the lamp manufacturing company expands into two divisions. The new division produces television picture tubes and display tubes used in computer terminals.

It is likely that most of the research and development would be transferred to the division headquarters so that each of the two divisions does its own research. The same would apply to marketing, since sales would be made to different markets. Some of the administration would also be transferred to the divisions. The guidelines as to how much of the corporate functions would be transferred will vary by company.

VARIATIONS IN MANUFACTURING AND NON-MANUFACTURING COSTS IN PRODUCT COSTING

In the preceding discussion of the breakdown of total product cost, only the categories were dealt with. No attempt was made to determine the relative size of the various categories in total product cost. Since the size of the categories varies from industry to industry, it is important that we consider this factor.

Comparison of Six Industries

The figures in Table 1–2 illustrate such a comparison for six different products. The same categories of cost used in Exhibit 1–1 are shown here as a percentage of total sales. Since percentage of sales is used as the base, the profit (operating income) is also included.

	Cosmetics	Word-Processing Equipment	Pharma-ceuticals	Consumer Products	Industrial Valves	Motor Vehicles 1980	Vehicles 1979
Manufacturing cost of sales*	37%	44%	45%	72%	74%	97%	89%
R&D, marketing, and administra-tion**	46	43	42	21	20	5	4
Operating income	17	13	13	7	6	(2)	7
Total	100%	100%	100%	100%	100%	100%	100%

*Includes depreciation and amortization of tools, where applicable.
**Combined because all companies did not break these figures down.
Note: The above figures are based on a selected company rather than an entire industry. Two years were selected for motor vehicles to show one profitable and one unprofitable year.

TABLE 1–2
ABBREVIATED INCOME STATEMENT

Note that nonmanufacturing costs for the first three industries range from 42 percent for pharmaceuticals to 46 percent of total sales for cosmetics. Consumer products and industrial valves require about 20 percent of the sales dollar for these items, while in the automobile company, in 1979, this figure was 4 percent. There are two factors to be considered in the application of nonmanufacturing costs to products:

- Nonmanufacturing costs should be applied individually—i.e., R&D, marketing, and administration. A well-established product line, or variations thereof, will have little or no R&D requirement—and probably much less marketing expense than a newly developed product. Administration, on the other hand, might be just as large as ever.
- When a company's product-line mix crosses industry lines, it is entirely possible that the percentages of nonmanufacturing costs may be different for different products. Many companies, however, overlook such differences and make the application of such costs on an overall basis. In the process of cost-estimating products for pricing or preparation of product-line income statements, it is entirely possible that incorrect conclusions could be formed from this approach.

Although this book is directed toward manufacturing cost control, potential costing errors such as the foregoing cannot be overlooked. This subject will be covered further in a later section.

EFFECT OF OPERATIONAL DIFFERENCES ON MANUFACTURING COST BREAKDOWN

The previous section broke down the total product cost by major categories—i.e., manufacturing, research and development (engineering), marketing, and administration. Manufacturing cost was broken down in column A into its three basic elements—material, direct labor, and overhead.

This section breaks down actual manufacturing cost to reflect the cost breakdown of four types of manufacturing operations. Exhibit 1–2 shows this in two steps:

- Cost breakdown of the three elements of cost.
- Cost breakdown of the major items in overhead.

Percentage Breakdown of the Three Elements of Cost

This breakdown is shown in the upper portion of the exhibit. The percentages of total manufacturing cost represented by material, direct labor, and overhead are shown for four different types of manufacturing operations.

Highly Labor-Paced Operations. These operations include machine shop work and finishing operations such as grinding, polishing, and assembly. Typical products would be machinery, valves, and turbines.

The percentage of material to total manufacturing cost is 30 percent, the smallest percentage for the four types of operations shown. The predominant material used by companies in this category is steel, while the other categories use more expensive materials in addition to steel. At 24 percent, direct labor accounts for the highest percentage for the four operations, while overhead is about double that of direct labor.

	(1) HIGHLY LABOR-PACED (3 COMPANIES)	(2) AUTOMATIC EQUIPMENT HIGHLY MACHINE-PACED (1 COMPANY)	(3) PRODUCT WITH HIGH MATERIAL CONTENT (2 COMPANIES)	(4) COMPOSITE OF COLUMNS 1, 2, 3 IN ONE COMPANY
Direct material	30%	59%	72%	62%
Direct labor	24	5	8	13
Overhead	46	36	20	25
Manufacturing Cost	100%	100%	100%	100%
Breakdown of Overhead				
Indirect labor and fringe benefits	60%	47%	65%	45%
Maintenance labor and repair material	7	17	4	14
Depreciation	5	12	4	13
Occupancy costs	6	7	10	6
All other (1)	22	17	17	22
Total Overhead	100%	100%	100%	100%
Number of items in "All other" (1)	26	23	18	16

**EXHIBIT 1–2:
BREAKDOWN OF MANUFACTURING COSTS FOR FOUR DIFFERENT TYPES OF OPERATIONS**

Case Example

The Harpor Company is a privately owned company that manufactures metal parts made of steel and brass and molded parts made of plastics. Much to his surprise, Mr. Harpor discovered that his company's pretax profit of 8.2 percent of sales was lower than that of similar companies in the industry. The 8.2 percent compared with 12.2 percent earned by competitors in the same type of manufacture. In the past, Harpor's accountant had suggested that the company become a member of the trade association. This would provide the company with cost data for the industry as well as an opportunity to meet with counterpart management executives at periodic conferences where problems are discussed.

Harpor had always played his cards close to the vest. He was reluctant to disclose his methods and successes to competitors. Now, however, with a pretax profit of 8.2 percent (less than 4 percent after taxes), Harpor was more than willing to participate. He became a member and planned to attend the upcoming conference.

The latest industry figures, which were distributed at the conference, showed that the past five years of pretax earnings had been higher than Harpor's. They were: 10.4, 9.5, 9.8, 12.3, and 12.2 percent.

In pursuing the analysis further, Harpor found that he was out of line on direct labor. His labor cost was 14 percent of sales (22 percent of manufacturing cost—highly labor-paced) compared with industry figures of 13.8, 12.1, 12.6, 9.1, and 9.0 percent for the current year. The industry had obviously made some important cost reductions in the past two years.

Harpor decided that he had been a loner long enough. He discussed his problems of high labor quite openly. The competitors were open as to how they had accomplished a reduction from 13.8 percent five years ago to 9.0 percent in the current year. Their answer was that they replaced certain manually operated equipment with fully automatic machines. Also, on the high-volume items, they substituted progressive dies for single-operation tooling. This confirmed Harpor's suspicion that he had been penny-wise and pound-foolish when he insisted on holding onto equipment and tooling because they were in good condition—not taking into account the savings of new automated equipment and better tooling. He reversed his previous false economy hangups and went into progressive automation with deliberate speed. In eighteen months, the Harpor Company's pretax profit became slightly higher than the average for the industry. Harpor anticipated that when his program for automation was complete in six months he would increase his profit further by about 25 percent.

As a small- to medium-size company, Harpor is not alone. Many small divisions of large companies also live or have lived within a cocoon, remaining oblivious to what is going on in the real world of competition. Trade associations are not the only answer. Industry trade magazines can be very helpful, but they must be read seriously rather than accumulating in bookcases. Likewise, seminars can be helpful because they bring together the executives of related industries, as well as the unrelated. Here again, attending seminars should not be an excuse to get a trip out of town. Participants should be required to write a summary of what was learned from the seminar and how the company (or division) can apply what has been learned from the experience. Company personnel such as salesmen and purchasing managers, who have contacts with other companies, are in a position to obtain information as to what is going on in the marketplace. All avenues of information sources must be explored.

Highly Machine-Paced Operations

The Electro-Tech company makes metal and plastic parts for the electronics industry. The predominant material is brass—although steel, phosphor bronze, and copper are also used. The equipment consists of metal stamping presses, multislide equipment, and plastics molding equipment. The equipment is highly automated so that direct-labor operators can run several machines simultaneously. Once started, the equipment, paces the operation-barring breakdown.

The percentage of material to total manufacturing cost is 59 percent—double that of the products listed under the labor-paced category. This relationship is not fixed—it will vary depending upon the types of material used by the companies making up these categories.

Direct labor is quite small at 5 percent because of the number of machines operated by each direct-labor operator. The percentage of overhead, on the other hand, is approximately seven times that of direct labor. This high ratio is not only caused by the reduced labor base in an automated operation, it is affected by the higher depreciation and maintenance as well.

Products with High Material Content

The two companies used to develop this breakdown of the three elements of manufacturing cost are predominantly assembly operations with some fabrication. The largest portion of the parts assembled is represented by outside purchases of the more expensive components. One of these companies manufactures test equipment. It purchases electronic tubes, some of which are in excess of $2000 each. The cabinetry is also purchased. The other company is a television set manufacturer that purchases its expensive picture tubes and cabinets from other divisions within the company.

As the figures indicate, the percentage of material for this category of operations is the highest of all four categories shown in Exhibit 1–2. Direct labor is relatively low at 8 percent because the assembly lines are conveyorized. This improves efficiency of labor and thus reduces cost.

The ratio of overhead to direct labor is 2.5:1, which is the second highest ratio of the four categories analyzed. Some of this is due to conveyorized production; some is also due to higher overhead because of the greater amount of space required for the volume of large items passing through the plant and the large storage areas needed for the products being made as well as the many components that are used.

Manufacturing Cost Report

The manufacturing cost report shown in Exhibit 1–3, which will be used in later sections to provide illustrations of costing and cost estimating for pricing, includes metal stamping presses, plastics molding equipment, and finishing (assembly) operations. These operations are a combination of labor-paced and machine-paced operations while the product content is high in material cost. The heavy use of brass and high-cost resins accounts for this.

Percentage Breakdown of Major Items in Overhead

Overhead is probably the least understood element of cost in modern business. Many think of it in terms of a rate—the percentage that is applied to labor in order to recover overhead in product costing. Others think of it in terms of dollars—potential additional dollars of profit; if only the magnitude of this "monster" could be reduced. To many, overhead is a mental image, hard to describe and difficult to measure and control. Later sections will deal with this in greater detail.

In analyzing the behavior of overhead, one usually finds that a few items make up a substantial portion of the total. The lower portion of Exhibit 1–2 illustrates this for the same four types of manufacturing operations discussed previously.

The major items in overhead are indirect labor and related fringe benefits, maintenance labor plus related fringes, depreciation, and occupancy costs. The direct-labor related fringe benefits were included with the smaller items of overhead in the "All other" category.

MANUFACTURING COST REPORT

Plant _____   Year of 19 _____

Summary	Year to Date		Month	
	Actual	Budget	Actual	Budget
Sales Value of Production	7,800,000			
Material	3,711,540			
Direct Labor	746,823			
Total Prime Cost	4,458,363			
Indirect Labor-Prod'n. Depts.	128,560			
Indirect Labor-Service Depts.	538,607			
Labor Connected Expenses	321,289			
Non-Payroll Expenses	511,400			
TOTAL OVERHEAD	1,499,856			
TOTAL COST OF PRODUCTION	5,958,219			

OPERATING STATISTICS	ACTUAL % OF COST	BUDGET % OF COST	ACTUAL % OF SALES VALUE	BUDGET % OF SALES VALUE
Sales Value of Production			100.0	
Material	62.3		47.5	
Direct Labor	12.5		9.6	
Indirect Labor-Prod'n. Depts.	2.2		1.7	
Indirect Labor-Service Depts.	9.0		7.0	
Labor Connected Expenses	5.4		4.1	
Non-Payroll Expenses	8.6		6.5	
TOTAL COST	100.0		76.4	

MATERIAL

Plant _____   Year of 19 _____

	Year to Date		Month	
	Actual	Budget	Actual	Budget
Steel	2,094,416			
Resins	1,242,062			
Packing Material	375,062			
TOTAL MATERIAL COST	3,711,540			

DIRECT LABOR

Department	Year to Date		Month	
	Actual	Budget	Actual	Budget
Molding Presses	283,151			
Punch Presses	225,646			
Finishing	238,026			
TOTAL DIRECT LABOR	746,823			

INDIRECT LABOR-PRODUCTION DEPARTMENTS

Department	Year to Date		Month	
	Actual	Budget	Actual	Budget
Molding Presses	48,151			
Punch Presses	48,965			
Finishing	31,444			
TOTAL INDIRECT LABOR-PROD'N.	128,560			

EXHIBIT 1–3:
OVERVIEW REPORT FOR MANUFACTURING COST

INDIRECT LABOR-SERVICE DEPARTMENTS

Plant _____ Year of 19 _____

Department	Year to Date		Month	
	Actual	Budget	Actual	Budget
General Manager's Staff	50,932			
Personnel	34,200			
Cost Accounting	39,370			
Material Control	86,679			
Engineering	45,356			
Quality Assurance	73,285			
Purchasing	27,278			
Maintenance	119,950			
Receiving and Shipping	61,557			
TOTAL INDIRECT LABOR-SV.	538,607			

LABOR CONNECTED EXPENSES

Account Name	Year to Date		Month	
	Actual	Budget	Actual	Budget
Overtime Premium	42,890			
Shift Premium	10,154			
Vacation Expense	27,166			
Unemployment Insurance	29,778			
Group Life Insurance	12,430			
Hospitalization	35,595			
Pension Expense	43,505			
Compensation & Liability Ins.	25,990			
Payroll Taxes	93,781			
TOTAL LABOR CONNECTED	321,289			

NON-PAYROLL EXPENSES

Plant _____ Year of 19 _____

Account Name	Year to Date		Month	
	Actual	Budget	Actual	Budget
UTILITIES				
Water	4,000			
Gas	4,100			
Electricity	46,900			
Telephone	9,120			
Acetylene	275			
FACILITIES COST				
Rent	2,000			
Property Taxes	8,290			
Purchased Services	5,400			
Depreciation	195,100			
Insurance	2,817			
Fuel Oil	34,600			
SUPPLIES				
Stationery	5,900			
Postage	3,100			
Expendable Tools	20,700			
Maintenance Materials	65,700			
Lubricants and Chemicals	8,000			
Factory Supplies	4,200			
Tool Maintenance & Amortization	58,648			
OFFICE EXPENSES				
Employment Expenses	4,750			
Subscriptions	500			
Dues & Memberships	500			
Computer Services	3,500			
Rental of Equipment	10,600			
Auto Expense	12,700			
TOTAL NON-PAYROLL EXPENSES	511,400			

EXHIBIT 1-3, continued

Indirect Labor and Fringe Benefits. This category of overhead is shown in Exhibit 1–2 as the highest percentage of total overhead in the highly labor-paced operations and products with a high material content—60 percent and 65 percent, respectively. These same percentages for the highly machine-paced operation and the case example in Chapter 9 are lower—47 percent and 45 percent, respectively. This case example is essentially a machine-paced operation, but has some finishing (assembly) operations. (See Column 4 in Exhibit 1–2.)

Based on the seven companies in Exhibit 1–2 used for this analytical study, it appears that indirect labor increases when the operations require a high degree of manual operations and also when the product has a high number of purchased material items. It also follows that when the operations become more automated, the indirect labor, as a percentage of total overhead, drops.

Maintenance Labor, Fringes, and Maintenance Repair Materials. This item of cost is lower for the highly manual operations and the products that have a high material content. The reason is that the equipment used for these operations is not as complex as the automated types of machines. The percentages are 7 and 4 percent, respectively—compared with 17 and 14 percent for the more highly machine-paced operations.

Case Example

Alcor, a division of a large company, monitored its key costs as shown in Exhibit 1–2. Although, historically, its maintenance labor and repair materials amounted to 15 percent of total overhead, recently it had been running at 18 percent. When the division vice-president raised the question as to the increase from 15 percent to 18 percent, the plant manager advised him that 3 percent of the 18 percent was actually capitalizable because of a machine rebuilding program. When asked to justify in-house rebuilding by a crew of maintenance men with limited facilities, the plant manager brought out a make-versus-buy study in which a machine manufacturer bid $195,000 for rebuilding six machines. The study showed that the in-house cost would be $155,000 including overhead assessment. To buttress the accuracy of the report, the plant manager cited that the cost of rebuilding the first machine was 28 percent less than it would have been if the machine manufacturer's bid had been accepted.

The division vice-president assigned one of his industrial engineers to review the study and the types of machines involved. The study revealed that the rebuilding cost was reasonably calculated—the costs appeared to be realistic. However, there was a new machine on the market that was more fully automated—permitting four machines to be run by one operator rather than two. The saving in direct labor plus the associated fringe benefits would result in a payback of 1½ years on the new machines.

The original make-versus-buy study was obviously too narrow in perspective because it did not consider all of the factors—one of which was the direct labor savings of the new machines. The division vice-president, who was new, realized the need in the future for clearing all such expenditure proposals through his office for review. Such a policy was instituted.

Depreciation. The depreciation costs follow the same pattern as maintenance. In short, the more machine-paced the operations, the greater the depreciation.

Occupancy. These rent-equivalent costs include such items as building depreciation, rent if applicable, real estate taxes, insurance, heat, and building maintenance. As might be expected, the occupancy costs for the product with high material content show the largest amount (10 percent of total overhead) because of the need for larger storage areas for material components.

It is obvious from the breakdown of manufacturing costs for the four different types of operations shown in Exhibit 1–2 that the nature of the operations affects the relative amount of cost associated with the products being manufactured.

In these examples, the assumption is made that all companies apply one of the four types of operations to cover their entire facility. But modern-day business is not that simple. More often than not, one will find a mixture of operations within a company. For example, one department may be labor-paced because the metal-forming equipment requires one or more operators per machine; another department of the same company may have automatic molding equipment that will make it machine-paced; while a third department, which puts together the final product, may be assembling the product with high-cost components purchased from the outside—as well as fabricated parts turned out by the metal-forming and plastics-molding departments.

The costs associated with the metal-forming presses would be different from those associated with molding and those associated with the assembly of a product with high material cost content. Obviously, for proper product costing, these differences in the type of operations must be taken into account. Subsequent chapters will discuss this further and will illustrate how these "multi-associations" are accounted for.

OVERVIEW OF MANUFACTURING COSTS

Exhibit 1–1 shows how manufacturing costs fit into total product costs. Exhibit 1–2 breaks these manufacturing costs down into major categories of expense and shows the variations in these expenses under different types of operations. Exhibit 1–3 goes into the detail of manufacturing costs. This is a monthly report with provision for comparing actual costs with the budgeted costs for the month and for the year to date. The actual report is a single 11" × 17" sheet that folds into an 11" × 8½" size and opens like a book made up of four pages.

The company makes molded parts used in the electronics industry as well as parts used in nonelectronics applications. It also forms metal parts on punch presses. These, too, are used in electronics applications. The metal parts are frequently assembled with the plastics parts to form sockets used in the base of television picture tubes as well as display tubes used in computer terminals. The molding and punch presses are automatic and, therefore, essentially machine-paced. Assembly operations that are fairly large are mostly labor-paced. The breakdown of the pertinent information contained in this report is shown below for each of the four pages.

Manufacturing Cost Summary

This is the summary of the information contained on pages 2, 3, and 4. The first item is *sales value of production,* showing the billing value of the items produced. This provides management with some idea of the volume for the period in terms of sales dollars. This figure is shown only on the summary page.

The summary, in dollars, also shows the total material that was consumed in production during the month and for the year to date. The total amount of direct labor is also shown. Total overhead is the third element of manufacturing cost that is included in the summary. However, since the total overhead figure is double that of direct labor, the company felt that it would like to see this item broken down by major categories within overhead as an overview before looking into the departmental detail.

The lower portion of the summary page shows the percentages that the dollar figures are of total manufacturing cost and of sales value of production. These percentages are useful in monitoring the trends of the major items in terms of total cost and also in terms of sales value—the latter trends providing some indication of trends in profitability.

Material, Direct Labor, and Indirect Labor in Production Departments. Page two shows the detail behind direct material, direct labor, and indirect labor-production departments. The direct material breakdown is made up of steel strip of various widths and thicknesses, resins, and packing materials. Direct labor costs are identified for the three departments—molding presses, punch presses, and finishing (assembly). The indirect-labor production departments are broken down for the same departments as the direct labor. These costs include the salaries of the departmental foremen, setup men, and material handlers.

Indirect Labor in Service Departments and Labor-Connected Expenses. The upper portion of page three lists the costs of the various support departments referred to as indirect-labor service departments. The lower portion lists the various labor-connected expenses for all labor. This includes direct labor, indirect-labor production departments, and indirect-labor service departments.

Nonpayroll Expenses. Page four lists the nonpayroll expenses under the categories of utilities, facilities costs, supplies, and office expenses.

The figures in this report will be used in a later section to demonstrate the development of departmental (cost center) overhead rates for more accurate association of costs with products.

USING COST SYSTEMS FOR ASSOCIATING MANUFACTURING COSTS WITH PRODUCTS

As mentioned earlier, there are two basic systems for identifying manufacturing costs with products: job costing and process costing. The distinguishing features of the two systems are:

- *Job Costing.* Costs are accumulated by individual customer order because of the uniqueness of the product specifications required to fit the customer's needs. A good example is elevators. Each elevator order is designed to fit the design of the building in which it is installed. While certain basic equipment such as motors, cables, electrical controls, and the like can be similar for many customers, the other features can be quite different from one customer to another. The same applies to transportation equipment such as locomotives, railroad cars, trucks, ships, turbines, and valves.

- *Process Costing.* Costs are accumulated by process (usually identified by department or cost center). No distinction is made by customer order because the products are standard and built to stock rather than to individual customer order. Examples are: household appliances, garments, shoes, radios, and television sets.

Job versus Process Costing—Production Flow

Exhibit 1–4 illustrates the production flow into work-in-process and finished goods.

Job Costing—Charges into Work-in-Process. Direct material is identified by job number which, in turn, identifies the customer. The work-in-process account is broken down by jobs that are in process. When standard components are required for two or more customer orders, these are frequently built for stock and identified as stock orders. When these are issued to a job, the appropriate job number is charged.

Job Costing—Finished Production. As orders are completed, they are shipped to customers. If the order calls for a number of units that must be shipped together, the finished units may be transferred to a finished goods inventory account until all units have been completed. Companies vary in the use of the finished goods inventory account. Some require all finished production to be recorded through this account to have a running record of all completed orders. Others ship directly from work-in-process.

Shipments to customers are recorded as cost of sales, and the work-in-process (or finished goods) inventory is relieved.

Process Costing—Charges into Work-in-Process. Material is issued to the department in which it is used (molding, punch presses, finishing) without identifying the customer order on which it is used, since the units are being produced to stock.

Direct labor and overhead are charged in the same way without identifying the customer order.

Process Costing—Completed Production. As orders are completed, they are moved into the finished goods inventory and work-in-process relieved. Customer orders are filled from the finished goods inventory and shipments are recorded as cost of sales.

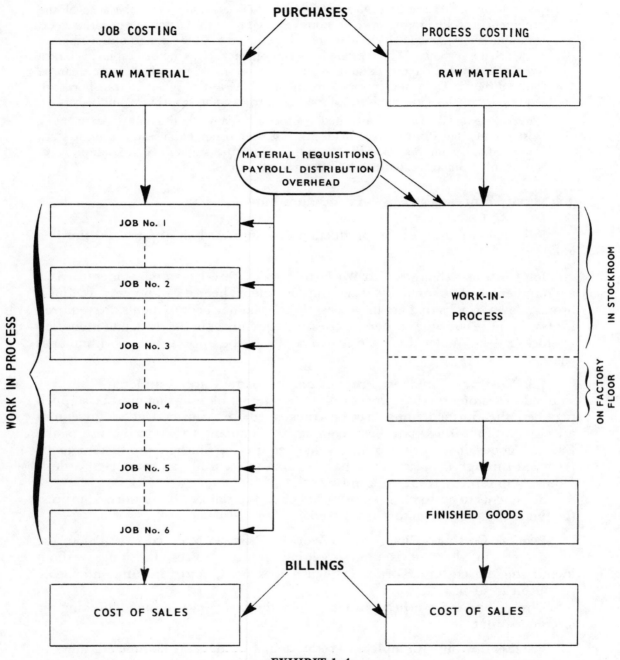

EXHIBIT 1–4:
TWO BASIC COST FLOWS

INTERRELATIONSHIP OF COST SYSTEM VARIATIONS

The underlying principles of job and process costing have remained the same since the early days of the Industrial Revolution. Any changes that have been introduced are essentially modifications to provide additional information. This is illustrated in Exhibit 1–5. This exhibit shows three levels of costing:

- Primary Costing Level   The basic costing system
- Secondary Costing Level   The option as to whether standard costs will be used rather than actual.
- Tertiary Costing Level   The option as to whether direct costing or full costing will be used.

Job Costing

The primary costing level shown in the exhibit was discussed in the previous section entitled "Using Cost Systems for Associating Manufacturing Costs with Products."

The primary (basic) costing system originally used actual costs on a full costing basis. With the acceptance of standard costs and variances during recent decades, a number of companies have adopted standard costs for job costing to facilitate control by monitoring the variations of actual costs from standards. Exhibit 1–5 shows this as the secondary level of costing.

The tertiary costing level provides the option of using direct costing and charging the fixed (nonvariable) costs to period expense. Direct costs would include direct material, direct labor, and variable overhead. Only these costs would be included in product cost. Inventory, then, would be valued at its variable costs. The nonvariable items would be excluded. Although there is some advantage to making analytical studies through use of direct costing, companies making products that are unique to a customer should always give close attention to actual costs on a full costing basis.

Process Costing

Process costing, like job costing, originally used actual costs on a full costing basis.

The secondary level of costing in the accompanying exhibit shows standard costs as an alternative to actual costs. Process costing, because of the standardized nature of the products and the continuous nature of production, lends itself well to use of standard costs. Undoubtedly, the majority of companies making standardized products on a repetitive basis use some form of standard costing.

The tertiary level of costing presents the alternatives of direct and full costing. Direct costing (the valuation of production and inventories at direct costs only) lends itself more to process costing than to job costing. Since the SEC and IRS will not accept direct costing for external reporting, its use must be limited to internal reporting and analysis.

KEY FEATURES OF COST SYSTEM VARIATIONS

The interrelationship of cost system variations shown in Exhibit 1–5 for the primary, secondary, and tertiary costing levels has been recast in Exhibit 1–6 for convenience in comparing the key features of each of the variations shown in the three levels. The second, third, and fourth columns are devoted to the three elements of manufacturing cost—material, direct labor, and overhead. The last column shows the type of product for which the different variations apply. These columns describe the treatment of each of the elements under the cost system variations. The fifth column shows the control features of each of the cost system variations.

   These cost system variations will be discussed in greater detail in the chapters that follow.

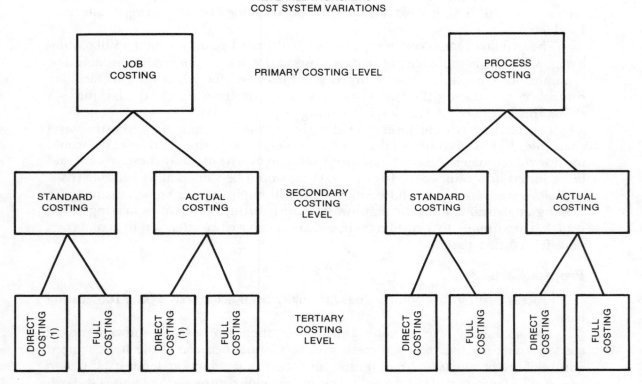

INTERRELATIONSHIP OF
COST SYSTEM VARIATIONS

(1) NOT RECOMMENDED FOR USE WITH JOB COSTING

EXHIBIT 1–5:
INTERRELATIONSHIP OF COST SYSTEM VARIATIONS

COST SYSTEM	DIRECT MATERIAL	DIRECT LABOR	OVERHEAD	CONTROL FEATURE	TYPE OF PRODUCT
Job Costing	Material usually is charged directly to job. Small items, normally charged to overhead would be charged to job as material when item cost is high, as in highly engineered products. Actual costs used.	Actual hours at actual hourly rates charged directly to job. Such costs as rework and setup, normally charged to overhead, would be considered as direct labor in highly engineered jobs.	Although predetermined rates are used, they are often revised semiannually (or at least reviewed) to assure that they reflect current costs.	Actual costs by job can be compared with original cost estimate on which sales price was based.	Customized to customer specifications. Orders normally are for small quantities of products at high unit prices. Examples: Locomotives Fire Trucks Elevators Airplanes Turbines Ships Research Projects
Process Costing	Standardized components assembled into finished products.	Direct labor less skilled than in job costing.	Predetermined rates revised annually.	Costs accumulated by department rather than by job.	Standard products built to stock rather than to customer order. Unit prices lower than for job costed products. Examples: Appliances Clothing Radios & TV Sets
Standard Costing	Standards established for material quantities and purchase prices. Standards can be used in job costing concurrently with actual costs.	Standards established for time allowances and hourly labor rates. Standards can be used in job costing concurrently with actual costs.	Predetermined rates revised annually. Variances calculated for spending and volume. These variances can be calculated for job costing.	Measurement of variances from standard. For material, direct labor and overhead.	Same as process costing.
Actual Costing	Used in job costing.	Used in job costing.	Predetermined rates often revised more frequently than once a year.	See job costing.	See job costing.
Direct Costing	Can be coupled with process costing and standard costing.	Can be coupled with process costing and standard costing.	Overhead costs identified by variable and fixed costs. Inventories valued at variable overhead rates only. Fixed costs treated as period costs.	Availability of variable and fixed breakdown for overhead facilitates use of flexible budgets and breakeven analysis.	Same as process costing and standard costing. Not recommended for job costing.
Full Costing	Mandatory for job costing and external reporting for all costing systems; variances must be included in inventory value.	Mandatory for job costing and external reporting for all costing systems; variances must be included in inventory value.	Fixed costs must be included in inventory value. Variances must also be included.	Provides assurance that all costs are included in product costs and inventory.	Applicable to inventories of all products for external reporting.

EXHIBIT 1–6:
KEY FEATURES OF COST SYSTEM VARIATIONS

2

Job Costing Systems

Job costing systems facilitate a more accurate identification of costs associated with the manufacture or construction of customized products. A job cost system would be used in the construction of a ship or an office building. Such a system would also be used for the manufacture of orders to a customer's specific requirements. This would include elevators that must fit a particular design of a building, castings made for a specific application, valves and turbines required for a particular use. Such items are not usually standard products that are built to stock and sold from stock when orders are received. Job costing is also used in rebuilding, overhauling, or repair projects. The average car owner is familiar with the customer repair order when a vehicle is brought to a garage for repair. This order lists the materials used and the labor charges for the various tasks that were performed. The labor charge usually includes an override for such overhead as office expenses, rent equivalent costs, and utilities.

If, on the other hand, the auto manufacturer is required to recall one or more models with a defect, the dealer is furnished with a standard allowance depending on the nature of the work to be performed. The manufacturer will reimburse the dealer on the basis of this standard inasmuch as the nature of the work is similar for all cars recalled.

This chapter will review job costing formats used by several industries to demonstrate the similarity of the costing principles even though the formats for accumulation will vary. Some case studies will also be illustrated.

JOB COSTING FORMAT FOR MANUFACTURE OF CARRIAGES IN THE EARLY 1800s

Job costing is not a new development (nor is process costing, for that matter). In his article, "Early Contributions to Cost Accounting," published in the December 1973 issue of *Management Accounting*, R. E. Feller, includes an exhibit illustrating the job costing format used for the manufacture of carriages. This is shown as Exhibit 2–1. Note that each of the three carriages, purchased by three different customers, shows the costs associated with each. The distribution of costs appears on the left side of the exhibit. The third item in the right-hand column shows the cost of

Carriage 1	305	Carpenter's	
2	102	Memo	407
Carriage 1	475	Smith's	
2	400	Memo	875
Carriage 1	440	Lumber	
2	310	Merchant's	
3	222	Memo	972
Carriage 1	340		
2	100	Wheelwright's	
3	205	Memo	645
Carriage 1	70		
2	65	Saddler's	
3	55	Memo	190
Carriage 1	345		
2	200	Painter's	
3	30	Memo	575
	3,664		3,664

Factory Warehouse			
Carriage 1			
Amounting to	1,975		
Carriage 2		Enterprise is discharged	
Amounting to	1,177	of accountability	
Carriage 3		by the transfer	
Amounting to	512	to warehouse	3,664
	7,328		7,328

EXHIBIT 2–1:
CARRIAGE PRODUCTION—JOURNAL IN KIND
Source: R. E. Feller, "Early Contributions to Cost Accounting," *Management Accounting,*
December 1973.

lumber, with the breakdown included in the three carriages appearing immediately to the left in the first column. The charges of the five craftsmen are shown in the column at the right, with each of the craft charges also distributed to the three carriages immediately to the left in the first column. The charges made by the five craftsmen include the labor, nonlabor expenses (overhead), and the smaller items of material such as paint, iron, and bolts. Although the carriage has long since been replaced by the automobile, the basic principles being followed in present-day job costing are similar to those followed by modern-day companies.

JOB COSTING IN THE CONSTRUCTION INDUSTRY

The illustrative job costing material for the construction industry was taken from the *Managerial Accounting and Cost Control Manual* prepared by the Mechanical Contractors Association of America. The breakdown of costs by category and by jobs is shown in Exhibit 2–2. The lower portion of the exhibit summarizes the charges made to Job 101 for the month of September.

(401) Direct Labor. Charges for such personnel as plumbers, steamfitters, and laborers are taken from the weekly payrolls and shown under the column labeled (401) Direct Labor.

(403) Materials. The next column represents materials that the mechanical contractor purchases and frequently keeps in his inventory for ready availability. These materials include items such as pipes, elbows, fixtures, and other materials used in water and drainage systems. The charges come from the purchase journal and cash disbursements.

(405) Equipment. This column includes such items as boilers, pumps, radiators, grills, and other equipment to which the pipes, fittings, and valves (403 items) are attached. The equipment is usually purchased from the manufacturer and is delivered directly to the construction site. To facilitate better control, the equipment is set up as a separate category rather than being merged with the 403 account.

(407) Subcontract. This column identifies the costs of work done by other contractors. Examples are sheet metal contractors who are called in to provide duct work. Another example is heating contractors called in to erect the boiler. This segregation of subcontract work can be helpful in determining whether the contractor should begin thinking of performing some of these services himself.

(410–499) Other Direct Costs. The final column might better be defined as on-site overhead. It includes such indirect personnel as the project manager or superintendent, the job engineer, and the on-site accountant. Also included would be the telephone charges, permits, truck expenses, and cost of utilities.

This portion of the exhibit summarizes the costs for Job 101 for the month— the total amount being $121,000. The upper portion of the exhibit accumulates similar costs for other jobs in process as well as those that have been completed during the month. In the general ledger, the total of these job costs is compared with the total of the control accounts.

Although the principle of breaking down the costs for both the production of carriages and the construction of an office building are similar, there is a difference in the mix of the elements of cost. The former has substantially more labor while the latter is heavier in its proportion of material plus equipment cost. The figures in Exhibit 2–2 are theoretical and therefore do not reflect the true breakdown. The

ILLUSTRATION OF TIE-IN OF JOB COSTS
   TO THE GENERAL LEDGER

As of September 30,___

General Ledger			Job Cost Ledgers				
Construction Costs: 400 Series	Account No.	Account Balances	Total	Job No. 101	Job No. 102	Job No. 103	Completed Jobs
Direct Labor	401	$194,000	$194,000	$ 35,000	$ 40,000	$ 19,000	$100,000
Materials	403	160,000	160,000	25,000	30,000	15,000	90,000
Equipment	405	192,000	192,000	30,000	35,000	17,000	110,000
Subcontract	407	112,000	112,000	22,000	25,000	10,000	55,000
Other Direct Costs .	410-499	40,000	40,000	9,000	7,000	4,000	20,000
Total Construction Costs To Date		$698,000	$698,000	$121,000	$137,000	$ 65,000	$375,000

JOB COST LEDGER

Job Name ___ABC Company___   Job No. ___101___

Date	Ref. Folio	Remarks	Total Costs	(401) Direct Labor	(403) Materials	(405) Equip- ment	(407) Sub- Contract	(410-499) Other Direct Job Costs
9/7	PR	Weekly Payroll	$10,000	$10,000				
9/14	PR	Weekly Payroll	9,500	9,500				
9/21	PR	Weekly Payroll	6,500	6,500				
9/28	PR	Weekly Payroll	9,000	9,000				
9/30	PJ	Purchase Journal	80,500		$23,000	$30,000	$22,000	$ 5,500
9/30	CD	Cash Disbursements	3,500		2,000			1,500
9/30	RJ	Recurring Journal	2,000					2,000
		Balance 9/30	121,000	35,000	25,000	30,000	22,000	9,000

EXHIBIT 2–2:
SUMMARIZING COSTS BY JOBS AND BY COST ELEMENTS
This illustrative material on job costing in the construction industry is taken from the
Managerial Accounting and Cost Control manual prepared by the Mechanical Contractors
Association of America.

manufacture of early automobiles required heavy labor, as in the case of the carriages. But modern-day automobile manufacturers utilize a mix of cost elements that more closely resembles construction. The reason is that many of the components are purchased in other divisions of the company as purchased components. Many components, such as tires, glass, and batteries, are purchased from outside suppliers. These purchased materials are then assembled in a conveyorized assembly plant equipped with automatic equipment—including robots. Modern-day industry, because of the heavy capitalization in automatic equipment, requires heavy overhead—which in many cases far exceeds the direct labor cost.

JOB COSTING FORMAT FOR DEVELOPING NEW SEMICONDUCTOR TYPES

The importance of semiconductors in modern-day computer technology is well known. The experimentation that was required in the development of newer and smaller types of semiconductors called for the use of job cost systems. The history of this product is full of examples in which type after type was introduced at $60, $90, $120, and more per unit. Inevitably, prices dropped after introduction and an increased volume of sales. It was not unusual for a semiconductor that was introduced at a price of, say, $93 to start dropping to $55, or thereabouts, then $30, then $8. Many prices dropped below $1. This was due to a combination of competition, better know-how, and better control of electrical characteristics because of longer runs.

Electrical characteristics of the final product are difficult to predict. The manufacturing process had to be conducted to completion, at which time the finished product was tested and classified according to the test readings.

Exhibit 2–3 provides the format for the processing stage of manufacture. Exhibit 2–4 shows the format for assembly of the finished semiconductor. Both formats are practically the same: both provide for the accumulation of labor, material, and overhead costs, as well as the per unit cost of each of the elements across the top. The horizontal breakdown is also the same except that on the processing sheet "transfers out" indicates "Assembly Department" and on the assembly sheet it indicates "To Classification Department." Since the processing department is the starting point, it does not show "transfers in" from other departments. The assembly sheet indicates that the "transfer in" was from the processing department.

Although the total unit cost is $0.9838 at completion of the assembly operations, it represents the average cost of the preclassified units. In the classification department, only labor and overhead were added. This plus the yield losses resulted in an average per unit cost of $6.351. The selling price of the mix (assortment of electrical characteristics) ranged from a high of $18.50 for the type most in demand to a low of $7.15 for the type least in demand.

The cost flow in both Exhibits 2–3 and 2–4 starts with the beginning inventory. To this is added the cost of additional units produced and the cost of units transferred in (when applicable). This adds up to the total units available.

Production Department—Processing

Month of August 19XX

Description	Units	Labor	Per Unit	Material	Per Unit	Overhead	Per Unit	Total	Per Unit
Beginning Inventory 7/31	857,779	35,101	.0409	17,963	.0210	77,663	.0905	130,727	.1524
August Operations:									
Departmental Costs		3,005	.0815	1,059	.0287	6,570	.1782	10,634	.2884
Transfers in:									
TOTAL	36,866	3,005	.0815	1,059	.2087	6,570	.1782	10,634	.2884
Total Available	894,645	38,106	.0426	19,022	.0213	84,233	.0941	141,361	.1580
Transfers Out:									
To Assembly Department	77,515	3,301	.0426	1,648	.0213	7,299	.0941	12,248	.1580
TOTAL	77,515	3,301	.0426	1,648	.0213	7,299	.0941	12,248	.1580
Ending Inventory 8/31	817,130	34,805	.0426	17,374	.0213	76,934	.0941	129,113	.1580

EXHIBIT 2–3:
JOB COST LEDGER (Production Department—Processing)

Production Department—Assembly

Month of August 19XX

Description	Units	Labor	Per Unit	Material	Per Unit	Overhead	Per Unit	Total	Per Unit
Beginning Inventory 7/31	17,679	2,552	.1440	3,537	.2002	8,297	.4695	14,386	.8137
August Operations:									
Departmental Costs		5,544	.1153	9,757	.2030	24,028	.4998	39,329	.8181
Transfers in:									
From Processing Department	48,075	2,958	.0615	1,477	.0307	6,540	.1360	10,975	.2282
TOTAL	48,075	8,502	.1768	11,234	.2337	30,568	.6358	50,304	1.0463
Total Available	65,754	11,054	.1681	14,771	.2246	38,865	.5911	64,690	.9838
Transfers Out:									
To Classification Department	60,772	10,217	.1681	13,652	.2246	35,920	.5911	59,789	.9838
TOTAL	60,772	10,217	.1681	13,652	.2246	35,920	.5911	59,789	.9838
Ending Inventory 8/31	4,982	837	.1681	1,119	.2246	2,945	.5911	4,901	.9838

EXHIBIT 2-4:
JOB COST LEDGER (Production Department—Assembly)

The total units available is reduced by the number of units transferred out to other departments. The remaining balance constitutes the ending inventory that is carried over as the beginning inventory of the new month's job cost ledger sheet.

Note that the first two examples of job costing differed from the format for semiconductors. The illustrations of the production of carriages and the construction of a building show the cost accumulation at a single level. There is no movement of the product from one department to another in the accounting records. The assumption is that the product is built in place.

In the case of the semiconductors, production starts in the processing department. The finished units are then transferred to the assembly department and then from assembly to the classification department. Another difference in the semiconductor example is that the quantities are relatively large, resulting in accumulations of inventories throughout the process.

The next example will deal with the manufacture of valves used for control of liquid flow. The liquid could be water, chemicals, or refinery products. Valves that are standard and used by a number of customers would normally utilize process costing. But the highly engineered valves, such as those used in nuclear applications, would be job-costed. The illustration that follows is based on the latter.

JOB COSTING FORMAT FOR HIGHLY ENGINEERED VALVES

Valves are made in various sizes and configurations. Exhibit 2–5 shows one of the larger sizes whose weight is equal to that of a passenger automobile. Exhibit 2–6 shows a smaller valve with an entirely different configuration which stands about twenty inches high. Also included in this exhibit are many forms and reports that illustrate the paperwork associated with some of the highly engineered valves. Our discussion will be centered on the larger valve, which is also highly engineered.

The highly engineered valves require intensive inspection of the castings and other components throughout the process—which includes machining, welding, and assembly/test. These inspections are more extensive than for similar valves of the standard variety. When flaws are uncovered in engineered valves, as they frequently are during the machining operation, the defects are gouged out, welded, remachined, and reinspected. On a standard valve, rework would not always be done because many of the sandholes can remain. In the more serious flaws, the casting for a standard valve would be scrapped rather than incurring the expense of rework.

Exhibit 2–7 displays the format followed in summarizing the job costs of highly engineered valves. The upper portion of this exhibit shows the breakdown of the unit costs of orders that were shipped in the current period. The material is broken down by the major sections of the valve—body, bonnet, disc, etc. Labor and overhead are broken down for machining, welding, and assembly/test. In addition to the total manufacturing cost, the selling price and gross profit are shown for each valve shipped. Nonmanufacturing direct charges are also shown. In addition to the actual costs incurred, the original estimates on which the selling prices were based are shown in the same breakdown as the actual costs. This information is useful in future estimating.

EXHIBIT 2–5:
VALVE (Large Size)

EXHIBIT 2–6:
VALVE (Smaller Size)

By permission of the Valve Manufacturers Association

The lower portion of this exhibit, the Cost History Record, recaps all completed orders that have been shipped. Note that two of the 20-inch 150# gate valves, order #23957, were shipped in the current month (upper portion of exhibit). These were the final two of the original order. With the order now complete, the history record of this order has been shown in the lower portion of the exhibit. This facilitates the comparison of the various material component costs with previous orders for the same valve. Instead of showing the labor/overhead dollars, labor hours are shown in the history record. This is particularly helpful because the hours are consistent—there is no need for adjusting dollars to compensate for changes in the hourly labor rates.

KEY FEATURES OF THE FOUR JOB COSTING FORMATS

Exhibit 2–8 summarizes the four job costing formats shown in Exhibits 2–1, 2–2, 2–3, 2–4, and 2–7. This summary lists the key features of the basic elements of cost, as well as identifying the best features of each format. The key features specify:

- Whether material is shown in total for the job or broken down by product components or departments—whichever is the more appropriate.
- Whether direct labor is shown in total for the job or broken down into controllable segments—e.g., by crafts or by departments.

UNIT COSTS OF ORDERS SHIPPED

Order No.	Quan.	Total Material Cost Body	Bonnet	Disc.	Operator	Other	Total	Tooling and Patterns	Machining	Welding	Assembly and Test	Total	Total Mfg. Cost	Selling Price	Gross Profit %	Non-Mfg. Direct Charges
4" 300# S.S.																
Actual 22113-11	2	$ 327	$268	$ 54	$ 966	$ 235	$1,850	$ 24	$ 617	$ 318	$ 299	$1,234	$ 3,108	$ 5,044	38.4%	$ 410
Estimate	2	620	460	35	834	213	2,162	—	721	350	371	1,442	3,604	5,044	28.5	580
12" 900# Ca. St.																
Actual 26126-12	1	3,123	991	165	3,904	1,341	9,524	2,140	3,174	1,597	1,578	6,349	18,013	16,602	(8.5)	1,040
Estimate	1	2,138	874	126	2,004	1,027	6,169	2,515	2,056	1,019	1,037	4,112	12,796	16,602	22.9	796
20" 150# Ca. St.																
Actual 23957-15	2	1,288	154	229	—	376	2,047	15	682	362	320	1,364	3,426	5,910	42.0	804
Estimate	5	1,015	148	297	—	260	1,720	—	607	365	342	1,314	3,034	5,910	48.7	760
30" 150# Ca. St.																
Actual 24628-16	2	2,943	349	441	—	688	4,421	—	1,474	716	757	2,947	7,368	20,200	63.5	1,149
Estimate	2	4,984	300	501	—	861	6,646	5,028	2,215	1,097	1,119	4,431	16,105	20,200	20.3	1,296

COST HISTORY RECORD
UNIT COST

Product 20" 150" GATE VALVE

Shop Order #	Quan.	Material Cost Body	Bonnet	Disc.	Operator	Other	Total Material	Upgrade	Machine Shop	Weld	Assembly	Total Hours	Total Mfg. Cost	Sales Price	Gross Profit	Non-Mfg. Direct Charges
21428-16	3	$1,285	$163	$246	—	$346	$2,040	3	57	14	21	95	$3,521	$5,910	$2,389	$1,519
21585-17	2	1,273	162	241	—	345	2,021	4	58	12	18	92	3,502	5,910	2,408	1,307
23561-14	2	1,311	189	220	—	298	2,018	5	71	29	22	127	3,982	5,910	1,928	1,275
23957-15	5	1,288	154	229	—	376	2,047	4	63	16	21	104	3,426	5,910	2,484	804

*Upgrade refers to Rework

EXHIBIT 2–7:
JOB COST HISTORY

PRODUCT	MATERIAL	DIRECT LABOR	OVERHEAD	BEST FEATURE
Carriage Production—Exhibit 2-1	Identifies major material. Smaller items included with labor by craft.	Identified by craft.	Included as part of craft labor.	Labor identified by craft. Profitability for each carriage produced.
Construction—Exhibit 2-2	Standard items of material segregated from equipment purchased for the job.	Labor reported in total. Subsidiary report needed for craft breakdown.	Overhead reported separately.	Segregation of major materials.
Semiconductors—Exhibits 2-3 and 2-4	Material reported by department.	Labor reported by department.	Overhead reported by department.	The three elements of manufacturing cost are broken down by department.
Valves—Exhibit 2-7	Material identified by major components of the product.	Labor identified by department.	Overhead included in labor.	Cost history of jobs by components and departments. Reporting of labor hours for past jobs improves cost estimating for future jobs. Calculation of profitability by job. Comparing actual costs with the original estimates.

EXHIBIT 2–8:
KEY FEATURES OF FOUR JOB COSTING FORMATS

- Whether overhead is shown separately from direct labor and is broken down by craft or department.
- Whether the format provides for showing the profitability by job.
- Whether the format provides for a convenient comparison with past costs of similar jobs.

Perfection versus the Real World of Costing

Accepting the four costing formats as being sufficiently representative for the selection of the best features of job costing systems, Exhibit 2–9 illustrates the application of these features for control. The "perfect" job costing system would

ITEMS	APPLICATION OF CONTROL	EXCEPTIONS
Material	*By major categories of material* when a wide range of material is used as in the mechanical contractor illustration.	Die and mold manufacturing in which material is a relatively small element of cost.
	By department when usage is controllable within the departments through which the product passes, as illustrated in the production of semiconductors.	
	By major product components when the materials can be associated with the components of the product, as in the case of the valve costing format.	
Direct labor	*By craft,* as in the production of carriages or general contracting, in which different skills are utilized.	Companies that do little or no fabrication, but instead, purchase components which are manually assembled.
	By department, as the product moves through two or more departments. Illustrated in the semiconductor job costing format.	
Overhead	*By department* when the product is processed through two or more departments, as in the case of the semiconductor job costing format.	When the operations are homogeneous and manual in nature, such as bench work, a single overhead rate will usually suffice. The same applies when the machines in a machine-oriented operation are fairly similar.
Profitability by job	Applicable to all job costing systems.	
Cost history	Applicable to all job costing systems.	

EXHIBIT 2–9:
USING THE BEST FEATURES OF THE FOUR JOB COSTING FORMATS FOR CONTROL

provide the maximum breakout of each of the elements of manufacturing cost. Material would be identified by major categories used in each of the departments. Direct labor would be segregated by department, or craft, to reflect labor rate differences in the manufacturing operations. Overhead would not be combined with labor but would be shown separately for each significant manufacturing process. Thus, as each job passed through the different processes, its costs would be accumulated precisely as incurred.

In efforts to achieve perfection, there is often an overconcentration on improving one of the smaller elements of manufacturing cost to the exclusion of a larger one. This was the case in the Powerflite Division of a large company that had eleven industrial engineers concentrating on direct labor which was the smallest element of the three (see Case Example of the Powerflite Division).

Case Example

The product made by this division had a large material content. The material was 76 percent of total manufacturing cost while labor was 9 percent and overhead 15 percent. The eleven industrial engineers concentrated almost entirely on time studying and developing efficiency analyses of the direct labor. The standards versus actuals were being reported by individual operations for each employee for each day. In many instances, very small amounts of time were being reported for the efficiency report. For example, .08 hours at standard was being compared with the actual. When such small amounts were involved, the daily efficiency report consisted of over 100 pages for each of the foremen. The foremen did not have too much faith in some of the small amounts of time per operation being reported because a small error in reporting could bias the efficiency percentage.

The recommendation was made to the division manager that at least one-third of the effort of the industrial engineering department be devoted to monitoring the efficiency with which the material was being utilized. Further, it was recommended that the splintering of the labor efficiency reports be eliminated by accumulating the efficiency by operator for a week. The weekly report of efficiency would be adequate for highlighting the poor performers. This would save the foremens' time and would make more time for the industrial engineers to concentrate on material efficiency.

The division manager agreed to deploy the effort of two industrial engineers to cost-reduction studies for material. He agreed that the monitoring of short-cycle operations by the direct-labor employees could be broadened to include a longer cycle. He also agreed that monitoring labor efficiency on a weekly rather than a daily basis would be adequate for identifying the poor performers.

Accordingly, one of the industrial engineers worked with the quality control department in closer monitoring of production defects. The addition of the industrial engineer was helpful because he understood the manufacturing processes more intimately than the inspector whose responsibility ended when he identified defective parts or products. Each time a different type of defect was discovered, the engineer would review the process or the operation performed at the station at which the defect occurred and take whatever corrective action was indicated.

The other industrial engineer analyzed the bills of material for products in which components could be standardized. There were many instances in which he found, for example, that two or three differently designed brackets were used when one design could be used instead. Standardization by adoption of a multiuse bracket designed to use less material resulted not only in a saving of material but also in a reduction of the size of inventory and the resulting losses through obsolescence. In another instance, the bills of material called for three different fractional motors purchased from different vendors. A decision was made to standardize on one of the three types. This permitted purchases in larger volume at lower prices. In another instance, it was found that savings could be realized by reducing the thickness of sheet metal used. This could be accomplished by utilizing a thinner gauge while maintaining the same strength by forming longitudinal grooves in the forming operation.

After a six-month trial, the percentage of material to total manufacturing cost dropped from 76 to 69 percent.

The Perfect Cost System—Too Costly for Most Businesses

It would be ideal if the attention given to control of direct labor in the Powerflite example could be duplicated for all three elements of cost in all companies. However, the realities of the real world of business will not allow this degree of perfection to be exercised. Take, for example, a company that has 100 customer orders in process with as many as 6 shop orders for each customer order in the various fabricating, finishing, and assembly operations. This could easily aggregate 600 individual shop orders from which costs must be continually extracted for posting to the customer job order. The greater the breakdown of the material, labor, and overhead elements, the greater the volume of paperwork that will be required—thus adding to the complexity and expense of product costing. Good business judgment must enter the picture in determining the degree of detail that is warranted in providing management with reasonably accurate costs—without imposing overly expensive costing procedures.

Take, for example, a company that makes dies and molds. This company's usage of material is relatively small compared with total manufacturing cost. The principal material is tool steel, which accounts for about 90 percent of the total material cost. There is little point in the job cost accumulation process to break out the nontool steel materials to identify their consumption separately. Nor is there much to be gained by accounting for material usage by individual departments when labor is the predominant cost. When labor is efficient, material usage should be close to standard (estimate). The same applies to departmentalization of direct labor and overhead. The operations do not vary so widely from department to department that a departmental breakdown is required. Like material, the total labor cost for the job can be compared with the standard (estimate) and the variance can be easily determined. The same applies to overhead.

If the company should buy a battery of numerically controlled (NC) machines to perform certain types of operations, a separate department (cost center) would have to be established to identify these costs separately. It is likely that there would be a saving of labor because in all likelihood one operator would operate two machines. The overhead to labor ratio for the NC equipment would also be different, so the overhead would be applied at a different rate for these operations than for the rest of the plant.

The Spectrum of Complexity

Just as the die and mold company example represents the lower end of the spectrum as to degree of costing complexity, the highly engineered valves (Exhibit 2–7) represent the upper end. Here, the breakdown of material is made by component parts of the valve. Labor and overhead are broken down by department. Labor hours are also shown by making comparisons with other departments with similar, readily available valves. Additional features include profitability by job—an important control feature. The higher degree of complexity is necessary for this product because material represents 60 percent of total manufacturing cost. The variation in types of labor operations dictates recognition of the differences through departmentalization. Although the semiconductor example falls into a similar category, it does not provide for determination of profitability by product or a convenient cost history analysis, both of which are highly desirable for such a dynamic product.

SUMMARY OF GUIDELINES TO SELECTION OF JOB COSTING FORMAT

There is no magic formula for selecting the proper job costing format. Each situation must be determined individually, taking into account the magnitude of the three elements of manufacturing cost and addressing questions such as the following:

- Is there more than one type of material that should be given visibility in the costing format?
- Should such visibility be extended to a departmental breakdown or shown only on a total job basis?
- Is there a wide spread of labor grades and skills that warrants the separate identification of departments (or crafts)?
- Do the departmental operations vary sufficiently to warrant departmental identification to recognize such differences as assembly versus fabrication, manual versus automatic, etc.?

These and related questions will be helpful in fitting the job-costing format into its proper place in the spectrum of simplicity versus complexity.

JOB COST CONTROL FOR THE LONG-TERM JOBS

Jobs with relatively short production cycles are provided with the tools for control that are available in the cost accounting system. The jobs that take longer periods of time—such as a large specialized machine, a construction project, or a government contract—require an "extension" to the accounting system. This will be referred to as the Job Cost Control and Cost of Completion Report. This report provides the means for monitoring the performance of each job against the latest cost estimate.

It also provides the documentation for progress billings to customers for whom such work is being done.

Cost Breakdown

The costs shown on the Job Cost Control and Cost of Completion Report (Exhibit 2–10) are listed vertically in the following sequence:

- Factory labor and burden (overhead) broken down by:
  - Machining
  - Assembly
- Factory material and material-related burden
- Purchased systems and designs
- Engineering and engineering burden
- Variances

Although engineering is shown as the fourth item, this list does not illustrate the true sequence. Engineering usually precedes production and is usually well along in the performance of its functions before actual production begins. Material-related burden consists of the costs of ordering, handling, and storing material before actual labor and machining operations begin. Since material must be ordered, received, stored, and issued before production can begin, the material burden rate is added to factory cost at the time such material is issued.

The Divisor

The divisor is shown on the line directly below the total cost. This is a useful index for monitoring job performance and is obtained by dividing the selling price into total costs throughout the job. The calculation is illustrated in Table 2–1 for Column 1–Sales Original (estimated costs on which the selling price was based), Column 3–Manufacturing Check (more definitive study of production costs), and Column 5–Projected (anticipated production costs for the job).

	Column 1 Sales Original	Column 3 Manufacturing Check	Column 5 Projected
Total cost	$120,000	$118,070	$119,058
Selling price	$180,000	$180,000	$180,000
Total cost/selling price			
(divisor)	.666	.656	.661
Gross profit	.334	.344	.339
	1.000	1.000	1.000

TABLE 2–1

The above figures, taken from Exhibit 2–10, illustrate how the divisor can change throughout the job. The effect of this on the gross profit is also shown. Any changes in the divisor should be traced to the cause—whether the cause has been

Contract No.
Equipment:
Customer:

Month End ___ Project Eng: ___ Sales Eng: ___
Profit Center ___
Contract Date: ___ Eng. Sate Date: ___ Prod. Start Date: ___
SIC ___ Sch. Ship Date: ___

	(1) SALES ORIGINAL	(2) ESTIMATE REVISION	(3) MFG. CHECK	(4) ESTIMATE DIFFERENCE	(5) PROJECTED COST	(6) PROJECTED CHANGE	(7) ACTUAL COST TO DATE	(8) ACTUAL COST CURRENT	(9) ESTIMATE TO COMPLETE	(10) PROJECTED VS. SALES ORIGINAL
Factory Labor and Burden:										
Machining hours	790		760	30	750		250	175	500	40
Machining labor	4,187		4,028	159	3,975		1,325	928	2,650	212
Machining burden	8,453		8,132	321	8,025		2,675	1,872	5,350	428
Assembly hours	800		800	—	800				800	—
Assembly labor	4,240		4,240	—	4,240				4,240	—
Assembly burden	8,560		8,560	—	8,560				8,560	—
Total Factory Labor/Burden	25,440		24,960	480	24,800		4,000	2,800	20,800	640
Factory Material and Burden:										
Material	35,000		33,663	1,337	32,550		10,848	7,594	21,702	2,450
Burden	3,040		2,927	113	2,825		941	658	1,884	215
Total Factory Material/Burden	38,040		36,590	1,450	35,375		11,789	8,252	23,586	2,665
Purchased Systems and Designs:	31,320		31,320	—	31,320		7,830		23,490	—
Engineering and Burden:										
Engineering hours	1,575		1,575	—	1,575		1,325	150	250	—
Engineering labor	11,812		11,812	—	11,812		9,938	1,125	1,874	—
Engineering burden	13,388		13,388	—	13,388		11,263	1,275	2,125	—
Total Engineering w/Burden	25,200		25,200	—	25,200		21,201	2,400	3,999	—
Subtotal	120,000		118,070	1,930	116,695		44,820	13,452	71,875	3,305
Variances:										
Machining labor					140		22	15	118	(140)
Assembly labor										
Material purchase price					1,953		597	418	1,356	(1,953)
Machining burden										
Assembly burden					270		44	31	226	(270)
Total Variance					2,363		663	464	1,700	(2,363)
TOTAL COST	118,070		118,070	1,930	119,058		45,483	13,916	73,575	942
Divisor	.666		.656		.661		.661		.661	
Gross profit %	33.4%		34.4%		33.9%		33.9%		33.8%	
Gross profit $	60,000		61,930		60,942		23,326		37,616	
Selling price	180,000		180,000		180,000		68,809		111,191	
Material variance %					6.0%		5.5%	5.5%	6.2%	
Machining labor variance %					3.6%		1.7%	1.6%	4.5%	
Machining burden variance										

EXHIBIT 2–10:
JOB COST CONTROL AND COST TO COMPLETE

favorable or unfavorable. An unfavorable change could be caused by an alternate method of manufacture, excess usage of materials, inefficiency, additional design changes, or engineering changes that were not included in the selling price.

The horizontal columns include the following:

Column   1—Sales Original. The initial cost estimate.

Column   2—Estimate Revision. Changes to initial cost estimate that may be made before production.

Column   3—Manufacturing Check. Review and adjustment of estimated costs to standards based on more detailed study.

Column   4—Estimate Difference. Amount of change in estimate due to results of manufacturing check.

Column { 5—Projected Cost. Review of previous projection to determine if any changes
Column { 6 are required.

Column { 7—Actual Cost. Cost to date and current period's actual cost.
Column { 8

Column   9—Estimate to Complete. Shows the cost to complete and the amount of billable sales based on latest information.

Column 10—Projected versus Sales Original. Deviation of latest projection from original estimate.

Making the Cost Estimate

The first four columns of the Percentage Completion Report deal with the estimates relating to the beginning phase of the job. Most of the other columns also deal with estimates, but these relate to the later phases of the job after production is underway.

Column 1—Sales Original. These are the raw estimates used as a guide in determining the selling price. Most companies receive a continuous flow of requests for quotation by potential customers. Frequently, because of lead-time limitations, insufficient time is available for detailed development of the cost estimates. Because of this and uncertainty of the problems that will be encountered in the production process, cost estimates are closer to being raw than finished standards. Frequently, these estimates are based on adjusted historical costs of similar jobs.

Column 2—Estimate Revision. This column provides for adjustments to the original cost estimate when changes are made in product specifications. Often, when communications break down, the changes in specifications may be made by the company without adjusting the costs and the selling price. Avoiding this type of breakdown is the responsibility of the contract administrator whose job it is to act as liaison with the customer. The contract administration function usually resides in the marketing department.

Column 3—Manufacturing Check. When the company is awarded the order and has started some production, it is in a better position to develop better estimates that come closer to standards. When this manufacturing check comes up with such changes, the new estimates (standards) are posted to this column.

Column 4—Estimate Difference. The estimate difference posted in this column is only a memo figure. It is the difference between:

1. The original estimate in column 1 and the manufacturing check in column 3, or

2. If there is a figure in the estimate revision in column 2, then, this column is compared to the manufacturing check in column 3.

Monthly Reappraisal—Making the Projection

The projected costs shown in column 5 must be reviewed, and where necessary, restated each month in light of the most recent actual costs. This is done in the following steps:

1. The bill of materials for each job is costed by determining the material and direct labor values taken from the revised estimates or standards. The variances, shown in the lower portion of the exhibit, will be measured from these estimates or standards.

2. Calculate a projected variance of factory material.
   - Divide the variance for each month by the month's standard material (or estimate) to arrive at each month's percentage.
   - Review the trend of the monthly percentages and, through judgment, ascertain what the average percentage will be for the year.
   - Put this percentage on the "Material Variance %" line in column 5.
   - Multiply this percentage (6 percent) by the standard material ($32,550).
   - Place the resulting projected material price variance of $1953 on the material variance line.

3. Calculate a projected variance for purchased systems and designs following the same procedures as in 2.

4. Compute a projected variance for labor following the same steps as for material.

5. The treatment of burden will follow the base used for application of the burden.

Accumulating the Actual Costs (Columns 7 and 8)

Cost-to-date figures are determined each accounting period. To arrive at the cost for the current month, the previous cost-to-date amounts are subtracted from the most recent cost-to-date figures.

1. **Machining Labor and Burden.** This cost represents the standard (or estimated) labor and burden cost content of the fabricated parts transferred to the assembly department.

2. **Assembly Labor and Burden.** This company records its assembly labor at actual. The reasoning is that there is an infinite number of operations that are not sufficiently repetitive within the same job to make development and application of standards economically feasible.

3. **Factory Material.** Material cost will be the standard material content of the finished parts transferred to the assembly department. The material burden rate will be applied to this material.

4. **Purchased Systems and Designs.** This item will be recorded at the invoice price.

5. **Engineering and Burden.** It is difficult to establish standards for engineering tasks related to nonstandard products. These costs will be recorded at actual.

Estimate to Complete

The Estimate to Complete in column 9 is the difference between the latest projected cost in column 5 and the year-to-date actual cost in column 7. Column 9 shows the amount of sales to be billed, the divisor on which the billable sales calculation was made, and the gross profit.

The estimated completion can be monitored by use of percentages for the major categories of cost. This is demonstrated in Table 2–2 for total factory labor and burden, total factory material and material burden, purchased systems and designs, variances, and engineering and burden. The computation of the percentage that the job has been completed for these categories is arrived at by dividing the figures in column 7 by the projections shown in column 5.

	Latest Projected Cost Column 5	Actual Cost Column 7	% Completed by Category
Total factory labor and burden	$ 24,800	4,000	16%
Total factory material and burden	35,375	11,789	33
Purchased systems and designs	31,320	7,830	25
Variances	2,363	663	28
Total Production Costs	$ 93,858	24,282	26%
Engineering and burden	25,200	21,201	84%
Total Cost	$119,058	45,483	38%
Selling Price	$180,000	68,809	38%

TABLE 2–2

Although Exhibit 2–10 refers to the Estimate to Complete in terms of dollars (column 9), it would be helpful, additionally, to issue a report showing the percentages of completion by the major categories, as shown in Table 2–2. A glance at the figures shows that the engineering effort is 84 percent complete, production is 26 percent complete, and the total job is 38 percent complete. Although the dollar figures shown in Exhibit 2–10 are necessary for accounting purposes, the report is not sufficiently concise for informing top management about the status of the various jobs. A report in the format shown in Table 2–2 would provide the key data for executive review in a more simplified, easy-to-read report.

Projected versus Sales Original

The figures in column 10 show the amount by which the various cost elements in the latest projection (column 5) deviate from Sales Original in column 1.

STANDARD AND CUSTOMIZED PRODUCTS UNDER THE SAME ROOF—WHICH COST SYSTEM TO USE

There is a misconception that when a manufacturing plant implements a new cost system to fit the product line being currently produced this same system should fit all related new products brought into the family.

This was the case with one manufacturer of flow control valves used in water and sewerage systems. When the utility companies began constructing nuclear plants, the demand for similar valves increased beyond the capacity of the industry to supply these needs.

The Decision to Expand Volume

Since this company had adequate capacity and good equipment, the decision was made to tap the nuclear market. The valves used by the utilities were basically the same as those used in industrial applications. The same equipment would be used and the same workforce, with some expansion, would be used to make the new valves. The accounting department's assessment of the cost system requirements was that the present process cost system could adequately handle the costing of the new addition to the family.

Disappointing Financial Results

The company had been manufacturing fifteen industrial-type valves per month. It maintained that volume until the new line came into the picture and increased the total volume of valves to twenty-five per month—fifteen industrial and ten nuclear. Gross profits had run at a level of about 25 percent for the industrials but had slipped during the period that the new line had been added because of disruptions and training of new employees. After the passage of almost a year—after the changeover and training had been completed—gross profits had stabilized at 11 percent. This was less than half that of previous years. True, there had been some downward pressure on prices, but the drop in gross profits should not have been as great. Company management was greatly concerned and requested that a diagnostic review be made to determine the reason for the eroding profits.

The Diagnosis

A review of past history revealed that when the company made the decision to get into the more highly engineered valves, they were then being built to the same specifications as those used for the industrial (commercial) types. Based on this, the company foresaw no problems and took on the nuclear line. Selling prices were established so that the nuclear valves would be priced approximately 10 percent higher than the industrial types. This would allow for any unforeseen contingencies.

Unanticipated Changes in Product Specifications and Impact on Expenses

Because of growing public fear of nuclear disaster, the Atomic Energy Commission pressed for codes with specifications that would guard against any remote possibility of accident. Valve manufacturers found that the resulting codes did not bring about standardization but did result in stricter codes that varied from customer to customer.

Expense items that would normally be considered overhead because of their small size and difficulty in making direct assignment to the product were considered as part of the overhead rate that was applied on the basis of the labor content of the product. Some of these overhead items, because of stricter codes for the nuclear valves, were costly and could be specifically identified with the product. Examples of these items follow:

Supplies. Such items as nuts, bolts, welding material, and gaskets were found to be relatively small for industrial valves—less than five dollars per valve. For the nuclear valve, the same class of items could amount to as much as $1500. These differences dictated that, in the future, the nuts, bolts, welding materials, and gaskets should be issued to the specific job and charged to that job. This meant that job costing had to be substituted for the process costing system.

Shipping Materials. The nuclear valves are completely crated to prevent damage in shipment while the regular industrial types are merely strapped to a skid. The cost of the lumber for crating and other protective material could amount to as much as $3000 per valve while the cost of strapping the other types to a skid cost less than $50. Here, again, was an item that should be charged directly to the product through the job costing process.

Incoming Freight. Several months ago, the company had discontinued its own foundry operations in favor of purchasing castings from outside suppliers. The overhead rate covered the relatively small incoming freight cost but had not been corrected to cover the increased shipping cost. Costs on both types of valves were understated, with the underabsorbed amount allocated to both types on the basis of material content. The amount of this cost had to be corrected for both types of valves.

Material Handling Costs. Both types of valves were large and heavy, so material handling was a fairly large cost. The nuclear valves had to be moved more frequently to holding areas awaiting tests by customers, and they remained in process longer because of these tests. The resulting material handling costs were higher for the nuclear types. The recommendation was made that this item be allocated between the two types of valves on the basis of a study that weighted this cost on the basis of 2.7 for nuclear and 1.0 for industrial valves. Job costing this item by accounting for the hours of material handling actually spent on both types was considered but would require too much paperwork for something that could be handled with a fair degree of accuracy on the 2.7 to 1 allocation.

Rework. Rework costs were relatively small for the industrial valves because subsurface porosity was not as serious as it was for the nuclear valves. In the latter, it was necessary to gouge out the sandholes, weld the opening, grind the surface, x-ray, heat treat, inspect, etc. In view of the amount of rework required to make an acceptable nuclear valve, the recommendation was made to reclassify this as direct labor and to record the time against the job.

Preparation for Shipping. This represented the labor in preparing the valves for shipment. Like the materials, the labor was small for the industrial valves and quite large for the nuclear types. This item was recommended for treatment as direct labor and was recorded against the job.

Quality Assurance. The numerous inspections, tests, and documentation (see Exhibit 2–6) resulted in about eight times as much effort being expended by the quality assurance department on nuclear valves as on the industrials. It was recommended that this item be treated as direct labor and be charged directly to the job rather than through overhead.

Engineering. Engineering and drafting, like quality assurance, required substantially more effort for the nuclear valves. Here, too, the recommended treatment was to account for this cost as direct labor and charge it directly to the job rather than through an overhead rate.

The comparative income statements showing the three elements of manufacturing cost, sales, and gross profit are shown in Exhibit 2–11 before and after the recommendations. The net effect on the individual elements of cost can be gleaned from the total columns. Overhead for both types of valves was decreased from $240,300 to $149,450. A portion of this was picked up in material, which increased from $206,300 to $218,850 while labor increased from $92,100 to $170,400.

	BEFORE RECOMMENDATIONS			AFTER RECOMMENDATIONS		
	TOTAL	INDUSTRIAL	NUCLEAR	TOTAL	INDUSTRIAL	NUCLEAR
Sales	$605,100	323,515	281,585	$605,100	323,515	281,585
Manufacturing Costs						
Material	206,300	103,349	102,951	218,850	102,827	116,023
Direct Labor	92,100	51,167	40,933	170,400	65,767	104,633
Overhead	240,300	133,498	106,802	149,450	83,026	66,424
Total	538,700	288,014	250,686	538,700	251,620	287,080
Gross Profit	$ 66,400	35,501	30,899	$ 66,400	71,895	(5,495)

EXHIBIT 2–11:
ABBREVIATED INCOME STATEMENT BEFORE AND AFTER RECOMMENDATIONS

The differences between the industrial and nuclear types show the impact if job costing is substituted for process costing when a relatively standard product and a highly customized product are made in common facilities. The process costing system in this company distributed the overhead between the two types of valves on the basis of the labor content. Under job costing, the indirect labor items that can be directly associated with the product would be reclassified to direct labor and charged directly to the valve on which the work is done. In this case example, such indirect labor items as quality assurance, shipping labor, material handling, and rework are large factors in the production of nuclear valves but small for the industrial valves. Use of job costing results in the reclassification of these items to direct labor and, therefore, direct assignment to the individual products that incur these costs. The same applies to shipping materials and incoming freight, which would be treated under job costing as materials and charged directly to the product that incurred the cost.

Exhibit 2–11 also shows the change in gross profit which is about the same percentage for both types of valves under the process costing system. Under job costing, industrial valves are found to be almost as profitable as in the past and nuclear valves show a loss of $5495 rather than a profit of $30,899.

Which Cost System Takes Precedence?

It should be obvious from the foregoing case example that job costing provides for more accurate product costing. This is only natural because there is a closer association of costs with products when all the major items in overhead are charged directly to the job rather than being allocated through an overhead rate. This is not to the detriment of process costing, which is a more economical system when standard products are being produced. This will be discussed in the next chapter.

Using Process Costing and Job Costing for the Same Product

There are instances, however, when a company can utilize two cost systems (process costing and job costing) for the same product. One of these products would be a standard type—telephone switching equipment, for example—which would utilize process costing. The other, relating very closely to the switching equipment, would be the installation of such equipment on the customer's premises to fit the customer's needs. Each installation would be unique and would require job costing to assure correct association of the costs with the job. Using two different costing systems is permissible in this case because the same facilities are not used for the installation.

Another situation in which both systems could be used for the same product is the case in which fabricated components are standard and interchangeable but the assembly varies by customer. The fabricated components (molded, stamped, machined, etc.) could utilize the process cost systems while the assembly operations would use job costing to reflect the different options. Here, as in the preceding example, there is a separation of the functions: Assembly is done in a different department. In the case of the telephone switching equipment, the manufacturing is done in the factory while the installation is done on the customer's premises.

WHICH SYSTEM IS SUPERIOR?

One cannot say that either job costing or process costing is the superior cost system. Both have advantages and disadvantages and each is the superior system in its proper application. Since this chapter has been devoted to job costing, a summary of advantages and disadvantages to that system follow. A similar summary will be included in Chapter 3, "Process Costing System."

Advantages of Job Costing

- Job costing results in more accurate costing because it "customizes" the costing to reflect the differences in the various jobs.
- The cost of each job can be directly associated with the resulting sales price.
- Costs of products can be compared with the original estimate on which the selling price was based.
- The profitability of each job can be quickly determined.
- Inventory control will be more reliable because the inventory will be identified separately for each job. As the job is completed and shipped, the inventory will be decreased. This should reduce the physical to book differences so characteristic of process costing.
- The detailed information for the various jobs will be useful in future estimating.

Disadvantages of Job Costing

- Job costing requires a good deal more work than process costing because of the greater detail of posting costs to individual jobs rather than to departments.
- Highly engineered jobs frequently must be supported by a great deal of documentation. This type of cost is difficult to estimate in advance.
- The practice of "borrowing" parts from one job to be used on another can greatly distort the costing procedures when paperwork adjustments are ignored—as they frequently are.

3

Process Costing System

Before proceeding with a discussion of the process cost system, it might be well to first restate the typical differences between job costing and process costing.

THE MAJOR DIFFERENCE BETWEEN JOB COSTING AND PROCESS COSTING

The major difference between these two systems lies in the classification given to certain overhead items. Normally, overhead costs are allocated to products through a vehicle such as direct labor, machine hours, or material. However, certain customized products consume overhead costs in amounts that may be far in excess of the amounts that would be applied through the vehicle of overhead rates. The examples cited in the chapter on job costing systems fall into two categories—indirect labor and indirect material. These are shown for both customized and standardized products.

Indirect Labor

CUSTOMIZED	STANDARDIZED
Engineering	
The end product must be designed according to specifications furnished by customer.	Manufacturing company establishes its own specifications and sells the standard product to all customers.
Spells out the specifications for purchase of material.	Specifications for material usually standardized and remain fairly fixed.
Provides detail drawings for shop based on customer specifications.	Once made, drawings remain the same except for periodic changes of the company's own making or of the demands of the marketplace.
Coordinates customer requirements with manufacturing procedures.	Customer orders standard product made under standardized manufacturing procedures.

CUSTOMIZED	STANDARDIZED

Inspection and Quality Assurance

Cost of inspection can be more than double that of equivalent commercial version. This interrupts production.	Inspections frequently can be made on random or sampling basis.
Audit and control of suppliers necessary to assure conformance to specifications.	Specifications not as rigid.
Monitoring programs for calibration of measuring equipment.	Specifications and requirements in calibration not as rigid.
Controls quality documentation.	Less documentation required.

Rework

In highly engineered work, rework is an unavoidable cost. Like much of the engineering, inspection, and quality assurance must be treated as direct labor.	Rework normally treated as overhead.

Shipping Labor

Unusual packing requirements are treated as direct labor to assure that the cost is properly associated with the product.	Packaging requirements usually less demanding for standard products sold commercially. Shipping labor treated as overhead unless packing is performed as part of the production line, in which case it would be considered to be direct labor.

CUSTOMIZED	STANDARDIZED

Indirect Material

Supply items used in highly engineered jobs can sometimes be quite expensive. Bolts for a nuclear valve can cost in excess of $10 each, whereas the equivalent commercial valve would utilize a bolt valued at ten cents. The same applies to other supply items.	The relatively low cost of indirect materials does not warrant identification as direct materials.

Those who are analytically inclined might argue that job costing, like process costing, should be based on accountability of costs by process rather than by customer order. They could point to machining, welding, heat treating, coating such as plating and painting, and assembly as individual processes for which costs are collected. True, they are processes and there also could be some automation. The difference is that, in a true job shop operation, product specifications are tighter than they are for standardized products. Also, products costed in a job shop operation are usually low in volume. This means that setup and changeover from one job to another may consume more time relative to "running time" than for standard products. Process costing would average out such costs.

The argument that job costing and process costing are the same because both involve processes should not be permitted to mask the need for delineation of the two costing systems. Financial executives responsible for the costing systems of multiplant companies have been known to issue edicts on standardization of cost systems within the company to the detriment of good product costing.

A Case in Point

The Elox Company was a $75 million a year company that manufactured electrical measuring instruments. It started as a development laboratory using a job costing system, and was a leader in this type of instrumentation. Its experienced costs, which through job costing revealed the difficulties in the various jobs, provided a reasonable basis for pricing. When the product gained market acceptance and a good volume was assured, it was moved out of the laboratory and transferred to one of the factory production lines, and repriced to reflect the more economical manufacturing procedures.

When a new controller came into the company, he argued that since 90 percent of the company's sales volume came from the standardized products, it was foolish to support two cost systems to satisfy the needs of only 10 percent of the volume. He therefore mandated a process cost system for the entire company.

As a result of the change in costing newly developed products, some were underpriced because they did not reflect the difficulties of manufacturing. Other new products that did not indicate problems in manufacturing were overpriced, thus providing competitors with an umbrella for getting into the business.

When management began to realize this, a mandate was issued that all laboratory products would revert to project costing (job costing). It took at least another year to obtain reliable costs on the new products since a number of them had been in process for a year or more under the process costing system. The controller learned a lesson from this experience but at great cost to the company, which subsequently replaced him because of another similar snap decision he made without considering all the factors.

MASS PRODUCTION—BIRTHPLACE OF PROCESS COSTING

The early automobiles, like the carriages, were handcrafted and production was low. For example, the 1903 Ford was built in an area about the size of a house—with less than a dozen cars in various stages of construction.

The modern automobile manufacturer can have a hundred or more manufacturing locations throughout the country, housing the fabrication, assembly, and warehouse storage areas. Engine manufacturing plants, component parts, plants, and other component producing facilities are located throughout the country to supply the assembly plants. The assembly cycle requires almost a day from start of the assembly to a finished auto—with finished vehicles coming off the end of the line at the rate of one a minute. This is mass production—another name for process flow. Because of the high volumes and well-organized material flow, it is possible to utilize the job shop feature in a process flow to satisfy each customer's options without delays for setup and changeover. This makes process costing sufficiently accurate for customized production when standard components are used.

Simplification of Operations and Specialization

The handcrafting of carriages and the early automobiles required skilled labor. With the advent of mass production and the breaking down of the operations into simple tasks, it was possible to utilize a greater percentage of semiskilled. This resulted in a lowering of production costs. The space requirements per unit also decreased because of the more rapid pace of production.

But somewhat offsetting the lower labor costs was the decrease in the spread of the wages paid to the semiskilled and the skilled operators. Although wages increased for both classes of labor, the rate of increase was greater for the less skilled. To offset this, many companies have introduced more automation. A relatively new type of automation is the use of robots for such operations as painting, welding, picking up boxes and moving them to another spot, and the loading and unloading of machines. Another characteristic of mass production is the high operating cost, which, including wages, can amount to $1500 per minute*—a high cost to pay for assembly line stoppages because of quality or other problems.

PROFITABLE OPERATIONS REQUIRE OPTIMUM LEAD TIMES AND OPTIMUM PRODUCTION RUN SIZES

The process type of manufacturing generally requires a substantial investment per employee. To be successful financially, the facilities of a process operation must be utilized efficiently at optimum size runs. This means continuous production with a minimum of downtime due to setup and changeover from one product specification to another. Reference was made earlier to automobile manufacturing in which various customer options are fed to the assembly line with no loss of momentum. This degree of efficiency requires proper lead time and sufficient standardization of the options to permit them to be accepted into the process without loss of momentum.

Lead Time. Lead time is necessary to facilitate the most efficient scheduling. In a product made in a steel, brass, or aluminum mill, for example, proper lead time allows scheduling by progressive gauges, widths, diameters, etc. This minimizes potential problems because of radical changes in production lines. To cite another example, in plastics molding it is important to make color changes efficiently. With proper scheduling, based on sufficient lead time, the lighter colors would be scheduled first. Progressively darker colors would follow. This reduces purging time between succeeding runs.

-----

* "Quality Controller, A Ford Plant Manager Tries to Limit Defects in Escort, Lynx Models," by John Koten, *The Wall Street Journal*, May 15, 1981, p. 1.

Production Run Size. Size of the production run of each specification is also very important. For very short runs, making changeovers from one specification to another could result in excessively high downtime in relation to running time.

One problem that many process-type manufacturers have experienced is a desire to increase volume and obtain a greater share of the market. This prompts them to emphasize good service to customers. What they overlook is that it is frequently necessary to accept orders with unreasonably short lead times. Short lead time reduces efficiency because of more frequent changeovers and shorter runs. With adequate lead time, proper scheduling would result in fewer changeovers and longer runs that are properly sequenced.

A Case in Point

A small plastics molding company that made parts in various colors scheduled its customer orders on a first-come, first-served basis. It prided itself on good service to its customers, who frequently had to wait several weeks when placing orders with competitors. What was overlooked, however, was that order 1 might call for use of a dark brown resin, while order 2, which arrived a day later, might call for pink, and order 3, received on the following day, calls for white.

In purging the press of the brown color, in preparation for running the pink, it took much longer to prepare for the lighter color than if the colors had been scheduled to be run in progressive darker shades. Following the pink with white had a similar result. Machine downtime due to excess purging time amounted to 36 percent more than if the sequence of colors had progressed from white to pink to brown. Although this plastics manufacturer scored an "A" for good service to customers, he lost numerous points in utilization of equipment, which in turn reduced profits.

PRODUCTION FLOW—GUIDE TO PROCESS COSTING FORMAT

In the section entitled "Perfection versus the Real World of Costing" in Chapter 2, it was pointed out that the "perfect" costing system would provide the maximum breakout of each of the elements of manufacturing cost. This means that the material, direct labor, and overhead would be shown for each of the departments (processes) through which the product passes. This section went on to say that a maximum breakout of the costs for the three elements was not always economically feasible. The manufacture of dies and molds was given as an example in which material was a relatively small cost, so a departmental breakdown would not be "worth the candle."

Although the foregoing can apply to process costing as well, it does not apply to the extent that it does to the job-shop operations. The reason is that the dollar volume is usually larger not only in number of units of product but the capital cost of the manufacturing facilities. In addition, the automation which is more prevalent in standardized products requires additional costs of maintenance and energy. It is more likely that a greater breakdown of the cost elements is necessary under process costing but less likely that overhead items would be reclassified to direct material and direct labor as was the case with manufacture of nuclear valves.

Brass Mill Production—Illustration of Interaction of Processes

A brass manufacturing company, which started in the brass button business, was the first in the United States to produce successfully a one-pound cast bar used for cold-rolling into brass strip from which the buttons were made. By 1970, the original one-pound cast bar had grown to well over a 3000-pound casting—which was used as the starting point in the cold-rolling operations of the continuous brass strip mill. The brass mill products were also expanded to include rod, wire and tube, as well as strip. Flowcharts A through F in Exhibit 3–1 illustrate the flow of the various brass products through the processes.

Casting—Flowchart A. The mill operations start with melting together (alloying) in various combinations the following metals: copper, zinc, lead, nickel, tin, and other metallic elements. These are melted electrically. The common high production alloys were continuously cast in Junghans-Rossi machines to make bars for sheet and strip products or billets for rod, wire, and tube products. The lower volume or the more difficult alloys were produced by semicontinuous bar or billet casting, continuous strand casting (rod), or by conventional mold casting.

Semifinished Tube, Rod, and Wire Shapes—Flowchart B. Hot extruding into a semifinished shape such as rod, tube, wire, or shapes consists of heating the cast billet until red hot and then forcing it under high pressure through a die in an extrusion press into the desired form. Flowchart B shows the steps from cast billet to material for further processing in the rod and tube mills.

Rod Mill—Flowchart C. Material for processing by the rod mill is received in the form of straight lengths or coils extruded from continuous-cast billets or as strand-cast coils. Material extruded in lengths is inspected for extrusion defects, drawn to finish size on draw benches, cut-to-length, cleaned, chamfered, inspected, and shipped.

Material extruded in coils, when finished as coils or redraw wire, is either drawn to finish size on single blocks or rolled to finish size on the twelve-strand tandem rolls. The tandem mill converts ¾"-diameter round wire to a square shape about ¼" each side by passing it through twelve pairs of rolls. Because this represents a high degree of cold reduction, only nonleaded alloys possessing high ductility can be processed in this manner. Material extruded in coils, when finished in lengths, is either sent directly to the Schumag-type machine which draws, straightens, burnishes, and cuts to length in one operation, or is drawn to a smaller size first on the single draw block, annealed, cleaned, and then finished on the Schumag-type machine. Leaded or less ductile alloys are processed in this manner. For extruded coils that go to the wire mill as redraw coils (leaded alloys or less ductile alloys) or to customers as coils, operations may be limited to single block draws with or without intermediate anneals.

Strip and Sheet—Flowchart D. The first operation on the continuous cast bars is to mill all four corners to prevent the corners from "fishtail" spreading while being processed through the cold-rolling operations.

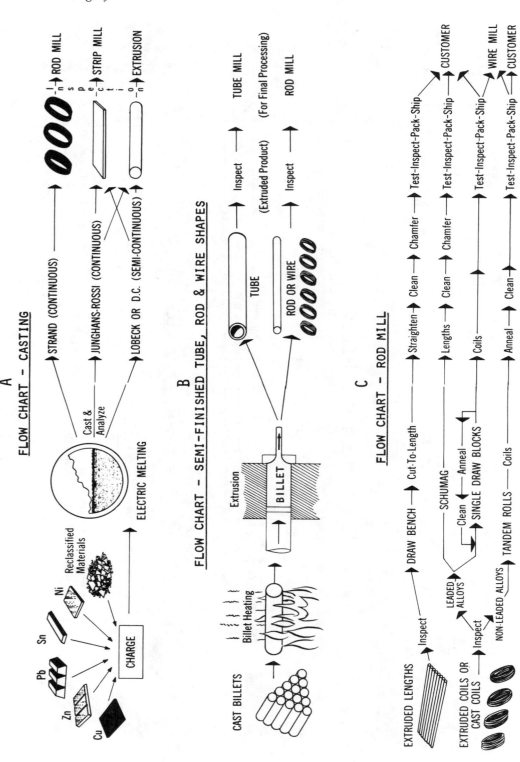

A

FLOW CHART – CASTING

B

FLOW CHART – SEMI-FINISHED TUBE, ROD & WIRE SHAPES

C

FLOW CHART – ROD MILL

EXHIBIT 3–1:

FLOW CHARTS ILLUSTRATING THE FLOW OF VARIOUS BRASS PRODUCTS THROUGH THE PROCESSES

Used with permission of the Scovill Manufacturing Company, Waterbury, CT.

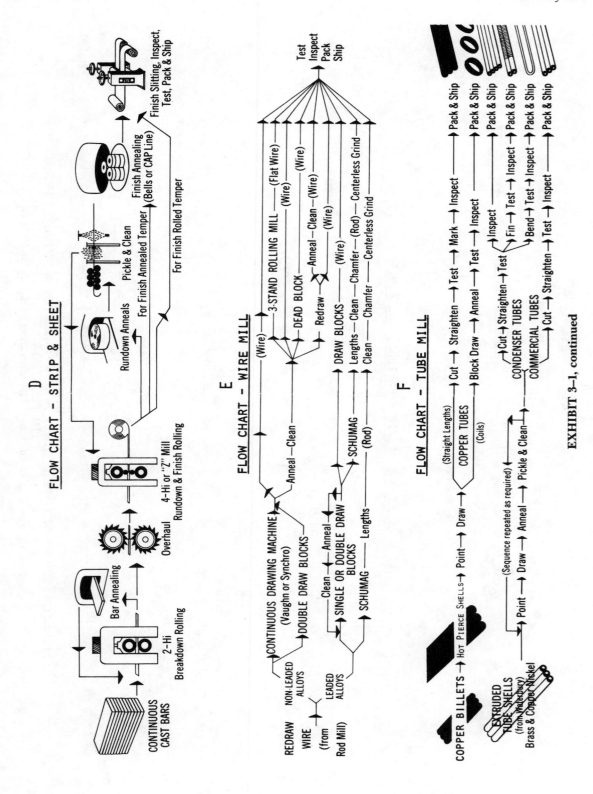

EXHIBIT 3–1, continued

The 2-Hi rolling mill reduces the cast bars from 3¼″ thick to 0.540″ thick in a series of rolling operations. These operations break up the cast structure and, at certain stages between the 3¼″ and 0.540″, the bars are softened for further rolling in one of two bar annealing furnaces, depending on the length of the bars. The softening changes the structure of the bars from work-hardened grains to soft equiaxed grains. Vacuum cup handling equipment moves flat bars through successive rolling, annealing, and milling operations until bars reach lengths up to sixty-four feet.

The 4-Hi rundown mill takes the overhauled (milled on both sides to remove surface oxides and imperfections) bars, reduces them in thickness, and forms them into coils.

After intermediate breakdown on the rundown mill, the coils are annealed in roller hearth furnaces which have accurate control of temperature and atmosphere. This controls the grain size and cleans the surfaces.

In order to produce longer coils up to 400 pounds per inch of width, two or three coils may be welded together. The longer coils are required for maximum nonstop runs on fabricating machines of the customers. Brass strip and sheet may be shipped to the customer either in the as-rolled condition, various hard tempers; or in the soft condition.

The final rolling passes are performed on a 4-Hi finishing mill similar to the rundown mill or on the "Z-mill."

For material shipped in the annealed or soft condition, the coils are either annealed in the controlled-atmosphere bell furnaces or on the CAP line (continuous annealing and pickling).

The final operation on the strip or sheet is to slit to the width ordered by the customer on one of the several slitters.

Wire Mill—Flowchart E. Coils of redraw wire are received from the rod mill for processing by the wire mill. Both leaded and nonleaded alloys are processed in a multiplicity of finished wire products such as flat wire, pin wire, cold heading wire, straight rods, single coils, spooled coils, and large packaged coils.

Large-size nonleaded wire is normally finished on the single of double-draw blocks, whereas small sizes are reduced on a multidie Vaughn or Syncro machine. The Vaughn machine has up to seven drawing dies and uses a dry lubricant. The Syncro has up to ten drawing dies and uses a wet lubricant. Both machines are run continuously by welding together the ends of wire coils to be drawn.

Leaded alloys and the more difficult to draw nonleaded alloys are reduced on single or double-draw blocks and may be finished in straight lengths on a Schumag machine. Material between drawing operations, or if finished soft (annealed), will be annealed in the Bell annealing furnace. Flat wire, edge-rolled wire, and rectangular wire is produced on a two-high, three-strand mill which rolls round wire to such shapes to close dimensional tolerances. (A well-known use of flat wire is the pull tab on slide fasteners.)

The Dead Block produces heavy weight coils on "stands" for long continuous wire fabrication runs by the customer.

The Schumag centerless grinder is capable of producing extremely straight, very close tolerance, small diameter rod.

Tube Mill—Flowchart F. Copper tube billets are hot-pierced to form a heavy-walled copper tube shell. Tubes are successively cold drawn, through dies and over mandrels, controlling the outside and inside diameters, respectively. The tubes become smaller in diameter and longer in length. This operation is performed on draw benches which can draw up to five tubes at a time. When the tube becomes too hard for further drawing, it is annealed (softened) and may be drawn again, annealed, and drawn until it reaches the final dimensions ordered by the customer. Pickling removes oxide coatings formed by the high temperatures and assures clean and bright surfaces.

Process Costing Format for Brass Mill Products

Flowcharts A through F identify a natural departmental structure for the production of brass mill products. These are:

Casting

Semifinished tube, rod and wire shapes

Rod mill

Strip and sheet

Wire mill

Tube mill

This departmental structure facilitates more accurate association of costs with products because the manufacturing cost elements are identified by departments (major groups of processes). This departmental format compares favorably with the listing of best features for control of the four job-costing formats (see Exhibit 2–9 on p. 36).

Material. The input of material takes place at the beginning of the casting process. This same material, in different forms and shapes, moves through the various departments with no additional material added.

Labor. This element of cost is identifiable by labor grade for each of the departments by process within the department.

Overhead. A breakdown of overhead by department should be readily available. It is also important that information on overhead be determined by processes within the department for more meaningful association of overhead costs with products. Flowchart D in Exhibit 3–1, for strip and sheet, provides an example of variations in work performed on the CAP line. A strip can be passed through the CAP line at 25 feet per hour or 250 feet per hour, depending on the alloy, gauge, and desired grain size and surface condition. The product running through at 25 feet per hour absorbs substantially more of the labor and overhead associated with the CAP line than the product running through at 250 feet per hour. This difference must be recognized if the cost association with the product is to be correct. Such variations can occur in other processes as well.

This illustration of brass mill products was selected to demonstrate the casting of a metal for making a range of products sold to other manufacturers for further processing. Another manufacturer might, for example, purchase its sheet (brass, aluminum, or steel) at a greater thickness and roll it down to the gauges desired by its customers. An electronics company might purchase wire in the larger diameter and draw it down to smaller diameters suitable for its needs and for the needs of its customers if it also makes sales to the outside. Manufacturers of products made of die castings might purchase ingots of zinc (or zamac) and mold their own castings rather than purchasing the molded parts.

The next illustration will deal with a manufacturer of tire valve stems. The stem is made of brass rod purchased from a brass mill. It is drilled out from both ends to provide for the insertion of the core which controls the flow of air into and out of the tire. A rubber disc is molded to the brass stem to secure the stem to the rim of the tire. Exhibit 3–2 illustrates some types of stems. Exhibit 3–3 illustrates the product build-up of the stem exclusive of the valve core. The valve core contains the mechanism that opens the valve when an air hose is applied. A spring mechanism closes the valve when the air hose is removed.

Tire Valve Stems—Product Build-up by Operations

The product build-up lists the operations to be performed for each product level. Using the brass stem as an example, level (04) calls for the following:

Cut off and head

Roll thread

Heading

Degrease

In the next higher level (03), a rubber disc whose operations are also shown separately is molded to the stem with the following operations:

Coat rubber disc and stem

Mold rubber disc to stem and cure

At the highest level (01), the operations include:

Make carton and apply label

Pack 1000 in carton

Weigh and seal

TUBELESS INDUSTRIAL VALVES
No. 3640S (TR416S) Clamp-in type
For rims having a .453″-diameter hole.
See description in Section A.

No. 412 (TR 412) Snap-in type.
For rims having a .453″-diameter hole.

TR No.	Schrader Number	Metal Insert	A	A₁	A₂	Valve Cap	Valve Core
TR 412	412	412UAH-1	1 $\frac{19}{64}$	$\frac{31}{32}$	$\frac{7}{8}$	660	8500T

Metal insert for tubeless snap-in valve

Schrader Number	A	A₁	E	M
412UAH-1	$\frac{61}{64}$	$\frac{9}{16}$	.242	.340

Motorcycle and Motor Scooter Tire Valves
These valves have broad general application on small tubes for motorcycles, motor scooters and other lightweight vehicles.

Dubltite tube type with full-threaded stems

TR No.	Schrader Number	Stem Without Rubber	A	Cm	Cr	Valve Cap	Valve Core	Rim Nut	Ring Washer	Hex Nut
11	1958	1958-1	1 ½	¾	2 ¼	6300C	6100T	6300-197	—	—
4	6006	6006-1	1 $\frac{5}{32}$	½	1 ½	6300C	6100T	4900	1022-4	5360-2

Manufactured to order only.

Metal stems for full-threaded type

Schrader Number	A	Cm	D	E	M
1958-1	1 ½	¾	1 $\frac{1}{16}$	.406″-28	½
6006-1	1 ⅛	½	—	.302″-32	$\frac{23}{64}$

Manufactured to order only.

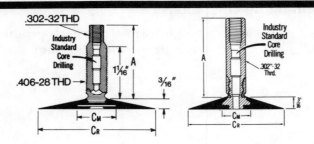

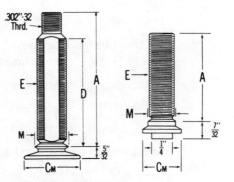

SCHRADER AUTOMOTIVE PRODUCTS

EXHIBIT 3–2:
SOME TYPES OF STEMS
Used With permission of the Scovill Manufacturing Company, Waterbury, CT.

62

PRODUCT BUILD-UP BY OPERATIONS

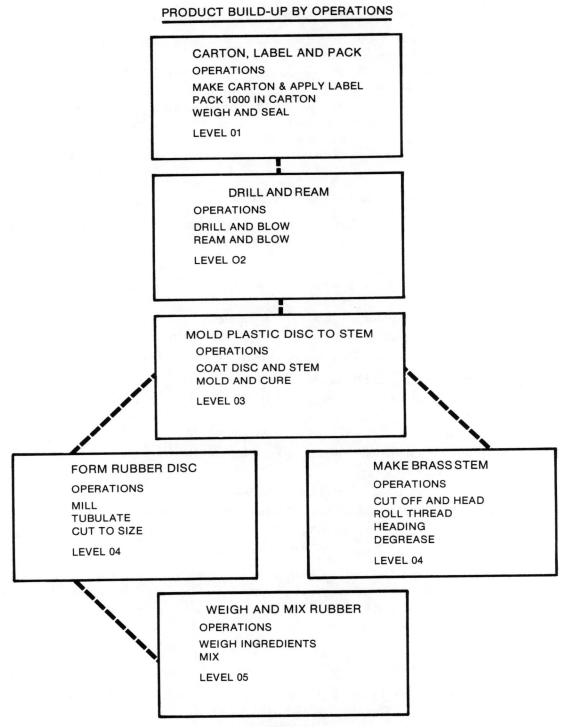

CARTON, LABEL AND PACK

OPERATIONS

MAKE CARTON & APPLY LABEL
PACK 1000 IN CARTON
WEIGH AND SEAL

LEVEL 01

DRILL AND REAM

OPERATIONS

DRILL AND BLOW
REAM AND BLOW

LEVEL O2

MOLD PLASTIC DISC TO STEM

OPERATIONS

COAT DISC AND STEM
MOLD AND CURE

LEVEL 03

FORM RUBBER DISC

OPERATIONS

MILL
TUBULATE
CUT TO SIZE

LEVEL 04

MAKE BRASS STEM

OPERATIONS

CUT OFF AND HEAD
ROLL THREAD
HEADING
DEGREASE

LEVEL 04

WEIGH AND MIX RUBBER

OPERATIONS

WEIGH INGREDIENTS
MIX

LEVEL 05

**EXHIBIT 3–3:
PRODUCT BUILD-UP BY OPERATIONS**

Use of Product Build-up Information

The format of the build-up of the various products varies from company to company. Many companies refer to this as bills of material, manufacturing, process sheets, and routing sheets. Some use combinations, such as bills of material, for specifying the materials required to make the product and the specifications for purchase—and routing sheets for listing the operations as well as time requirements for performing these operations. Whatever the terminology, this information serves an important function, not only as a guide to making and costing the product, but as a guide to factory layout based on the latest mix of product families.

Importance of Good Layout of Factory Floor

The more standardized the products and continuous the sequence of operations, the more important it is to have a good layout.

Features of a Good Layout

- Provides the shortest distance for travel of production consistent with the available facilities.
- Promotes better utilization of labor and equipment.
- Conserves floor space.
- Minimizes inventory levels because of increased productivity of the facilities.

Steps in Determining the Best Layout

- Determine the number and variety of parts, subassemblies, and finished products to be made.
- Identify those items that will be manufactured and those that will be purchased.
- Determine the capacity required for near-term growth.
- List the operations needed.
- Establish the logical sequence of these operations.
- Determine the relationship of the equipment to the operations.
- Determine the floor space needs of individual departments.
- Provide for flexibility in case of need for expansion.

Exhibit 3–4 shows the factory floor layout in which the tire valve stems are manufactured along with other related products. The operational steps are indicated on the layout with arrows showing the production flow. The stems used in this illustration are sold without the cores.

Process Costing Format for Tire Valve Stems

This company utilizes a computer in its costing system. It can therefore obtain cost information by operation and by cost centers within departments. The

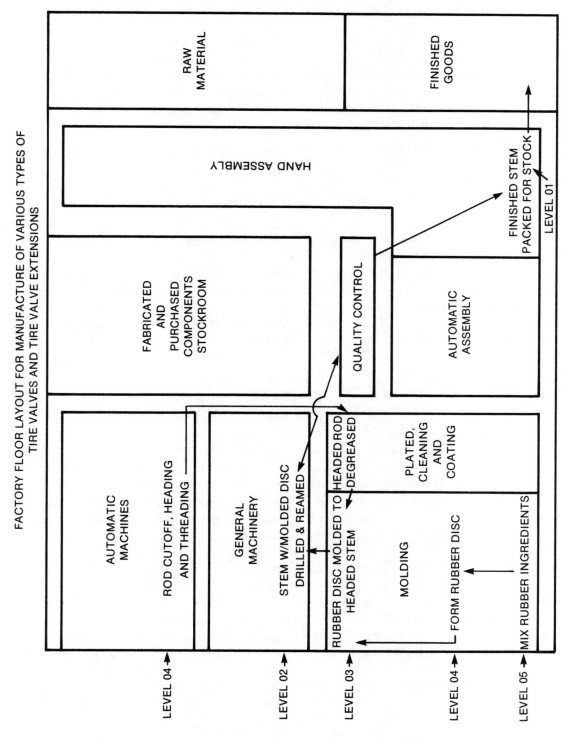

FACTORY FLOOR LAYOUT FOR MANUFACTURE OF VARIOUS TYPES OF
TIRE VALVES AND TIRE VALVE EXTENSIONS

RAW MATERIAL

FINISHED GOODS

HAND ASSEMBLY

FABRICATED AND PURCHASED COMPONENTS STOCKROOM

QUALITY CONTROL

AUTOMATIC ASSEMBLY

FINISHED STEM PACKED FOR STOCK

LEVEL 01

AUTOMATIC MACHINES

ROD CUTOFF, HEADING AND THREADING

GENERAL MACHINERY

STEM W/MOLDED DISC DRILLED & REAMED

RUBBER DISC MOLDED TO HEADED ROD

HEADED ROD DEGREASED

PLATED, CLEANING AND COATING

MOLDING

FORM RUBBER DISC

MIX RUBBER INGREDIENTS

LEVEL 04

LEVEL 02

LEVEL 03

LEVEL 04

LEVEL 05

HEADED STEM

EXHIBIT 3–4:
**FACTORY FLOOR LAYOUT FOR MANUFACTURE OF VARIOUS TYPES OF TIRE VALVES
AND TIRE VALVE EXTENSIONS**

overhead can be broken down by the portion that is considered to be variable and the portion considered to be fixed.

Material. Exhibit 3–5 illustrates the calculation of brass costs in cost center 0447. This is the cost of the brass rod issued for cutoff, heading, and threading.

The rubber ingredients issued to cost center 1291 are listed in the lower portion of the cost routing sheet. These can be identified as Product No. 97-00019-0000. Cartons and labels, which are used in cost center 1369, appear on the first two lines of the cost routing sheet.

Direct Labor. The cost routing sheet shows, for the various cost centers, the standard hours per thousand and the hourly rate of pay for each of the labor grades (see Exhibit 3–6). Multiplying the standard hours per thousand by the hourly rate for the cost center determines the labor cost by cost center.

Overhead. Although the cost routing sheet (same form in both Exhibit 3–5 and 3–6) shows a single variable overhead rate and a single fixed overhead rate in each cost center, there are actually a number of rates depending on the nature of the operations within the cost center. Manually operated machines (one operator for each machine) would have a different rate than machines operated by one-third of an operator, one-fourth of an operator, etc. The rates shown on the cost routing represent a composite of all the rates within the cost center after weighting according to the time allowances in the operations within each cost center.

Key Features of Two Process Costing Formats (See Exhibit 3–7)

The previous chapter on job-costing systems examined four formats while only two formats have been shown in this chapter on process costing systems. Actually, one of the four job-costing formats (semiconductors) is also used in the same company for all fully developed products that have become part of the standard line. The difference is that products under development are each costed individually through job costing while the fully developed products are costed in the aggregate by process costing without dealing with them on an individual basis. How this is done will be discussed in subsequent chapters.

Chapter 2 discussed the use of both job costing and process costing for the same product line. This had reference to telephone-switching equipment that was manufactured under process-costing procedures but was installed on the customer's premises on a job-costing basis.

Chapter 2 also covered the use of both job costing and process costing under the same roof. The manufacture of interchangeable components would be accomplished under a process-costing system, but the assembly of these to fit many different customer options would be done under a job-costing system of accounting. (Exception: When high volume permits conveyorized assembly line.)

This chapter, in an earlier section, also referred to various customer options being provided within the framework of a process-costing system. The difference is that, under process costing, there must be sufficient lead time and sufficiently large

COST ROUTING SHEET
PRODUCT 01-02608-5036

	1	2	3	4	5	6	7	8	9	10	11	12	13	14	15
PRODUCT ID	OPR NO.	BM LEVL	QUANTITY	START OPN.	COST CNTR.	STND HRS/M	LABOR RATE	VARBLE OVHEAD	FIXED OVHEAD	R/M CODE	R/M GROSS	R/M NET	SCRAP RECOVY	STANDARD R/M COST	U M
01—02608—5036	010	01	1.00000	010	1369	.02	2.497	1.749	3.407	018751				128.6900	2
01—02608—5036	010	01	1.00000	010						011856				8.0500	2
01—02608—5036	020	01	1.00000	020	1369	.05	2.497	1.749	3.407						
. 01—02608—0537	010	02	1.00000	010	0267	1.67	2.473	2.093	3.678						
. 01—02608—0537	020	02	1.00000	010	0267	1.18	2.473	2.093	3.678						
.. 01—02608—0005	010	03	1.00000	010	0568	.05	2.752	6.022	4.282						
.. 01—02608—0005	020	03	1.00000	010	0981	1.16	2.790	1.942	3.237						
... 01—02608—0008	010	04	1.00000	010	0447	.15	1.335	4.182	7.121	202800	(37.80)	(17.0)	(313.75)	(638.17)	2
... 01—02608—0008	020	04	1.00000	010	0450	.50	1.335	4.182	7.122						
... 01—02608—0008	030	04	1.00000	010	0761	.81	3.396	3.326	4.933						
... 01—02608—0008	050	04	1.00000	010	0568	.07	2.752	6.022	4.282						
... 01—02608—0002	010	04	1.00000	010	1294	.08	2.773	2.978	4.413						
.... 97—00019—0000	010	05	.00990	010	1291	4.65	2.773	2.978	4.413	059562	350.75000	350.75000		250.0000	2
.... 97—00019—0000	010	05	.00990	010						055461	17.54000	17.54000		88.0000	2
.... 97—00019—0000	010	05	.00990	010						051202	3.86000	3.86000		530.0000	2
.... 97—00019—0000	010	05	.00990	010						058110	4.56000	4.56000		530.0000	2
.... 97—00019—0000	010	05	.00990	010						057326	7.02000	7.02000		34.5000	2
.... 97—00019—0000	010	05	.00990	010						054202	35.08000	35.08000		260.0000	2
.... 97—00019—0000	010	05	.00990	010						057320	87.69000	87.69000		114.2100	2
.... 97—00019—0000	010	05	.00990	010						055407	86.64000	86.64000		160.0000	2
.... 97—00019—0000	010	05	.00990	010						057315	3.51000	3.51000		225.0000	2
.... 97—00019—0000	010	05	.00990	010						059536	70.15000	70.15000		102.5000	2
.... 97—00019—0000	010	05	.00990	010						059537	224.48000	224.48000		60.0000	2
.... 97—00019—0000	010	05	.00990	010						051214	21.05000	21.05000		11.7500	2
.... 97—00019—0000	010	05	.00990	010						054213	87.67000	87.67000		72.5000	2

```
COSTING THE BRASS
(COSTS ARE PER/M)

1. MULTIPLY GROSS WEIGHT (COL. 11) × STANDARD COST (COL. 14)
   (37.8) Lbs. X (638.17)/M = $24.13/M

2. SUBTRACT NET WEIGHT (COL. 12) FROM GROSS WEIGHT (COL. 11)
   37.8 Lbs. MINUS (17.0) Lbs. = 20.8 Lbs.

3. MULTIPLY DIFFERENCE BY SCRAP RECOVERY COST (COL. 13)
   20.8 Lbs. X (313.75)/M = $6.53/M

4. FROM LINE 1 SUBTRACT LINE 3
   $24.13 MINUS $6.53 = $(17.60)/M
```

2,255 UNITS @ $17.60 = ($39.68)

COST OF SALES

PRODUCT ID	OPR NO.	QUANTITY	BRASS	NON-BRASS MATERIAL	LABOR	VARIABLE OVERHEAD	CUMULATIVE OPERATING COST	FIXED OVERHEAD	TOTAL COST
01 00131 AP1	0004 000 R	315,000	4,191.36	17.71	310.16	731.31	5,250.54	837.66	6,088
01 00131 A1782	0013 000 R	57,500	773.78	240.59	481.82	524.23	2,020.42	756.87	2,777
01 00131 17829	0017 000 R	243,800	3,167.79	899.12	2,187.49	2,315.74	8,570.14	3,324.75	11,894
01 01651 UAH1	0086 000 R	277,500	3,605.67	15.45	287.09	676.08	4,584.29	760.57	5,344
01 02351 7913	5250 000 R	1,200	15.59	11.59	17.31	14.93	59.42	20.94	80
01 02870 7913	5179 000 R	757	12.58	5.29	31.35	20.25	69.47	27.18	96
01 02608	5036 000 R	2,255	39.68	3.77	33.28	33.49	110.22	54.50	164
01 03407 0178	5032 000 R	8,550	137.70	29.88	148.94	186.67	503.19	241.74	744
PRODUCT TOTALS	R	952,062	12,535.35	1,472.22	3,904.79	4,940.38	22,852.74	6,655.99	29,508
PERCENT OF TOTAL COST			42.49	4.99	13.23	16.75	77.46	22.54	100.00

LEGEND: R = Rod

EXHIBIT 3–5:
DEVELOPING THE PRODUCT COST—MATERIAL

COST ROUTING SHEET
PRODUCT 01-02608-5036

	1	2	3	4	5	6	7	8	9	10	11	12	13	14	15
PRODUCT ID	OPR NO.	BM LEVL	QUANTITY	START OPN.	COST CNTR.	STND HRS/M	LABOR RATE	VARBLE OVHEAD	FIXED OVHEAD	R/M CODE	R/M GROSS	R/M NET	SCRAP RECOVY	STANDARD R/M COST	U M
01—02608—5036	010	01	1.00000	010	1369	.02	2.497	1.749	3.4u7	018751				128.6900	2
01—02608—5036	010	01	1.00000	010						011856				8.0500	2
01—02608—5036	020	01	1.00000	020	1369	.05	2.497	1.749	3.407						
. 01—02608—0537	010	02	1.00000	010	0267	1.67	2.473	2.093	3.678						
. 01—02608—0537	020	02	1.00000	010	0267	1.18	2.473	2.093	3.678						
.. 01—02608—0005	010	03	1.00000	010	0568	.05	2.752	6.022	4.282						
.. 01—02608—0005	020	03	1.00000	010	0981	1.16	2.790	1.942	3.237						
... 01—02608—0008	010	04	1.00000	010	0447	.15	1.335	4.182	7.121	202800	37.800	17.000	313.75000	638.1700	2
... 01—02608—0008	020	04	1.00000	010	0450	.50	1.335	4.182	7.122						
... 01—02608—0008	030	04	1.00000	010	0761	.81	3.396	3.326	4.933						
... 01—02608—0008	050	04	1.00000	010	0568	.07	2.752	6.022	4.282						
... 01—02608—0002	010	04	1.00000	010	1294	.08	2.773	2.978	4.413						
.... 97—00019—0000	010	05	.00990	010	1291	4.65	2.773	2.978	4.413	059562	350.75000	350.75000		250.0000	2
.... 97—00019—0000	010	05	.00990	010						055401	17.54000	17.54000		88.0000	2
.... 97—00019—0000	010	05	.00990	010						051202	3.86000	3.86000		530.0000	2
.... 97—00019—0000	010	05	.00990	010						058110	4.56000	4.56000		530.0000	2
.... 97—00019—0000	010	05	.00990	010						057326	7.02000	7.02000		34.5000	2
.... 97—00019—0000	010	05	.00990	010						054202	35.08000	35.08000		260.0000	2
.... 97—00019—0000	010	05	.00990	010						057320	87.69000	87.69000		114.2100	2
.... 97—00019—0000	010	05	.00990	010						055407	86.64000	86.64000		160.0000	2
.... 97—00019—0000	010	05	.00990	010						057215	3.51000	3.51000		225.0000	2
.... 97—00019—0000	010	05	.00990	010											
.... 97—00019—0000	010	05	.00990	010											
.... 97—00019—0000	010	05	.00990	010											
.... 97—00019—0000	010	05	.00990	010											

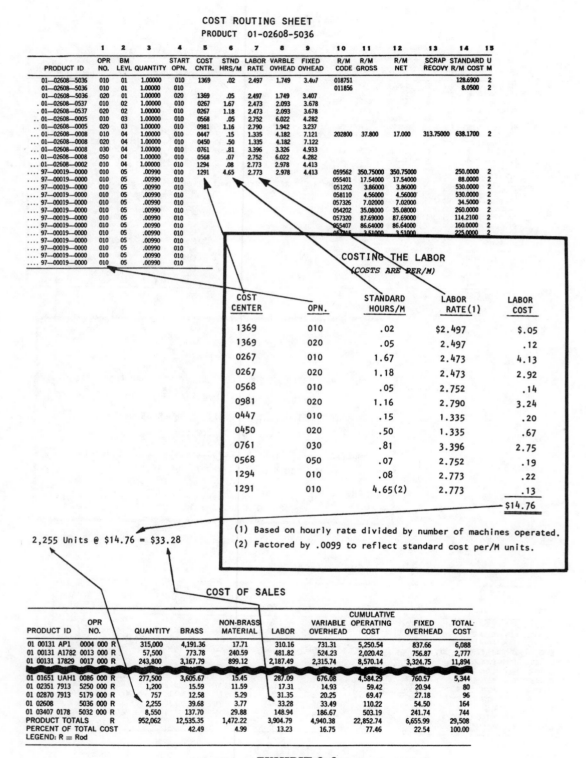

COSTING THE LABOR
(COSTS ARE PER/M)

COST CENTER	OPN.	STANDARD HOURS/M	LABOR RATE(1)	LABOR COST
1369	010	.02	$2.497	$.05
1369	020	.05	2.497	.12
0267	010	1.67	2.473	4.13
0267	020	1.18	2.473	2.92
0568	010	.05	2.752	.14
0981	020	1.16	2.790	3.24
0447	010	.15	1.335	.20
0450	020	.50	1.335	.67
0761	030	.81	3.396	2.75
0568	050	.07	2.752	.19
1294	010	.08	2.773	.22
1291	010	4.65(2)	2.773	.13
				$14.76

(1) Based on hourly rate divided by number of machines operated.
(2) Factored by .0099 to reflect standard cost per/M units.

2,255 Units @ $14.76 = $33.28

COST OF SALES

PRODUCT ID	OPR NO.	QUANTITY	BRASS	NON-BRASS MATERIAL	LABOR	VARIABLE OVERHEAD	CUMULATIVE OPERATING COST	FIXED OVERHEAD	TOTAL COST
01 00131 AP1	0004 000 R	315,000	4,191.36	17.71	310.16	731.31	5,250.54	837.66	6,088
01 00131 A1782	0013 000 R	57,500	773.78	240.59	481.82	524.23	2,020.42	756.87	2,777
01 00131 17829	0017 000 R	243,800	3,167.79	899.12	2,187.49	2,315.74	8,570.14	3,324.75	11,894
01 01651 UAH1	0086 000 R	277,500	3,605.67	15.45	287.09	676.08	4,584.29	760.57	5,344
01 02351 7913	5250 000 R	1,200	15.59	11.59	17.31	14.93	59.42	20.94	80
01 02870 7913	5179 000 R	757	12.58	5.29	31.35	20.25	69.47	27.18	96
01 02608	5036 000 R	2,255	39.68	3.77	33.28	33.49	110.22	54.50	164
01 03407 0178	5032 000 R	8,550	137.70	29.88	148.94	186.67	503.19	241.74	744
PRODUCT TOTALS	R	952,062	12,535.35	1,472.22	3,904.79	4,940.38	22,852.74	6,655.99	29,508
PERCENT OF TOTAL COST			42.49	4.99	13.23	16.75	77.46	22.54	100.00

LEGEND: R = Rod

EXHIBIT 3–6:
DEVELOPING THE PRODUCT COST—LABOR

PRODUCT	MATERIAL	DIRECT LABOR	OVERHEAD	BEST FEATURE
Brass mill products (steel, aluminum, and other metals are somewhat similar in manufacturing process)	Same basic material is used throughout the entire process	Identified by process (department)	Identified by process (department)	Identification of labor by process (department) Identification of overhead by process (department)
Brass tire valve stems	Material identified two ways: • Brass and nonbrass • By department	Identified by operation within cost center (department)	Identified by operation within cost center (department)	Two-way breakdown of material Breakdown of labor by operation and by cost center Breakdown of overhead by operation and by cost center

EXHIBIT 3–7:
KEY FEATURES OF TWO PROCESS–COSTING FORMATS

production runs to assure that the momentum of production will not be slowed. If either of these two conditions is missing, utilization of facilities could be adversely affected, with a deleterious effect on profitability.

The Best Features of the Two Process Costing Formats

The two formats selected for analysis provide a representative range of costing formats for related products. The brass mill products are manufactured in a manner similar to other metals such as aluminum and steel. The end products from the various processes are made from the same material that originated in the first process; only one material is used throughout.

The manufacture of brass tire valve stems demonstrates how a product of the brass mills is processed from rod to an end product used on tires of various types of vehicles. Nonbrass products are also used so that material is identified by type of material as well as by department. Similar processes would be followed if the material were steel or aluminum—or some other metal.

The features of these two formats are quite representative of the process-costing system. Because process manufacturing requires relatively heavy investment in facilities and support labor, good controls are important. In both formats, and also in the semiconductor format referred to in Chapter 2, both labor and overhead are identifiable by department. Through use of a computerized cost system, the valve stem format demonstrates how labor and overhead can be broken down even further.

ADVANTAGES AND DISADVANTAGES OF PROCESS COSTING

The breakdown is as follows:

Advantages
• Process costing is simpler.

- Not necessary to accumulate costs for many individual orders; costs are accumulated by department.
- Availability of departmental costs facilitates responsibility reporting.
- Standardized nature of products facilitates measurement of productivity.
- Repetitiveness of production permits establishment of standards for determination of variations from standard cost.

Disadvantages
- Profitability by customer order not practical to compute.
- Inventory more difficult to control because of greater number of parts and subassemblies in process. Physical to book inventory differences more likely in process costing.

Comparison of Job Costing and Process Costing Features

Exhibit 3–8 compares various features of job and process costing. These include costing accuracy, relationship of cost to selling price, control features, maintenance costs, and measurement of job profitability. Exhibit 3–9 lists guidelines to selection of the proper cost system.

FEATURES	JOB COSTING	PROCESS COSTING
Accuracy of costing	Greater accuracy because of greater number of direct charges to the job	Greater averaging of costs
Relation of cost to selling price	Selling price usually has some relationship to estimated cost	Marketplace dictates selling price
Inventory control	Better controls because work-in-process is identified by job	Work-in-process inventory usually carried on books as a total
Other control features	Controls are by customer order	Controls are by department
Maintenance cost of system	Costlier because of greater volume of work	Less costly because data accumulation is by department rather than by individual job
Measurement of product profitability	Profitability of each job can be determined	Process costing does not provide for determination of profitability by customer

EXHIBIT 3–8:
COMPARISON OF JOB COSTING AND PROCESS COSTING FEATURES

PRODUCT CHARACTERISTICS	JOB COSTING	PROCESS COSTING
Made to Customer Specifications—Not Built to Stock Highly engineered products such as components used in nuclear applications	X	
Nonstandard product made to one customer's specifications. Examples: Airport firefighting equipment; special-purpose machinery; mill products made of special alloys.	X	
Standard, High-Volume Product with Customer Options— Not Usually Built to Stock Examples are automobiles, lathes, milling machines, grinders		X
Built to Manufacturer's Specifications—Built to Stock Standard high volume products such as television sets, radios, household appliances		X
Book publishing—The product would actually be written by a nonemployee who would fulfill the general requirements of the publisher	X	

EXHIBIT 3–9:
GENERAL GUIDELINES TO SELECTION OF COST SYSTEM

These guidelines are necessarily general in nature because it would be impossible to take into account every case. The guidelines have been identified in three categories:

- Made to customer specifications—not built to stock
- Standard, high-volume products with customer options—final product not built to stock
- Built to manufacturer's specifications—built to stock

Made to Customer Specifications—Not Built to Stock

When a product is built to a customer's requirements, there is ordinarily little likelihood that this product would be sold to any other customer. There is always the possibility, however, that such a product could increase in demand. With the increase in demand, standardization of specifications would further increase volume, reducing prices and encouraging competition. If our society accepts increased construction of nuclear power plants, it is conceivable that the nuclear components could be produced through standardized processes that provide for strict quality standards. In such a situation, process costing could be substituted for job costing. The government has sponsored numerous development contracts that have subsequently become production contracts, so a transition of this kind is not unusual.

Standard, High-Volume Products with Customer Options—Not Built to Stock

The key to which cost system would be appropriate is "standard high volume products." This sets the stage for use of process costing. An earlier section emphasized that lead time is also a factor. The greater the number of options and frequency in the changes in the variety of options, the more important a factor lead time will be.

Built to Manufacturer's Specifications—Built to Stock

The previous two categories were based on selections made by the customer. In this category, the manufacturer establishes the specifications and offers for sale a standardized product that is geared to high-volume process manufacturing. This method of manufacture dictates process costing.

Although the manufacturer (publisher) would establish the specifications for the books and the general requirements as to content, books cannot be categorized as a standard product such as television sets or radios. Actually, they would fall more in the category of a contractor constructing a building according to the customer's requirements. Each book would be somewhat different from the other books, as would be true in the case of the building. This uniqueness feature calls for job costing.

ASSOCIATING COSTS WITH MANUFACTURING PROCESSES AND PRODUCTS

Exhibit 1–5 in Chapter 1 summarizes graphically the cost system variations that affect the association of costs with processes and products. At this point, we have completed discussion of job costing and process costing, the primary costing levels. The next two chapters will cover the secondary costing level, which includes standard costing and actual costing.

4

Actual Costing

Although the cost system variations referred to earlier in Exhibit 1–5 (see p. 22) contain the three elements of manufacturing cost, these were not dealt with in detail for the primary level of costing. The intent for this level was to identify the differences in treatment accorded the three elements in the two systems. These differences related to the classification of certain overhead items as either direct material and direct labor when job costing is used. Conversely, these items would be considered to be overhead for process costing.

Material and direct labor will be dealt with in greater detail in this chapter on actual costing and the following chapter on standard costing (see Exhibit 4–1). These chapters will illustrate the mechanics for charging material into production, development of the labor rates, and the application of labor to products.

CHARGING MATERIAL INTO PRODUCTION (PRODUCT COST)

Important in its effect on the amount charged to product cost is the method used for valuation of materials put into production. The most common methods are first-in-first-out (FIFO), last-in-first-out (LIFO), and average cost. The figures shown in Exhibit 4–2 were applied to each of these three methods. Seven periods were assumed, with purchases ranging from 200 units to 800 units. Issues ranged from 200 in the lowest period to 500 in the highest, while the units remaining in inventory ranged from 100 units in period 1 to 600 units in periods 5 and 6. The calculations were based on a period of falling prices as well as a period of rising prices. During the period of falling prices, the purchase price per unit ranged from $0.62 to $0.40, while during a period of rising prices the cost ranged from $0.40 to $0.62.

Use of these basic figures will show the results of pricing under a wide variety of conditions—showing radical changes in price as well as a rapid build up of inventory, with stabilization of the number of units during the fifth and sixth periods and then a decrease in the seventh period.

First-In-First-Out Method

Under this method, the material put into production is valued at the price of the earliest material purchased. The material remaining in stores inventory would

73

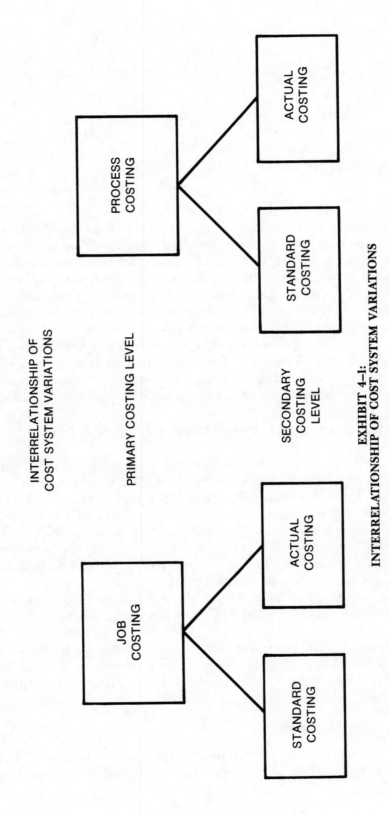

INTERRELATIONSHIP OF
COST SYSTEM VARIATIONS

PRIMARY COSTING LEVEL

SECONDARY
COSTING
LEVEL

PROCESS
COSTING

ACTUAL
COSTING

STANDARD
COSTING

JOB
COSTING

ACTUAL
COSTING

STANDARD
COSTING

EXHIBIT 4–1:
INTERRELATIONSHIP OF COST SYSTEM VARIATIONS

	QUANTITIES PURCHASED	QUANTITIES ISSUED	QUANTITIES IN INVENTORY	PURCHASE PRICE FALLING PRICES	RISING PRICES
Period 1	300	200		$.62	$.40
To date	300	200	100		
Period 2	400	400		.60	.42
To date	700	600	100		
Period 3	300	200		.55	.45
To date	1,000	800	200		
Period 4	200 & 600	500		.52 & .50	.50 & .52
To date	1,800	1,300	500		
Period 5	300	200		.45	.55
To date	2,100	1,500	600		
Period 6	400	400		.42	.60
To date	2,500	1,900	600		
Period 7	300	500		.40	.62
To date	2,800	2,400	400		

EXHIBIT 4–2:
BASIC FIGURES USED FOR VALUING PRODUCTION

therefore tend to be valued at the more recent prices. Using the basic figures shown in Exhibit 4–2, the method of pricing under FIFO is demonstrated in Exhibit 4–3.

The first issue of 200 units in period 1 was costed at $0.62 (period of falling prices), leaving the balance in inventory of 100 units at a unit cost of $0.62. During the second period, 400 units were purchased at $0.60. Likewise, 400 units were issued. However, the first 100 were costed at $0.62 (thus cleaning up the original purchase of 300 units at $0.62) and the other 300 units were issued at $0.60 resulting in a total of $242 or an average issue cost of $0.605 per unit. The same procedure is followed in the period of rising prices as well.

Note that the unit cost of issues to production during a period of falling prices is consistently higher than the unit cost of purchases while the unit cost of the balance remaining in inventory is consistently lower. Cumulative figures for the seven periods show:

Unit cost of purchases	$0.507
Unit cost of issues	0.523
Unit cost of inventory	0.405

During a period of falling prices, FIFO results in valuation of production at higher than current costs—thus resulting in higher product cost. During a period of rising prices, the unit cost of issues is consistently lower than the unit cost of purchases while the unit cost of material in inventory is consistently higher. Comparative figures, based on a total for the seven periods as shown in Exhibit 4–3 follow:

Unit cost of purchases	$0.509
Unit cost of issues	0.492
Unit cost of inventory	0.615

PERIOD OF FALLING PRICES UNDER FIFO

	Purchases			Issues to Production			Balance		
	Quantity	Unit Cost	Total Cost	Quantity	Unit Cost	Total Cost	Quantity	Unit Cost	Total Cost
Period 1	300	$.62	$186	200	$.62	$124	100	$.62	$62
Period 2	400	.60	240	400	.605	242			
Total to date	700	.609	426	600	.610	366	100	.60	60
Period 3	300	.55	165	200	.575	115			
Total to date	1000	.591	591	800	.601	481	200	.55	110
Period 4	200 & 600	.52–.50	404	500	.528	264			
Total to date	1800	.553	995	1300	.573	745	500	.50	250
Period 5	300	.45	135	200	.500	100			
Total to date	2100	.539	1130	1500	.563	845	600	.475	285
Period 6	400	.42	168	400	.488	195			
Total to date	2500	.519	1298	1900	.547	1040	600	.430	258
Period 7	300	.40	120	500	.432	216			
Total to date	2800	.507	1418	2400	.523	1256	400	.405	162

PERIOD OF RISING PRICES UNDER FIFO

	Purchases			Issues to Production			Balance		
Period 1	300	$.40	$120	200	$.40	$ 80	100	$.40	$40
Period 2	400	.42	168	400	.415	166			
Total to date	700	.412	288	600	.410	246	100	.420	42
Period 3	300	.45	135	200	.435	87			
Total to date	1000	.423	423	800	.416	333	200	.450	90
Period 4	200 & 600	.50–.52	412	500	.484	242			
Total to date	1800	.464	835	1300	.442	575	500	.520	260
Period 5	300	.55	165	200	.520	104			
Total to date	2100	.476	1000	1500	.453	679	600	.535	321
Period 6	400	.60	240	400	.528	211			
Total to date	2500	.496	1240	1900	.468	890	600	.583	350
Period 7	300	.62	186	500	.580	290			
Total to date	2800	.509	1426	2400	.492	1180	400	.615	246

EXHIBIT 4–3:
FIRST-IN-FIRST-OUT METHOD

In a period of rising prices, production is valued at less than current costs, thus resulting in lower product cost. As a result of this price lag in costing of production, current costs are not matched with current income—with the result that profit and loss statements are not representative of actual conditions, nor are inventories valued at current costs.

Last-In-First-Out Method

This method was devised in order to remedy some of the disadvantages of FIFO. Under this system, material is put into production at the most recent purchase price. If the current month's consumption of material were exactly the same as the quantity purchased during that month, product cost would be neither over- nor understated. If, on the other hand, the purchases were less than the month's consumption and it were necessary to dip into inventory, product cost would be understated or overstated, depending upon the price which was paid for the materials drawn out of inventory.

The first issue of 200 units during the period of falling prices was costed at $0.62 and the balance of 100 units was put into inventory at the same price. In the second period, the issue of 400 units was exactly the same as the quantity purchased that period. Since the procedure under LIFO is to cost issues at the most recent purchase price, the entire 400 units issued were priced at $0.60, leaving intact the 100 units in inventory which were purchased at $0.62. In the third period 200 units were issued. These were costed at the latest purchase price of $0.55 while the remaining 100 units purchased during that period were also put into inventory at $0.55. The first 100 units in inventory at a value of $62, plus the second 100 units at a total of $55, resulted in a total valuation of $117, which divided by 200 units equals an average unit cost of $0.585.

Exhibit 4–4 shows that production was costed at exactly the same unit cost as the purchases in all the periods except period 4 and period 7.

The variation in these two periods was due to the fact that the quantity issued was greater than the quantity purchased, thus necessitating withdrawal out of inventory at the next most recent purchase price. Under FIFO, during a period of falling prices, the unit cost of material in inventory was consistently lower than the cumulative purchase price while during a period of rising prices the unit cost of inventory was consistently higher. Under LIFO, however, there was no consistency in one direction or the other. In three of the periods the unit cost of inventory was higher than the cumulative unit cost of purchases and in three periods it was lower. Whenever purchases exceeded issues in a particular month, the excess amount was added to inventory to await its turn to be issued at such time as issues exceeded purchases. Under LIFO, if the current month's purchases are exactly equal to the current month's issues, there will be no over- or understatement of product cost because production will be costed at the current purchase price. In the case of FIFO, even if issues are equal to purchases in any period, there will usually always be some over- or understatement because the issues will be costed at prices paid for material in prior periods. LIFO, then, results in product costs which are more closely attuned to current market prices. As long as the volume of purchases closely approximates the volume of material issued to production, this method of inventory valuation will result in product costs which are correctly valued, and profit and loss statements will match current costs with revenue.

Weighted Average Method

Under this method of costing, the most recent purchase of materials is added to the cost of materials in inventory and the entire quantity is divided by the total number of units in order to obtain an average price per unit. As each period's issues of material is costed, the latest average price is used (see Exhibit 4–5).

PERIOD OF FALLING PRICES—LIFO

	Purchases			Issues to Production			Balance		
	Quantity	Unit Cost	Total Cost	Quantity	Unit Cost	Total Cost	Quantity	Unit Cost	Total Cost
Period 1	300	$.62	$186	200	$.62	$124	100	$.62	$62
Period 2	400	.60	240	400	.60	240			
Total to date	700	.609	426	600	.607	364	100	.62	62
Period 3	300	.55	165	200	.55	110			
Total to date	1000	.591	591	800	.592	474	200	.585	117
Period 4	200 & 600	.52–.50	404	500	.50	250			
Total to date	1800	.553	995	1300	.556	724	500	.542	271
Period 5	300	.45	135	200	.45	90			
Total to date	2100	.539	1130	1500	.542	814	600	.527	316
Period 6	400	.42	168	400	.42	168			
Total to date	2500	.519	1298	1900	.516	982	600	.527	316
Period 7	300	.40	120	500	.43	215			
Total to date	2800	.507	1418	2400	.498	1197	400	.553	221

PERIOD OF RISING PRICES—LIFO

	Quantity	Unit Cost	Total Cost	Quantity	Unit Cost	Total Cost	Quantity	Unit Cost	Total Cost
Period 1	300	$.40	$120	200	$.40	$80	100	$.40	$40
Period 2	400	.42	168	400	.42	168			
Total to date	700	.412	288	600	.413	248	100	.40	40
Period 3	300	.45	135	200	.45	90			
Total to date	1000	.423	423	800	.423	338	200	.425	85
Period 4	200 & 600	.50–.52	412	500	.52	260			
Total to date	1800	.464	835	1300	.460	598	500	.474	237
Period 5	300	.55	165	200	.55	110			
Total to date	2100	.476	1000	1500	.472	708	600	.487	292
Period 6	400	.60	240	400	.60	240			
Total to date	2500	.496	1240	1900	.499	948	600	.487	292
Period 7	300	.62	186	500	.586	293			
Total to date	2800	.509	1426	2400	.517	1241	400	.463	185

EXHIBIT 4–4:
LAST-IN-FIRST-OUT METHOD

Using the second period during a period of falling prices as an example, the costing of issues would be as follows:

100 units in inventory	$ 62
400 units purchased	240
Total value of 500 units	$302

$302 divided by 500 units = $0.604 per unit. This is the unit cost used for costing issues in the second period. The weighted average method is a modified version of

FIFO because, like FIFO, it has a similar, though less pronounced, distorting effect on product cost. In a period of falling prices, both methods result in costing of production at consistently higher than current purchase prices. During a period of rising prices both methods result in costing of production at consistently lower prices than the current purchase price. The only difference is in degree—the weighted average method does not distort as greatly as does FIFO.

PERIOD OF FALLING PRICES—WEIGHTED AVERAGE

	Purchases			Issues to Production			Balance		
	Quantity	Unit Cost	Total Cost	Quantity	Unit Cost	Total Cost	Quantity	Unit Cost	Total Cost
Period 1	300	$.620	$186	200	$.62000	$124	100	$.62000	$62
Period 2	400	.600	240	400	.60400	242			
Total to date	700	.609	426	600	.60900	366	100	.60400	60
Period 3	300	.550	165	200	.56350	113			
Total to date	1000	.591	591	800	.59800	478	200	.56350	113
Period 4	200 & 600	.52–.50	404	500	.51670	258			
Total to date	1800	.553	995	1300	.56670	736	500	.51670	258
Period 5	300	.450	135	200	.49169	98			
Total to date	2100	.539	1130	1500	.55667	835	600	.49169	295
Period 6	400	.420	168	400	.46301	185			
Total to date	2500	.519	1298	1900	.53690	1020	600	.46301	278
Period 7	300	.400	120	500	.44201	221			
Total to date	2800	.507	1418	2400	.51717	1241	400	.44201	177

PERIOD OF RISING PRICES—WEIGHTED AVERAGE

	Quantity	Unit Cost	Total Cost	Quantity	Unit Cost	Total Cost	Quantity	Unit Cost	Total Cost
Period 1	300	.400	$120	200	$.40000	$80	100	$.40000	$40
Period 2	400	.420	168	400	.41600	166			
Total to date	700	.412	288	600	.41100	246	100	.41600	42
Period 3	300	.450	135	200	.44150	88			
Total to date	1000	.423	423	800	.41830	335	200	.44150	88
Period 4	200 & 600	.50–.52	412	500	.50030	250			
Total to date	1800	.464	835	1300	.44990	585	500	.50030	250
Period 5	300	.550	165	200	.51894	104			
Total to date	2100	.476	1000	1500	.45909	689	600	.51894	311
Period 6	400	.600	240	400	.55136	221			
Total to date	2500	.496	1240	1900	.47851	909	600	.55136	331
Period 7	300	.620	186	500	.57424	287			
Total to date	2800	.509	1426	2400	.49845	1196	400	.57424	230

EXHIBIT 4–5:
WEIGHTED AVERAGE METHOD

Comparison of Three Methods of Charging Material into Production

The deviation of the cumulative unit cost of issues to production from the cumulative unit purchase price is compared for each of the periods for

- Period of falling prices
- Period of rising prices

This comparison is shown in cents per unit in Exhibit 4–6. Exhibit 4–7 makes a comparison of the same data graphically.

The deviations are greatest for the FIFO method, with the weighted average close behind. The LIFO deviations run fairly close to the zero line and show the smallest deviations. This means that use of LIFO will result in the least amount of distortion in product costing from period to period.

The rate of change is somewhat large in the purchase prices used in these comparisons. This tends to exaggerate the deviations within the seven periods. The relationships among the three methods, however, are not distorted.

Before going on to direct labor, it should be noted that material is purchased directly for the job in many job costing systems. In such situations, when an inventory of the raw material is not maintained separately, the entire purchase price will be charged directly to the job.

PERIOD OF FALLING PRICES

	FIFO	LIFO	Wgtd. Avg.
Period 2 to date	+ .001	− .002	—
Period 3 to date	+ .010	+ .001	+ .007
Period 4 to date	+ .020	+ .003	+ .014
Period 5 to date	+ .024	+ .003	+ .018
Period 6 to date	+ .028	− .003	+ .018
Period 7 to date	+ .016	− .009	+ .010

PERIOD OF RISING PRICES

	FIFO	LIFO	Wgtd. Avg.
Period 2 to date	− .002	+ .001	− .001
Period 3 to date	− .007	—	− .005
Period 4 to date	− .022	− .004	− .014
Period 5 to date	− .023	− .004	− .017
Period 6 to date	− .028	+ .003	− .017
Period 7 to date	− .017	+ .008	− .011

EXHIBIT 4–6:
DEVIATION OF CUMULATIVE UNIT COST OF ISSUES FROM CUMULATIVE UNIT PURCHASE PRICE

Deviation of Cumulative Cost of Issues
from Cumulative Unit Purchase Price

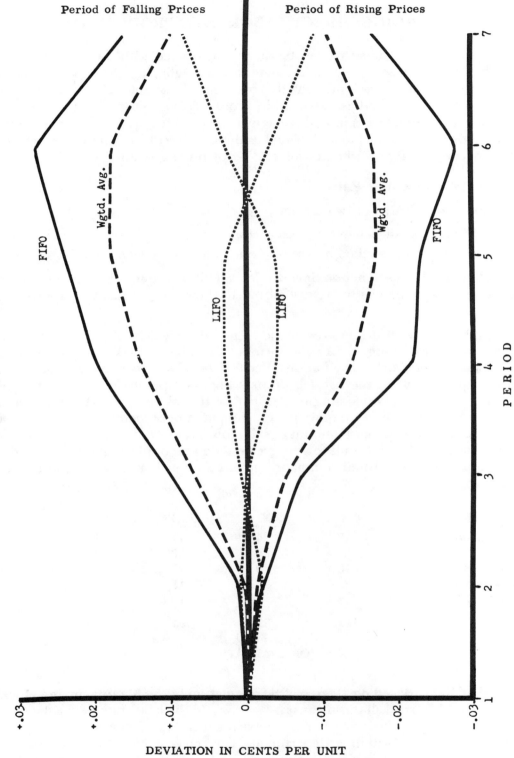

Period of Falling Prices   Period of Rising Prices

FIFO

Wgtd. Avg.

LIFO

LIFO

Wgtd. Avg.

FIFO

+.03   +.02   +.01   0   -.01   -.02   -.03

DEVIATION IN CENTS PER UNIT

PERIOD

1   2   3   4   5   6   7

EXHIBIT 4–7:
DEVIATION OF CUMULATIVE COST OF ISSUES FROM CUMULATIVE UNIT PURCHASE
PRICE

81

CHARGING DIRECT LABOR INTO PRODUCTION

Direct labor is that labor that can be directly associated with the product. If the amount of such labor (as well as material) is negligible, the labor would be considered to be indirect—and treated as overhead. In Chapter 2 it was pointed out that certain items treated as overhead in process costing should be reclassified as direct labor (and material) in highly engineered products. Here, our treatment of direct labor refers to the labor classified as direct. Direct labor, therefore, could be different, depending on whether job costing or process costing is used.

Development of Labor Rates

Labor rates consist of two factors:

- Labor grades assigned to the specific jobs.
- The labor rates based on degree of segmentation of the manufacturing operation.

Labor Grades Assigned to Specific Jobs. This is frequently referred to as job evaluation. Its purpose is to classify jobs as to their skill, difficulty, responsibility, etc.

Exhibit 4–8 illustrates a job evaluation schedule in which Jobs A, B, C, D, and E are evaluated according to five job factors: mental effort, skill, physical effort, responsibility, and working conditions. Each of the jobs is given a rating according to the requirements of the five job factors. The total points for each of the jobs becomes the basis for evaluating the "worth" of the job in terms of pay per hour. Jobs D and A, for example, require the greatest amount of mental effort, while Jobs A and B call for the greatest amount of skill. Job A requires the greatest amount of responsibility, while Job C calls for the greatest amount of physical effort. Based on this evaluation, Job A would command the largest hourly rate, while Job E would receive the lowest.

JOB FACTORS	JOB A	JOB B	JOB C	JOB D	JOB E
Mental effort	27	24	17	28	14
Skill	37	34	22	11	19
Physical effort	16	19	27	19	19
Responsibility	22	17	15	15	17
Working Conditions	5	5	10	6	9
Total Points	107	99	91	79	78

EXHIBIT 4–8:
JOB EVALUATION

Labor Rates Based on Degree of Segmentation of the Manufacturing Operation. In simple terms, all this means is: What would the labor rate be for the entire plant? What would it be for each of the departments? And what would it be for each of the cost centers within a department? For purposes of illustration, we will demonstrate a direct labor rate for the entire plant and a departmental rate.

Single Labor Rate for Entire Plant

The plantwide rate would be determined by dividing the total hourly direct labor payroll cost for the plant by the number of direct labor employees. This calculation is shown in Table 4–1.

Department	Employees	Labor grade	Hourly wage rate	Total wages per hour
Molding	28	8	$5.50	$154.00
Presses	25	6	4.40	110.00
Assembly	28	5	4.25	119.00
Total Plant	81			$383.00

TABLE 4–1

The calculation of the plantwide direct labor rate would be made as follows:

$$\frac{\text{Total wages per hour}}{\text{Total direct labor employees}} = \frac{\$383.00}{81} = \$4.73 \text{ per hour}$$

This $4.73 charge would be applied to the total hours required to make a product regardless of the nature of the manufacturing operations performed. This method of associating direct labor costs with products will work satisfactorily if the manufacturing operations are homogeneous and the labor rates are about the same. However, when such operations as molding, metal press work, and assembly work are performed, with labor grades ranging from $4.25 per hour to $5.50, there will be distortions. In such cases, the hourly labor rates must be calculated individually for molding, metal presses, and assembly.

Departmental Labor Rates

The association of labor costs with products will be demonstrated for plant-wide and for departmental application of these costs. The product consists of a molded bracket and molded support which are assembled together. The method of costing is to multiply the hours per thousand required for performance of each of the operations by:

• The plantwide direct labor rate per hour
• The departmental direct labor rate per hour

The total direct labor cost applied to the product by these two methods can then be compared to determine the amount of variation (see Table 4–2).

Operation	Standard Hours per 1000	Direct Labor Cost Plantwide Rate	Plantwide Cost	Departmental Rate	Departmental Cost
Mold bracket	.3768	$4.73	1.78	5.50	2.07
Mold support	.4072	4.73	1.93	5.50	2.24
Assemble	.6000	4.73	2.84	4.25	2.55
Total Labor Cost			$6.55		$6.86

TABLE 4–2

The total labor cost based on use of the plantwide average hourly rate is $6.55 for this product. The departmental rates, on the other hand, show a total labor cost of $6.86. Use of the plantwide rate would understate the product's labor cost by $0.31. Conversely, some products would be overstated.

Segmentation of the manufacturing operations should go below the departmental level in some instances. As an example, if one of the labor tasks within a department requires an unusually high skill, the labor grade may be higher than the normally required skill level. It may therefore be necessary to recognize this difference in product costing (as in budgeting) rather than using the departmental average.

USE OF ACTUAL COSTS IN JOB COSTING AND PROCESS COSTING SYSTEMS

Exhibit 4–1 indicates at the secondary level of costing that actual costs and standard costs can be used in both job costing and process costing systems. Although this is true, the probability is that actual costs are used to a greater extent in job costing, while standard costs are used to a greater extent in process costing systems.

The degree of usage of actual costs is likely to vary with increases and decreases in defense contracts. Paul M. Trueger, CPA, author of numerous editions of *Accounting Guide for Defense Contracts* states in his chapter on "Management Practices and Accounting Systems for Government Contracts":

> It should be expected that Government auditors seeking to determine the costs incurred under a particular contract will feel most kindly disposed toward an accounting system which reflects the accumulation of actual costs on a job costing basis, as such procedures are easiest to audit.

The methods employed should be productive of accurate costs by Government contracts. Trueger goes on to say, "This does not mean 'Actual' costs to the exclusion of acceptable standard cost systems, nor does it imply job order costs to the restriction of process, parts and assembly costs, etc."

Effect of Rising Prices on Costing System

Rapidly rising prices are another factor that can swing some companies, or segments thereof, from standard to actual costing. The financial vice-president of OGM Corporation decided that the rapidly rising costs of materials used by his company—as well as the labor increases—required such frequent adjustments to the standards that the standard cost system produced unreliable variances that became more and more inconsistent from one time period to another.

A Case in Point

This executive, in a meeting with his outside accountants, stated: "I know our products' specifications rarely change—and that they are built to stock for sale to many customers. We're a natural for standard costing, I admit. But what do I do when variances due to price increases get so large that I have to change standards at least twice during the year? This is expensive. We'll be better off using an actual cost system. I'm planning to use the weighted average method for my inventories. Cost of sales will also be costed at the weighted average method. In addition to these changes, I'm planning to give the marketing department their income statement showing the cost of sales based on replacement costs. I want them to see the profitability based on current market conditions."

The following outline showing the treatment of the various inventories was distributed to those attending the meeting:

INPUT	INVENTORY	ISSUES
Based on:		*Based on:*
Actual prices paid	Raw Material	Weighted average unit cost
Material at weighted average unit cost	Work-in-Process	
Direct labor at actual cost × predetermined[1] overhead rates		Weighted average unit cost
Work-in-process items at weighted average unit cost	Finished Goods	Sales costed at weighted average unit cost
Additional raw material added at weighted average unit cost		
Direct labor at actual cost × predetermined[1] overhead rates		

[1]Predetermined rates continued to be revised annually.

The one disagreement that was raised with the above related to the use of actual labor costs for application of predetermined (standard) overhead rates. The financial executive acknowledged that a base which changed in value during the year could not be used as the denominator for applying overhead rates that remained constant for the year. He agreed to a suggestion that direct labor hours be used in the future as the denominator for charging overhead to the product.

Another question that came up was: "As long as the company is going to an actual cost system, why not use LIFO rather than the weighted average since LIFO will come closer to actual costs?" The response was that the company was, indeed, agreeable to use of LIFO because it would be more advantageous in matching costs with current prices. With the present computer facilities, the company can handle the weighted average costing of its 11,800 items. It is making a study of procedures required for changing to LIFO. As soon as this study is completed and permission is granted by the Treasury Department to make the change, the appropriate steps will be taken. Since it would take about a year to make all the necessary preparations, the date of implementation of LIFO would be a year hence. In the meantime, the weighted average method can eliminate the most troublesome current problems.

ACTUAL OVERHEAD

The plan by the OGM Corporation to substitute actual costing in place of standard costs did not include abandonment of predetermined (standard) overhead rates that are revised annually. Some companies, however, do calculate the actual overhead rates each month and distribute overhead to the products made in that month. Others make their overhead calculations on a quarterly or semimonthly basis.

There are inherent weaknesses in such calculations that are made more frequently than once a year for standard products. For nonstandard products made by lot or by contract, it may be necessary to calculate interim rates. But in so doing, it is important to adjust the figures for distortions that occur when the period used for the calculation is not fully representative of the true costs.

The weaknesses in semiannual or quarterly rates are due to two basic factors:

1. Denominator used for application of overhead rates.
2. Behavior of overhead expense.

Denominator Used for Application of Overhead Rates

A period of less than a year might cover an unusually low (or high) period of activity. An unusually low period will minimize the denominator during a period when expenses are high. As an example, the months of July and August frequently show low activity because of vacations and accompanying plant shutdowns. During such shutdowns, expenses could be high—maintenance labor and maintenance materials, for example. Thus, in keeping with the philosophy of actual costing, the overhead rates in such periods would be unusually high and would overstate the costs of products.

Conversely, during a period of unusually high activity, which does not permit catch-up maintenance work to be done on a large scale, the costs due to this factor will be low and would understate the costs of products made in such a period.

A number of the overhead expenses are indicated as being stable in Exhibit 4–9. Here, again, when the denominator (direct labor, and/or machine hours, for example) is unusually low or unusually high—and the major costs are stable, there will be a distortion in the overhead charged to products. The importance of using the proper base for the calculation of overhead rates becomes obvious.

Behavior of Overhead Expenses

As noted above, expenses can vary in magnitude from one period to another; some remain fairly stable throughout the year; some are seasonal; others fluctuate with production, etc.

If we classify these by behavior, we would obtain the following:

Constant Costs—Those that remain fairly stable

Variable—Those that move with changes in level of activity

OVERHEAD EXPENSE	SIZE	STABILITY OF USAGE
Indirect Labor		
Salaried (supervisory & staff)	Large	Stable
Hourly (material handling and shipping)	Large	Fluctuates with production level
Maintenance	Large	Stable during year; high during shutdown periods
Overtime premium (nonmaintenance)	Large	Fluctuates with production level
Utilities		
Water	Small unless used in manufacturing process	Stable
Gas	High if used for heat treating	Stable if used in heat treating or drying ovens
Electricity	High if used for heat treating	Stable if used in heat treating or drying ovens
Telephone	Small for a factory	Stable
Facilities Costs		
Occupancy (except heating fuels)	Medium	Stable
Occupancy (heating fuels)	Medium	Seasonal
Equipment depreciation	High to medium	Stable
Supplies		
Maintenance materials	High to medium	High during low production periods
Expendable tools	Medium	Fluctuates with production
Tool maintenance	Small	Stable
Office Expenses		
Subscriptions and memberships	Small	Stable
Data processing services	Medium	Stable
Stationery	Small	Stable

EXHIBIT 4–9:
MANUFACTURING OVERHEAD EXPENSES—SIZE AND STABILITY OF USAGE

Contra Costs—Those that are high when activity is low and vice versa

Cyclical—Those costs that occur on a seasonal basis

Matching Overhead Expense Behavior with Three Levels of Volume

Rather than attempt to identify the Volume Level for a month, a quarter, or six-month period, three levels will be identified. These are:

- Low volume
- Annual volume
- High volume

The month, quarter, six-month period—or any other segmentalized portion of a year—could be represented by low or high volume.

The matching process, demonstrates the impact on product costing, and is shown in the table below:

OVERHEAD EXPENSE CLASSIFICATIONS	LOW VOLUME	LEVEL OF ACTIVITY ANNUAL VOLUME	HIGH VOLUME
Constant (fixed)	Overstated	Normal	Understated
Variable	Normal	Normal	Normal
Contra	Overstated	Normal	Understated
Cyclical	Overstated	Normal	Understated

The matching of the four classifications of overhead expense with the three indicated levels of activity shows that the annual volume produces normal overhead expense application to products because annual volume is matched with annual expenses. The variable overhead expenses show normal costs for all three volume levels because the expenses fluctuate with changes in production volume. For the variable items, the time span would not be a factor to be considered since the costs follow the volume. But for the other three classifications, these overhead costs would be overstated at low volume and understated at high volume.

The above applies to a process costing system in which standard products are made. For a highly engineered product or a government contract in which direct charging is required, some of the overhead expenses would be reclassified to direct material and direct labor—leaving a smaller pool of overhead expenses to be applied to product cost.

This discussion of overhead concentrated on the difficulties encountered in accounting for this element on an actual basis. A later section will be devoted to the development of predetermined (standard) rates and the application of these to product cost.

ADVANTAGES AND DISADVANTAGES OF ACTUAL COSTING

Although actual costing is looked upon as passe by many accountants, it is far from obsolete. As long as there are customized products and government development contracts, there will be a need for the accumulation of actual costs by jobs. However, it is necessary to be conscious of the disadvantages as well as the advantages of using actuals.

Advantages of Actual Costing

Actual costing is more accurate because more of the cost items are directly associated with the product on which the work was done. This applies particularly to production lots, customized products, and government contracts. Availability of actual costs can be helpful for future estimating for selling price purposes. The reclassification of certain overhead items to direct material and direct labor will reduce the pool of overhead costs that must be allocated on a less direct basis. Finally, actual costing minimizes the need for adjusting figures for the effect of inflation.

Disadvantages of Actual Costing

One of the costs that is difficult to associate with products is downtime. This can be a larger factor when the production runs are short. The difficulty arises in trying to determine the amount of the downtime due to a specific product. The questions that must be answered are: "When a time-consuming changeover affects several successive products, how is this cost apportioned?" "If the downtime is caused by a machine that cannot hold the tolerances required by the product, is the excess time caused by the design of the product or because of machine failure?"

Another cost that is difficult to associate accurately with products is the attempt to identify the actual overhead chargeable to the product made in a specific time period. If the run was made during a period of unusually high or unusually low volume, and actual overhead were applied, the amount of such application could be distorted because of the unusually high or low levels of activity. Likewise, any unusually high or low overhead expenses during the period in which the production run was made could distort the amount of cost associated with the product.

5

Standard Costing

Standards are not new. The January 10, 1980, issue of the *Wall Street Journal,* in the article "For Men Who Build Railroads, Not Much Seems to Change," makes the following statement with reference to what might be referred to as informal standards:

> In the 1860s, a newspaper reporter vividly recorded the sounds of railroad building. "It's a grand anvil chorus that those sturdy sledges are playing across the plains," he wrote. "Triple time, three strokes to a spike, 10 spikes to a rail, 400 rails to a mile"....

Although standards were known in the 1860s and before, it wasn't until 1908 that an engineer named Emerson recognized that one of the tasks of modern scientific management is to convert efficiency records into cost records—since the language of cost is understood by all and the language of efficiency only by a few.*

CONVERTING EFFICIENCY RECORDS INTO COST RECORDS

Standard costing might be defined as the conversion of efficiency records into cost records. The following steps would be required in the establishment of standards for the three elements of cost—material, direct labor, and overhead:

- Specifications of material to be used
- Allowable quantity of material
- Standard material prices
- Types of operations and equipment required
- Time allowances for operations
- Standard labor rates by nature of operation
- Predetermined overhead rate(s)

Efficient Performance and Good Layout—Prerequisite to Good Standards

Before any standards are set, it is important to assure that the operations are being efficiently performed and the equipment properly laid out.

---

*Harrington Emerson, "The Twelve Principles of Efficiency," *The Engineering Magazine,* New York, 1913.

A Case in Point on Efficiency

The EPG Corporation purchased steel tubing in 8-, 10-, 12-, and 15-foot lengths. These were threaded at both ends and used in the construction of equipment. Quite frequently, it was found that only 7-foot lengths were needed, in which case an 8-foot length was used with waste of a foot. When 11-foot lengths were needed, a 12-foot length was used, and so on. This resulted in a great deal of loss of material, which concerned management. If a greater number of different lengths were stocked, the size of the inventory and the associated carrying costs would increase. When the company was making preparations for installation of standards for standard costing, it was decided to purchase the tubing in coils and cut it to the various sizes as needed. This eliminated the waste pieces and reduced the size of the inventory because the various standard-size lengths were no longer needed. The cost to the company was a straightener and an automatic cutter, both of which were relatively inexpensive.

A Case in Point on Factory Layout

In reviewing the factory layout, it was found that there were two NC (numerically controlled) machines located in different parts of the plant because the plant was separated into two different product manufacturing areas. Since two machines of this type could be operated by one operator, the company was incurring excess labor costs by using a full-time operator for each of the two machines. An investigation showed that there were other similar potential economies if the company combined the similar processes even though they served two different end products. The development of standards was delayed until the study was completed and the potential economies realized. The standards were then established with these economies taken into account.

It is also important that the work flow throughout the factory follows efficient patterns and that there is good control over quality to assure that work of one department forwarded to another meets the specifications required in the finished product. In addition, the steps required at the various work stations must be committed to writing in the form of a routing. (See, for example, Exhibit 5–4, Manufacturing Process Sheet, discussed later in this chapter, which shows the steps in making the tire valve stem.)

Specifications of Material to Be Used

The engineering department determines the most suitable material, consistent with economic factors, to use in the manufacture of the product. This considers not only the basic materials but the coating, finish, and application of the product as well.

The specifications must also take into account the allowable quantity of material to be used in the manufacture of the part, subassembly and finished product. The specifications are supported by drawings that provide descriptions of the parts, subassemblies, and finished products. Part numbers and dimensions are also indicated.

Allowable Quantity of Material

The allowable quantity of material must provide for "necessary losses," such as blanking scrap and turnings. Depending on the type of material used, the scrapped material can be reprocessed and the proceeds applied to reduce the cost of the material content of the product. This can be demonstrated in the figures for manufacture of a tire valve stem which are shown in Exhibit 3–5, Developing the Product Cost-Material, on page 67 and Exhibit 3–3, Product Build-up by Operations, on page 63. The latter exhibit, at level 04, lists the operations as cut off and head, roll thread, heading, and degreasing. The former exhibit, in the cost routing sheet, operation 010, cost center 0447, lists the material allowances per thousand tire valve stems as:

Gross weight	37.8 pounds brass per 1000 stems
Finished stem weight	17.0 pounds brass per 1000 stems
Necessary scrap	20.8 pounds brass per 1000 stems

Standard Material Prices

The function of establishing standard purchase prices is the responsibility of the purchasing department. The prices should be based on reasonable expectations of what the prices will average out to in the coming year.

Some companies prefer to establish material price standards based on the prices at the beginning of the new year (actually at the end of the current year). These companies prefer to measure the price variances from the beginning of the new year rather than making the measurement from an estimated average for the new year.

In some instances in which a particular material has a high degree of volatility, it may be necessary to revise the standards more frequently than once a year—probably semiannually.

In instances in which the company purchases a large amount of material during the year, it should investigate the possibility of more favorable prices through annual contracts in which the material would be shipped through releases scheduled by the company at specified dates. A purchased parts history should be maintained as a guide to past trends. This history experience should be utilized by the accounting function to review the standard prices established by the purchasing department (see Exhibit 5–1 for a specimen copy of a purchased parts history).

The Material Cost Standard

The standard material cost will be obtained by multiplying the standard (allowable) quantity by the standard material price. In instances in which scrap credits are involved, the purchasing department will also furnish the standard price to be used for this purpose. Using the gross weight, finished weight, and weight of the necessary scrap for the valve stem, we would calculate the standard cost for the material as in Table 5–1.

PART NO.	VENDOR NAME	STANDARD UNIT COST	U/M	PURCHASE ORDER NUMBER	INVOICE NUMBER	INVOICE DATE	QUANTITY	ACTUAL UNIT COST	ACTUAL TOTAL COST
1049		$ 5.40	c						
	Hanset Hanger			4219	48978	1-15-85	100	5.55	555.00
	Hanset Hanger			4300	49126	1-15-85	150	5.50	825.00
	Hanset Hanger			5316	51320	2-20-85	100	5.55	555.00
	Hanset Hanger			6300	1425	3-20-85	100	5.45	545.00
	Hanset Hanger			6315	1430	3-25-85	100	5.45	545.00
	Total—20 Plas-bound Caps								3025.00
1096		$24.75	ea.						
	National Metal			4500	1250	2-10-85	10	24.50	245.00
	National Metal			7125	2790	5-15-85	5	25.10	125.00
	Total—Metal Case Caps								370.50
1080		$ .35	lb.						
	Keystone			5120	26500	2-18-85	500	.35	175.00
	Keystone			7155	35200	5-16-85	500	.36	180.50
	Total—Polycorn								355.50

EXHIBIT 5–1:
PURCHASED PARTS HISTORY

	Pounds of Brass	Standard Cost per M Pounds	Cost per M Pieces
Gross material cost	37.8	$638.17	$24.13
Less necessary scrap	20.8	$313.75	(6.53)
Net material cost	17.0		$17.60

TABLE 5–1

Time Allowances for Operations

The amount of time that each of the operations should take can be determined in several ways:

- Estimates based on past performance adjusted for the unusual
- Time studies
- Predetermined tables of allowances

Estimates Based on Past Performance Adjusted for the Unusual. The earlier example of hammering spikes to hold rails in place is an example of using past performance.

Time Studies. Exhibit 5–2 illustrates how a time study is developed. The drilling of two holes in a bearing cup has been broken down into eight steps. For each of these steps, ten observations have been made and the readings for elapsed time recorded. In the last column, the ten observations have been averaged after adjustment for abnormal conditions that occurred during the time the time study was conducted. The eight steps add up to a total allowance of 0.92 minutes.

To this must be added such other allowances as bringing stock to and from work areas and making tool changes. These are estimated on a one-time basis rather than making ten observations, as was done for the drilling operations. These other allowances add up to 0.09 minutes. Adding the 0.92 minutes for the drilling operations to the 0.09 minutes for other allowances gives us a total allowance of 1.01 minutes per piece.

BEARING CUP	DRILL 2 ¹⁷⁄₃₂″ HOLES 24″ DRILL PRESS										Average
	—— Elapsed time in decimal minutes ——										
Place part on fixture (25″)	.03	.04	.04	.04	.05	.03	.07	.03	.04	.05	.04
Clamp part (socket wrench & nut)	.08	.07	.09	.09	.08	.10	.09	.10	.08	.07	.06
Lower drill head (3″)	.03	.03	.02	.03	.04	.04	.03	.04	.02	.03	.02
Drill 2 holes (17/32″)	.68	.66	.65	.69	.67	.66	.68	.67	.65	.65	.65
Machine feed trip-raise head	.02	.04	.03	.02	.02	.02	.03	.04	.02	.03	.02
Release part (socket wrench/nut)	.05	.05	.06	.07	.08	.05	.06	.07	.06	.08	.05
Remove 1 part (15″)	.03	.03	.04	.05	.04	.03	.03	.05	.04	.05	.03
Blow out fixture (air hose)	.05	.05	.06	.05	.05	.05	.04	.05	.06	.04	.05
Allowance for drilling operations											.92
Other allowances											
Bring stock to work area											.02
Remove stock from work area											.02
Tool change											.05
Total other allowances											.09
Total Time Allowed Per Piece											1.01

EXHIBIT 5–2:
ILLUSTRATIVE TIME STUDY

Predetermined Tables of Allowances. Using the drilling operations as an example, predetermined tables would provide operational allowances for drilling various sizes and various numbers of holes. The appropriate time allowance could be looked up in the table rather than requiring a study to be made.

The Manufacturing Process Sheet (Exhibit 5–4) lists the steps in making the brass tire valve stem. It also lists the time allowances by operation. These cover the setup hours for the machines that must be set up, as well as the production hours. In addition to the hours allowed for both setup and production, the manufacturing process sheet (routing) also shows the labor grade to be paid. How the labor grade is established will be discussed next.

Standard Labor Rates by Nature of Operation

The determination of labor grades for the various jobs, as discussed in Chapter 4, is based on evaluating several factors and their importance to the job being performed. These include mental effort, skill, physical effort, responsibility, working conditions, and, conceivably, other factors in jobs that have special requirements. The earlier job evaluation exhibit has been expanded in Exhibit 5–3 to add an additional job that is required to provide labor grades needed in Exhibit 5–4. These are developed in the following steps:

Machines/Operations	Setup	Production
Header	X	X
Rolling machine	X	X
Heading	X	X
Degreasing		X

Job Factors	Job A	Job B	Job C	Job D	Job E	Job F
Mental effort	27	24	21	20	14	12
Skill	37	34	22	19	19	15
Physical effort	16	19	27	19	19	17
Responsibility	22	17	15	15	17	16
Working conditions	5	5	10	6	9	12
Total Points	107	99	95	79	78	72
Grade	14	12	10	8	6	4

EXHIBIT 5–3:
JOB EVALUATION

These jobs can be covered by the six job categories shown in Exhibit 5–4. Even numbers have been assigned to the labor grades, which are shown in the lower portion of the exhibit just below the total points used as the basis for ranking the grades.

Machines/Operations	Setup Jobs	Production Jobs
Header	Job C	Job E
Rolling machine	Job C	Job E
Heading	Job A	Job B
Degreasing		Job F

When the job evaluation factors have been rated for each of the jobs and totaled, the number of points for each of the jobs is used as the basis for assigning grade numbers. The highest number of points identifies the highest labor grade. Thus, the grade assignments for the jobs listed above become:

MANUFACTURING PROCESS SHEET

SHEET 1 OF 1

ISSUE DATE	ISSUE NO.	SUPERCEDED DATE	P.C.	BASIC 02608	LINE NO. 1	MACH. CODE 0008	REFERENCE	SHOP ORDER NO.

DRAWING NO.   LAST C.A.   PART NAME STEM   DATE ISSUED

MATERIAL CODE 20-208   KIND BRASS   SIZE .280 DIAMETER   QTY. TO MAKE

SHAPE COIL   SPEC. 26-4   TEMPER   HARDNESS   RAW MATERIAL REQ.

UNIT POUNDS   PER/M GROSS 37.8   PER/M NET 17.0   REQUIRED COMPLETION DATE

ROUTING: MACHINING, COATING, INSPECTION, COMPONENTS STOCKROOM

OPER. NO.	OPERATION DESCRIPTION	EQUIPMENT	DEPT.	SET-UP HRS.	LAB. GRD.	PROD. HRS./M	LAB. GRD.	NO. MACH.	NO. MEN	REFERENCE
010	CUT-OFF AND HEAD	HEADER	MCHG.	3.0	10	.15	6	3	1	0447
020	ROLL THREAD	ROLLING MACHINE	MCHG.	2.0	10	.50	6	3	1	0450
030	HEADING	HEADER	MCHG.	12.0	14	.81	12	2	1	0761
050	DEGREASE	DEGREASER	COATG.			.07	4			0568

PROCESS ENGINEER   STANDARD ENGINEER

PROCESSED FOR A MAXIMUM-MINIMUM RUN OF _____ PCS.

EXHIBIT 5-4:
MANUFACTURING PROCESS SHEET

Machines/Operations	Setup Grades	Production Grades
Header	10	6
Rolling machine	10	6
Heading	14	12
Degreasing		4

These labor grades provide the basis for establishing standard labor costs which, like material standards, are frozen for a year. Although standards are established for setup, these are used as a means of control but are not included as direct labor standards. They are part of the overhead cost.

Calculating the Labor Standards

To determine the standard labor cost per thousand tire valve stems, the following data is required:

- Operations
- Production hours per M
- Standard hourly labor rate

This information is contained in the Manufacturing Process Sheet, shown as Exhibit 5–4. The calculations are shown in Table 5–2.

Cost Center	Operations	Production Hours per M	Standard Hourly Labor Rate	Standard Cost per M
0447	010 Cut-off and head	.15	$1.335	$ .20
0450	020 Roll thread	.50	1.335	.67
0761	030 Heading	.81	3.396	2.75
0568	050 Degrease	.07	2.752	.19
				$3.81

TABLE 5–2

The standard hourly labor rate takes into account the number of machines that are run by the operator. In the heading operation, for example, the operator's hourly rate of $6.79 is divided by two to arrive at $3.396 per machine.

Predetermined Overhead Rate(s)

Predetermined overhead rates are actually standards for overhead. These will be covered in Chapter 9.

VARIANCE ANALYSIS AND MANAGEMENT BY EXCEPTION

The differences between standard and actual costs are usually referred to as variances, which can be either favorable or unfavorable. When the major variances (either favorable or unfavorable) are singled out for management attention, this is referred to as *management by exception*. This means that management would ignore the smaller variances and concentrate on the factors causing the larger ones.

THE SIX KEY MANAGEMENT VARIANCES

Although there are more than six possible types of variances, this discussion will be limited to six—two for each element of manufacturing cost. These are:

Material Variances
Material purchase price variance
Material usage variance

Direct-Labor Variances
Labor rate variance
Labor efficiency variance

Overhead
Volume variance
Overhead spending variance

Material Purchase Price Variance

This is the difference between the actual price paid and the standard price that has been established for the current year. For illustrative purposes, to calculate the standard material cost let us assume the same standard price for brass that was used earlier in the chapter—$.63817 per pound. For simplicity in demonstrating how the purchase price calculation is made, let's assume a purchase of one coil of brass weighing 15,000 pounds at an invoice price of $0.70.

Standard cost (15,000 pounds at $0.63817)	=	$ 9,572.55
Actual cost (15,000 pounds at $0.70)	=	10,500.00
Unfavorable Variance	=	(927.45)

Material Usage Variance

This variance represents the difference between the quantity of material that should have been used (standard quantity) to make a given number of items and the actual quantity that was used. Following are the steps in making the calculation:

Finished good pieces	1,000,000
Pounds of brass per 1,000 pieces	37.8
Pounds of material for 1,000,000 pieces	37,800 lbs.
Actual pounds of material used	39,600 lbs.
Material usage variance in pounds	(1,800) lbs.
Standard price per pound	$ .63817
Unfavorable material usage variance	($1,148.71)

Importance of Determining Material Usage Variances Correctly

In listing the disadvantages of process costing, it was stated in Chapter 3 that:

> inventory is more difficult to control because of a greater number of parts and subassemblies in process. Physical to book inventory differences are more likely in process costing than in job costing.

A company making thousands of different parts of relatively low unit cost will find it difficult (and expensive) to calculate material usage variances with accuracy. Most writers and speakers on the subject of cost accounting and inventory control look to scrap reports (spoiled production reports) for the required adjustments to relieve inventories of spoiled work. Although this is technically correct, it does not work in many cases.

Case Example

The AKL Company manufactures stamped metal parts, molded plastic parts, and metal/plastic subassemblies sold to outside customers. The metal parts are stamped out of steel while the plastic parts are made of general-purpose plastics for the most part. The parts are of a low unit cost and are made in very high volume. Because of the small size of the parts, they are weigh-counted. This eliminates the need of handcounting items that are so numerous they are stored in large steel barrels that have to be moved by lift trucks.

The company had a history of fairly large inventory differences whenever physical inventories were compared with the book inventories. This occurred in both the metal and the plastic parts. When the company auditor criticized the factory controller because of inaccurate reporting of spoiled work by the factory, the controller made the following rebuttal to the auditor's report:

"When we purchase steel strip, there is a min-max range of thicknesses that the supplier is given for any specification. Obviously, the mill cannot roll the strip to the exact thickness required. Business being what it is, it's logical to expect the supplier to ship steel that tends toward the thicker end of the range that is allowed, while the standard weight allowance per fabricated piece will be closer to the average. Since the conversion factor for converting weigh-counted production to pieces is based on a different weight per piece than the actual weight per piece based on the steel shipped by the suppliers, there is bound to be an inventory discrepancy when the physical is compared with book." The auditor had, on a previous occasion, objected to the suggestion that an adjustment factor be added to the conversion factor to adjust for the difference. He didn't openly suggest that actual counts in lieu of weigh counting be made, but the thought seemed to be lurking in his mind.

The count problem with the plastic parts was somewhat the same. As the molds wore, more plastic material was used. As a result, the usage was greater than the standard weight allowance—which was based on new molds. I'm afraid our auditor has read too many textbooks but has spent too little time in the real-world of manufacturing.

Labor Rate Variance

The labor rate variance reflects the difference between the actual hourly rates of pay and the standard rates. This calculation would not be made for individual products. It would be made for major segments of the operations, such as cost centers, departments, or total plant. Table 5–3 shows how the calculation would be made for a manufacturing operation with four departments.

CALCULATION OF STANDARD LABOR COST

	Production Hours	Standard Hourly Rate	Total Standard Cost
Dept. 1	2,800	$5.50	$15,400
Dept. 2	1,300	5.00	6,500
Dept. 3	2,800	4.25	11,900
Dept. 4	1,200	3.75	4,500
TOTAL			$38,300

CALCULATION OF ACTUAL LABOR COST

	Production Hours	Actual Hourly Rate	Total Actual Cost
Dept. 1	2,800	$5.60	$15,680
Dept. 2	1,300	5.10	6,630
Dept. 3	2,800	4.20	11,760
Dept. 4	1,200	3.85	4,620
TOTAL			$38,690

CALCULATION OF LABOR RATE VARIANCE

	Standard Labor Cost	Actual Labor Cost	Variance
Dept. 1	$15,400	$15,680	($280)
Dept. 2	6,500	6,630	(130)
Dept. 3	11,900	11,760	(140)
Dept. 4	4,500	4,620	(120)
TOTAL	$38,300	$38,690	($390)

TABLE 5–3

In the foregoing example, the production hours are multiplied first by the standard hourly rates and then by the actual hourly rates. These calculations result in the total standard labor cost for each of the four cost centers and the total actual labor cost for the same cost centers. The difference between the standard and the actual labor cost for each of the cost centers indicates the amount of labor rate variance.

Labor Efficiency Variance

This calculation is made by first calculating the difference between the standard production hours and the actual hours. This difference is then multiplied by the standard hourly labor rate to arrive at the efficiency variance (Table 5–4).

	Production Hours			Standard Hourly Labor Rate	Variance in Dollars
	Standard	Actual	Variance		
Dept. 1	2,800	3,276	(476)	$5.50	($2,618)
Dept. 2	1,300	1,580	(280)	5.00	(1,400)
Dept. 3	2,800	3,750	(950)	4.25	(4,038)
Dept. 4	1,200	1,360	(160)	3.75	(600)
TOTAL	8,100	9,966	(1,866)		($8,656)

TABLE 5–4

The material and labor variances discussed in this chapter (and overhead variances that will be discussed in a later chapter) are reported in dollars. These are reported at the end of each accounting period—usually monthly.

Effectiveness of Variance Reporting

Calculation of the foregoing material and direct-labor variances provides the means for reconciling the actual manufacturing costs with the standard costs for financial reporting purposes. This is illustrated in Table 5–5.

INCOME STATEMENT
(Standard Costing)

Sales	$7,800,000
Cost of Sales at Standard	5,500,000
Gross Profit at Standard	2,300,000
Manufacturing Variances	
Material	111,540
Direct labor	46,823
Indirect expenses (Overhead)	249,856
Total	408,219
Gross Profit—Actual	1,891,781
Selling Expenses	546,000
General and Administrative Expenses	312,000
Pre-Tax Income	$1,033,781

TABLE 5–5

The format of the income statement can vary. Some companies show the breakdown of the material, direct-labor, and overhead variances. Others argue that developing this detail will unduly delay the issuance of the statement. They prefer to issue the detail later showing the individual types of variance within each cost element by cost center or department.

Operating executives frequently argue that they do not find the accounting-developed variances of much help to them in controlling their operations. Their argument is that they cannot wait until the end of the accounting period to obtain information on the labor efficiency variances. In some instances, they need this information on a daily basis, in other instances, at least weekly. Furthermore, they prefer to convert the actual and standard hours into percentage efficiency factors rather than delaying the analysis until the dollar values are calculated. This calculation is shown in Table 5–6.

PRODUCTION HOURS

	Standard	Actual	% Effcy.
Dept. 1	2,800	3,276	85%
Dept. 2	1,300	1,580	82
Dept. 3	2,800	3,750	75
Dept. 4	1,200	1,360	88
TOTAL	8,100	9,966	81%

TABLE 5–6

These figures could be calculated for as short a time frame as necessary—per shift, day, week, or month. The cost centers, identified as departments in this company, could be broken down further into work stations, if desired. The factory manager of the EG Company had the following philosophy:

"Reports cost money. I don't want an efficiency report (or any other report, for that matter) prepared routinely just to prepare a report. I want a weekly report by department every Monday to review with my department managers at our weekly meeting. However, if in this meeting I find that there appears to be a problem in one of the departments, I'll immediately request that a report be prepared for that department for each shift each day until I'm convinced that the problem has been corrected. In fact, if there is a high-cost work station with a problem, I will request a daily report for that specific work station. But when the problem has been cleared up, I want that report discontinued. If I didn't work this way, our files would be loaded with reports for every work station for every shift." When asked how he would know if that work station should slip again, he replied: "I'll spend some time in that work station during my morning tour to see how things are going. Once you have become aware of a problem, it takes only a few minutes to determine whether that problem has been corrected. After all, we have a department manager in each department who should be aware of existing and recurring problems. If he can't monitor a problem after being alerted to the existence of that problem, a pile of reports can't take the place of good supervision."

Unlike the pragmatic philosophy of this factory manager, the equivalent executive of another company demanded a weekly efficiency report showing each new week added to the previous weeks. This report was nineteen columns across and covered twenty-six weeks per page, plus each month's totals. The total report was over fifty pages long and included a total of 21,200 figures. Although the factory manager of this company used the report, the industrial engineer and departmental foremen shrugged their shoulders when asked if they found the report helpful.

Variance Reporting for Too Short a Time Frame

In their desire to "nail down" areas of weakness, some factory managers will insist on reporting labor efficiencies by work station for each shift. Frequently, this will result in efficiency percentages that can be highly misleading.

A Case in Point

Work station 6E in the Hawkins Company provided such an example. Work station 6E was a finishing operation for castings. The finishing operation was done in two steps: a smoothing operation in which the surface was sanded and a spray painting operation.

Depending on the product characteristics, some products have curved surfaces that require more sanding time than other products with flat surfaces. The spray painting operation is slightly longer for the curved surface, but the difference is very slight. The procedure is to do all the spray painting for like products at one time. When one product has been spray painted, the spray painter starts the next batch after a starting inventory has been accumulated. Earned hours (standard hours) are based on the number of items spray painted of each type. At certain times during the day, more hours have been put into the sanding operation than are reflected in the spraying production count for the same product. This would result in a low reported efficiency. After the spray painter has worked off the backlog, the production would be at a high point—resulting in high earned hours.

The figures in Table 5–7 illustrate some of the fluctuations in reported efficiency due to the foregoing.

PRODUCTION COUNT LOW BECAUSE SPRAY PAINTING LAGS SANDING

Product	Earned Hours (Standard)	Actual Hours	% Efficiency
348G11	0.4	2.7	14.8
457H21	2.3	7.2	31.9
539I32	4.1	7.5	54.7

PRODUCTION COUNT HIGH BECAUSE SPRAY PAINTING PRODUCTION IS HIGHER THAN SANDING

Product	Earned Hours (Standard)	Actual Hours	% Efficiency
549H54	7.2	3.0	240.0
667P45	5.7	2.2	259.1
332R90	15.5	7.3	212.3

TABLE 5–7

The above figures show distorted efficiencies because the time frame—one shift—is too short to reflect balanced production. A possible solution would be to separate the sanding operation from painting and to calculate the efficiencies individually. This is impractical, however, because the employee doing the spray painting assists in the sanding while the backlog for spraying is being built up.

When Direct Labor Does Not Vary with Production

Before the modern-day advances that have been introduced into manufacturing in recent decades, most machines required a full-time operator. As the production increased, labor cost increased proportionately. It varied with the volume of production.

As the more sophisticated equipment was developed, it provided for automatic stops when material started to jam. The buckling of the material pressing against a solenoid valve automatically shuts down the equipment before the die is damaged. Previously, it was necessary for the full-time operator to shut off the machine manually.

With this new feature, it is possible for the operator to attend two, three, four, or more machines. Thus, direct labor took on the nature of a fixed cost. If the operator was in charge of four machines, and only three were operating, the operator was still needed. The variable factor is machine hours rather than direct-labor hours. In costing products, direct labor would be assigned to products as part of the machine-hour rate. (This will be discussed in the chapter on overhead.) Accordingly, the measure of efficiency would be based on machine hours rather than direct-labor hours. Some companies use the terminology *machine efficiency* and *machine utilization* interchangeably. This was the case with the RPG Company, a brass mills company similar to the one illustrated in an earlier chapter.

Monitoring Machine Utilization

The RPG Company used scheduled hours as the base for measurement of the percentages of:

- Nonstandard work to scheduled hours
- Downtime to scheduled hours
- Scheduled hours during which no crew was assigned

Percentage of Nonstandard Work to Scheduled Hours. This percentage provides management with an indication as to how many of the jobs fall under the classification of nonstandard. When this percentage gets high, the orders are analyzed to determine if the dimensions of a standard size were changed slightly, whether they would fulfill the needs of several nonstandard items that cluster around a certain central dimension. This would facilitate longer runs and fewer changeovers.

Percentage of Downtime to Scheduled Hours. The percentage of downtime to scheduled hours measures the magnitude of downtime due to changeovers, adjustments, and maintenance.

Percentage of Scheduled Hours During which No Crew Was Assigned. This percentage indicates the downtime due to reductions in planned production.

The four-week experience of the company in monitoring machine utilization is shown in Exhibit 5–5.

Machine	% NONSTANDARD WORK TO SCHEDULED HOURS			
	Week 1	Week 2	Week 3	Week 4
#1 Rundown Mill	12.1	11.5	1.6	8.9
#2 Rundown Mill	80.6	88.3	86.0	63.7
Annealer A	21.8	20.9	26.1	21.7
Annealer B	44.8	64.8	72.8	86.1

Machine	% DOWNTIME TO SCHEDULED HOURS			
	Week 1	Week 2	Week 3	Week 4
#1 Rundown Mill	12.4	9.3	7.9	7.2
#2 Rundown Mill	12.8	11.7	14.0	8.5
Annealer A	39.9	37.4	33.3	39.1
Annealer B	14.9	26.9	12.6	.3

Machine	SCHEDULED HOURS DURING WHICH NO CREW WAS ASSIGNED			
	Week 1	Week 2	Week 3	Week 4
#1 Rundown Mill	13.3	6.3	21.3	11.8
#2 Rundown Mill	—	—	—	27.8
Annealer A	3.4	7.6	10.8	—
Annealer B	36.3	8.3	14.6	5.2

EXHIBIT 5–5:
FOUR-WEEK EXPERIENCE IN MONITORING MACHINE UTILIZATION

Rundown Mills 1 and 2

The exhibit, under "% Nonstandard Work," shows that mill 2 does a large percentage of nonstandard work as compared with mill 1. The percentage of nonstandard work drops from 86.0 percent in week 3 to 63.7 percent in week 4. Correspondingly, under "Scheduled Hours During Which No Crew Was Assigned," week 4 showed 27.8 percent as compared with 0 percent in weeks 1, 2, and 3. The percentage of downtime for both rundown mills shows a generally declining trend.

Annealers A and B

Annealer B shows an increasing trend in the percentage of nonstandard work while annealer A shows figures that are relatively flat. With the increasing trend in nonstandard work for annealer B, the scheduled hours during which no crew was assigned shows a downward trend. The percentage of downtime for annealer B shows a downward trend while A shows downtime to be fairly level.

ADVANTAGES OF STANDARD COSTING

Process costing lends itself to the use of standard costs because of the standard nature of the products and the use of standardized procedures for manufacturing. This does not preclude the use of standards for job costing operations.

Standards are advantageous because record keeping is simplified. Use of predetermined standard allowances eliminates the need for detailed records in which the actual costs must be closely monitored.

Standard costing permits the use of variances to boil down the degree of efficiency attained in the operation for each accounting period. These variances facilitate the reconciliation of financial results with management plans. Although the financial statements generally only summarize the variances, the more detailed reports that follow permit an analysis by individual items. Through use of the variances, management's control of the manufacturing operations is improved.

Although by their nature the standard cost-accounting systems produce information on a monthly basis, good controls could be made available more frequently. The quantitative allowances to which the dollars are applied can be used on a selective basis more often than once a month. This advantage is overlooked by many accountants who feel that controls must be expressed in dollars.

DISADVANTAGES OF STANDARD COSTING

Standard costing reduces the clerical cost that would be required under actual costing, but like any sophisticated system it requires constant maintenance.

One of the disadvantages of standard costing during periods of high inflation is that standards can get out of date quickly. In such circumstances, the credibility of the variances and standards from which they are derived become suspect. This may require interim revisions to adjust for inflation.

When standards are being revised, it is difficult to determine which items will be inactive during the coming year. As a result, standards may be established for hundreds of items that may not even be produced. This can be costly.

Many of the items for which standards must be established may be small in volume and run only once. This too can be costly.

6

Implementing a Standard Cost System— A Case Example

Vanity Products produces a line of plastic products used in toiletries sold to women. The principal products are cosmetic cases and lipstick holders. Although these were made for different customers to their own specifications, the processes were standard and the volume of production was in the millions. The standardized nature of the processes and the long production runs made use of standard costs a natural.

SYSTEM PHILOSOPHY

The philosophy followed in the design of this system is that accountability for costs must be based on the natural flow of production through the plant.

Tie-in of Cost System with Production Control Procedures

To be an effective tool of management, the cost system must reflect the flow of costs through the factory and warehouses with a reasonable degree of accuracy. Since the production control department is responsible for controlling the quantities of material, components, and subassemblies that are produced and shipped, it is logical that the accounting system be based on the paperwork flow used by the production control function. In short, production control quantifies, the cost department "dollarizes."

Production Scheduling

The steps followed in the production control function of scheduling production and issuing the work order are illustrated in Exhibit 6–1.

The scheduling process starts with the three-month forecast of sales, which is maintained on a three-month moving basis. The sales forecast is converted to a production forecast by adjusting for backorders and taking into account the inventory level of items currently in stock.

Production requirements are then exploded to determine the components needs. These requirements are converted into material requirements after taking

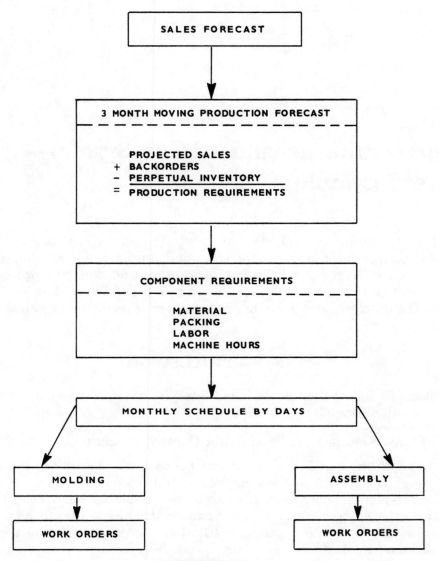

EXHIBIT 6–1:
STEPS IN PRODUCTION SCHEDULING

the inventory levels into account. Labor and machine-loading factors are also determined at this time. When the component requirements have been determined, a monthly schedule, by days, is made for molding and assembly. From this schedule, work orders are prepared and issued to the factory.

WORK ORDER CONTROL

The work order is basic to the production control system. Since it is the focal point in the procedure for determining the status of production within the plant, it is a key to the monitoring and collection of cost data.

Cost Flow

Exhibits 6–2 and 6–3 illustrate the cost flow through the injection molding and assembly departments—indicating the source of the costs, identification of the variances, and movement of finished production through the inventory accounts. Costs are collected by individual work order with input based on the following:

Material: Issues are based on actual quantities valued at standard prices.

Labor: Input is at actual labor hours costed at standard labor rates.

Overhead: Based on the predetermined overhead rate applied on machine hours for molding and on labor hours for assembly.

Work orders are relieved at standard cost for completed goods production. The difference between the standard value of this production and the accumulated input cost to the work order becomes the variance. Since production is valued at standard costs, inventories are also carried at standard costs.

Types of Work Orders Issued

Four types of work orders are issued to identify the types of production. These are:

• Molding and assembly of parts that are transferred directly to the finished goods inventory. These would be the large, continuous orders in which the molding and assembly operations are balanced.

• Molding of parts that are moved to stores for later issuance. Many of the products made by this company did not warrant more than one mold because of economic factors. In such instances, all of the parts would be molded and stored until sufficient parts are available to begin assembling the finished product. Certain of the components are standard and can be used on more than one product. These parts are frequently scheduled during low production periods in preparation for higher production periods.

• Assembling components (parts) to make the finished product. This would be the second of a two-step approach to making the finished product, the first step being the fabrication of the parts.

• Making subassemblies. Some products require the intermediate assembly of two or more parts that must be put together as a single unit, called the subassembly. In such instances, a separate subassembly work order would be prepared.

Information on the Work Order

The work order, shown in Exhibit 6–4, is used for all four types of production listed above. It contains the following types of information:

• Particulars of the product, such as product number and description.

• Operations to be performed—showing production standards, quantities produced, and actual hours compared with standard hours.

• Material requirements, showing quantity actually used, compared with the amount that should have been used.

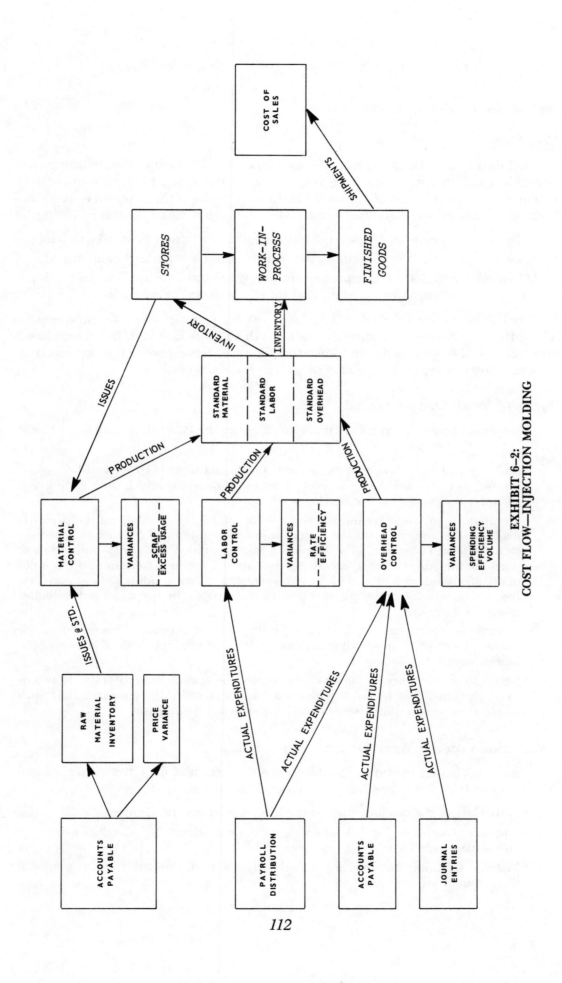

EXHIBIT 6–2:
COST FLOW—INJECTION MOLDING

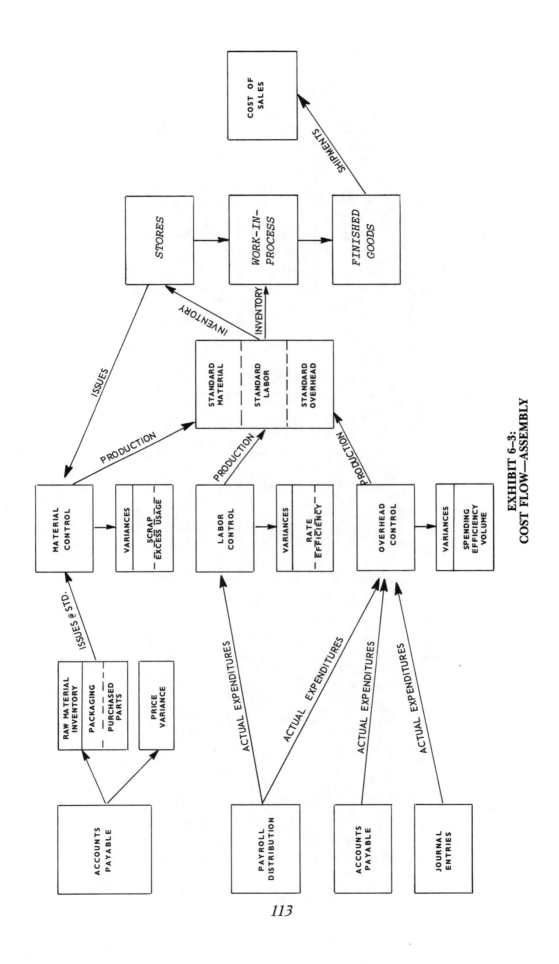

EXHIBIT 6–3:
COST FLOW—ASSEMBLY

113

WORK ORDER

MACH. SZ./NM.	MACH. NO.	DIE NO.	DATE STARTED	DATE COMPLETED	LOCATION	PRODUCT NUMBER	PRIORITY NO.	NO. OF OPER.	WORK ORDER NUMBER
			5-8	5-26		1003			8056

SCHEDULED QUANTITY	NUMBER OF CAVITIES	STANDARD CYCLE	STD. PIECES PER HOUR	LOT NUMBER	REMARKS
456,000					Assemble & Pack Cosmetic Cases

MATERIAL NUMBER	MATERIAL DESCRIPTION	WORK ORDER QUANTITY	DATE REQUIRED	DATE ISSUED	DATE REQUIRED	DATE ISSUED	DATE REQUIRED	DATE ISSUED	TOTAL	RETURN	TOTAL USAGE	QUANTITY STANDARD	QUANTITY ACTUAL
003	Carton	912									853		896
#1	Crate	912									853		896
#2	Bag	22,800									23,200		22,391
029	Tops	456,000									428,000		435,030
0032	Bottoms	456,000									525,500		435,030

OPER. NO.	DEPT. NO.	PROCESS FLOW	PART NO.	WORK CEN.	EMP. REQD.	STANDARD HOURS/100	STANDARD PCS./HR.	QUANTITY STANDARD	QUANTITY ACTUAL	HOURS STANDARD	HOURS ACTUAL
025		A-LINE 07 + 08			11	.0934	1070	435,030	426,500	398.6	407.3

$$\frac{426{,}500 \text{ pieces}}{1070 \text{ Pcs./Hour}} = 398.6 \text{ Std. Hrs.}$$

853 cs.

WORK ORDER CLOSED AND APPROVED BY	DATE	PRODUCTION PLANNER APPROVAL	DATE
	6-3		6-4

REMARKS

EXHIBIT 6–4: WORK ORDER

Exhibit 6–4 covers the assembly portion of producing cosmetic cases. The operations that are shown relate to the assembly—the molding having been covered in the work order that placed the plastic parts (tops and bottoms) in the stores area. It is for this reason that the information relating to the molding operations is not shown. Likewise, the material requirements are limited to the parts issued out of stores for assembly.

Summary Cost Sheet

This form (Exhibit 6–5) is used to summarize the actual material, labor, and overhead costs—as well as the standard material, labor, and overhead. An individual Summary Cost Sheet is used for each work order.

The actual material costs are based on actual quantities issued, multiplied by the standard material prices. Standard material cost is determined by extending the reported production by the standard cost per unit.

Actual labor cost represents the hours reported on the direct labor job cards priced at the standard labor rates. Standard labor cost is based on the reported production, extended by the standard labor cost per unit.

Actual overhead absorbed is determined by extending the machine and labor reported hours by the standard overhead rate. Standard overhead absorbed is determined by extending the reported production by the standard overhead cost per unit.

Work Order Summary

The Work Order Summary is a listing of work orders completed for the month, showing:

- Actual costs by individual work order.
- Transfers from work-in-process by individual work order.

Actual Costs. Actual costs for work order 8056C are illustrated on the first page of the Work Order Summary (Exhibit 6–6). Material is segregated to show packing supplies used ($922.66) separately from parts issued out of stores ($5899.25). The latter figure is made up of $2539.33 in material and $3359.92 in molding labor and overhead.

Transfers from Work-in-Process. The actual costs, discussed above, deal with the input of costs into the work order (work-in-process). Transfers from work-in-process deal with the output or relief of costs from the work orders. Since relief is at standard cost, the difference between the actual costs and transfers from work-in-process represents the variance.

The second page of the Work Order Summary (Exhibit 6–7) shows the standard costs as well as the variances. In the case of work order 8056C, again, standard costs of $8834.52 represent the value of product transferred out of work-in-process and transferred to finished goods inventory. In the amount of $497.09, the variances added to the standard cost of $8834.52 equal actual costs of $9331.61.

SUMMARY COST SHEET

$ TOTAL ACTUAL COSTS			
MATERIAL	LABOR	BURDEN	TOTAL
3461.99	1002.69	4866.93	9331.61

$ TOTAL FAVORABLE (UNFAVORABLE) VARIANCE			
MATERIAL	LABOR	BURDEN	TOTAL
(261.53)	(1.69)	(233.87)	(497.09)

DATE STARTED	DATE COMPLETED	LOCATION		WORK ORDER NO.
		WEST	EAST	
5/8	5/26			8056

NO. OF GOOD PARTS	PRODUCT DESCRIPTION	PRODUCT NO.
426,500	100X 15 "l" Plate	1003

ACTUAL AND STANDARD COSTS COMPARISON

OPER. NO.	DEPT. NO.	DESCRIPTION OF COST ELEMENT	ACTUAL			STANDARD		
			MATERIAL	LABOR	BURDEN	MATERIAL	LABOR	BURDEN
		Raw Material Usage	922 66			912 71		
		Packing Supplies Usage						
		Component Supply Usage						
		Stores Usage	2539 33	(1)	3359 92	2287 75	15 78	3071 22
		Machine Time Charges						
		Mold Amortization						
		Direct Labor and Burden:						
		Machine Operator						
		Extruder						
		Assembler(s) 25 = 407.3		814 60	1507 01		797 13	1474 41
		Other						
		Laboratory Costs		188 09			188 09	
		Finished Goods Loss						87 43
		TOTALS	3461 99	1002 69	4866 93	3200 46	1001 00	4633 06

ACTUAL → 9331. 61   STANDARD → 8334. 52

ACTUAL COST PER 1000 PARTS		
MATERIAL	LABOR	BURDEN

COST CLERK PREPARATION BY	DATE

COST ACCOUNTANT APPROVAL	DATE

(1) Included with burden (overhead)

EXHIBIT 6–5:
SUMMARY COST SHEET

WORK ORDER NUMBER	STATUS	RAW MATERIAL USAGE	PACKG. SUPPLY USAGE	COMPONENT SUPPLY	STORES USAGE	MACHINE TIME CHARGES	MOLD AMORT.	DIRECT LABOR	BURDEN ON LABOR	LAB COSTS	TOTAL CHARGES
8040	C	3,689.01				3,425.63					7,114.64
8041	C	14.50									14.50
8042	C	9.50									9.50
8043	C	1,834.73				2,630.15		48.80	90.28		4,453.96
8044	C	106.90				721.00					827.90
8045	C	30.08				189.00					219.08
8046	C	161.28				676.00		73.40	135.79		1,046.47
8054	C		3,222.92		17,551.42			2,049.80	3,792.13	581.46	27,197.73
8055	C		2,474.39		14,238.83			2,016.00	3,729.60	457.32	22,916.14
8056	**C**		**922.66**		**5,899.25**			**814.60**	**1,507.01**	**188.09**	**9,331.61**
8057	C		359.53		1,891.46			242.80	449.18	51.60	2,994.57
8058	C		283.58		2,082.76			762.00	1,409.70	104.52	4,642.56
8059	C		441.97		1,958.35			639.60	1,183.26	137.81	4,360.99
TOTALS		5,696.00	7,705.05		43,622.07	7,641.78		6,647.00	12,296.95	1,520.80	85,129.65
OPEN	X										
CLOSED	C	5,696.00	7,705.05		43,622.07	7,641.78		6,647.00	12,296.95	1,520.80	85,129.65

Status Symbols: X = OPEN
C = CLOSED

EXHIBIT 6–6:
WORK ORDER SUMMARY

WORK ORDER NUMBER	STATUS	STANDARD COSTS		VARIANCES				STD. COST	ACTUAL COSTS
		STORES WORK-IN-PROCESS	FINISHED GOODS	SCRAP MATERIAL USAGE	LABOR EFFICIENCY	OVERHEAD EFFICIENCY	MACHINE EFFICIENCY	FINISHED GOODS	TOTAL TRANSFERS
8040	C	8,624.70		310.99			1,199.07		7,114.64
8041	C	0		(14.50)					14.50
8042	C	0		(9.50)					9.50
8043	C	6,498.73		(47.78)	687.79	1,272.52	132.24		4,453.96
8044	C	884.27		5.43			50.94		827.90
8045	C	365.61		2.03			144.50		219.08
8046	C	761.29		2.58	(73.40)	(135.79)	(78.51)		1,046.47
8054	C		29,032.05	366.49	414.48	765.92		287.43	27,197.73
8055	C		22,833.70	(85.97)	(77.85)	(144.69)		226.07	22,916.14
8056	**C**		**8,834.52**	**(534.45)**	**(17.47)**	**(32.60)**		**87.43**	**9,331.61**
8057	C		2,916.81	(102.06)	(1.66)	(2.94)		28.90	2,994.57
8058	C		4,822.71	(30.70)	73.90	136.95			4,642.56
8059	C		4,114.69	(300.01)	4.46	8.62		40.63	4,360.99
TOTALS		17,134.60	72,554.48	(437.45)	1,010.25	1,867.99	1,448.18	670.46	85,129.65
OPEN	X								
CLOSED	C	17,134.60	72,554.48	(437.45)	1,010.25	1,867.99	1,448.18	670.46	85,129.65

Status Symbols: X = OPEN
C = CLOSED

EXHIBIT 6–7:
WORK ORDER SUMMARY (Second Page)

ACCOUNTING FOR MATERIAL

Accountability for material includes the accountability for usage as well as control of the flow of production through the plant and warehouses. The cost department plays an important role in reporting on the usage of various types of material consumed in production, while the dispatcher (expediter) is responsible for monitoring the flow of production through the plant.

Accountability for Usage

This includes the determination of material usage by part number as well as by type of material.

Raw Material Usage and Variance Report (Exhibit 6–8). The *Raw Material Usage and Variance Report* is concerned with accountability by part number. Exhibit 6–8 illustrates this for three plastic parts that have been molded with HF-77 G.P. bulk material.

The first column indicates the total good parts that have been produced during the period. This production is converted to pounds by multiplying the units produced by the "pounds per piece" conversion factor. Column 3 shows the total pounds of plastic contained in finished goods production.

PART #	GOOD PARTS PRODUCED	POUNDS PER PIECE	TOTAL POUNDS PRODUCED	REJECTION ALLOWANCE (POUNDS)	ACTUAL SCRAP GENERATED (POUNDS)	SCRAP VARIANCE (POUNDS)	TOTAL POUNDS MATERIAL USED
	(1)	(2)	(3)	(4)	(5)	(6)	(7)
1034-2	481,500	.01266	6,096	610	518	92	6,614
1054-1	589,500	.02403	14,166	1,416	2,278	(862)	16,444
1058-1	186,200	.10803	20,115	2,012	2,326	(314)	22,441

(   ) Unfavorable Variance
Column (3) = (1) × (2)
Column (6) = (5) − (4)
Column (7) = (3) + (5)

**EXHIBIT 6–8:
RAW MATERIAL USAGE AND VARIANCE REPORT**

The difference between the rejection allowance (column 4) and the actual amount of scrap generated (column 5) is reflected in the material usage variance (column 6).

The actual scrap generated for the period (column 5) is added to the total pounds produced (column 3) to arrive at the total pounds of material used.

Raw Material Consumption (Exhibit 6–9). This report develops the total material usage and the material usage variance by type of material. This determina-

MONTH OF _____

DESCRIPTION OF PLASTIC RAW MATERIAL	POUNDS						DOLLARS		
	BEGINNING INVENTORY	PURCHASES	MATERIALS CONSUMED	ENDING BOOK INVENTORY	ENDING PHYSICAL INVENTORY	MATERIAL USAGE VARIANCE	STD. COST/LB.	PHYSICAL INVENTORY	MATERIAL USAGE VARIANCE
HF-77-GP 347 (Bulk)	29,015	313,250	305,124	37,141	32,640	(4,501)	.12500	4,080	(563)
HF-77-GP 347 (Bag)	19,650	0	0	19,650	19,650	0	.13500	2,653	0
HF-77 Extrusion 300 (Bulk)	22,171	53,860	39,747	36,284	37,612	1,328	.12500	4,702	166
HF-77 Extrusion 300 (Bag)	39,600	0	27,158	12,442	11,800	(642)	.13500	1,593	(87)
Sinclair Koppers	2,600	0	0	2,600	2,600	0	.12750	332	0
Hercules 6323	26,400	10,000	16,322	20,078	19,410	(668)	.1700	3,300	(114)
Gulf 4112	3,600	0	260	3,340	3,400	60	.13750	468	8
Marlex–TR 880	14,600	0	8,734	5,866	5,490	(376)	.19000	1,043	(71)
Dow 666 U Amber	2,300	0	0	2,300	2,300	0	.17500	403	0
Dow 456-27-7	6,400	0	0	6,400	6,400	0	.18000	1,152	0
Marlex–TR 885 (Sweetheart)	9,450	95,280	52,764	51,966	51,033	(933)	.16750	8,548	(156)
Dow 900 M	6,650	0	0	6,650	6,650	0	.12250	815	0
TOTALS:	182,436	472,390	450,109	204,717	198,985	(5,732)		29,089	(817)

Unfavorable variances indicated by ( ).

EXHIBIT 6–9:
RAW MATERIALS CONSUMPTION

120

tion is made through a physical inventory taken at the end of each accounting period.

The beginning inventory by type of material is the starting point. To these figures, the purchases made during the period are added. From the aggregate of these two figures, the book inventory at the end of the accounting period is subtracted to determine total consumption, or usage. This is demonstrated below for material HF-77-347 bulk:

	Pounds		
Beginning inventory	29,015		
+ Purchases	313,250		
Total available		342,265	
− Ending book inventory		37,141	
Materials consumed			305,124

Material usage variance is determined by taking the difference between the ending book and physical inventories:

Ending book inventory	37,141	
Ending physical inventory	32,640	
Material usage variance		(4,501)

The dollar value of the physical inventory and the material usage variance are determined by extending the pounds by the standard cost per pound. These dollar figures are shown at the right of the report.

Control of Production Flow

The dispatcher (expediter) is responsible for all movement of material authorized by work orders. His approval stamp must appear on move papers before the material can be transferred. The various forms used to record production data and authorize movement of materials are discussed in this section.

Box Tags. This form (Exhibit 6–10) is attached to each box to identify its contents. It shows the part number, day and shift produced, the quantity, and the pallet control number.

Pallet Control (Exhibit 6–11). This form serves as a log of the box tags that are affixed to the cartons stacked on the pallets.

Scrap Notice (Exhibit 6–12). This is primarily used in the molding department. It identifies molding scrap that originates in the molding area—such as purged material, sprues, and defective molded parts. If the material can be reprocessed, the "To Be Reground" square is checked. If not reprocessable or if the part is an assembly that cannot be salvaged, the "To Be Scrapped" square is checked.

<table>
<tr><td>

PART NO.
7529-1

DATE 12/30

BOX NO.   2

PALLET CONTR. NO.   29-2

QUANTITY   Day 20,400
           Night 1,600
               22,000

(ATTACH TO GOOD PARTS TOTE BOX)

</td><td>

PART NO.
7529-2

DATE 12/30

BOX NO.   6

PALLET CONTR. NO.   31-1

QUANTITY   Day 4,600
           Night 18,600
               23,200

(ATTACH TO GOOD PARTS TOTE BOX)

</td></tr>
</table>

EXHIBIT 6–10:
SAMPLE BOX TAGS

ASSEMBLY   DATE: LOT NO.   SHIFT:

MOLDING   DATE: _____ SHIFT: _____

SAMPLE SIZE–   Act.   Sort   Rej.

MACH. & PALLET CONTROL NO: _____ DIE NO: _____

BOX NO'S: _____ AMOUNT _____ AMT/BOX _____

CHECK NO.	BOX	1	2	3	4	5	6	7	8	9	10	11	12	13	14	15	16	17	18	19	20	21	22	23	24	25
	1																									
	2																									
	3																									
	4																									
	5																									
	6																									
	7																									
	8																									
	9																									
	10																									
	11																									
	12																									
	13																									
	14																									
	15																									
	16																									
	17																									
	18																									
	19																									
	20																									
	21																									
	22																									
	23																									
	24																									
	25																									
	26																									
	27																									
	28																									
	29																									
	30																									

EXHIBIT 6–11:
FORM USED FOR PALLET CONTROL

SCRAP NOTICE					3457
PART NUMBER	OPERATION NUMBER		DATE	SHIFT	WORK ORDER NUMBER

DEPARTMENT	MACHINE NUMBER	PALLET CONTROL NUMBER	BOX NUMBER

☐ Purges ☐ Sprues ☐ Sweeping ☐ Overflow   ACTUAL COUNT ➤   ☐ To Be Reground   ☐ To Be Scrapped

REASON FOR SCRAPPING: _____

_____

_____

_____

_____

_____

Q.C. _____   Foreman _____   Dispatcher _____

QUALITY CONTROL

EXHIBIT 6–12:
SCRAP NOTICE FORM

TIME AND PRODUCTION REPORTING

Time reporting includes machines as well as direct labor employees. The card used for direct labor is called a *direct labor job card*. The form used for reporting machine time is the *in-process control traveler-molding*. These reports will be discussed separately.

Direct Labor Job Card (Exhibit 6–13)

The following information appearing on the card will be filled in:

a. Employee number

b. Group number for multiple-operator assignments

c. Start time

d. Stop time

e. Direct and indirect labor codes

f. Employee's signature

g. Foreman's approval

When a team of operators is used, the group leader will inform each employee of the production count and time so that the required information will be uniformly recorded.

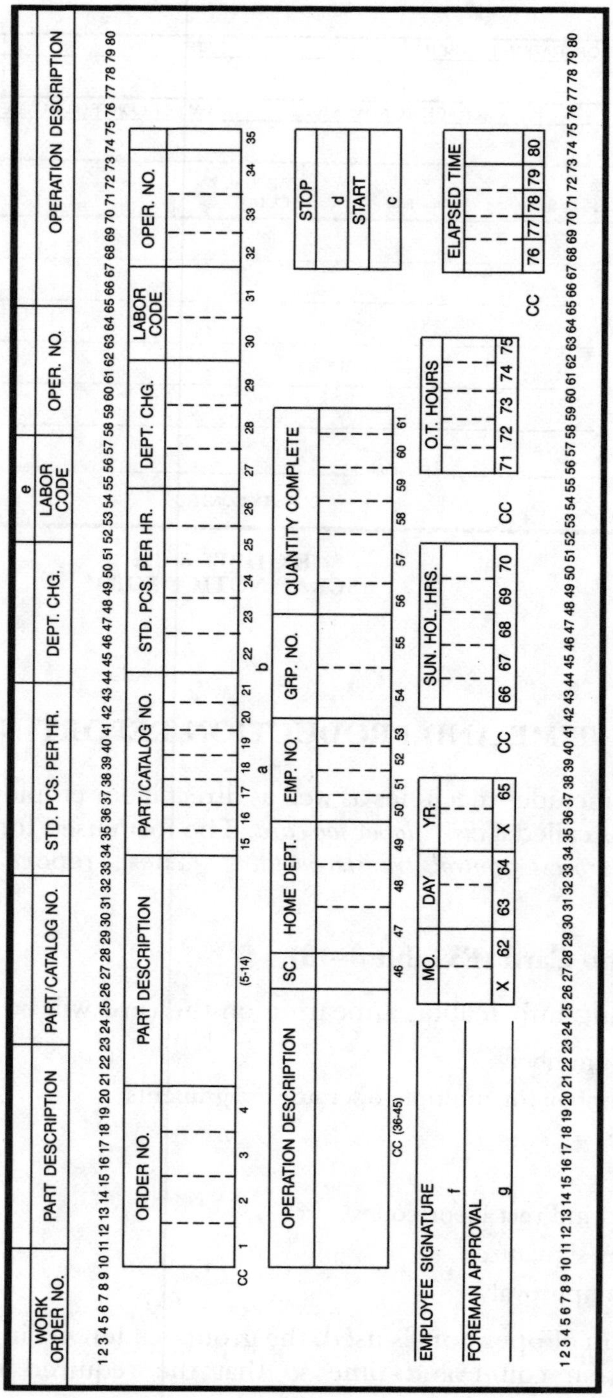

EXHIBIT 6–13:
DIRECT LABOR JOB CARD

IN PROCESS CONTROL TRAVELER II MOLDING

PART NUMBER	DESCRIPTION	TYPE OF MAT'L.	DATE	SHIFT	WORK ORDER NO.
MACHINE NO.	DIE NUMBER	EMPLOYEE NO.	NO. OF OPERATORS REQD.	NO. CAVITIES	ACTUAL CAVITIES	STANDARD CYCLES

DOWN STOP	TIME START	TOTAL HOURS	INITIAL	REASON LABOR CODE	REMARKS	GOOD UNITS PRODUCED

TOTAL DOWNTIME

RUNNING TIME

TOTAL HOURS

SUPERVISOR SIGNATURE

TOTAL OF UNITS

EXHIBIT 6–14:
IN-PROCESS CONTROL TRAVELER—MOLDING

In-Process Control Traveler-Molding (Exhibit 6–14). This form is filled out for each machine on each shift.

It serves as a "time card" for the molding machines in that downtime and running time are recorded in the same way that time would be recorded for a direct labor employee. The cause of the downtime must be shown along with the length of the delay.

The work order number, appropriate product identification data, type of material, and other pertinent machine-related information is shown along the upper edge of the card. The number of good units produced is listed along the right edge.

Like the direct labor job ticket, the form must be approved by the appropriate supervisor who attests to the accuracy of the information.

The Dispatcher's Responsibility

In addition to his responsibility to distribute job cards to each work station as required, the dispatcher will also oversee the following:

- Audit reported downtime to assure correctness of the figures.
- Maintain tally of quantities produced on the reverse side of the work orders.
- Audit total quantity produced on the pallet control sheet.
- Audit the production quantities on all job cards after they have been approved.
- Monitor all movement of material authorized by work orders.

Importance of Using Common Data for Production Control and Cost Accounting

The system philosophy expressed in the beginning of this chapter emphasized the importance of using the same paperwork in the cost accounting system as is used in the control of the physical units.

A computerized cost accounting system for a different product is described in Chapter 8. Here, too, the concept of using common data is illustrated in the computerized exhibits.

7

Direct Versus Full (Absorption) Costing

Direct costing is one of the more recent innovations adopted in the field of accounting. While it is new to the modern large company, variations of the direct costing concept have been used by a number of small companies for some time. Many small fabricators have for years set selling prices by adding a markup factor to prime cost (material plus direct labor).

Direct costing provides statements which are easier to understand because of the elimination of volume variances. Even though the modern manager is a professional, his knowledge and understanding of the flow of costs in an absorption accounting system is limited. The closer correlation of profits with sales—a characteristic of direct costing—provides the manager with a more understandable financial picture than absorption accounting which tends to correlate profits with volume of production.

Direct costing also demonstrates quite forcefully the impact of period cost on profits, providing a financial statement which spells out the profit-volume relationship.

INCREASING INTEREST IN DIRECT COSTING

The impetus given to direct costing stems from the ever-increasing mechanization of American industry. With automation on the increase, overhead becomes an even larger element of cost. Since a portion of this element is non-variable in nature, seasonal variations in production and sales tend to cause a distortion in profit which is difficult to justify when preparing operating statements for management. When production volume is increasing at a faster rate than sales, fixed costs build up in the inventory, thus deferring a portion of the current period's costs until such time as the inventory is sold. During this period of heavy production, profits may be high even though sales are low. During the reverse cycle, the opposite will usually be true.

Under direct costing, inventories would be valued at direct (variable) costs while fixed costs would be charged directly to expense in the current period. The basic difference in the operating statement (profit and loss) format between the full costing principle (in which fixed costs are included in inventory) and direct costing (which includes only direct or variable costs) is illustrated in the examples shown in Exhibit 7–1.

DIRECT COSTING FORMAT*		FULL COSTING FORMAT*	
Sales	$7,800,000	Sales	$7,800,000
Variable Manufacturing Costs		Cost of Sales	
Direct material	3,711,540	Direct material	3,711,540
Direct labor	746,823	Direct labor	746,823
Overhead	547,739	Overhead	1,449,856
Variable Operating Costs			
Selling expenses	61,200		
General & administrative expenses	51,000		
Total Variable Costs	$5,118,302	Total Cost of Sales	$5,908,219
Profit before fixed costs	$2,681,698	Profit before operating costs	$1,891,781
Fixed Costs		Operating Costs	
Manufacturing	952,117	Selling expenses	546,000
Operating		General & administrative	312,000
Selling expenses	484,800		
General & administrative expenses	261,000		
Total Fixed Costs	$1,697,917	Total Operating Costs	$ 858,000
Pre-tax Profit	$ 983,781	Pre-tax Profit	$1,033,781

*Although the company represented by these figures utilizes standards, the variances were not shown separately in the interest of simplicity.

EXHIBIT 7–1:
DIFFERENCE BETWEEN DIRECT COSTING AND FULL COSTING FORMAT

Both statement formats are split into two parts. In direct costing, this split is between variable (direct) costs shown in the upper section and fixed costs in the lower section. The full costing format breaks costs down between manufacturing costs (cost of sales) shown in the upper section and operating costs in the lower section.

Differences in Composition of the Profit in Direct Costing and Full Costing

The differences in the layering of costs in the two types of statements results in profits that reflect the financial results differently.

Direct Costing Format

Profit before fixed costs, frequently called *contribution to profit,* reflects profits after the direct or variable costs are deducted from sales. This figure can then be compared with the fixed (nonvariable) costs—the difference being the pretax profit.

Full Costing Format

The profit before operating costs (usually referred to as *gross profit* or *gross margin*) measures the profit after manufacturing costs are deducted from sales. The operating costs (sometimes referred to as *below-the-line costs*) are then deducted to arrive at the pretax profit.

Difference in Reported Profits by the Two Methods. Pretax profits are the same for both methods of costing when there is no increase or decrease in inventories. The pretax profit under full costing in Exhibit 7–1 is $50,000 greater than it is in direct costing. The reason is that in-process and finished inventories increased. The added production absorbed $50,000 in overhead that is deferred until the inventory is sold. The combinations making up the $50,000 difference are shown below.

Direct Costing Statement		
Variable overhead	$547,739	
Fixed overhead	952,117	$1,499,856
Full Costing Statement		1,449,856
Difference		$ 50,000

The initiative for introducing the direct costing format in operating statements usually stems from the financial executive. Operating executives, unfamiliar with differences between direct and full costing adapt quickly to the new format once they understand how it works. When a changeover is contemplated, a pre-implementation test period, such as was used at the E. I. Company, is highly desirable.

Introducing the Direct Costing Statement in the E. I. Company—A Case Example

The controller of the E. I. Company felt that the direct costing format might provide more effective controls because it recognizes differences in cost behavior of the various expenses, as well as providing a statement that is better understood by operating executives. Accordingly, he began distributing operating statements to the plants in both formats for a three-month test period. During this period, the controller met with each of the plant managers to answer questions.

One of the plant managers objected to using products shipped as a basis for measurement of profitability. His argument was that manufacturing costs were incurred in producing what went into stock rather than what was taken out of stock to meet sales commitments. The controller countered that the purpose of production was to replenish stocks that had been sold, therefore a relationship does exist between production and sales. The plant manager then pointed out that there was a lag between shipments and replenishment because machines could not be turned on and off to meet the replenishment needs of every item sold in the exact quantities that were sold that month. He also called attention to the increases and decreases in inventory as evidence of the correctness of his argument.

Further discussion revealed that the controller agreed with the objections that were raised. His hangup was a reluctance to undertake the additional task of valuing production at sales prices each month to accommodate the objection of the plant manager. When this came to light, the plant manager suggested that the sales figure be adjusted by the amount of inventory change each month. This could be accomplished by adding the standard cost of the inventory increase to the sales figure or, conversely, subtracting in the case of a decrease. If further refinement were required, a percentage factor could be applied at a later date to the amount of inventory change to adjust it to an equivalent selling price. A decision was agreed upon to issue the direct costing report in the format shown in Exhibit 7–2.

		% BREAK-DOWN
Sales (current month's shipments)	$7,800,000	
Plus inventory increase (at cost)	50,000	
Adjusted sales (Sales Value of Production)	$7,850,000	100.0%
Variable Manufacturing Costs		
Direct material	3,711,540	47.3
Direct labor	746,823	9.5
Overhead	547,739	7.0
Variable Operating Costs		
Selling expenses	61,200	.8
General & administrative expenses	51,000	.6
TOTAL VARIABLE COSTS	$5,118,302	65.2
Profit before fixed costs	$2,731,698	34.8%
Fixed Costs		
Manufacturing (overhead)	952,117	
Operating		
Selling expenses	484,800	
General & administrative expenses	261,000	
TOTAL FIXED COSTS	$1,697,917	
Pretax Profit	$1,033,781	
Breakeven Sales Volume	$4,879,100 (see calculation below)	

EXHIBIT 7–2:
DIRECT COSTING FORMAT

The revised direct costing statement was adjusted to the format illustrated in this exhibit. The percentage breakdown was included to facilitate analysis. The variable percentage, if increased, would indicate a lower profit before fixed costs (a smaller contribution to fixed costs and profit). If decreased, the contribution to fixed costs and profit would be higher.

The percentages were added for still another reason—to facilitate breakeven calculations, which are made in the following manner:

$$\frac{\text{Fixed Costs}}{\text{\% Profit before Fixed Costs}} = \frac{\$1,697,917}{.348} = \$4,879,100 \text{ (breakeven point)}$$

The breakeven point is inserted at the bottom of each month's statement. This will serve as another type of control to show deviations from the breakeven point established through the profit plan for the current year.

This case example at the E. I. Company demonstrates how one company introduced a new cost system. The method of introduction was good because dual systems were used during the test period. The operational personnel had the opportunity to appraise the new report, ask questions, and express their opinions. As a result of these questions and expressions of opinion, the report was modified to satisfy objections. This approach is in contrast to the approach followed by many companies that mandate a new report without first making a test and providing two-way communications.

Other Management Uses for the Direct Costing Concept

Identification of fixed and variable costs is the key to direct costing. Availability of this information makes it feasible to project potential profitability at various volumes within the normal range of activity. It facilitates the determination of the breakeven volume of activity; profitability of various product mixes and facilitates selective selling by identifying the products with the best potential profit.

We have already illustrated the use of fixed and variable costs in the preparation of direct costing statements and have made a comparison with the conventional full costing format. The breakeven calculation has also been demonstrated. The next step will concern itself with product mix and selective selling. Use of the fixed and variable concept for pricing (also referred to as marginal pricing) will be discussed in Section III of this book.

Product Mix and Profitability

Product mix refers to the variety of products and the units of each that are produced or sold. Since the contribution to profit will be different for each item, a change in the quantities will result in a change in the aggregate profit contribution for the period.

The separation of fixed and variable costs facilitates the measurement of the profit contribution of the various products. Exhibit 7–3 illustrates this with four products in which the unit statistics show the selling price, variable costs, and profit before fixed costs. Also shown is the percentage of profit for each of the four products before fixed costs. Note that product A, with a profit of 42.1 percent (and the lowest selling price), makes the highest profit contribution of the four products shown. Product C shows the lowest profit before fixed costs (30.2 percent). These unit figures were used in calculating the profit before fixed costs (as well as the profit after fixed costs) for the two product mixes.

In product mix 1, the sales of the two most profitable products, A and D, are shown at the lowest volumes—5,000 and 10,000 units, respectively. This results in a sales volume of $7,253,400 with a pretax profit of $736,431. In product mix 2, products A and D were calculated at higher volumes—40,000 and 30,000, respectively—while products B and C were calculated at 5,000 and 10,000 units,

	PRODUCT A	PRODUCT B	PRODUCT C	PRODUCT D	TOTAL
Unit Statistics:					
Selling price	$67.51	90.08	75.36	105.19	
Variable costs	39.07	59.25	52.60	67.56	
Profit before fixed costs	28.44	30.83	22.76	37.63	
%Profit before fixed costs	42.1 %	34.2 %	30.2 %	35.8 %	
Product Mix 1					
Units sold	5,000	40,000	30,000	10,000	85,000
Sales dollars	$ 337,550	3,603,150	2,260,800	1,051,900	7,253,400
Variable costs	195,350	2,370,102	1,578,000	675,600	4,819,052
Profit before fixed costs	142,200	1,233,048	682,800	376,300	2,434,348
Less fixed costs	Fixed costs not allocated in direct costing				1,697,917
Pretax profit					$ 736,431
Product Mix 2					
Units sold	40,000	5,000	10,000	30,000	85,000
Sales dollars	$2,700,400	450,400	753,600	3,155,700	7,060,100
Variable costs	1,562,800	296,250	526,002	2,026,848	4,411,900
Profit before fixed costs	1,137,600	154,150	227,598	1,128,852	2,648,200
Less fixed costs	Fixed costs not allocated in direct costing				1,697,917
Pretax profit					$ 950,283

EXHIBIT 7–3:
EFFECT OF TWO DIFFERENT SALES MIXES ON PRETAX PROFITS

respectively—the same figures that were used for A and D in product mix 1. The sales dollars in mix 2 dropped by $193,300 with pretax profits increasing by $213,852.

Monitoring Profitability of the Sales Mix through the Breakeven Point

The breakeven point is determined by division of the percentage of sales left after covering variable costs into the fixed cost. This percentage is affected by changes in the mix as the variable costs rise and fall. Exhibit 7–2 demonstrates the direct costing statement format in which the variable cost percentage is shown as well as the percentage left after deducting variable costs from sales. It also shows the breakeven point.

These differences in breakeven sales volume can be demonstrated in the three different mixes discussed in this chapter. The first of these, referred to above (Exhibit 7–2), is compared with the two product mixes shown in Exhibit 7–3 (see Table 7–1).

Note that as the percentage left for profit before fixed costs (contribution to profit) increases, the breakeven point decreases. The inclusion of the current month's breakeven point on the operating statement can be helpful as an indication of the changing profitability of the mix. Executives who become accustomed to using direct costing statements made in this manner become conscious of the impact of various products on profitability.

	Product Mix Used in Exhibit 7–2		Product Mixes in Exhibit 7–3			
			Mix 1		Mix 2	
Sales	$7,850,000	100.0%*	7,253,400	100.0%	7,060,100	100.0%
Variable costs	5,118,302	65.2	4,819,052	66.5	4,411,900	62.5
Profit before fixed costs	2,731,698	34.8	2,434,348	33.5	2,648,200	37.5
Fixed costs	1,697,917		1,697,917		1,697,917	
Pretax profit	1,033,781		736,431		950,383	
Breakeven Sales Volume	$4,879,100		5,068,400		4,527,800	

*Inventory increase of $50,000 added to sales of $7,800,000 for consistency.

TABLE 7–1

Importance of Allocating Corporate Costs to Segments of the Company

We have demonstrated the use of direct costing operating statements, breakeven analyses based on each month's operating results, and the impact of selective changes in mix on profitability.

In keeping with the principles followed in direct costing, items considered to be fixed were not allocated to products. Research and development was such an item in this company. Investigation revealed that product D was a newly launched product that had incurred a fairly substantial amount of development cost that was identifiable with this product, although other products would benefit by some of the research work. The figures shown in Exhibit 7–3 for product D are shown in Table 7–2 together with the figures after allocating research and development.

The new figures show that the percentage of profit before fixed costs was 29.8 percent rather than 35.8 percent. The sales manager objected to making this change because the development costs will have been completely recovered by the

UNIT STATISTICS FOR PRODUCT D

	As Shown in Exhibit 7–3	Including Research and Development
	---	---
Selling price	$105.19	105.19
Less research and development		6.30
Competitive selling price	105.19	98.89
Less variable costs	67.56	67.56
Profit before fixed costs	$ 37.63	31.33
% Profit	35.8%	29.8%

TABLE 7–2

end of the year. Product D, therefore, would not be correctly evaluated in profit potential after recovery of the research costs. The general manager disagreed with the sales manager. He pointed out that competitors were already copying this newly developed product. Since the competitors had not incurred research costs, the probability was that they would adjust the selling price downward by that amount. The E. I. Company would, naturally, have to follow suit. The adjusted sales figure of $98.89 was therefore adopted. Although this type of allocation smacks of full (absorption) costing, it merits serious consideration. New product development cost is not the only expense of the allocable type often treated as a nonallocable fixed cost. Examples are:

Centralized Data Processing Functions. With the advent of centralized computer services, more and more functions previously performed by the individual segments on a manual basis have been taken over by regional or corporate offices. The treasurer of one conglomerate stated it this way: "We are a conglomerate. All our segments were independent companies before they were acquired. They had their own payroll departments, they paid their own bills and did their own invoicing of customers. After acquisition, we transferred these operations to our central office. The same functions are now being performed at less cost. If these costs were previously included in the costs of the products that were manufactured, what has changed to exclude them from the cost of the same products?"

Purchasing. When a number of segments within a company use the same type of material, companies will often centralize the purchase of such materials. This provides the purchasing function with greater bargaining power. The remaining smaller items would continue to be purchased locally with reduced staffs. In this case, as in the previous one, purchasing at the corporate level is just as much a product cost as it was before centralization. Allocating the cost back to the segments is more difficult, but it is no reason to exclude it—or to use "quick and dirty" methods for making the allocation.

Industrial Relations (Personnel Services). The increasing complexity of union relations, pension administration, and administration of various types of insurance coverages has made it necessary for many companies to centralize this operation. This permits the use of higher skilled personnel at the headquarters locations—thus permitting the segments to be operated with fewer and lesser—skilled employees.

Too many of those responsible for furnishing their managements with more effective tools are unfamiliar with the basics underlying the manufacturing processes and problems. They fail to devote sufficient time in learning the mechanics of manufacturing, the nature and purpose of the various processes, types of equipment used, and the problems encountered in producing a quality product at optimum cost. This type of individual, in demonstrating the workings of a cost reporting system, will sometimes illustrate with an example based on the manufacture of "widgets" rather than an actual product. This is a dead giveaway of a paucity of knowledge of the manufacturing process. Obviously, the audience instead of being turned on is tuned out. An individual who is not sufficiently knowledgeable in the basics of manufacturing will be at a disadvantage in determining the cost behavior of key expenses—knowledge of which is important in making a direct costing system effective.

Common Errors in Determining Cost Behavior

Knowledge of cost behavior is an important ingredient when direct costing procedures are used. This applies to the calculation of breakeven sales volume, profit volume analyses, marginal pricing of products, and developing flexible budgets. Simply stated, cost behavior refers to the separation of variable and fixed costs. The variable costs are applied as a percentage of the activity level. The measure of activity would be sales or units of product for determining the breakeven volume and profit volume analyses. For marginal pricing of products and flexible budgets, direct labor, machine hours, or units of product could be used. Fixed (also referred to as constant and nonvariable) costs are applied as so much per period—usually a month.

Identification of variable and fixed costs is far from an exact science—it is highly subjective. Estimates of what is variable and what is fixed can vary from person to person. Such variations can affect the final results as demonstrated in Table 7–3. The breakeven analysis shown in Exhibit 7–2 was compared with example 2 and example 3. Example 2 shows the effect on the breakeven point when the variable costs are reduced from 65.2 to 55.2 percent. Example 3 illustrates the result when the variable costs are increased from 65.2 to 75.2 percent.

	Example 1 (From Exhibit 7–2)	Example 2	Example 3
Sales	$7,850,000	7,850,000	7,850,000
Total variable	5,118,302	4,333,200	5,903,200
Profit before fixed	2,731,698	3,516,800	1,946,800
Fixed	1,697,917	2,483,019	913,019
Pretax profit	1,033,781	1,033,781	1,033,781
Breakeven sales*	$4,879,100	5,542,453	3,681,528
Variable %	65.2	55.2	75.2
% Profit before fixed	34.8	44.8	24.8

*Breakeven sales = Fixed costs divided by % profit before fixed

TABLE 7–3

The comparative percentages for the three examples are based on sales. It is also possible to express the percentages of variable and fixed costs on the basis of the total cost being broken down into these two categories. For the above three examples, the comparison would be as seen in Table 7–4.

	Example 1 (From Exhibit 7–2)		Example 2		Example 3	
Variable portion	$5,118,302	75%	4,333,200	64%	5,903,200	87%
Fixed portion	1,697,917	25	2,483,019	36	913,019	13
Total Variable and Fixed Costs	$6,816,219	100%	6,816,219	100%	6,816,219	100%

TABLE 7–4

On the basis of total cost, the percentages for the variable and fixed costs range from 64/36 to 87/13 percent. The figures are hypothetical and the spread of the percentages is relatively small compared to variations that have been observed in some companies. One of these is described in the following case example:

> The HG Company had five plants making the same product with minor variations. The equipment was quite similar, permitting products in high demand to be manufactured in more than one of the plants with only minor adjustments to the equipment. The company controller made the decision to change to a direct costing system to provide for internal reports to be prepared in the format illustrated in Exhibit 7–2. For external reporting, the appropriate adjustments to full costing would be made.
>
> In implementing the new system, the identification of the variable and fixed costs was done in each plant by the resident cost accountant. When the range of percentages based on total cost were reviewed, the analysis showed the following extremes:

	Plant 2	Plant 5
Variable	61%	37%
Fixed	39	63
Total	100%	100%

> This is too wide a range for the five plants included in this comparison inasmuch as the manufacturing activities are quite similar. It is natural that when five different individuals apply their own subjective judgment, wide differences can be expected.
>
> An evaluation based on conversations with these five resident cost accountants revealed that two of them were familiar with the manufacturing operations. Their results were quite similar. The widest differences were contained in the data developed by the other three. These three were more office than factory-oriented, a circumstance that worked to the detriment of the study.
>
> Among the recommendations made to the controller were the following:
>
> 1. That preference be given to individuals who are factory-oriented when factory related tasks of this type are required, even if only two are available to do the work of identifying variable and fixed costs in five plants. The other three could be assigned to assist in the more mechanical features of the work, such as summarizing the figures and making the required calculations.
> 2. Prior to starting the work, and at suitable intervals in the course of the work, all five should meet to discuss any problem areas that may arise. At these meetings, an operations-oriented individual should be assigned to the group to offer recommendations and to answer any questions that arise.

3. The plant managers of each of the plants should be apprised of progress and they should be given a preliminary copy of the completed study prior to finalization.

There are circumstances in which it is fallacious to assume that an item of cost will retain a single cost behavior characteristic during its existence. This can be illustrated by the following case example involving litigation because of a breach of warranty:

The Rockhill Company purchased new automatic equipment to replace the existing manual operations. The company had received written assurances from the supplier that this new automatic equipment would cut direct labor by more than one-third. Such a saving would provide a payback of three years, certainly a worthwhile investment.

However, as is frequently the case, expectations are not always realizations. The new equipment broke down frequently. When it did run, the operating speed was only a bit more than half the speed warranted by the supplier. Rockhill waited patiently during the first two months while the supplier's maintenance personnel attempted to correct the problems. Finally, Rockhill management realized that the equipment had a serious deficiency in design that had to be changed before the promised speeds could be attained. The supplier was advised that Rockhill would institute a lawsuit for loss of production potential until the equipment redesign has been completed. A smaller number of units of product were being forced to bear all of the overhead costs—which would have been spread over a far greater number of units if the equipment were operating as warranted.

In making the fixed overhead cost calculations, the company defined fixed costs as outlined in its accounting policy and procedures which had been in effect during the past nine years. A partial list of some of the classifications is shown below:

	% Fixed	% Variable
Factory supervision	100	—
Factory clerical	90	10
Depreciation	100	—
Repair of production equipment	85	15
Plant rearrangement	85	15
Tools and fixtures	80	20
Sales and service	90	10
New product development	100	—
Administration and general	95	5

In testing the company's planned approach in the lawsuit, an analysis was made of the cost behavior of factory supervision and depreciation, both of which were considered by the company to be 100 percent fixed. Since the claim covered a three-year period, the study compared the supervisory costs and the depreciation for each of the years with the volume of production for the same years. The figures are shown below:

	Factory Supervision	Depreciation	Units of Production
Year 1	$102,150	$ 89,100	4,126,010
Year 2	156,284	111,300	6,147,740
Year 3	193,064	155,800	7,921,920

Using year 1 as the base year (100%), the percentage increase of years 2 and 3 over year 1 are shown below.

	Factory Supervision	Depreciation	Units of Production
Year 1	100%	100%	100%
Year 2	153	125	149
Year 3	189	175	192

It was obvious from the percentages shown above that factory supervision and depreciation costs were not 100 percent fixed, as indicated by the accounting policy and procedures. On the contrary, there was a fairly high degree of variability since the amount of the expenses increased to about the same degree as the level of activity represented by the units of production.

Factory supervision was increased as additional sections of the automatic system were added. Although automation reduced direct labor requirements, the greater complexity of the operations required closer supervision.

The reason that *depreciation* proved to be highly variable is that:

1. The company held back payments and made releases to the supplier as sections of the automatic system were corrected and put into production.
2. During the redesign process, the Rockhill Company requested changes which required additions. This increased the depreciation charges as each section was completed. Such additions are not unusual when companies embark on cost reduction programs.

The Rockhill Company's attorneys were advised that any attempt to specifically identify fixed costs would provide the opposition with ammunition for proving that Rockhill's claim was greatly overstated because of overstatement of fixed costs. The recommended alternative was to determine for each of the three years:

• The total units produced
• The total overhead (without attempting to distinguish between variable and fixed costs)
• Determine the overhead per unit by dividing total units produced into the total overhead.

Using year 3 as the standard (because it represents normalized operations), compare it with the unit overhead cost of years 1 and 2 to determine the amount of excess cost per unit in each of the two years. Multiply by the number of units produced in each of the two years to arrive at the total unabsorbed overhead.

The company decided to follow this recommended alternative with some adjustments because of other operations not related to the automatic equipment. The lawsuit never reached trial because Rockhill and the supplier came to terms in an out-of-court settlement.

Precautions to Be Followed in Identification of Variable and Fixed Costs

The determination of cost behavior by the fixed and variable components should be determined individually for each factory unit even though there appears to be a similarity in the products being produced. This will assure that the relationship of activity and the complement of costs associated with each unit's normal level of activity will be more meaningful. In addition to this, the following guidelines should also be followed:

- The chart of accounts should not be structured to break down the natural expenses by their fixed and variable segments.
- Cost behavior of a natural expense item can change with the application. Electricity, for example, is highly variable when used for operating motors. But when used for heating annealing furnaces, it will be highly fixed.
- In an automated operation in which one operator operates two or more machines, direct labor can behave as a fixed cost when volume drops because the operator will still be needed even when some of the machines have been idle.
- Inflation (or deflation) can affect cost behavior because costs can be affected by price changes even though the level of activity, as measured by labor hours or machine hours, remains relatively stable.
- Don't rely on mathematical formulas for determining cost behavior. The determination of cost behavior, and under what conditions behavior changes, can only be determined by knowing the business and the nature of the manufacturing (or service) operations.

The company pondering a decision as to whether direct costing or full costing is the more suitable for its needs is not dealing with an either/or decision as in the case of job costing versus process costing. Even though a full costing system is mandated for external reporting, there is no reason why the company cannot utilize the direct costing features to maximize the benefits of its cost system. However, to be effective, the precautions listed above must be followed to break down the various items correctly by their fixed and variable components. (See Exhibit 7–4 for a comparison of direct costing and full costing features.)

FEATURES OF THE SYSTEMS	DIRECT COSTING	FULL COSTING
Income statements (See Exhibit 7–1)	Easier for nonaccounting operating personnel to understand	Complicated by effect of over- and underabsorbed overhead on reported profit
Difference in reported profits by the two methods (see section by this title in this chapter)	Profits vary with changes in sales volume	Profits vary with production volume rather than with sales volume
Inventory valuation	Inventory value excludes fixed costs and therefore understates the value of the inventory	Inventory included fixed costs and is therefore fully valued
Product costs (See Section II—Costing and Pricing Products to Maximize Profits)	Product costs understate the true product cost	Products are fully costed
Product pricing (See Section II—Costing and Pricing Products to Maximize Profits)	Understatement of product costs could result in underpriced products	Full costing would reduce the possibility of underpricing
Analytical features (See Exhibits 7–2 and 7–3)		
Breakeven sales volume	Facilitates calculation of breakeven sales volume based on each month's income statement (see Exhibit 7–2)	Cannot be calculated without knowledge of variable and fixed costs
Make-buy decisions	Facilitates determination of economics of making the product in-house versus purchasing on the outside	Cannot be calculated without knowledge of variable and fixed costs
Product mix changes	Effect on profits of product mix changes is facilitated through availability of variable and fixed cost breakdown	Cannot be calculated without knowledge of variable and fixed costs
Variable and fixed cost breakdown	Incorrect determination of variable and fixed costs can impair accuracy of the system	Not a problem since variable and fixed costs are not identified separately
Legality of cost system	Can be used for internal analysis and reporting but not for external reporting.	Treasury department and SEC mandates use full costing for external reporting

EXHIBIT 7–4:
DIRECT COSTING VERSUS FULL COSTING

8

Computerizing the Cost Accounting System

The explosive increase in the demand for a proliferation of products and product types, coupled with the trend toward larger and larger manufacturing units, has resulted in a massive increase in the number of different items carried in inventory by many companies. This does not apply to finished goods and raw materials alone—it applies to the multiplicity of components, assemblies and subassemblies in various stages of completion as well. A fairly common mass-produced product can have as many as 20,000 items in inventory. An "order of magnitude" analysis by raw material, work-in-process and finished goods might typically show the following breakdown of the total of 20,000:

Raw Material	500
Work-in-process	14,500
Finished goods	5,000
	20,000

When manufacturing units were smaller and the items in inventory fewer in number, accountability for physical units and dollar value could be accomplished manually. But as the number of items expanded, companies found it more and more difficult to achieve proper accountability. Production and inventory control records were laboriously posted by hand. Accountants responsible for preparing financial statements found it exceedingly difficult to apply dollar values to movement of inventories through the production processes and through cost of sales.

Companies that found it impractical to price thousands of individual inventory cards, which were constantly in use by production personnel, were forced to find other means of costing production and inventories. Many cost accountants determined their manufacturing cost of sales by applying historical percentages of cost of sales to sales. Frequently, because the historical percentages proved to be incorrect for the current year, the year-end reconciliation of the physical to book inventory showed a large difference—indicating that profits during the earlier part of the year had been greatly overstated (sometimes understated). The general manager of one company stated the problem this way:

We had 15,000 to 16,000 items in inventory, of which 2600 were end products. Computers were still very expensive so we could not track the costs through the various manufacturing operations in order to come up with the correct finished product cost with which to relieve the inventory when such products were sold. My accountant used the historical cost of sales to sales percentage (64 percent) that was fairly stable. One year when we compared our priced-up physical inventory with the value carried on the books, we came up with a shortage of almost a quarter million dollars. We took a second physical, but the results were not much different. Applying our 20/20 hindsight, we then realized that the inflation rate for material and labor had jumped between 11 and 13 percent. Because of competition from overseas, we were limited in the amount that we could increase our selling prices. It was only natural for the inventory to be overstated if our cost of products sold was understated. It was no fun facing top management at one of the board meetings and explaining how this happened. The only good that came out of it was that the board authorized the purchase of computer equipment.

THE COMPUTER COMES TO THE RESCUE

The engineering bill of material is the "blueprint" of how the product is made. It provides a list of the various items, processes, and processing times at the different stages of production. Just as a bill of material is important to the physical production process in the manufacture of a product, so is the computerized cost routing sheet the central point in the computerized inventory and cost accounting control system. Exhibit 8–1 illustrates diagrammatically the relationship of the input and output documents to the Engineering B/M. On the input side, it shows the various types of transaction documents that are run against the bill of material information to produce such output documents as product costs, transaction costing, cost of sales, and variance analyses. Also, as an important part of the computerized procedures are the ongoing and year-end maintenance programs, the edit lists to assure more accurate input of information, and the "where-used" file.

This chapter will illustrate and explain the content of the cost routing sheet, where the information comes from, and how the product costs are developed. It will also illustrate transaction reports and describe the procedure for summarizing these and developing the closing journal entries and cost analyses.

Rather than use hypothetical figures in discussing the computerization of the cost accounting system, this chapter, like other chapters in this book, will use case examples based on actual figures. This chapter will discuss and illustrate:

- Sources of the basic data
- Manufacturing process sheets containing data culled from records maintained by the design engineering and manufacturing engineering departments
- How the manufacturing process sheets are "treed-up" (see Exhibit 8–2) to develop the product structure of a tire valve stem (exclusive of the tire valve core)
- The cost routing sheet shown in Exhibit 8–3 (referred to as an "indented bill of material" by the company)
- How the material and labor costs for this product are calculated in arriving at the product cost shown in the cost of sales transaction report (see Exhibits 8–5 and 8–6). Overhead will be discussed in another chapter.

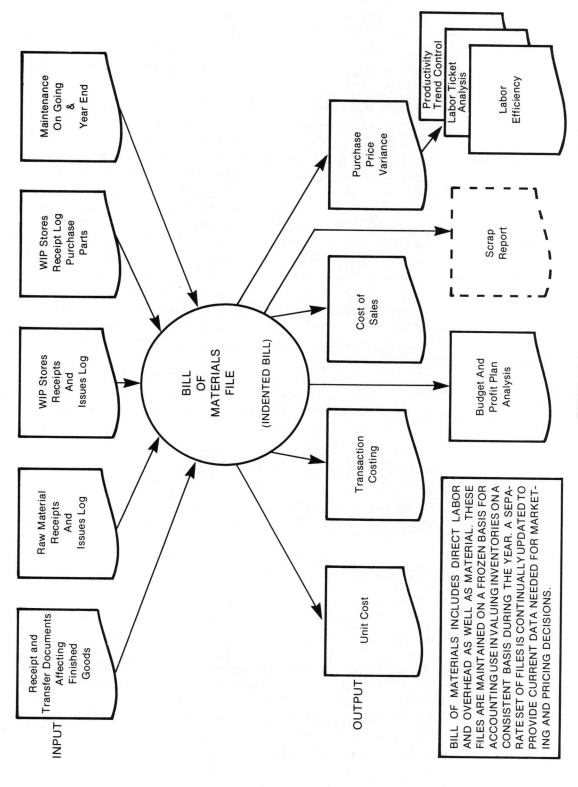

INPUT

Maintenance On Going & Year End

WIP Stores Receipt Log Purchase Parts

WIP Stores Receipts And Issues Log

Raw Material Receipts And Issues Log

Receipt and Transfer Documents Affecting Finished Goods

BILL OF MATERIALS FILE (INDENTED BILL)

Purchase Price Variance

Productivity Trend Control

Labor Ticket Analysis

Labor Efficiency

Scrap Report

Cost of Sales

Budget And Profit Plan Analysis

Transaction Costing

Unit Cost

OUTPUT

BILL OF MATERIALS INCLUDES DIRECT LABOR AND OVERHEAD AS WELL AS MATERIAL. THESE FILES ARE MAINTAINED ON A FROZEN BASIS FOR ACCOUNTING USE IN VALUING INVENTORIES ON A CONSISTENT BASIS DURING THE YEAR. A SEPARATE SET OF FILES IS CONTINUALLY UPDATED TO PROVIDE CURRENT DATA NEEDED FOR MARKETING AND PRICING DECISIONS.

EXHIBIT 8–1:

RELATIONSHIP OF INPUT AND OUTPUT DOCUMENTS TO COMPUTERIZED BILL OF MATERIAL

- The various transaction reports used to track production costs through the various departments (cost centers) and stockrooms (see Exhibit 8–14)
- Accounting for the work-in-process floor inventory value (see Exhibit 8–15)
- Manufacturing cost summary for use in developing the income statement and breakdown of variances (see Exhibit 8–16)

In addition to the above, this chapter will demonstrate how the transaction reports can be used to develop such byproduct reports as percent breakdown by cost elements of various product categories appearing on the cost of sales transaction report (Exhibit 8–9); purchased parts price history (Exhibit 8–10); purchase price variances by major item (Exhibit 8–11); material receipts compared with plan (Exhibit 8–12); and vendor performance report (Exhibit 8–13).

An important step in the mechanics of automation for inventory management and for cost accounting is the treeing up of the product structure. For purposes of illustrating this procedure, the tire valve stem (exclusive of the valve insert) will be used. This is the product line that showed a breakdown of 20,000 parts in raw materials, work-in-process, and finished goods. The process of "treeing up" an end product manually would require a day to a day and a half each, at a minimum. Herein lies the advantage of the computer which can track the physical movement of the thousands of items from raw material to finished goods at lightning speed and issue transaction reports for movement in and out of the various processing and stockroom points.

Source of Manufacturing Data

The required data is provided by the engineering, industrial relations, purchasing, and cost accounting departments. A listing of the required data is shown below:

1. Material specifications
2. Quantity of material required
3. Manufacturing operations to be performed
4. Cost centers in which operations are to be performed
5. Setup hours
6. Production hours
7. Labor grades of employees
8. Material cost
9. Direct labor cost
10. Overhead cost

The data listed above is based on the requirements per thousand units. A reasonable allowance for losses of material must be included. In a component such as the brass tire valve stem, the starting weight per thousand stems is 37.8 pounds. However, because of the drilling and reaming operations that hollow out the inside of the rod to provide space for the valve, the finished weight of the brass stem is 17 pounds. This means that 55 percent of the material becomes a production loss.

This is shown in the manufacturing process sheet in Exhibit 8–2, ("Product Structure of Tire Valve Stem"), level 04, machine code 0008. This process sheet also shows the material specifications, as well as the operations related to this level. The drilling and reaming operations that clean out the space for the insertion of the valve are shown at level 02, along with the other related data for operations performed, time allowances, routing and cost centers through which the work flows.

Reasonable allowances must also be made in the production hours required for the various operations to provide for such factors as start-up time, rest periods, and fatigue allowances where applicable. The sources of the data listed above are shown below:

1.	Material specifications	Engineering (Design Engineering)
2.	Quantity of material	Engineering (Design Engineering)
3.	Manufacturing operations	Engineering (Manufacturing Engineering)
4.	Cost centers	Engineering (Manufacturing Engineering)
5.	Setup hours	Engineering (Manufacturing Engineering)
6.	Production hours	Engineering (Manufacturing Engineering)
7.	Labor grades	Industrial Relations
8.	Material cost	Purchasing Department & Cost Accounting
9.	Direct labor cost	Cost accounting
10.	Overhead rates	Cost accounting

The above-listed items are considered to be standards that will remain fixed for a year unless a major change in processing or product design takes place. Although the standard material costs would also be considered to be fixed for a year, changes in the inflation rate could require changes to be made midyear to avoid unrealistic variances. Since labor rates are usually controlled by three-year contracts in many companies, these would not fluctuate to as great extent as would material costs. Overhead rates are usually predetermined for the year except in unusual circumstances. An example of an unusual circumstance could be the introduction of, say, highly automated equipment that would alter the labor and depreciation costs.

Treeing Up the Manufacturing Process

Exhibit 8–2, referred to earlier, illustrates the treeing up process diagrammatically. The underlying manufacturing process sheets are shown for each of the levels. These include:

Item identification and machine code

Material specifications

Quantity of material required

Routing through the cost centers

Number and description of each operation

MANUFACTURING PROCESS SHEET

ISSUE DATE	ISSUE #	REVISED:	P.C. 01	BASIC 02608	SUFFIX 172-2	MACH. CODE 0005	REFERENCE		SHOP ORDER #
DRAWING #		LAST C.A.	PART NAME	STEM W/PLASTIC DISC – OPERATION 20					DATE ISSUED
			MTL. CODE	TUBE	KIND ASSEMBLY		SIZE		QTY. TO MAKE
			SHAPE		SPEC.	TEMPER		HARDNESS	RAW MTL. REQMT.
			UNIT	PER/M GROSS		PER/M NET			REQD. COMPLETION DATE
			ROUTING	COATING, MOLDING, MACHINING					LEVEL (03)

OPN. #	OPERATION DESCRIPTION	EQUIPMENT	DEPT.	SET-UP HRS.	LAB. GRD.	PROD. HRS./M	LAB. GRD.	NO. MACH.	NO. MEN	COST CENTER
	01-02608-1-0008 SEMI-FINISHED STEM									
	01-02608-173-2-0002 PLASTIC DISC									
010	FINISH STEM PER SPEC. #29	COATING TANKS	PLATE			.05	7			0568
020	MOLD & CURE	MOLDING PRESS #5	MOLD			1.16	7			0981

MANUFACTURING PROCESS SHEET

ISSUE DATE	ISSUE #	REVISED:	P.C. 01	BASIC 02608	SUFFIX 173-2	MACH. CODE 0002	REFERENCE		SHOP ORDER #
DRAWING #		LAST C.A.	PART NAME	PLASTIC DISC					DATE ISSUED
			MTL. CODE		KIND PLASTIC #316		SIZE 1" x 3/8"		QTY. TO MAKE
			SHAPE		SPEC.	TEMPER		HARDNESS	RAW MTL. REQMT.
			UNIT	PER/M GROSS		PER/M NET			REQD. COMPLETION DATE
			ROUTING						LEVEL (04)

OPN. #	OPERATION DESCRIPTION	EQUIPMENT	DEPT.	SET-UP HRS.	LAB. GRD.	PROD. HRS./M	LAB. GRD.	NO. MACH.	NO. MEN	COST CENTER
	.0099 LBS. 97-00019-0000 PLASTIC D785A									
010	MILL, TUBULATE & CUT TO SIZE	41" MARK	MOLD			.08	6		1	1294
		#25 REGAL & CUTOFF	MOLD			.08	6		1	1294

MANUFACTURING PROCESS SHEET

ISSUE DATE	ISSUE #	REVISED:	P.C. 97	BASIC 00019	SUFFIX 0000	MACH. CODE 0000	REFERENCE		SHOP ORDER #
DRAWING #		LAST C.A.	PART NAME	PLASTIC D 785A					DATE ISSUED
			MTL. CODE		KIND		SIZE		QTY. TO MAKE
			SHAPE		SPEC.	TEMPER		HARDNESS	RAW MTL. REQMT.
			UNIT	PER/M GROSS		PER/M NET			REQD. COMPLETION DATE
			ROUTING	MOLDING					LEVEL (05)

OPN. #	OPERATION DESCRIPTION	EQUIPMENT	DEPT.	SET-UP HRS.	LAB. GRD.	PROD. HRS./M	LAB. GRD.	NO. MACH.	NO. MEN	COST CENTER
010	WEIGH OUT AND MIX PLASTIC INGREDIENTS	BENCH W/SCALE, MIXER	MOLD			4.65	88		3	1291
	MATERIAL CODE DESCRIPTION	BREAKDOWN PER M/LBS.								
	05-9562 PLASTIC #276	350.75								
	05-4213 HEXO CL	87.67								
	TOTAL POUNDS OF INGREDIENTS 1,000.00		PROCESS ENG'G.		STDS. ENG'G.					

EXHIBIT 8–2:
PRODUCT STRUCTURE OF TIRE VALVE STEM

MANUFACTURING PROCESS SHEET

ISSUE DATE	ISSUE #	REVISED:	P.C. 01	BASIC 02608	SUFFIX 172-2	MACH. CODE 5036	REFERENCE	SHOP ORDER #
DRAWING #		LAST C.A.	PART NAME	STEM WITH PLASTIC DISC				DATE ISSUED
			MTL. CODE		KIND		SIZE	QTY. TO MAKE
			SHAPE		SPEC.	TEMPER	HARDNESS	RAW MTL. REQMT.
			UNIT	PER/M GROSS		PER/M NET		REQD. COMPLETION DAT
			ROUTING	PACKING & FINISHED GOODS			LEVEL 01	

OPN. #	OPERATION DESCRIPTION	EQUIPMENT	DEPT.	SET-UP HRS.	LAB. GRD.	PROD. HRS./M	LAB. GRD.	NO. MACH.	NO. MEN	COST CENTE
	01-02608-172-2-0537 STEM W/PLASTIC DISC									
010	MAKE CARTON 018751 & APPLY LABEL 011856	BENCH	PKG.			.02	2			1369
020	PACK 1000 IN 018751 CARTON; WEIGH & SEAL	BENCH W/SCALE	PKG.			.05	2			1369

MANUFACTURING PROCESS SHEET

ISSUE DATE	ISSUE #	REVISED:	P.C. 01	BASIC 02608	SUFFIX 172-2	MACH. CODE 0537	REFERENCE	SHOP ORDER #
DRAWING #		LAST C.A.	PART NAME	STEM W/PLASTIC DISC				DATE ISSUED
			MTL. CODE		KIND		SIZE	QTY. TO MAKE
			SHAPE		SPEC.	TEMPER	HARDNESS	RAW MTL. REQMT.
			UNIT	PER/M GROSS		PER/M NET		REQD. COMPLETION DATE
			ROUTING	MACHINING, MACHINING, INSPECTION, PACKING			LEVEL 02	

OPN. #	OPERATION DESCRIPTION	EQUIPMENT	DEPT.	SET-UP HRS.	LAB. GRD.	PROD. HRS./M	LAB. GRD.	NO. MACH.	NO. MEN	COST CENTER
	01-02608-172-2-0005									
010	DRILL & BLOW	BENCH MACHINE	MACHG.			1.67	2			0267
020	REAM & BLOW	BENCH MACHINE	MACHG.			1.18	2			0267
	INSPECT		QC							

MANUFACTURING PROCESS SHEET

ISSUE DATE	ISSUE #	REVISED:	P.C. 01	BASIC 02608	SUFFIX 1	MACH. CODE 0008	REFERENCE	SHOP ORDER #
DRAWING #		LAST C.A.	PART NAME	STEM				DATE ISSUED
			MTL. CODE 20-2800		KIND BRASS		SIZE .280 DIAMETER	QTY. TO MAKE
			SHAPE COIL		SPEC. 26-4	TEMPER	HARDNESS	RAW MTL. REQMT.
			UNIT LBS.	PER/M GROSS 37.8		PER/M NET 17.0		REQD. COMPLETION DATE
			ROUTING	MACHINING, COATING, INSPECTION, COMPONENTS STOCKROOM			LEVEL 04	

OPN. #	OPERATION DESCRIPTION	EQUIPMENT	DEPT.	SET-UP HRS.	LAB. GRD.	PROD. HRS./M	LAB. GRD.	NO. MACH.	NO. MEN	COST CENTER
010	CUT-OFF & HEAD	HEADER	MACHG	3.0	10	.15	5	2	1	0447
020	ROLL THREAD	ROLLING MACHINE	MACHG	2.0	10	.50	5	2	1	0450
030	HEADING	HEADER	MACHG	12.0	13	.81	12			0761
050	DEGREASE	DEGREASER	COATG			.07	4			0568
	INSPECT		QC							

EXHIBIT 8–2, continued

Equipment required

Setup hours (where applicable)

Labor grades for setup

Production hours

Labor grades for production

Cost centers

COST ROUTING SHEET

The cost structure of the tire valve stem (minus the valve) is shown in Exhibit 8–3, "Cost Routing Sheet." The product ID (part number—level 01) is shown as 01-02608-5036. As is typical in many companies converting their systems to the computer, difficulties arose in this company in trying to use existing product ID numbers. There was no consistency in the numbering procedures that had been developed over the years. In some instances, a combination of numerals and alphabetical designations had been used. In some, additional digits were added for designation of special finishes or colors. To avoid the problems of attempting to use these, a new four-digit "machine code" was added to the regular number. Thus, the old product ID—familiar to the operating people—would always print out with the machine code used in the computer for identification purposes. In the cost routing sheet illustrated in Exhibit 8–3, the first two digits, identified as PC for "product code," precede the basic five-digit number—which is then followed by the four-digit machine code. Note in the manufacturing process sheets that a suffix is also used, thus requiring fifteen digits to be shown on some documents. While this may seem unnecessary, practical considerations deemed it to be obligatory.

Column 1, Opr. No. The operation number identifies the product by stage of completion within each level. These numbers are shown as 010, 020, 030, 040, 050, etc. Number 010 may identify a drilling operation in one cost center but in another, the same number would mean a coating process.

Column 2, B/M Level. The B/M (bill of material) level designates the position of the part number in the "treeing up" process.

Column 3, Quantity. Specifies how many of the specific items are required per completed part at that level. This must be viewed in conjunction with the last column, headed "UM," which stands for unit of measure. In this instance, the code 2 under UM means per thousand. For example, the quantity of 1.00000 therefore means that 1,000 components are required per 1,000 units completed at that level. When two units are required per finished unit, the quantity will be shown as 2.00000. In the case of raw materials shown as the ninety-seven series of items at the bottom portion of the cost routing sheet, the quantity is shown as .00990. This means that .00990 pounds of material are required per thousand units of product.

Column 4, Start Operation. The operation number in this column identifies the point in the process at which processing starts on an incoming component. Note

COST ROUTING SHEET

PRODUCT ID	(1) OPR. NO.	(2) BM LEVEL	(3) QUANTITY	(4) START OPERATION	(5) COST HRS.	(6) STANDARD HRS./M	(7) LABOR RATE	(8) VARIABLE OVERHEAD	(9) FIXED OVERHEAD	(10) R/M CODE	(11) R/M GROSS	(12) R/M NET	(13) SCRAP RECOVERY	(14) STANDARD R/M Cost	(15) U M
01-02608-5036	010	01	1.00000	010	1369	.02	2.497	1.749	3.407	018751				128.6900	2
01-02608-5036	010	01	1.00000	010						011856				8.0500	2
01-02608-5036	020	01	1.00000	020	1369	.05	2.497	1.749	3.407						
.01-02608-0537	010	02	1.00000	010	0267	1.67	2.473	2.093	3.678						
.01-02608-0537	020	02	1.00000	010	0267	1.18	2.473	2.093	3.678						
..01-02608-0005	010	03	1.00000	010	0568	.05	2.752	6.022	4.282						
..01-02608-0005	020	03	1.00000	010	0981	1.16	2.790	1.942	3.237						
...01-02608-0008	010	04	1.00000	010	0447	.15	1.335	4.182	7.121						
...01-02608-0008	020	04	1.00000	010	0450	.50	1.335	4.182	7.122						
...01-02608-0008	030	04	1.00000	010	0761	.81	3.396	3.326	4.933						
...01-02608-0008	050	04	1.00000	010	0568	.07	2.752	6.022	4.282						
...01-02608-0002	010	04	1.00000	010	1294	.08	2.773	2.978	4.413	202800	37.800	17.00	313.75000	638.1700	2
....97-00019-0000	010	05	.00990	010	1291	4.65	2.773	2.978	4.413	059562	350.75000	350.75000		250.0000	2
....97-00019-0000	010	05	.00990	010						055401	17.54000	17.54000		88.0000	2
....97-00019-0000	010	05	.00990	010						051202	3.86000	3.86000		530.0000	2
....97-00019-0000	010	05	.00990	010						058110	4.56000	4.56000		530.0000	2
....97-00019-0000	010	05	.00990	010						057326	7.02000	7.02000		34.5000	2
....97-00019-0000	010	05	.00990	010						054202	35.08000	35.08000		260.0000	2
....97-00019-0000	010	05	.00990	010						057320	87.69000	87.69000		114.2100	2
....97-00019-0000	010	05	.00990	010						055407	86.64000	86.64000		160.0000	2
....97-00019-0000	010	05	.00990	010						057315	3.51000	3.51000		225.0000	2
....97-00019-0000	010	05	.00990	010						059536	70.15000	70.15000		102.5000	2
....97-00019-0000	010	05	.00990	010						059537	224.48000	224.48000		60.0000	2
....97-00019-0000	010	05	.00990	010						051214	21.05000	21.05000		11.7500	2
....97-00019-0000	010	05	.00990	010						054213	87.67000	87.67000		72.5000	2

EXHIBIT 8–3:
COST ROUTING SHEET

149

that the first operation in cost center 1369 (level 01) relates to raw material (packaging and labels). The first operation is 010, which consists of making up the carton and applying the label. The incoming component from level 02 is packaged in operation 020. Thus, the start operation for the latter is indicated as 020.

Column 5, Cost Center. The first two digits identify the department while the second two identify various work centers within the department.

Column 6, Standard Hrs./M. This means the number of hours per thousand units that it should take to perform an operation. The hours would mean labor hours when a hand operation is performed or machine hours when the operation is machine-paced. (Machine hours could be synonymous with labor hours when there is a full-time operator for the machine being used.)

Column 7, Labor Rate. Quantifies the labor cost per hour for performing the particular operation. This rate, multiplied by the hours per M, provides the standard direct-labor cost.

Column 8, Variable Overhead. This represents the variable portion of indirect costs. It is based on a flexible budget that identifies separately those costs that are likely to fluctuate with changes in volume of production. This would include such costs as supplies, material handling, and equipment servicing.

Column 9, Fixed Overhead. This is also determined through the flexible budget. This category includes such costs as occupancy, supervision, and depreciation. Segregation of the variable and fixed overhead facilitates additional analysis beyond that required in the routine cost system procedures.

Column 10, R/M Code. This identifies the material to which no labor has yet been applied. Included in this coding in the cost routing sheet are the following:

- Cartons and labels used at level 01
- Brass rod for making the stem in level 04
- Ingredients required for making the plastic disc at level 05

Column 11, R/M Gross. This refers to the starting quantity of material for making the component or assembly. When material is unavoidably lost in the processing of a component, the finished weight is shown in Column 12 as R/M Net. An illustration of this is operation 10 of level 04. The brass rod must be drilled out and threaded. The gross weight of the rod is shown in Column 11 as R/M Gross while the finished weight is indicated in Column 12 as R/M Net.

Column 13, Scrap Recovery. This shows the standard cost per thousand pounds of metal recovered from the process.

Column 14, Standard R/M Cost. This shows the standard cost of the raw material used in the product.

Column 15, UM (Unit of Measure). The numeral "2" indicates "per thousand."

In comparing Exhibit 8–2 with Exhibit 8–3, it will be noted that the cost routing sheet doesn't provide for setup hours as a separate item. The reason is that setup, for costing purposes, is included in the overhead category.* The manufacturing process sheets used in Exhibit 8–2 indicate, however, the setup cost allowances where applicable for purposes of monitoring the efficiency with which the setups are made.

The "Where Used" File

Another feature that must be built into the program is a "where used" file that can access parts that are common to two or more end products. Note in Exhibit 8–4 that component 06100746 is used in 684 end products and component 06100100 is used in 3 end products.

The cost standards as well as the stock status "on hand" balances reside in an item master file. Both are updated with single rather than multiple entries.

Component #06100746 used in 684 End Products:

02026910209	02026910307	02026910308	02026910309	02052950002
02054310003	02054310004	02054310020	02054310198	02054310209
02054310298	02054320003	02054320004	02054330001	02054330002
02054330129	02054340001	02054340002	02054340197	02054350002
02054350003	02054350020	02054350021	02054350197	02054350209
02054350210	02054360002	02054360003	02054360197	02054360198
02054360200	02054360209	02054360210	02054370003	02054370020
02054380003	02054380020	02055720002	02055720003	02055720019
02055720020	02055720021	02055720209	02055720210	02055730002
02055730003	02055730019	02055730020	02055730021	02055730209
90057620099	90057620090	90057620092	90057620096	90057620197
99009900099	99009900100	99052880336	99052890126	99052932401
99053880097	99052453212	99052567820	99061880132	99073201063
99132647761	99133677642	99213674541	99224675132	99567362111

Component #06100100 used in 3 End Products:

39031001001	39076160419	39078131335

EXHIBIT 8–4:
"WHERE USED" FILE

THE MECHANICS OF COSTING

The program format illustrated in the cost routing sheet not only provides for tracking production and inventory quantities for use in inventory management, it also provides for costing the production and inventory for cost accounting purposes. Illustrative examples for costing material and labor are shown in Exhibits 8–5 and 8–6.

---

*When production runs are long, as in this product, the cost of setup per 1,000 units is so small that setup is included as part of the overhead rate.

COST ROUTING SHEET
PRODUCT 01-02608-5036

	1 OPR NO.	2 BM LEVL	3 QUANTITY	4 START OPN.	5 COST CNTR.	6 STND HRS/M	7 LABOR RATE	8 VARBLE OVHEAD	9 FIXED OVHEAD	10 R/M CODE	11 R/M GROSS	12 R/M NET	13 SCRAP RECOVY	14 STANDARD R/M COST	15 U M
PRODUCT ID															
01—02608—5036	010	01	1.00000	010	1369	.02	2.497	1.749	3.407	018751				128.6900	2
01—02608—5036	010	01	1.00000	010						011856				8.0500	2
01—02608—5036	020	01	1.00000	020	1369	.05	2.497	1.749	3.407						
. 01—02608—0537	010	02	1.00000	010	0267	1.67	2.473	2.093	3.678						
. 01—02608—0537	020	02	1.00000	010	0267	1.18	2.473	2.093	3.678						
.. 01—02608—0005	010	03	1.00000	010	0568	.05	2.752	6.022	4.282						
... 01—02608—0005	020	03	1.00000	010	0981	1.16	2.790	1.942	3.237						
... 01—02608—0008	010	04	1.00000	010	0447	.15	1.335	4.182	7.121	202800	37.80	17.0	313.750	638.17	2
... 01—02608—0008	020	04	1.00000	010	0450	.50	1.335	4.182	7.122						
... 01—02608—0008	030	04	1.00000	010	0761	.81	3.396	3.326	4.933						
... 01—02608—0008	050	04	1.00000	010	0568	.07	2.752	6.022	4.282						
... 01—02608—0002	010	04	1.00000	010	1294	.08	2.773	2.978	4.413						
.... 97—00019—0000	010	05	.00990	010	1291	4.65	2.773	2.978	4.413	059562	350.75000	350.75000		250.0000	2
.: 97—00019—0000	010	05	.00990	010						055401	17.54000	17.54000		88.0000	2
.. 97—00019—0000	010	05	.00990	010						051202	3.86000	3.86000		530.0000	2
... 97—00019—0000	010	05	.00990	010						058110	4.56000	4.56000		530.0000	2
... 97—00019—0000	010	05	.00990	010						057326	7.02000	7.02000		34.5000	2
... 97—00019—0000	010	05	.00990	010						054202	35.08000	35.08000		260.0000	2
... 97—00019—0000	010	05	.00990	010						057320	87.69000	87.69000		114.2100	2
... 97—00019—0000	010	05	.00990	010						055407	86.64000	86.64000		160.0000	2
... 97—00019—0000	010	05	.00990	010						057315	3.51000	3.51000		225.0000	2
.... 97—00019—0000	010	05	.00990	010						059536	70.15000	70.15000		102.5000	2
.... 97—00019—0000	010	05	.00990	010						059537	224.48000	224.48000		60.0000	2
.... 97—00019—0000	010	05	.00990	010						051214	21.05000	21.05000		11.7500	2
.... 97—00019—0000	010	05	.00990	010						054213	87.67000	87.67000		72.5000	2

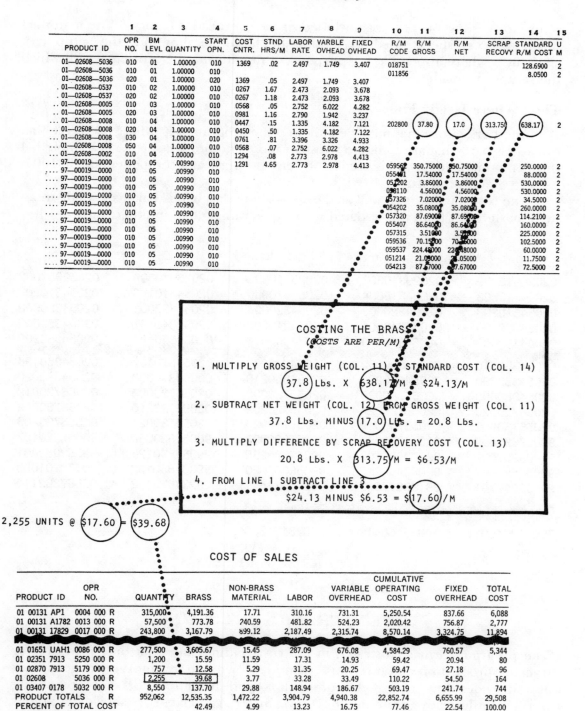

COSTING THE BRASS
(COSTS ARE PER/M)

1. MULTIPLY GROSS WEIGHT (COL. 11) X STANDARD COST (COL. 14)

   37.8 Lbs. X 638.17/M = $24.13/M

2. SUBTRACT NET WEIGHT (COL. 12) FROM GROSS WEIGHT (COL. 11)

   37.8 Lbs. MINUS 17.0 Lbs. = 20.8 Lbs.

3. MULTIPLY DIFFERENCE BY SCRAP RECOVERY COST (COL. 13)

   20.8 Lbs. X 313.75/M = $6.53/M

4. FROM LINE 1 SUBTRACT LINE 3

   $24.13 MINUS $6.53 = $17.60/M

2,255 UNITS @ $17.60 = $39.68

COST OF SALES

PRODUCT ID	OPR NO.	QUANTITY	BRASS	NON-BRASS MATERIAL	LABOR	VARIABLE OVERHEAD	CUMULATIVE OPERATING COST	FIXED OVERHEAD	TOTAL COST
01 00131 AP1	0004 000 R	315,000	4,191.36	17.71	310.16	731.31	5,250.54	837.66	6,088
01 00131 A1782	0013 000 R	57,500	773.78	240.59	481.82	524.23	2,020.42	756.87	2,777
01 00131 17829	0017 000 R	243,800	3,167.79	899.12	2,187.49	2,315.74	8,570.14	3,324.75	11,894
01 01651 UAH1	0086 000 R	277,500	3,605.67	15.45	287.09	676.08	4,584.29	760.57	5,344
01 02351 7913	5250 000 R	1,200	15.59	11.59	17.31	14.93	59.42	20.94	80
01 02870 7913	5179 000 R	757	12.58	5.29	31.35	20.25	69.47	27.18	96
01 02608	5036 000 R	2,255	39.68	3.77	33.28	33.49	110.22	54.50	164
01 03407 0178	5032 000 R	8,550	137.70	29.88	148.94	186.67	503.19	241.74	744
PRODUCT TOTALS R		952,062	12,535.35	1,472.22	3,904.79	4,940.38	22,852.74	6,655.99	29,508
PERCENT OF TOTAL COST			42.49	4.99	13.23	16.75	77.46	22.54	100.00

LEGEND: R = Rod

EXHIBIT 8–5:
DEVELOPING THE PRODUCT COST—MATERIAL

152

COST ROUTING SHEET
PRODUCT 01-02608-5036

	1	2	3	4	5	6	7	8	9	10	11	12	13	14	15
PRODUCT ID	OPR NO.	BM LEVL	QUANTITY	START OPN.	COST CNTR.	STND HRS/M	LABOR RATE	VARBLE OVHEAD	FIXED OVHEAD	R/M CODE	R/M GROSS	R/M NET	SCRAP RECOVY	STANDARD R/M COST	U M
01—02608—5036	010	01	1.00000	010	1369	.02	2.497	1.749	3.4u7	018751				128.6900	2
01—02608—5036	010	01	1.00000	010						011856				8.0500	2
01—02608—5036	020	01	1.00000	020	1369	.05	2.497	1.749	3.407						
. 01—02608—0537	010	02	1.00000	010	0267	1.67	2.473	2.093	3.678						
. 01—02608—0537	020	02	1.00000	010	0267	1.18	2.473	2.093	3.678						
.. 01—02608—0005	010	03	1.00000	010	0568	.05	2.752	6.022	4.282						
.. 01—02608—0005	020	03	1.00000	010	0981	1.16	2.790	1.942	3.237						
... 01—02608—0008	010	04	1.00000	010	0447	.15	1.335	4.182	7.121	202800	37.800	17.000	313.75000	638.1700	2
... 01—02608—0008	020	04	1.00000	010	0450	.50	1.335	4.182	7.122						
... 01—02608—0008	030	04	1.00000	010	0761	.81	3.396	3.326	4.933						
... 01—02608—0008	050	04	1.00000	010	0568	.07	2.752	6.022	4.282						
... 01—02608—0002	010	04	1.00000	010	1294	.08	2.773	2.978	4.413						
.... 97—00019—0000	010	05	.00990	010	1291	4.65	2.773	2.978	4.413	059562	350.75000	350.75000		250.0000	2
.... 97—00019—0000	010	05	.00990	010						055401	17.54000	17.54000		88.0000	2
.... 97—00019—0000	010	05	.00990	010						051202	3.86000	3.86000		530.0000	2
.... 97—00019—0000	010	05	.00990	010						058110	4.56000	4.56000		530.0000	2
.... 97—00019—0000	010	05	.00990	010						057326	7.02000	7.02000		34.5000	2
.... 97—00019—0000	010	05	.00990	010						054202	35.08000	35.08000		260.0000	2
.... 97—00019—0000	010	05	.00990	010						057320	87.69000	87.69000		114.2100	2
.... 97—00019—0000	010	05	.00990	010						055407	86.64000	86.64000		160.0000	2
.... 97—00019—0000	010	05	.00990	010						057415	3.51000	3.51000		225.0000	2
.... 97—00019—0000	010	05	.00990	010											
.... 97—00019—0000	010	05	.00990	010											
.... 97—00019—0000	010	05	.00990	010											
.... 97—00019—0000	010	05	.00990	010											

COSTING THE LABOR
(COSTS ARE PER/M)

COST CENTER	OPN.	STANDARD HOURS/M	LABOR RATE(1)	LABOR COST
1369	010	.02	$2.497	$.05
1369	020	.05	2.497	.12
0267	010	1.67	2.473	4.13
0267	020	1.18	2.473	2.92
0568	010	.05	2.752	.14
0981	020	1.16	2.790	3.24
0447	010	.15	1.335	.20
0450	020	.50	1.335	.67
0761	030	.81	3.396	2.75
0568	050	.07	2.752	.19
1294	010	.08	2.773	.22
1291	010	4.65(2)	2.773	.13
				$14.76

(1) Based on hourly rate divided by number of machines operated.

(2) Factored by .0099 to reflect standard cost per/M units.

2,255 Units @ $14.76 = $33.28

COST OF SALES

PRODUCT ID	OPR NO.	QUANTITY	BRASS	NON-BRASS MATERIAL	LABOR	VARIABLE OVERHEAD	CUMULATIVE OPERATING COST	FIXED OVERHEAD	TOTAL COST
01 00131 AP1	0004 000 R	315,000	4,191.36	17.71	310.16	731.31	5,250.54	837.66	6,088
01 00131 A1782	0013 000 R	57,500	773.78	240.59	481.82	524.23	2,020.42	756.87	2,777
01 00131 17829	0017 000 R	243,800	3,167.79	899.12	2,187.49	2,315.74	8,570.14	3,324.75	11,894
01 01651 UAH1	0086 000 R	277,500	3,605.67	15.45	287.09	676.08	4,584.29	760.57	5,344
01 02351 7913	5250 000 R	1,200	15.59	11.59	17.31	14.93	59.42	20.94	80
01 02870 7913	5179 000 R	757	12.58	5.29	31.35	20.25	69.47	27.18	96
01 02608	5036 000 R	2,255	39.68	3.77	33.28	33.49	110.22	54.50	164
01 03407 0178	5032 000 R	8,550	137.70	29.88	148.94	186.67	503.19	241.74	744
PRODUCT TOTALS	R	952,062	12,535.35	1,472.22	3,904.79	4,940.38	22,852.74	6,655.99	29,508
PERCENT OF TOTAL COST			42.49	4.99	13.23	16.75	77.46	22.54	100.00

LEGEND: R = Rod

EXHIBIT 8–6:
DEVELOPING THE PRODUCT COST—DIRECT LABOR

Developing the Product Cost–Material

Earlier in this chapter it was noted that the starting quantity for making the brass tire valve stem was 37.8 pounds per 1000. It was further noted that because of the "hollowing out" of the stem through a drilling operation 20.8 pounds of brass, or 55 percent of the starting quantity, was considered to be necessary scrap.

Exhibit 8–5 identifies these figures in the cost routing sheet and illustrates the application of standard costs in the section labeled "Costing the Brass." The costing is illustrated in four steps:

1. The gross weight is multiplied by the standard cost per thousand pounds of brass with a resulting cost of $24.13 per thousand stems.

2. The net finished weight is subtracted from the starting weight to arrive at the pounds of brass lost.

3. The 20.8 pounds of brass lost is multiplied by the standard cost of scrap recovery—showing a credit of $6.53 per thousand stems.

4. The product cost per thousand stems at level 04 is arrived at by subtracting the $6.53 from the $24.13. This indicates a brass cost of $17.60 per thousand stems.

The cost of sales summary shown in the lower third of the exhibit indicates that 2255 units of product 01 02608 5036 stem were sold at a total standard cost of $164. Of this, the standard cost of the brass content is shown as $39.68 (2255 × $17.60).

Developing the Product Cost–Labor

Exhibit 8–6 illustrates the procedure for arriving at the labor cost for product 01 02608 5036. The standard hours per thousand units are added up (see section entitled "Costing the Labor") for all the operations in all cost centers through which this product passes. These hours are then multiplied by the labor grade rates to arrive at a total labor cost by cost centers. The addition of the total labor cost by cost center results in a total labor cost of $14.76 per thousand units. Then, multiplying the $14.76 by the 2255 units that were sold, $33.28 of the total cost of sales of this product is accounted for. The balance of the cost is made up of the nonbrass material and the overhead. The nonbrass material is calculated in much the same manner as brass while the overhead is based on the applicable direct labor or machine hours, whichever is applicable to the particular operation performed. Determination of overhead costing rates will be covered in another chapter.

COSTING THE TRANSACTIONS

The costing of brass and labor, in the cost of sales summary shown in Exhibits 8–5 and 8–6, should fall under the heading of this section. Obviously, there are other transactions that precede the relief of inventory when products are sold.

Transactions for the parts fabricated and assembled in this company would involve the following stockrooms:

• Raw material

• Fabricated and purchased components (parts)

• Finished goods

The fabricating and assembly cost centers would include cost centers in the following departments:

1. Automatics
2. General machinery
3. Molding
4. Plating, cleaning, and coating
5. Hand assembly and packaging
6. Automatic assembly including packaging

Departments 1, 2, 3, and 4 are fabricating departments in the primary work-in-process area, while departments 5 and 6 are assembly departments in the secondary work-in-process area.

The transactions relating to issues out of raw material affect the primary work-in-process area. The fabricated parts are then listed as transactions through the various cost centers within primary work-in-process until ready for transfer into the fabricated and purchased components stockroom.

Reissue of the fabricated and purchased components into the secondary work-in-process area is treated as transactions much like issues out of the raw material stockroom, and finally, the fully assembled products are transferred into finished goods stock. The final stage in the transactions is, of course, the transfers out of finished goods to cost of sales.

Raw Material Issues

Exhibit 8–7 illustrates the costing of issues of raw material. These are categorized by broad types of material. The example shown covers chemicals. The individual items are listed in the sequence of the part numbers, each showing the unit of measure "2," indicating cost per thousand. The column headed "Extended Cost" is the result of multiplying the quantity by the standard unit cost per thousand. Note that item 96-5408 shows a negative quantity and therefore a negative cost. This indicates either a return to stock or correction of a previous issue. The extended costs showing a single asterisk to the right indicate sub-totals. The double asterisks are group totals. The final total, $346,340.81, is the total of all items issued during the month including the other categories as well as chemicals. This total for all issues will be shown later in a journal entry that relieves the raw material inventory account and charges work-in-process.

Fabricated Parts Transferred into the Stockroom

Most companies that fabricate parts for use in assembly at a later date utilize a work-in-process stockroom as a storage and staging area for fabricated components and subassemblies. When completed, they are transferred into the fabricated and purchased components stockroom. Exhibit 8–8 shows a typical transaction listing of the items being moved into the stockroom. Since no production operations are performed in the stockroom, the operation number used is 999. Note that the columnar format for costing is similar to that used for cost of sales, referred to in

CHEMICALS	DESCRIPTION	U/M	QUANTITY	STANDARD UNIT COST	EXTENDED COST
96-5408	Powder = 6 H	2	30	4750.0000	− 142.50
			30		− 142.50 *
96-5410	Tetrafluoroethylene Resin = 6	2	184	4750.0000	874.00
96-5410	Tetrafluoroethylene Resin = 6	2	138	4750.0000	655.50
	Resin = 6				
96-5410	Tetrafluoroethylene Resin = 6	2	140	4750.0000	665.00
			683		3,244.25 *
965411	Naphtha	2	30	45.0700	1.35
965411	Naphtha	2	60	45.0700	2.70
965411	Naphtha	2	30	45.0700	1.35
			120		5.40 *
			2,062		3,313.98**
TOTAL ALL MATERIAL CATEGORIES					346,340.81

EXHIBIT 8–7:
RAW MATERIAL ISSUES

the lower third of Exhibits 8–5 and 8–6. In fact, all transfers through the manufacturing process will show the same format, because the work-in-process and finished goods inventories show this breakdown. Note, also, that the costs transferred to the stockroom are summarized by "To" department totals and "From" department totals. Since this transaction listing includes parts used on the valve inserts as well as other related products, the brass column is broken down to show the brass strip and brass wire separately from the rod.

Cost of Sales

Although cost of sales was discussed in connection with Exhibits 8–5 and 8–6 it is included here again as Exhibit 8–9. Since the costing was previously explained, the purpose here is to point out that the computer automatically calculates the percentage that each element of cost is to the total cost. This is not only done for total cost of sales but for the various categories of products making up the total. This type of percentage breakdown can be helpful for analytical purposes.

Since the issues of material into work-in-process, transfers of fabricated items into the fabricated and purchased parts stockroom, and the cost of sales are representative of the method of costing transactions, there is no need to discuss the others at this time.

PRODUCT ID	OPR. NO.	QUANTITY	BRASS	NONBRASS MATERIAL	LABOR	VARIABLE OVERHEAD	CUMULATIVE OPERATING COST	FIXED OVERHEAD	TOTAL COST
31 05163	0009 999 R	360	3.16	4.54	34.96	43.52	86.18	70.52	156.70
33 00798 D15	0016 999	250		13.13	.00	.00	13.13	.00	13.13
39 01451 198	0019 999 R	1,900	2.36	.00	27.49	3.49	34.87	4.52	39.39
	W		1.53						
39 04414 6	0019 999 R	710	4.36	2.65	18.59	7.40	33.19	9.90	43.09
	S		.19						
39 09155 6	0048 999 R	830	1.75	8.78	51.24	12.54	74.37	21.36	95.73
	W		.06						
41 00931 5	0049 999	300		.17	1.84	1.62	3.63	2.74	6.37
51 01593 4	0029 999	1,000		25.55	9.68	11.15	46.38	13.38	59.76
53 07642 2	0019 999	1,000		2.61	.00	.00	2.61	.00	2.61
53 08385 A3	0109 999	41,620		19.98	155.02	129.55	304.55	223.07	527.62
67 03670 197	0079 999	10		5.85	.00	.00	5.85	.00	5.85
67 08600 16	0119 999	8		.15	.11	.06	.32	.12	.44
67 08600 22	0159 999	7		.24	.57	.63	1.44	1.00	2.44
67 08600 23	0169 999	7		.11	.67	.81	1.59	1.32	2.91
67 08600 45	0269 999	9		.57	.49	.68	1.74	.83	2.57
67 08601 12	0089 999	10		5.20	.00	.00	5.20	.00	5.20
"TO" DEPT. TOTALS	R	48,021	11.63	89.53	300.66	211.45	615.05	348.76	963.81
	S		.19						
	W		1.59						
"FROM" DEPT. TOTALS	R	48,021	11.63	89.53	300.66	211.45	615.05	348.76	963.81
	S		.19						
	W		1.59						

LEGEND: R = Rod; S = Strip; W = Wire

EXHIBIT 8–8:
FABRICATED PARTS TRANSFERRED TO STOCKROOM

PRODUCT ID	OPR. NO.	QUANTITY	BRASS	NONBRASS MATERIAL	LABOR	VARIABLE OVERHEAD	CUMULATIVE OPERATING COST	FIXED OVERHEAD	TOTAL COST
01 00131 AP1	0004 000 R	315,000	4,191.36	17.71	310.16	731.31	5,250.54	837.66	6,088
01 00131 A1782	0013 000 R	57,500	773.78	240.59	481.82	524.23	2,020.42	756.87	2,777
01 00131 17829	0017 000 R	243,800	3,167.79	899.12	2,187.49	2,315.74	8,570.14	3,324.75	11,894
01 01651 UAH1	0086 000 R	277,500	3,605.67	15.45	287.09	676.08	4,584.29	760.57	5,344
01 02351 7913	5250 000 R	1,200	15.59	11.59	17.31	14.93	59.42	20.94	80
01 02870 7913	5179 000 R	757	12.58	5.29	31.35	20.25	69.47	27.18	96
01 02608	5036 000 R	2,255	39.68	3.77	33.28	33.49	110.22	54.50	164
01 03407 0178	5032 000 R	8,550	137.70	29.88	148.94	186.67	503.19	241.74	744
PRODUCT TOTALS	R	952,062	12,535.35	1,472.22	3,904.79	4,940.38	22,852.74	6,655.99	29,508
PERCENT OF TOTAL COST			42.49	4.99	13.23	16.75	77.46	22.54	100.00

**EXHIBIT 8–9:
COST OF SALES**

LEGEND: R = Rod

158

BYPRODUCT CONTROL REPORTS

Availability of the computer speeds up many of the routine tasks previously performed by hand. Much of the data that provides information needed for cost accounting and inventory management contains valuable information that could be used for more complete management control.

When the work was performed manually, time did not permit culling out such data and reassembling it into more comprehensive controls. The computer now makes such data more readily accessible and programmable into useful reports. Since material accounts for almost half of the total manufacturing cost in most companies, and in many instances far in excess of half, material will be used to provide illustrative examples.

Purchased Parts Price History

Price information on purchases is maintained manually in the purchasing departments of many companies. Since much of this information is posted by hand, any meaningful analysis would require burdensome manual analysis that would be both time-consuming and costly. Introduction of the computer provides an excellent opportunity to develop a price history by individual items for various suppliers over a period of time.

Exhibit 8–10 illustrates an example of two items for which such an analysis is made. The listing shows the vendor (or vendors when more than one source is used), the invoice number, invoice date, quantity purchased, the unit in which purchased, the total actual cost, the unit cost, and the average unit cost in a desired period of time.

The unit cost history is useful in monitoring the historical price trends and the influence of quantity purchases on individual unit prices. The report can be rearranged so that price comparisons can be made of similar items supplied by more than one vendor. This type of report can also be very useful in setting material price standards for cost accounting purposes.

Purchase Price Variance Report

In companies using standard costs, the purchase price variances are usually calculated at the time the vendor invoices are being processed for payment. This facilitates the matching of the purchase price variance with the specific invoice to which it applies. Introduction of the computer facilitated the preparation of purchase price variance reports that listed every single purchase—showing the quantity purchased, the standard unit cost, total actual cost, total standard cost, and the variance of the total actual cost from the total standard cost. Such a report is illustrated in the upper half of Exhibit 8–11.

Many data processing departments, when initially programming such reports, list every item purchased irrespective of the magnitude of the variance between actual and standard cost. The result has been complaints by operating personnel such as the following, which was made by the plant manager of a company using many different parts that were purchased from the outside:

PART NO.	VENDOR	INVOICE NO.	P.O. #	INVOICE DATE	QUANTITY	U/M	TOTAL ACTUAL COST	ACTUAL UNIT COST
01-2868	Ajax Supply Company	42367	02873	2/2	100	ea.	53.80	.538
01-2868	Ajax Supply Company	42367	05091	3/5	400	ea.	215.20	.538
01-2868	Ajax Supply Company	42646	03047	3/6	100	ea.	53.80	.538
01-2868	Ajax Supply Company	43359	06068	5/7	100	ea.	53.80	.538
01-2868	Ajax Supply Company	43363	06949	6/7	900	ea.	522.90	.581
01-2868	Ajax Supply Company	43424	06729	6/8	300	ea.	176.40	.588
01-2868	Ajax Supply Company	43426	07657	7/12	600	ea.	352.80	.588
01-2868	Ajax Supply Company	43468	07657	8/18	600	ea.	352.80	.588
01-2868	Ajax Supply Company	43686	07729	9/12	300	ea.	176.40	.588
01-2868	Ajax Supply Company	45898	07892	10/13	500	ea.	345.00	.690
01-2868	Ajax Supply Company	46667	07884	10/16	502	ea.	376.50	.750
01-2868	Ajax Supply Company	48882	08861	11/23	501	ea.	375.75	.750
01-2868	Ajax Supply Company	52601	08960	12/14	500	ea.	375.00	.750
					5403		3,430.15	.635*
43-9267	Berkshire Products	41031	02802	1/30	25	ea.	408.17	16.327
43-9267	Berkshire Products	42308	02815	2/5	125	ea.	2,040.85	16.327
43-9267	Berkshire Products	42309	05020	2/18	25	ea.	408.17	16.327
43-9267	Berkshire Products	42656	03023	3/6	50	ea.	816.34	16.327
43-9267	Berkshire Products	42333	05621	4/2	75	ea.	1,224.51	16.327
43-9267	Berkshire Products	43852	06842	5/9	25	ea.	408.17	16.327
43-9267	Berkshire Products	43962	06731	6/17	25	ea.	416.50	16.660
43-9267	Berkshire Products	43975	07662	7/12	35	ea.	583.10	16.660
43-9267	Berkshire Products	44502	07894	8/14	85	ea.	1,416.10	16.660
43-9267	Berkshire Products	45652	07992	9/16	65	ea.	1,082.90	16.660
43-9267	Berkshire Products	46867	08012	10/18	15	ea.	249.90	16.660
43-9267	Berkshire Products	49001	08862	11/21	56	ea.	932.96	16.660
43-9267	Berkshire Products	51621	09002	12/16	57	ea.	949.62	16.660
					663		10,937.29	16.496*

EXHIBIT 8–10:
PURCHASED PARTS PRICE HISTORY

*Average unit price.

BY ITEM

P.O. NO.	ITEM CODE	QUANTITY	U/M CODE	U/M	STD. UNIT COST	ACTUAL COST	STANDARD COST	VARIANCE
49999	03 3472	3346	2	LBS	702.700	2,754.43	2,351.23	−403.20
50344	20 2980	810	2	LBS	620.190	490.21	502.35	12.14
49760	21 3190	1851	2	LBS	625.000	1,110.97	1,156.88	45.91
50134	21 3476	4372	2	LBS	625.000	2,733.37	2,732.50	.87
50333	21 3476	7378	2	LBS	625.000	4,428.28	4,611.25	182.97
50050	21 3650	344	2	LBS	724.490	206.47	249.22	42.75
50217	21 4450	555	2	LBS	580.000	306.75	321.90	15.15
49799	21 4450	1238	2	LBS	580.000	684.24	718.04	33.80
50591	22 0781	127	2	LBS	1,287.780	109.83	163.55	53.72
50218	22 1562	110	2	LBS	828.000	89.56	91.08	1.52
49215	22 1660	1000	2	LBS	828.000	814.20	828.00	13.80
49216	22 1660	6018	2	LBS	828.000	4,899.86	4,982.90	83.04
49216	22 1660	4383	2	LBS	828.000	3,130.34	3,629.12	498.78
49185	23 0245	6810	2	LBS	625.000	4,087.36	4,256.25	168.89
49186	23 0245	26689	2	LBS	625.000	16,152.18	16,680.63	528.45
49186	23 0245	17314	2	LBS	625.000	10,391.86	10,821.25	429.39
49186	23 0245	20517	2	LBS	625.000	12,416.89	12,823.13	406.24
48958	23 0332	6614	2	LBS	630.000	4,002.79	4,166.82	164.03
48958	23 0332	3726	2	LBS	630.000	2,329.50	2,347.38	17.88
49398	23 0437	7152	2	LBS	585.0000	3,988.67	4,183.92	195.25
48971	23 0437	13939	2	LBS	585.000	7,773.78	8,154.32	380.54
49996	23 0438	534	2	LBS	585.00	297.81	312.39	14.58
49670	23 0467	2522	2	LBS	585.000	1,454.44	1,475.37	20.93
50345	23 0531	5066	2	LBS	576.000	2,777.18	2,918.02	140.84
49659	23 0625	1010	2	LBS	549.000	524.90	554.49	29.59
50222	23 0625	1520	2	LBS	549.000	789.94	834.48	44.54
						232,934.06	249,125.73	16,191.67

BY MAJOR ITEM*

P.O. NO.	ITEM CODE	QUANTITY	U/M CODE	U/M	STD. UNIT COST	ACTUAL COST	STANDARD COST	VARIANCE**
49997	03 3472	3346	2	LBS	702.700	2,754.43	2,351.23	403.20U
50333	21 3476	7378	2	LBS	625.000	4,428.28	4,611.25	182.97F
50050	21 3650	344	2	LBS	724.490	206.47	249.22	42.75F
50591	22 0781	127	2	LBS	1,287.780	109.83	163.55	53.72F
49216	22 1664	4383	2	LBS	828.000	3,130.34	3,629.12	498.78F
49185	23 0245	6810	2	LBS	625.000	4,037.36	4,256.25	168.89F
49186	23 0245	26689	2	LBS	625.000	16,152.18	16,680.63	528.45F
49186	23 0245	17314	2	LBS	625.000	10,396.86	10,521.25	429.39F
49180	23 0245	7859	2	LBS	625.000	4,716.97	4,911.85	194.91F
49186	23 0245	20517	2	LBS	625.000	12,416.89	12,823.13	406.24F
48958	23 0332	6614	2	LBS	630.000	4,280.85	4,116.82	164.03U
49398	23 0437	7152	2	LBS	585.000	3,988.67	4,183.92	195.25F
48971	23 0437	13939	2	LBS	585.000	7,773.78	8,154.32	380.54F
50345	23 0531	5066	2	LBS	576.020	2,777.18	2,918.02	140.84F

*Major items are those variances that are 5% or more and those that exceed $100.
**U = Unfavorable   F = Favorable.

EXHIBIT 8–11:
PURCHASE PRICE VARIANCES

I think the theory of standard costs and variances is great but why must I receive a printout each month that requires me to pore through fifty to seventy-five pages of items purchased during the month? I have more important things to do. First of all, weekly reports would be more useful to me than monthly reports. Additionally, I would like only the major items reported on an exception basis. This would include:

1. Those items in which the variance exceeds 5 percent of the standard cost.

2. Those items in which the variance is in excess of $100 regardless of the percentage.

This plant manager, in describing the format that would be more useful to him, commented further that the previous month's total purchase price variance was favorable in the amount of $16,191.69. He expressed his reaction in the following words:

I get very suspicious of the type of effort that went into setting standard prices when I see a 6.4 percent favorable price variance—particularly when the wholesale price index showed an 8 percent increase during the year. This tells me that the purchasing department was playing it safe. What also bothers me is that the cost department accepted these standards without a single question or challenge.

The lower portion of Exhibit 8–11 illustrates a purchase price variance report showing only the major items on an exception basis. Note that this excludes such minor items as $.87 on a purchase of over $2700 and the small items whose percentage variance is less than 5 percent. The comments by this plant manager showed that he was interested in controlling his costs and that he was able to do so without requiring voluminous reports. Other operating executives may prefer to establish different guidelines for exception reporting. Another company wanted no variances of under $100 reported even if they exceeded 5 percent. Such determinations vary from company to company depending upon the nature of the materials used and the demand and supply situation in the marketplace.

Material Receipts Compared with Plan

The controller of one company noted that a large number of invoices were being received from suppliers in advance of the delivery date specified on the purchase order. This meant that the material might also be delivered in advance of the date specified for delivery. In a sample of 100 such cases, it was found that material was being received 3.2 days early, on the average. This premature delivery meant that the company's inventory was excessive to the extent that orders were received early. It also meant that some invoices with a discount allowed for payment within ten days were being paid prematurely, thus depriving the company of the use of such cash. Additionally, this tended to dilute the calculation of return on investment because inventories were higher than planned.

Exhibit 8–12 illustrates the format of a report that was prepared weekly to monitor deliveries against planned (scheduled) dates. This report lists the part number, purchase order number, description of the material ordered, quantity and standard cost. The total standard cost of the material received during each week was compared with the standard cost of the material scheduled for delivery during

PART NO.	PURCHASE ORDER NO.	DESCRIPTION	U/M	QUANTITY	STANDARD UNIT COST	TOTAL STANDARD COST
01-0126	46236	Casting	ea.	1	22.994	20.994
01-0326	46337	Casting	ea.	10	93.789	937.890
02-0462	40454	Casting	ea.	10	275.000	2,750.000
02-0561	46567	Casting	ea.	10	181.030	1,810.300
03-0102	46567	Casting	ea.	1	148.870	148.870
04-9362	47668	.067″ × 48″ Coiled Steel	lb.	20,000	.105	2,100.000
04-9867	47887	.051″ × 36″ Coiled Steel	lb.	20,000	.108	2,160.000
05-0002	48882	.020″ × 10″ Coiled Steel	lb.	5,000	.122	610.000
05-0763	46567	.018″ × 9″ Coiled Steel	lb.	5,000	.108	540.000
05-0972	46338	.016″ × 12″ 70/30 Brass	lb.	1,000	.100	100.000
05-2707	43536	.010″ × 16″ 70/30 Brass	lb.	2,000	.580	1,160.000
06-9872	43678	Teflon Tetraflouride	lb.	184	4.750	874.000
06-9962	44587	Teflon Tetraflouride	lb.	138	4.750	655.500
07-3212	45867	#110 Switch Plates	ea.	35	500	17.500
07-3336	43633	#220 Switch Plates	ea.	1,000	1.500	1,500.000
07-5456	42337	Nylon Grommets	ea.	25,000	.028	700.000
07-6768	41246	Plastic Washers	ea.	100,000	.030	3,000.000
20-3246	46687	#10 Webbing	yd.	1,000	3.070	3,070.000
20-4678	46667	#26 Webbing	yd.	5,000	4.020	20,100.000
20-5762	45452	#32 Plastic Material	yd.	10,000	.500	5,000.000
20-6879	46601	#41 Plastic Material	yd.	5,000	1.100	5,500.000
22-1334	45827	2122 Ferrules	ea.	100	2.100	210.000
22-2377	45990	3538 Ferrules	ea.	200	3.000	600.000
23-3679	42876	½ HP. Motor	ea.	100	10.000	1,000.000
23-4627	43378	1 HP. Motor	ea.	300	46.500	13,950.000
		Total w/e 10/7				95,968.000*
		Planned Purchases				87,690.000

*Actual receipts in excess of plan by 9.4%.

Note: Although this report shows a single percentage for the week's purchases, some may prefer to calculate a percentage by line item.

EXHIBIT 8–12:
MATERIAL RECEIPTS COMPARED WITH PLAN

that same week. The difference indicates the dollar value of material shipped prematurely. The difference between actual receipts and planned purchases in this case was in excess of 9 percent compared with 2 percent which was the amount allowed. This report was forwarded to the purchasing department each week as well as to the general manager. The purchasing department was instructed to notify the suppliers of the premature shipment and to advise them that discounts would be calculated from the date the delivery was scheduled to have arrived rather on the date of receipt. In the event that material was received late, the date from which the discount allowance would be counted would be from the date of receipt. After this report was in use for six weeks, the difference between the actual date of receipt and the planned date of receipt dropped from over 9 percent to 3 percent, based on the standard cost of the material involved.

The treasurer of another company was also quite conscious of early and late deliveries of material by suppliers. He expressed his views somewhat as follows:

> Timeliness to me means delivery on schedule—not late and not too early. The objection to late delivery is obvious; to early delivery, not so obvious. It is to the advantage of the vendor to ship to the customer as soon as possible—even if ahead of schedule. The vendor thus reduces the amount of capital tied up in inventory and improves his return on investment. While advantageous to the seller, this practice has the opposite effect on the buyer. If the buyer company receives the shipment ahead of schedule, its investment is needlessly increased and its return on investment reduced.

The report format used by this company is shown in Exhibit 8–13. The basis of the report is to compare the scheduled delivery date, contained in the purchase order data base, with the date of receipt of the material. The last column, headed "Vendor Performance," indicates the number of days that delivery was made ahead of or behind the authorized delivery date. Such a report is useful in determining which vendors come closest to approximating the authorized receipt date. Those who habitually make delivery several days ahead of time can be dealt with by:

1. Refusing to accept the material
2. Accepting the material but basing payment and discount (when applicable) on the authorized delivery date.

Exhibits 8–12 and 8–13, although different in format, are similar in principle and intent. Companies seeking to control the size of their inventories will find that monitoring vendor adherence to scheduled delivery date (within reason) is one of the many methods of accomplishing this goal.

SUMMARIZING THE TRANSACTION REPORTS

In an earlier section entitled "Costing the Transactions," the mechanics of costing was demonstrated for the brass required in making the stem, as well as the direct labor cost for the various cost centers. The format of the transaction reports was also illustrated. The following section, "Byproduct Control Reports," discussed the modifications that could be made to the information contained in the transaction reports to provide management with additional information. Although the illustrative examples were limited to material, the concept could be applied to the other elements of cost as well.

This section will deal with the consolidation of the various transaction reports with a view toward determining the cost of production for the month and the changes in inventory. The transaction reports, listed below, are shown in Exhibit 8–14 together with a listing of the closing journal entries. The transactions are numbered from one to ten, as are the journal entries.

VENDOR	PART. NO.	DESCRIPTION	PURCH. ORDER NUMBER	QTY.	U/M	TOTAL STANDARD COST	SCHEDULED DELIVERY DATE	RECEIVED DATE	VENDOR PERFORMANCE[1]
ABC Corp.	1440 202	Angle	C45100	1,440	In	514.00	5 17 85	5 23 85	6
ABC Corp.	1452 316	Channel	C45101	2,400	In	1,200.00	5 22 85	5 19 85	3-
ABC Corp.	1535 360	Flat	C45205	2,400	In	1,320.00	5 22 85	5 23 85	1
						3,034.00*			
ABZ. Corp.	1440 220	Angle	C45100	1,440	In	576.00	5 15 85	5 22 85	7-
						576.00*			
B.Z. Co.	1535 274	Flat	C45206	240	In	144.00	5 09 85	5 20 85	11
B.Z. Co.	1622 334	Bar Round	C46170	240	In	120.50	5 15 85	5 21 85	6

3,996.50**

[1]Indicates the number of days ahead of or behind schedule.

EXHIBIT 8–13:
VENDOR DELIVERY PERFORMANCE

Transaction #

1. Purchase price variance
2. Raw material issues
3. Fabricated parts transferred into fabricated and purchased parts inventory
4. Transfers from finished goods to fabricated and purchased parts inventory
5. Transfers from fabricated and purchased parts inventory to production
6. Omitted because there were no transactions
7. Components in finished goods stock returned to production
8. Completed production transferred to finished goods inventory
9. Change in work-in-process floor inventory
10. Cost of sales

Purchase Price Variance Report

This report was discussed in the section "Byproduct Control Reports" in which it was suggested that the analysis of variances be presented to the purchasing department and to management on an exception basis to avoid numerous pages of detail. Note in closing journal entry 1 that the total purchase price variance is $16,352.54, made up of $16,191.67 relating to purchases into raw material inventory and $160.87 relating to purchases into the fabricated and purchased parts inventory. Note that the purchase price variance of $16,352.54 is favorable because the standard cost is greater than the actual cost. Since the company values its production and inventory at standard cost, the raw material inventory was increased in value by the amount of the variance to bring it up to the standard cost.

Before proceeding to the other transaction reports, it would be well to first discuss the method of recording the variances and to give some explanation of the "uncosted items" shown in the various reports.

2 — RAW MATERIAL ISSUES

CHEMICALS	DESCRIPTION	U/M	QUANTITY	STANDARD UNIT COST	EXTENDED COST
96-5408	Powder ≡6 H	2	30	4750.0000	− 142.50
			30		− 142.50 *
96-5410	Tetrafluoroethylene Resin ≡ 6	2	184	4750.0000	874.00
96-5410	Tetrafluoroethylene Resin ≡ 6	2	138	4750.0000	655.50
96-5410	Resin ≡ 6	2	140	4750.0000	665.00
	Tetrafluoroethylene Resin ≡ 6		683		3,244.25 *
965411	Naphtha	2	30	45.0700	1.35
965411	Naphtha	2	60	45.0700	2.70
965411	Naphtha	2	30	45.0700	1.35
			120		5.40 *
			2,062		3,313.98 **
					346,340.81 **

1 — PURCHASE PRICE VARIANCE

P.O. NO.	ITEM CODE	QUANTITY	U/M CODE	U/M	UNIT COST	ACTUAL COST	STANDARD COST	VARIANCE
49999	03 3472	3346	2	LBS	702.700	2,754.43	2,351.23	− 403.20
50344	20 2980	810	2	LBS	620.190	490.21	502.35	12.14
49260	21 3190	1851	2	LBS	625.000	1,110.97	1,156.38	45.81
48958	23 0332	6614	2	LBS	630.000	4,002.79	4,166.82	164.03
48958	23 0332	3726	2	LBS	630.000	2,329.50	2,347.38	17.88
49398	23 0437	7152	2	LBS	585.000	3,988.67	4,183.92	195.25
48971	23 0437	13939	2	LBS	585.000	7,773.78	8,154.32	380.54
49996	23 0438	534	2	LBS	585.000	297.81	312.39	14.58
49670	23 0467	2522	2	LBS	585.000	1,454.44	1,475.37	20.93
50345	23 0531	5066	2	LBS	576.000	2,777.18	2,918.02	140.84
49659	21 0625	1010	2	LBS	549.000	524.90	554.49	29.59
50222	23 0625	1520	2	LBS	549.000	789.94	834.48	44.54
						232,934.06	249,125.73	16,191.67

STANDARD COST EQUALS QUANTITY X UNIT COST

3 — FABRICATED PARTS TRANSFERRED INTO FABRICATED AND PURCHASED PARTS INVENTORY

From:	Brass	Non-Brass	Direct Labor	Variable Overhead	Fixed Overhead	Total
01	$ 13.41	89.53	300.66	211.45	348.76	963.81
02	1.50	38.12	4.08	3.20	4.75	51.65
03	2,085.47	81.80	302.92	678.81	1,029.06	4,178.08
04	4,098.41	11,928.58	2,080.78	2,055.62	2,889.39	23,050.78
05	229,804.96	16,932.22	39,916.46	69,870.01	93,891.07	450,414.72
06	2,913.91	591.33	1,796.39	2,041.96	2,879.65	10,223.24
07	1,408.39	63.53	388.42	433.52	654.23	2,948.09
08	15,413.32	2,473.79	10,881.12	14,917.32	22,872.35	66,557.90
09	541.54	1,204.47	3,340.78	3,096.48	4,880.48	13,063.75
10	97.36	246.72	26.32	38.35	39.43	438.18
11	1,390.27	1,611.96	539.96	628.49	950.28	5,120.96
12		36.72				36.72
Total Costed	257,768.54	35,296.77	59,577.89	93,965.23	130,439.45	577,047.88
Uncosted items	6,666.95	2,003.78	1,495.59	2,368.74	3,444.58	15,979.64
	$ 264,435.49	37,300.55	61,073.48	96,333.97	133,884.03	593,027.52
			301,736.04		230,218.00	

4 — TRANSFERS FROM FINISHED GOODS TO FABRICATED AND PURCHASED PARTS INVENTORY

	Brass	Non-Brass	Direct Labor	Variable Overhead	Fixed Overhead	Total
Total Costed	$ 47.72	537.22	217.03	188.69	273.50	1,264.16
Uncosted items	31.60	471.41	69.30	47.90	72.19	692.40
	$ 79.32	1,008.63	286.33	236.59	345.69	1,956.56

5 — TRANSFERS FROM FABRICATED AND PURCHASED PARTS INVENTORY TO PRODUCTION

To:	Brass	Non-Brass	Direct Labor	Variable Overhead	Fixed Overhead	Total
01	$ 48,524.50	21,270.43	18,750.18	23,636.47	32,404.98	144,586.56
02	14,120.43	5,520.33	9,464.68	13,374.62	20,628.73	63,108.79
04	2,454.31	15,257.61	1,861.74	2,285.78	3,029.04	24,888.48
05	152,774.51	6,920.74	14,377.23	24,868.29	34,414.69	233,355.46
06	5,803.94	15,186.86	1,737.66	2,538.59	3,463.66	28,730.71
07	25,787.14	495.34	9,930.40	21,765.50	28,195.78	86,174.16
08	189.76	565.40	41.22	50.95	70.46	917.79
11	1,769.73	373.78	1,077.12	1,791.47	1,738.56	6,750.66
12	14,507.04	59,294.59	5,319.20	7,813.14	10,714.46	97,648.43
13	.34		.07		.11	.17	.69
Total Costed	265,931.70	124,885.08	62,559.50	98,124.92	134,660.53	686,161.73
Uncosted items	4,389.27	1,867.91	1,208.45	1,969.62	2,788.12	12,223.37
	$ 270,320.97	126,752.99	63,767.95	100,094.54	137,448.65	698,385.10

CLOSING JOURNAL ENTRIES

(1)
Material Variance 16,191.67
  Raw Material Inventory 16,352.54
  Fabricated and Purchased Stores (WIP) 160.87
    To record purchase price variance.

(2)
Material Variance 346,340.81
  Raw Material Inventory 346,340.81
    To record issues of raw material to production floor.

(3)
Fabricated and Purchased Parts Inventory ... 593,027.52
  Material Variance 301,736.04
  Labor Variance 61,073.48
  Indirect Labor and Overhead Variance ... 230,218.00
    To record production of fabricated parts transferred into fabricated and purchased parts stores.

(4)
Fabricated and Purchased Parts Inventory ... 1,956.56
  Finished Goods Inventory 1,956.56
    To record transfers of items in finished goods to fabricated and purchased parts stores.

(5)
Work-in-Process Floor Inventory 698,385.10
  Fabricated and Purchased Parts Inventory ... 698,385.10
    To record issues of fabricated and purchased parts to production floor.

(6)
No entry this month.

(7)
Work-in-Process Floor Inventory 14,269.22
  Finished Goods Inventory 14,269.22
    To record items in finished goods transferred to the production floor.

(8)
Finished Goods Inventory 782,001.14
  Work-in-Process Floor Inventory ... 782,001.14
    To record production transferred to finished goods.

(9)
Work-in-Process Floor Inventory 69,347.82
Material Usage Variance (brass & non-brass) .. 52,720.65
  Labor Variance 47,587.73
  Indirect Labor and Overhead Variance ... 74,480.74
    To record standard cost of production.

(10)
Cost of Sales 753,596.69
  Finished Goods Inventory 753,596.69
    To record shipments during month.

Cost of Sales 62,364.67
Indirect Labor and Overhead Variance 40,740.02
  Material Variance 81,133.75
  Labor Variance 21,970.94
    To close out Variance Accounts.

7 — COMPONENTS IN FINISHED GOODS STOCK RETURNED TO PRODUCTION

To:	Brass	Non-Brass	Direct Labor	Variable Overhead	Fixed Overhead	Total
01	$ 347.41	119.19	243.64	277.24	413.38	1,400.86
02	16.48	96.01	17.43	15.64	25.46	171.02
04	13.08	1.58	28.39	29.87	46.15	119.07
06		61.99	.50	.35	.68	63.52
07	37.87	.12	1.57	3.41	5.89	48.66
08	.05	.21	.50	.37	.57	1.70
11	315.01	850.44	213.87	215.11	333.43	1,927.86
12	1,637.18	1,887.21	1,504.84	1,419.30	2,173.41	8,621.94
32	21.28	77.66	21.30	20.58	31.88	172.70
41	1.42	1.92	2.27	2.20	3.26	11.07
42	.58	.49	.51	.66	.81	3.05
43	1.12	1.06	.62	.60	.93	4.33
47	269.84	63.51	172.31	186.96	289.44	982.06
Total Costed	2,661.32	2,161.39	2,207.75	2,172.29	3,325.09	13,527.84
Uncosted items	547.84	85.95	40.25	47.92	19.42	741.38
	$ 3,209.16	3,247.34	2,248.00	2,220.21	3,344.51	14,269.22

8 — COMPLETED PRODUCTION TRANSFERRED TO FINISHED GOODS INVENTORY

	Brass	Non-Brass	Direct Labor	Variable Overhead	Fixed Overhead	Total
Costed	$214,710.48	123,008.74	108,217.04	121,741.51	181,154.82	748,832.59
Uncosted	7,264.81	5,825.78	5,386.64	5,965.95	8,725.37	33,168.55
	$221,975.29	128,834.52	113,603.68	127,707.46	189,880.19	782,001.14

9 — CHANGE IN WORK-IN-PROCESS FLOOR INVENTORY

	Brass	Non-Brass	Direct Labor	Variable Overhead	Fixed Overhead	Total
Finished Goods Produced:	$221,975.29	128,834.52	113,603.68	127,707.46	189,880.19	782,001.14
From Finished Goods to Production Floor:	3,209.16	3,247.34	2,248.00	2,220.21	3,343.51	14,268.22
From Fabricated Stores to Production Floor:	270,320.97	126,752.99	63,767.95	100,094.54	137,448.65	698,385.10
	(51,554.84)	(1,165.81)	47,587.73	25,392.71	49,088.03	69,347.82

COST OF SALES

10

PRODUCT ID	OPR NO.	QUANTITY	BRASS	NON-BRASS MATERIAL	LABOR	VARIABLE OVERHEAD	CUMULATIVE OPERATING COST	FIXED OVERHEAD	TOTAL COST
01 00131 AP1	0004 000 R	315,000	4,191.36	17.71	310.16	731.31	5,250.54	837.66	6,088
01 00131 A1782	0013 000 R	57,500	773.78	240.59	481.82	524.23	2,020.42	756.87	2,777
01 00131 17829	0017 000 R	243,800	3,167.79	899.12	2,315.74	2,187.49	8,570.14	3,324.75	11,894
01 01651 UAH1	0086 000 R	277,500	3,605.67	15.45	287.09	676.08	4,584.29	760.57	5,344
01 02351 7913	5250 000 R	1,200	15.59	15.59	17.31	14.93	59.42	20.94	80
01 02870 7913	5179 000 R	757	12.58	5.29	31.35	20.25	69.47	27.18	96
01 02608	5036 000 R	2,255	39.68	3.77	33.28	33.49	110.22	54.50	164
01 03407 0178	5032 000 R	8,550	137.70	29.88	148.94	186.67	503.19	241.74	744
PRODUCT TOTALS	R	952,062	12,535.35	1,472.22	3,904.79	4,940.38	22,852.74	6,655.99	29,508
PERCENT OF TOTAL COST			42.49	4.99	13.23	16.75	77.46	22.54	100.00

LEGEND: R ≡ Rod   TOTAL ALL SALES CATEGORIES $753,597

EXHIBIT 8–14:
SUMMARY OF TRANSACTION REPORTS

Recording Variances. Since actual costs must be compared with standard in a standard cost system, it is necessary to use a "clearing account" to measure the difference. This clearing account is referred to by different names. Some call it a manufacturing cost control account while others call it variance clearing account. The company used in this case example identifies the clearing account as:

• Material variance

• Labor variance

• Indirect labor and overhead variance

The more detailed breakdown of the above variance accounts is illustrated later in the chapter.

Uncosted Items. One of the "real world" problems in establishing standard costs at the beginning of each year is the determination of which of the thousands of items fabricated and assembled will be active in the coming year—after a period of inactivity. Another problem is the determination of what new parts and end products will be introduced in the coming year. Failure to predict uncertainties of this nature accurately results in transactions that cannot be costed in the normal computerized costing process. As a result, when such uncosted items are discovered, temporary standards are introduced manually until the more permanent standards can be added to the files. Although the "uncosted" category is difficult to avoid, the dollar value should be only a small percentage of the value of the transactions that are costed.

Raw Material Issues

This transaction report was explained earlier to provide the groundwork for the discussion of byproduct reports that would be helpful for better management control. The total standard cost of issues ($346,340.81) is charged to the material variance clearing account and credited to raw material inventory to reflect the issues.

Fabricated Parts Transferred into Fabricated and Purchased Parts Inventory

This transaction report lists and costs the fabricated parts that have been *accepted* into the fabricated and purchased parts stockroom. Although the computer accumulates the input costs as they are incurred, the standard cost of the part at the point when it is accepted into stock is the value added to inventory. This avoids dependence on the accuracy of spoilage reports, which, in many cases are incomplete. This will be explained in greater detail when Transaction Report 9 is discussed.

It should be noted that although many fabricated items physically bypass the stockroom and move on to the assembly operations, they are nonetheless recorded as if they had been received into stock and issued. The "From" and "To" entries are made simultaneously.

The total of $593,027.52 transferred into this stockroom is shown in journal entry 3 (corresponds with the number shown for this transaction report in Exhibit 8–14) as a debit (charge) to the fabricated and purchased parts inventory. The breakdown of this total by material, direct labor, and overhead are shown as credits to the respective variance clearing accounts.

Transfers from Finished Goods to Fabricated and Purchased Parts Inventory

Fabricated parts are found in the finished goods stockroom for several reasons:

- They are sold as replacement parts.
- They may be sold to companies that purchase the parts and make the end products.
- When goods are returned from customers because of a defect, the returned item may be disassembled and the salvaged parts returned to the fabricated and purchased parts stockroom.

In this month, the $1956.56 total value of some or all of the above has been transferred back to the parts stockroom. The journal entry bearing the same number as this transaction report (4) shows the charge into the parts stockroom and the credit to finished goods inventory.

Transfers from Fabricated and Purchased Parts Inventory to Production

These transfers could be made up of some of the parts that move directly from the fabrication area to assembly without physically being received into the stockroom. This was mentioned in the discussion of Transaction Report 3 when reference was made to the "From" and "To" entries that are made simultaneously. The bulk of the items have been transferred to such departments as 01 (Automatic Machinery), 04 (General Machinery), and 05 (Plating, Coating, and Cleaning). Although some of these may return to the parts stockroom, most are moved to the assembly departments. Note the reference "To Production" in the caption of this transaction report. Journal entry 5 shows a charge of the total standard cost of transfers in the amount of $698,385.10 to the work-in-process floor inventory, and a credit of the same amount to the fabricated and purchased parts inventory. Both are work-in-process inventories but a separation is made between the work-in-process in stock that is maintained on a perpetual basis and the work-in-process that remains on the factory floor at the various work stations. This will be discussed further when we cover Transaction Report 9 (Change in Work-in-Process Floor Inventory).

Customer Returns

Customer returns for which credits have been issued are covered by this transaction report and the journal entry bearing the same number. Because there were no credits issued in this period, no transaction report is shown and no charges or credits are shown in the related journal entry.

Components in Finished Goods Stock Returned to Production

These transactions are similar to those covered earlier in (4), except that the transfer is being made to work-in-process floor inventory rather than to the fabricated and purchased parts inventory. The journal entry charges the work-in-process floor inventory and credits the finished goods inventory in the amount of $14,269.22.

Completed Production Transferred to Finished Goods Inventory

This transaction report shows the cost of finished products that have been transferred to the finished goods inventory. Accordingly, journal entry 8 charges the finished goods inventory and credits the floor work-in-process inventory for the total amount of $782,001.14.

Change in Work-in-Process Floor Inventory

One of the difficult problems in accurate reporting of production is correct accountability for spoilage. When spoiled production is understated, inventory value will naturally be overstated with the result that a phantom inventory will build up on the books. This results in overstatement of profits during the year followed by a writedown of these profits at year-end when the value of the physical inventory is compared with the book value. With the advent of automatic equipment that spews out parts by the million, many parts fall through open areas around the machines. These are difficult to retrieve economically. At best, such parts can be swept up and placed in scrap barrels for recovery of the scrap value.

In operations in which the material can be remelted—plastics molding and die casting material, for example—production counts are often determined by multiplying the number of cavities in the mold by the number of cycles registered on the counting mechanism. Frequently, because of variations and unevenness in mold temperatures, as well as defects in some of the cavities, many parts counted as good production are thrown back for remelting. These are counted as production the second time they are used.

The solution to this problem is to recognize production only when the component (part) is accepted into the work-in-process stockroom (fabricated and purchased parts stockroom) or into finished goods stock. This leaves only the floor work-in-process to be accounted for and it becomes a two-step process:

1. Net out the production transferred into finished goods with the issues of components transferred out of the stockrooms to the production floor.
2. Account for the inventory in the "pipeline" on the factory floor through a constant figure. If the pipeline inventory fluctuates widely, then a monthly physical inventory of major items will have to be taken and the work-in-process inventory adjusted. If the adjustment is not made, the difference will be reflected as a variance. The transactions in Transaction Report 9 assume a constant pipeline inventory.

The transaction reports from which the figures in Transaction Report 9 were taken are shown in Exhibit 8–15, which shows the interaction of Transaction Reports 7, 8, and 5 with 9.

7 COMPONENTS IN FINISHED GOODS STOCK RETURNED TO PRODUCTION

To:	Brass	Non-Brass	Direct Labor	Variable Overhead	Fixed Overhead	Total
01	$ 347.41	119.19	243.64	277.24	413.38	1,400.86
02	16.48	96.01	17.43	15.64	25.46	171.02
04	13.08	1.58	28.39	29.87	46.15	119.07
06		61.99	.50	.35	.68	63.52
07	37.87	.12	1.57	3.41	5.69	48.66
08	.05	.21	.50	.37	.57	1.70
11	315.01	850.44	213.87	215.11	333.43	1,927.86
12	1,637.18	1,887.21	1,504.84	1,419.30	2,173.41	8,621.94
32	21.28	77.66	21.30	20.58	31.88	172.70
41	1.42	1.92	2.27	2.20	3.26	11.07
42	.58	.49	.51	.66	.81	3.05
43	1.12	1.06	.62	.60	.93	4.33
47	269.84	63.51	172.31	186.96	289.44	982.06
Total Costed	2,661.32	2,161.39	2,207.75	2,172.29	3,325.09	13,527.84
Uncosted items	547.84	85.95	40.25	47.92	19.42	741.38
	$ 3,209.16	3,247.34	2,248.00	2,220.21	3,344.51	14,260.22

8 COMPLETED PRODUCTION TRANSFERRED TO FINISHED GOODS INVENTORY

	Brass	Non-Brass	Direct Labor	Variable Overhead	Fixed Overhead	Total
Total Costed	$214,710.48	123,008.74	108,217.04	121,741.51	181,154.82	748,832.59
Uncosted	7,264.81	5,825.78	5,386.64	5,965.95	8,725.37	33,163.55
	$221,975.29	128,834.52	113,600.68	127,707.46	189,880.19	782,001.14

5 TRANSFERS FROM FABRICATED AND PURCHASED PARTS INVENTORY TO PRODUCTION

To:	Brass	Non-Brass	Direct Labor	Variable Overhead	Fixed Overhead	Total
01	$ 48,524.50	21,270.43	18,750.18	23,636.47	32,404.98	144,586.56
02	14,120.43	5,520.33	9,464.68	13,374.62	20,628.73	63,108.79
04	2,454.31	15,257.61	1,861.74	2,285.78	3,029.04	24,888.48
05	152,774.51	6,920.74	14,377.23	24,868.29	34,414.69	233,355.46
06	5,803.94	15,186.86	1,737.66	2,538.59	3,463.66	28,730.71
07	25,787.14	495.34	9,930.40	21,765.50	28,195.78	86,174.16
08	189.76	565.40	41.22	50.95	70.46	917.79
11	1,769.73	373.78	1,077.12	1,791.47	1,738.56	6,750.66
12	14,507.04	59,294.59	5,319.20	7,813.14	10,714.46	97,648.43
13	.34		.07	.11	.17	.69
Total Costed	265,931.70	124,885.08	62,559.50	98,124.92	134,660.53	686,161.73
Uncosted items	4,389.27	1,867.91	1,208.45	1,969.62	2,788.12	12,223.37
	$ 270,320.97	126,752.99	63,767.95	100,094.54	137,448.65	698,385.10

9 CHANGE IN WORK-IN-PROCESS FLOOR INVENTORY

	Brass	Non-Brass	Direct Labor	Variable Overhead	Fixed Overhead	Total
Finished Goods Produced:	$221,975.29	128,834.52	113,603.68	127,707.46	189,880.19	782,001.14
From Finished Goods to Production Floor:	3,209.16	3,247.34	2,248.00	2,220.21	3,343.51	14,288.22
From Fabricated Stores to Production Floor:	270,320.97	126,752.99	63,767.95	100,094.54	137,448.65	698,385.10
	(51,554.84)	(1,165.81)	47,587.73	25,392.71	49,088.03	69,347.82

*This exhibit is an excerpt of Exhibit 14

EXHIBIT 8–15:
CALCULATING THE WORK-IN-PROCESS FLOOR INVENTORY

Cost of Sales

The cost of sales format was referred to several times in the earlier parts of this chapter. Like the others, the columnar format showing the elements of cost is the same.

The balance of the three variance clearing accounts is closed out into the Cost of Sales account. Although this is shown in journal entry 11, no transaction listing has been made because this entry is the result of posting balances from previously made journal entries.

MANUFACTURING COST SUMMARY

Shown in Exhibit 8–16, the manufacturing cost summary lists the following data:

- Closing journal entries that were used in Exhibit 8–14 to reconcile the entries with the transaction reports from which these entries were taken.
- Factory ledger accounts to which the journal entries were posted.
- Abbreviated income statement.
- Breakdown of variances.

As can be seen from Exhibit 8–14, the journal entries summarize the ten transaction reports. The function of the ledger accounts is to recast the journal entries into the various accounts to determine the impact of the transactions on these accounts. This facilitates the determination of the month's income statement. Note that the standard cost of sales is subtracted from the sales (not included in this exhibit) and the standard gross profit is determined. When the total variances which had been closed into the cost of sales account are deducted from the standard gross profit, the actual gross profit is reflected.

Variance Summary

The variances are usually shown on the income statement in total, in the interest of a faster closing and earlier determination of the results for the month. However, the variances are broken down further beyond the detail contained in the journal entries. The right side of the upper part of the exhibit starts with a broad breakdown which, within material, shows the purchase price variance and material usage variance separately. Direct labor is broken down to reflect the rate variance and efficiency variance separately. The spending variance for overhead was calculated first and then subtracted from total overhead to arrive at the volume variance.

Breakdown of Variances

The further breakdown was required to pinpoint the figures by responsibility. The purchase price variance, for example, is shown for brass and nonbrass material, so the appropriate buyers would be shown the amount of variance they

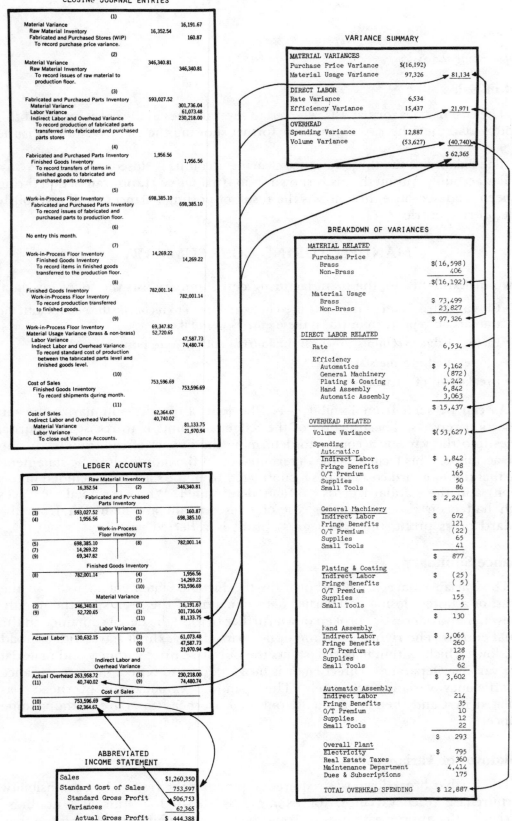

CLOSING JOURNAL ENTRIES

(1)

Material Variance		16,191.67
Raw Material Inventory	16,352.54	
Fabricated and Purchased Stores (WIP)		160.87
To record purchase price variance.		

(2)

Material Variance	346,340.81	
Raw Material Inventory		346,340.81
To record issues of raw material to production floor.		

(3)

Fabricated and Purchased Parts Inventory	593,027.52	
Material Variance		301,736.04
Labor Variance		61,073.48
Indirect Labor and Overhead Variance		230,218.00
To record production of fabricated parts transferred into fabricated and purchased parts stores		

(4)

Fabricated and Purchased Parts Inventory	1,956.56	
Finished Goods Inventory		1,956.56
To record transfers of items in finished goods to fabricated and purchased parts stores.		

(5)

Work-in-Process Floor Inventory	698,385.10	
Fabricated and Purchased Parts Inventory		698,385.10
To record issues of fabricated and purchased parts to production floor.		

(6)

No entry this month.

(7)

Work-in-Process Floor Inventory	14,269.22	
Finished Goods Inventory		14,269.22
To record items in finished goods transferred to the production floor.		

(8)

Finished Goods Inventory	782,001.14	
Work-in-Process Floor Inventory		782,001.14
To record production transferred to finished goods.		

(9)

Work-in-Process Floor Inventory	69,347.82	
Material Usage Variance (brass & non-brass)	52,720.65	
Labor Variance		47,587.73
Indirect Labor and Overhead Variance		74,480.74
To record standard cost of production between the fabricated parts level and finished goods level.		

(10)

Cost of Sales	753,596.69	
Finished Goods Inventory		753,596.69
To record shipments during month.		

(11)

Cost of Sales	62,364.67	
Indirect Labor and Overhead Variance	40,740.02	
Material Variance		81,133.75
Labor Variance		21,970.94
To close out Variance Accounts.		

LEDGER ACCOUNTS

Raw Material Inventory

(1)	16,352.54	(2)	346,340.81

Fabricated and Purchased Parts Inventory

(3)	593,027.52	(1)	160.87
(4)	1,956.56	(5)	698,385.10

Work-in-Process Floor Inventory

(5)	698,385.10	(8)	782,001.14
(7)	14,269.22		
(9)	69,347.82		

Finished Goods Inventory

(8)	782,001.14	(4)	1,956.56
		(7)	14,269.22
		(10)	753,596.69

Material Variance

(2)	346,340.81	(1)	16,191.67
(9)	52,720.65	(3)	301,736.04
		(11)	81,133.75

Labor Variance

Actual Labor	130,632.15	(3)	61,073.48
		(9)	47,587.73
		(11)	21,970.94

Indirect Labor and Overhead Variance

Actual Overhead	263,958.72	(3)	230,218.00
(11)	40,740.02	(9)	74,480.74

Cost of Sales

(10)	753,596.69		
(11)	62,364.67		

ABBREVIATED INCOME STATEMENT

Sales	$1,260,350
Standard Cost of Sales	753,597
Standard Gross Profit	506,753
Variances	62,365
Actual Gross Profit	$ 444,388

VARIANCE SUMMARY

MATERIAL VARIANCES

Purchase Price Variance	$(16,192)	
Material Usage Variance	97,326	81,134

DIRECT LABOR

Rate Variance	6,534	
Efficiency Variance	15,437	21,971

OVERHEAD

Spending Variance	12,887	
Volume Variance	(53,627)	(40,740)
		$ 62,365

BREAKDOWN OF VARIANCES

MATERIAL RELATED

Purchase Price		
Brass	$(16,598)	
Non-Brass	406	
		$(16,192)
Material Usage		
Brass	$ 73,499	
Non-Brass	23,827	
		$ 97,326

DIRECT LABOR RELATED

Rate		6,534
Efficiency		
Automatics	$ 5,162	
General Machinery	(872)	
Plating & Coating	1,242	
Hand Assembly	6,842	
Automatic Assembly	3,063	
		$ 15,437

OVERHEAD RELATED

Volume Variance		$(53,627)
Spending		
Automatics		
Indirect Labor	$ 1,842	
Fringe Benefits	98	
O/T Premium	165	
Supplies	50	
Small Tools	86	
	$ 2,241	
General Machinery		
Indirect Labor	$ 672	
Fringe Benefits	121	
O/T Premium	(22)	
Supplies	65	
Small Tools	41	
	$ 877	
Plating & Coating		
Indirect Labor	$ (25)	
Fringe Benefits	(5)	
O/T Premium	-	
Supplies	155	
Small Tools	5	
	$ 130	
Hand Assembly		
Indirect Labor	$ 3,065	
Fringe Benefits	260	
O/T Premium	128	
Supplies	87	
Small Tools	62	
	$ 3,602	
Automatic Assembly		
Indirect Labor	214	
Fringe Benefits	35	
O/T Premium	10	
Supplies	12	
Small Tools	22	
	$ 293	
Overall Plant		
Electricity	$ 795	
Real Estate Taxes	360	
Maintenance Department	4,414	
Dues & Subscriptions	175	
TOTAL OVERHEAD SPENDING	$ 12,887	

EXHIBIT 8–16:
MANUFACTURING COST SUMMARY

were responsible for. In the case of the favorable variance for brass, it was mentioned earlier that this was not necessarily an indication of better buying but rather of establishing standards too high.

The material usage variance was also broken down by brass and nonbrass material for better pinpointing as to the cause. Although not shown here, the breakdown of brass by rod, wire, and strip permitted identification of the foreman whose cost center caused the excess usage in these brass items.

The industrial relations department was responsible for further pinpointing the direct labor rate variance. This could have been caused by the assignment of labor to tasks that were rated lower than the grade of the individual assigned.

The labor efficiency variances are identified by the departments in which the variances were incurred.

The overhead related variances were broken down as follows:

- Management was considered to be responsible for any volume variances because sales affected the volume of production. In this period, the variance was favorable because the plant operated above normal capacity. It is possible, however, that a fully loaded plant could have an unfavorable variance if a high percentage of production is defective or if the scheduling of production is not properly made. This cannot be determined without further analysis.

- The spending variance for most expenses has been broken down by the cost centers for the expenses considered to be controllable by the foremen. The indirect category includes only the factory foremen and some part-time clerical help. The administrative type of indirect labor such as the plant manager, cost accounting, industrial engineering, production control, purchasing, and quality control are included in fixed overhead and are therefore reflected in the volume variance.

- Certain expenses, which might be considered to be applicable to the individual cost centers, are shown in the overall plant category because they are monitored by the following individuals:
  - Chief electrician (electricity)
  - Management (real estate taxes)
  - Plant engineer (maintenance costs)
  - Industrial relations department (dues and subscriptions)

The cost of computerizing the cost system is not small—even with the great reductions that have taken place in computer costs and the availability of software. When a company embarks on a program for computerizing the cost accounting system, it should computerize its materials management procedures as well. The reverse is also true. The physical units reported in the transaction listings and providing the basis for inventory management should be the same units that are valued by the cost department in arriving at general ledger inventory values.

As competitive pressures continue to intensify, computerized inventory management and cost accounting will contribute increasingly to the economic survival of American industry. The procedures outlined in this chapter provide a framework that should buttress management's needs for more effective controls.

9

Developing the Overhead Costing Rates and the Flexible Budget Formula

Chapters 2 through 7 discuss the two primary cost systems—job costing and process costing—as well as the variations such as standard versus actual and direct versus full costing features that can be built into the basic systems. In these chapters, direct material and direct labor were discussed in greater detail than the indirect expenses (overhead). For this reason, overhead will be discussed more fully in this chapter. The overhead expenses in Exhibit 9–1 will be allocated to the three producing cost centers; they will be broken down into their fixed and variable segments; overhead costing rates will be calculated for each of the three cost centers; and, finally, these figures will be used to develop a flexible budget formula.

Before embarking on this, it may be well to first recapitulate the three elements of manufacturing cost as to assignability to products, source of information needed for costing, relative magnitude of the three elements, types of items in each of the three elements, and the degree of control generally exercised over each of the three. This recapitulation follows:

RECAPITULATION OF THE THREE ELEMENTS

	DIRECT MATERIAL	DIRECT LABOR	INDIRECT EXPENSES (OVERHEAD)
Assignability to products	Engineering bills of material (specifications) provide good measures of quantity of material required for each type of product.	Industrial engineers provide information on time required for each step in making the product.	Indirect cost items by their nature are not directly identifiable with specific products. Assignment of costs to products must be made by an overhead rate applied to the product through an appropriate base.

Costing	Purchasing department furnishes prices.	The industrial relations (personnel) department identifies labor grade information.	Accounting department establishes overhead rates and the appropriate base for applying the rates.
Magnitude of cost of the three elements.	Usually the largest of the three.	Smallest of the three. Growing smaller as automation increases.	Usually second largest. This element grows as automation increases.
Number and types of items in each element.	Consists of two basic categories: raw materials and purchased components.	Consists of direct labor by operation and labor grade.	Consists of indirect labor (support labor), indirect material, depreciation of equipment and tools, and purchased services.
Degree of control exercised.	Poorest control of the three because of difficulty (sometimes impracticality) in obtaining correct reporting of production losses.	Generally the most tightly controlled.	Control most effective when activity level remains stable.

WHAT ARE THE CATEGORIES THAT MAKE UP OVERHEAD?

Exhibit 9–1 shows the breakdown of manufacturing costs for the company whose figures were used in Chapter 7 to illustrate the differences between the direct cost and full cost formats for presenting operating statements. The summary on page 1 of Exhibit 9–1 provides a breakdown of overhead by major categories:

Indirect labor—production departments	$ 128,560
Indirect labor—service departments	538,607
Labor-connected expenses	321,289
Nonpayroll expenses	511,400
Total Overhead	$1,499,856

Indirect Labor—Production Departments

This classification includes foremen, supervisors, and clerks as well as maintenance personnel and material handlers assigned to a specific production department—as distinguished from a service department that provides services to all departments on an as-needed basis. The production departments include the molding presses that make the plastic parts, the punch presses (metal forming presses), and the finishing (assembly) department that assembles the plastic and metal parts as called for in the product.

MANUFACTURING COST REPORT

Plant _____   Year of 19 _____

Summary	Year to Date		Month	
	Actual	Budget	Actual	Budget
Sales Value of Production	7,800,000			
Material	3,711,540			
Direct Labor	746,823			
Total Prime Cost	4,458,363			
Indirect Labor-Prod'n. Depts.	128,560			
Indirect Labor-Service Depts.	538,607			
Labor Connected Expenses	321,289			
Non-Payroll Expenses	511,400			
TOTAL OVERHEAD	1,499,856			
TOTAL COST OF PRODUCTION	5,958,219			

OPERATING STATISTICS	ACTUAL % OF COST	BUDGET % OF COST	ACTUAL % OF SALES VALUE	BUDGET % OF SALES VALUE
Sales Value of Production			100.0	
Material	62.3		47.5	
Direct Labor	12.5		9.6	
Indirect Labor-Prod'n. Depts.	2.2		1.7	
Indirect Labor-Service Depts.	9.0		7.0	
Labor Connected Expenses	5.4		4.1	
Non-Payroll Expenses	8.6		6.5	
TOTAL COST	100.0		76.4	

MATERIAL

Plant _____   Year of 19 _____

	Year to Date		Month	
	Actual	Budget	Actual	Budget
Steel	2,094,416			
Resins	1,242,062			
Packing Material	375,062			
TOTAL MATERIAL COST	3,711,540			

DIRECT LABOR

Department	Year to Date		Month	
	Actual	Budget	Actual	Budget
Molding Presses	283,151			
Punch Presses	225,646			
Finishing	238,026			
TOTAL DIRECT LABOR	746,823			

INDIRECT LABOR-PRODUCTION DEPARTMENTS

Department	Year to Date		Month	
	Actual	Budget	Actual	Budget
Molding Presses	48,151			
Punch Presses	48,965			
Finishing	31,444			
TOTAL INDIRECT LABOR-PROD'N.	128,560			

EXHIBIT 9–1:
OVERVIEW REPORT FOR MANUFACTURING COST

INDIRECT LABOR-SERVICE DEPARTMENTS

Plant _____   Year of 19 _____

Department	Year to Date		Month	
	Actual	Budget	Actual	Budget
General Manager's Staff	50,932			
Personnel	34,200			
Cost Accounting	39,370			
Material Control	86,679			
Engineering	45,356			
Quality Assurance	73,285			
Purchasing	27,278			
Maintenance	119,950			
Receiving and Shipping	61,557			
TOTAL INDIRECT LABOR-SV.	538,607			

LABOR CONNECTED EXPENSES

Account Name	Year to Date		Month	
	Actual	Budget	Actual	Budget
Overtime Premium	42,890			
Shift Premium	10,154			
Vacation Expense	27,166			
Unemployment Insurance	29,778			
Group Life Insurance	12,430			
Hospitalization	35,595			
Pension Expense	43,505			
Compensation & Liability Ins.	25,990			
Payroll Taxes	93,781			
TOTAL LABOR CONNECTED	321,289			

NON-PAYROLL EXPENSES

Plant _____   Year of 19 _____

Account Name	Year to Date		Month	
	Actual	Budget	Actual	Budget
UTILITIES				
Water	4,000			
Gas	4,100			
Electricity	46,900			
Telephone	9,120			
Acetylene	275			
FACILITIES COST				
Rent	2,000			
Property Taxes	8,290			
Purchased Services	5,400			
Depreciation	195,100			
Insurance	2,817			
Fuel Oil	34,600			
SUPPLIES				
Stationery	5,900			
Postage	3,100			
Expendable Tools	20,700			
Maintenance Materials	65,700			
Lubricants and Chemicals	8,000			
Factory Supplies	4,200			
Tool Maintenance & Amortization	58,648			
OFFICE EXPENSES				
Employment Expenses	4,750			
Subscriptions	500			
Dues & Memberships	500			
Computer Services	3,500			
Rental of Equipment	10,600			
Auto Expense	12,700			
TOTAL NON-PAYROLL EXPENSES	511,400			

EXHIBIT 9–1, continued

The breakdown of indirect labor costs in the production departments is shown on page 2 of the Manufacturing Cost Report:

Molding presses	$ 48,151
Punch presses	48,965
Finishing (assembly)	31,444
Total	$128,560

Indirect Labor—Service Departments

These departments provide support services for the entire factory rather than only the production departments. The breakdown of the service department costs is:

General manager's staff	$ 50,932
Personnel	34,200
Cost accounting	39,370
Material control	86,679
Engineering	45,356
Quality assurance	73,285
Purchasing	27,278
Maintenance	119,950
Receiving and shipping	61,557
Total	$538,607

It should be noted that some classifications such as material handling and maintenance can be categorized as indirect labor in production departments as well as indirect labor in service departments—the difference being that, in the former, the employee is assigned to a specific production department under the supervision of the department foreman rather than being under the jurisdiction of the service department manager who would make assignments on an as-needed basis throughout the plant. The division accountant of the company objected to this approach. His reason is that this approach splintered the costs of the various disciplines. He felt that he wanted to be able to report costs of indirect labor by job description. The plant manager, on the other hand, insisted on responsibility reporting—he wanted to hold each department head responsible for the costs under his jurisdiction; he was not interested in structuring costs to fit a standard mold that distorted control by responsibility. In evaluating both arguments, the corporate controller sided with the plant manager.

Labor-Connected Expenses. These are frequently referred to as fringe benefits. The expenses include overtime premium, shift premium, vacation expense, unemployment insurance, group life insurance, hospitalization, compensation and liability insurance, and payroll taxes. These expenses cover direct labor as well as indirect labor employees. (See lower portion of page 3 in Exhibit 9–1.)

Nonpayroll Expenses. This section, shown as page 4 in Exhibit 9–1, includes purchased services such as utilities; indirect materials (supplies); facilities costs, such as equipment depreciation and rent-equivalent types of expenditures; and office expenses.

These are the items making up the overhead expenses in the ACR Company. Since these are all indirect items that cannot be specifically identified with the products, an overhead rate or rates must be developed.

Six-Step Procedure for Developing Overhead Rates

The six steps include the following:

1. Determine the Amount of Expense

Determine the amount of expense for the activity level being projected. Although the figures in the manufacturing cost report (Exhibit 9–1) used as the basis for calculating overhead rates are the actual costs incurred during the past year, the general manager decided that the costing (overhead) rates would be calculated on the basis of "actuals." This would provide the marketing department with a comparison of the actual cost/selling price relationships as they existed during the preceding year. Exhibit 9–2 lists the expenses for the various cost categories.

2. Determine Most Appropriate Bases for Allocating Expenses to Production Cost Centers

The general manager was highly critical of past attempts at arriving at overhead costing rates. His complaint was that many of the expenses were arbitrarily allocated to production cost centers on the basis of the production hours in each of the centers. He objected to these "quick and dirty" methods that did not reflect the true costing rates.

He cited specific figures from the last overhead rate study in which the costing rate for the finishing (assembly) department was $9.95 per hour while the molding department rate was $7.20 and the punch press department rate came to $8.80 per hour. He went on to say: "My accountant used a direct labor base for most of the service departments in allocating their costs to the three production centers. The service department costs amount to over a half million dollars a year and represent more than one third of total overhead. If you use the wrong basis for allocating such a large 'nut,' you're swinging a lot of dollars the wrong way, because you're saying that the more people in a department, the more it costs to support them. Bunk! The service labor spends substantially more of its time (in proportion to direct labor) in the molding and punch press departments. This is where 85 percent of the maintenance labor spends its time; that's where we encounter most of our quality problems. The demands on material control and engineering services is also high in the molding and punch press departments....If my assembly costs for overhead were practically $10 per hour we would have to drop the products that required a large amount of assembly work—I know that $10 per hour is wrong....It should be less than $7.00."

The general manager called in the plant manager and the accountant. His instructions were to use good business judgment in distributing overhead costs in

STEP 1

	TOTAL OVERHEAD
Molding presses	$ 48,151
Punch presses	48,965
Finishing	31,444
Total Indirect Labor—Production Departments	128,560
General manager's staff	50,932
Personnel	34,200
Cost accounting	39,370
Material control	86,679
Engineering	45,356
Quality assurance	73,285
Purchasing	27,278
Maintenance	119,950
Receiving and shipping	61,557
Total Indirect Labor—Service Departments	538,607
Labor connected expenses (except O/T)	278,399
Overtime premium	42,890
Total Labor-Connected Expenses	321,289
Electricity	46,900
Telephone	9,120
All other utilities	8,375
Total Utilities	64,395
Depreciation	195,100
All other facilities costs	53,107
Total Facilities Cost	248,207
Maintenance materials	65,700
Mold maintenance and amortization	58,648
All other supplies	41,900
Total Supplies and Mold Costs	166,248
Computer services	3,500
Rental of (computer) equipment	10,600
Travel expenses	12,700
All other office expenses	5,750
Total Office Expenses	32,550
Total Overhead	$1,499,856

EXHIBIT 9–2
DETERMINING AMOUNT OF EXPENSE FOR ACTIVITY LEVEL BEING PROJECTED

the current study. All department heads whose costs are to be distributed were to participate in the determination of the proper basis. As a result of a series of meetings with various department heads, the following allocation bases were developed:

Direct charges	Expenses could be specifically identified with a cost center. *Example:* Foreman, clerk, material handler working in a cost center full-time, and maintenance man assigned full-time to a production cost center.
One-third of the cost to each of the three cost centers	Functions that existed on a "readiness to serve" basis would be allocated equally to each of the three production cost centers. *Example:* General manager's staff, office expenses.
Total employees	Certain costs, like personnel, would be distributed to the three cost centers on the basis of the breakdown of total employees in each of the centers.
Number of items	An item in the material control department would be a requisition for ordering material. In engineering it would be the number of different part numbers used in a production center. The appropriate item to be used for allocation would be determined in conjunction with the department head concerned.
Total payroll	The percentage that each production center's payroll is to the total of the three centers. *Example of such an expense:* Labor-connected expenses.
Analysis	A study would be required. *Example:* Maintenance costs would be allocated on the basis of hours of service rendered to each of the service centers. This would require analysis of job tickets.
Floor space	The floor space occupied by each center as a percentage of floor space occupied by all three centers. *Example:* Rent-equivalent costs.
Direct labor employees	The number of employees in each center as a percentage of total direct labor employees. *Example:* Supplies.

Exhibit 9–3 lists the various allocation bases to be used for each of the expenses.

3. Identify Production Cost Centers

This plant of the ACR Company had a natural breakdown because of the three distinctively different processes: molding, punch presses (metal forming), and finishing (assembly). The company had on order two NC machines for its punch press department. Since these were much more sophisticated and therefore more expensive than the conventional presses, the decision was made to establish a separate rate for the NC machines. However, this would not be done until the equipment had been in operation for three months. During the discussion on this

STEP 2

	Allocation Basis	Total Overhead
Molding presses	Direct	$ 48,151
Punch presses	Direct	48,965
Finishing	Direct	31,444
Total Indirect Labor—Production Departments		128,560
General manager's staff	1/3 each	50,932
Personnel	Total empl.	34,200
Cost accounting	Total empl.	39,370
Material control	No. of items	86,679
Engineering	No. of items	45,356
Quality assurance	No. of items	73,285
Purchashing	No. of items	27,278
Maintenance	Analysis	119,950
Receiving and shipping	No. of items	61,557
Total Indirect Labor—Service Departments		538,607
Labor connected expenses (except O/T)	Total payroll	278,399
Overtime premium	Analysis	42,890
Total Labor-Connected Expenses		321,289
Electricity	Analysis	46,900
Telephone	Purch. & GM[1]	9,120
All other utilities	Analysis	8,375
Total Utilities		64,395
Depreciation	Analysis	195,100
All other facilities costs	Floor space	53,107
Total Facilities Cost		248,207
Maintenance materials	Analysis	65,700
Mold maintenance and amortization	Analysis	58,648
All other supplies	D. L. empl.	41,900
Total Supplies and Mold Costs		166,248
Computer services	Analysis	3,500
Rental of (computer) equipment	Analysis	10,600
Travel expenses	Analysis	12,700
All other office expenses	1/3 each	5,750
Total Office Expenses		32,550
Total Overhead		$1,499,856

[1] GM means same allocation as General Manager's staff

EXHIBIT 9 –3
DETERMINING MOST APPROPRIATE BASES FOR ALLOCATING EXPENSES TO PRODUCTION COST CENTERS

topic, it was pointed out that the NC machines would require full-time electronic maintenance, and unlike the other equipment in the punch press department, the NCs would be operated on three shifts. This would mean that the higher overhead would be partly offset by a higher level of activity that would reduce the cost per hour. The new machines would make obsolete several of the existing presses— which would result in reduced hours for the non-NC equipment and therefore a probable increase in that production center's overhead rate because of the reduced volume. Exhibit 9–4 illustrates the distribution of expenses that was made to reflect current operations.

4. Distribute (Allocate) Expenses to the Production Cost Centers

The distribution is essentially mathematical once the allocation bases have been determined. Each expense is distributed among the three production centers on the basis of its specific allocation base. The summary of the totals after distribution follows:

Molding presses	$ 651,692
Punch presses	427,514
Finishing (assembly)	420,650
Total	$1,499,856

Allocating overhead costs to production cost centers for development of costing rates can be classified into two types—direct (one-step) and two-step.

One-Step. This means that service department indirect labor (personnel, for example) is allocated directly to the production cost centers even though some personnel work is done for other service departments. In addition, the personnel department, like the other service departments, incurs nonlabor expenses such as forms, telephone, electricity, and depreciation—in addition to indirect labor. Under the one-step method, these are allocated directly to the cost centers without running them through their respective service departments before making the allocation. The philosophy behind making the allocation direct is that the amount of these expenses, in relation to the indirect labor, is small, and does not warrant the additional work—which is time-consuming. There is a justifiable exception, however, in the case of stockroom storage areas because these can occupy as much as 40 percent (or more) of the factory floor space. The rent-equivalent costs of the storage areas should be accumulated and then allocated on the same basis as the material control department indirect labor. (The material handlers and other personnel in the storage areas are part of the indirect labor in the material control department.)

Two-Step. Under this method, all overhead costs would be departmentalized before any allocations are made. Thus, personnel indirect labor plus all the nonlabor costs would be accumulated. Then, the services rendered by the personnel department to the other service departments would be charged to them—and they, in turn, would charge back any services that they rendered to the personnel department. After this recirculation process has been completed by all depart-

STEPS 3 AND 4

	ALLOCATION BASIS	BREAKDOWN OF OVERHEAD BY PRODUCTION CENTER			
		MOLDING PRESSES	PUNCH PRESSES	FINISHING	TOTAL OVERHEAD
Molding presses	Direct	$ 48,151			$ 48,151
Punch presses	Direct		$ 48,965		48,965
Finishing	Direct			$ 31,444	31,444
Total Indirect Labor—Production Departments		48,151	48,965	31,444	128,560
General manager's staff	1/3 each	16,977	16,977	16,978	50,932
Personnel	Total empl.	13,680	8,550	11,970	34,200
Cost accounting	Total empl.	15,748	9,843	13,779	39,370
Material control	No. of items	26,004	17,335	43,340	86,679
Engineering	No. of items	13,607	9,071	22,678	45,356
Quality assurance	No. of items	21,985	14,657	36,643	73,285
Purchasing	No. of items	8,183	5,456	13,639	27,278
Maintenance	Analysis	71,970	35,985	11,995	119,950
Receiving and shipping	No. of items	18,467	12,311	30,779	61,557
Total Indirect Labor—Service Departments		206,621	130,185	201,801	538,607
Labor connected expenses (except O/T)	Total payroll	108,576	77,952	91,871	278,399
Overtime premium	Analysis	23,460	10,330	9,100	42,890
Total Labor-Connected Expenses		132,036	88,282	100,971	321,289
Electricity	Analysis	23,450	14,070	9,380	46,900
Telephone	Purch. & GM	2,736	1,824	4,560	9,120
All other utilities	Analysis	3,769	2,931	1,675	8,375
Total Utilities		29,955	18,825	15,615	64,395
Depreciation	Analysis	110,100	78,200	6,800	195,100
All other facilities costs	Floor space	13,489	8,710	30,908	53,107
Total Facilities Cost		123,589	86,910	37,708	248,207
Maintenance materials	Analysis	39,420	19,710	6,570	65,700
Mold maintenance and amortization	Analysis	46,918	11,730		58,648
All other supplies	D. L. empl.	14,665	12,570	14,665	41,900
Total Supplies and Mold Costs		101,003	44,010	21,235	166,248
Computer services	Analysis	1,050	1,050	1,400	3,500
Rental of (computer) equipment	Analysis	3,180	3,180	4,240	10,600
Travel expenses	Analysis	4,190	4,190	4,320	12,700
All other office expenses	1/3 each	1,917	1,917	1,916	5,750
Total Office Expenses		10,337	10,337	11,876	32,550
Total Overhead		$651,692	$427,514	$420,650	$1,499,856

EXHIBIT 9–4
IDENTIFYING PRODUCTION COST CENTERS
DISTRIBUTING EXPENSES TO THE PRODUCTION COST CENTERS

ments, the net total of each department would then be allocated to the production cost centers.

The one-step method was used in Exhibit 9–4 because of its simplicity and directness. The cost-effectiveness of departmentalizing and recirculating the costs of the service departments to other service departments is highly questionable—inasmuch as the purpose of all service departments is to lend support to production. The one-step method is therefore the preferred method.

5. Determine Production Hours for Projected Level of Operations

Although the general manager wanted to use the actual expenses incurred in the previous year as a guide in the development of overhead (costing) rates, he wanted to approach the calculation of the divider differently. Previously, direct-labor dollars actually incurred for each production center were used as the divider for determining the percentage that overhead costs in each center were to the direct-labor cost. The new method was to work as follows:

Direct labor dollars would no longer be used as the base for calculating costing rates. The reason is that:

- Changes in the direct labor rates of pay during the year complicate the costing rate structure.

- Direct labor bases (both dollars and hours) distort the costing rate when the direct labor to machine ratio varies within a department. A case in point: some machines require a full-time operator, while the automatics may require only a half-operator (one operator for two machines). With the emphasis on further automation, new machines requiring only one operator for four machines are being considered. Accordingly, machine hours would now be used for the molding and punch press centers, while direct labor hours (rather than dollars) would be used for the finishing center.

Determination of the production hours to be used as the base for calculating costing rates will include the following steps:

- Determine the available hours in each of the three production centers, using machine hours in the molding and punch press centers and direct labor hours in the finishing center. Available hours will be determined by extending the total hours per shift by the number of shifts that each center normally operates.

- Allow for such normal downtime as maintenance, and changeovers to arrive at percentage utilization of available hours.

- Factor the available hours down to expected production hours by applying the percentage utilization to the available hours.

The production hours would be obtained through the following calculations:

	AVAILABLE HOURS	UTILIZATION %	PRODUCTION HOURS
Molding presses	93,500	65%	60,800
Punch presses	69,300	72	49,900
Finishing (assembly)	108,500	60	65,100

STEPS 5 AND 6

	ALLOCATION BASIS	BREAKDOWN OF OVERHEAD BY PRODUCTION CENTER			
		MOLDING PRESSES	PUNCH PRESSES	FINISHING	TOTAL OVERHEAD
Molding presses	Direct	$ 48,151			$ 48,151
Punch presses	Direct		$ 48,965		48,965
Finishing	Direct			$ 31,444	31,444
Total Indirect Labor—Production Departments		48,151	48,965	31,444	128,560
General manager's staff	1/3 each	16,977	16,977	16,978	50,932
Personnel	Total empl.	13,680	8,550	11,970	34,200
Cost accounting	Total empl.	15,748	9,843	13,779	39,370
Material control	No. of items	26,004	17,335	43,340	86,679
Engineering	No. of items	13,607	9,071	22,678	45,356
Quality assurance	No. of items	21,985	14,657	36,643	73,285
Purchasing	No. of items	8,183	5,456	13,639	27,278
Maintenance	Analysis	71,970	35,985	11,995	119,950
Receiving and shipping	No. of items	18,467	12,311	30,779	61,557
Total Indirect Labor—Service Departments		206,621	130,185	201,801	538,607
Labor connected expenses (except O/T)	Total payroll	108,576	77,952	91,871	278,399
Overtime premium	Analysis	23,460	10,330	9,100	42,890
Total Labor-Connected Expenses		132,036	88,282	100,971	321,289
Electricity	Analysis	23,450	14,070	9,380	46,900
Telephone	Purch. & GM	2,736	1,824	4,560	9,120
All other utilities	Analysis	3,769	2,931	1,675	8,375
Total Utilities		29,955	18,825	15,615	64,395
Depreciation	Analysis	110,100	78,200	6,800	195,100
All other facilities costs	Floor space	13,489	8,710	30,908	53,107
Total Facilities Cost		123,589	86,910	37,708	248,207
Maintenance materials	Analysis	39,420	19,710	6,570	65,700
Mold maintenance and amortization	Analysis	46,918	11,730		58,648
All other supplies	D. L. empl.	14,665	12,570	14,665	41,900
Total Supplies and Mold Costs		101,003	44,010	21,235	166,248
Computer services	Analysis	1,050	1,050	1,400	3,500
Rental of (computer) equipment	Analysis	3,180	3,180	4,240	10,600
Travel expenses	Analysis	4,190	4,190	4,320	12,700
All other office expenses	1/3 each	1,917	1,917	1,916	5,750
Total Office Expenses		10,337	10,337	11,876	32,550
Total Overhead		$651,692	$427,514	$420,650	$1,499,856
➤ Production hours		60,800	49,900	65,100	
➤ Overhead costing rates		10.72	8.56	6.46	

EXHIBIT 9–5
DETERMINING PRODUCTION HOURS FOR THE PROJECTED LEVEL OF OPERATIONS
CALCULATING COSTING RATES

6. Calculate Costing Rates

The total overhead distributed to each of the three production cost centers is divided by the production hours (see above) to arrive at the hourly overhead costing rates (see Exhibit 9–5).

	MOLDING PRESSES	PUNCH PRESSES	FINISHING (ASSEMBLY)
Distributed expenses by production center (Step 4)	$651,692	427,514	420,650
Production hours (Step 5)	60,800	49,900	65,100
Overhead costing rates (Step 6)	$ 10.72	8.56	6.46

Calculating Fixed and Variable Overhead Costing Rates

A breakdown of the overhead costing rates by their fixed and variable components is helpful in making marginal pricing decisions—a topic that will be discussed in a later section of this book. The steps in making the conversion from full costing rates are:

- The distributed amount of expense for each production cost center is broken down by its fixed and variable segments for each item.
- The total of the fixed and the total of the variable are each divided by the same production hours used in calculating the total costing overhead rates in each production cost center (see Exhibit 9–6).

The approach for breaking down the overhead in the three production cost centers into fixed and variable segments must follow the same philosophy outlined by the general manager for distributing the overhead costs to the three production centers:

- The appropriate department heads should participate.
- This applies to service department heads as well as production department heads.

The service department involvement is required for items such as maintenance, utilities, and accounting since these departments are most knowledgeable in the cost behavior of the expenses that come under their jurisdiction. Correct determination of the breakdown of fixed and variable expenses cannot be done by snap judgment—as is done in many companies. It must be a participative and coordinated effort.

IMPORTANCE OF PROPER ALLOCATION OF EXPENSES TO PRODUCTION COST CENTERS

Of the six steps outlined in this chapter for developing overhead rates, the execution of step 4 is the most difficult. Improper implementation can result in overhead rates that produce incorrect product costs. Improper implementation can take the form of:

BREAKDOWN OF OVERHEAD BY PRODUCTION COST CENTER / BREAKDOWN OF FIXED & VARIABLE COSTS BY PRODUCTION COST CENTER

	ALLOCATION BASIS	MOLDING PRESSES	PUNCH PRESSES	FINISHING	TOTAL OVERHEAD	MOLDING PRESSES FIXED	MOLDING PRESSES VARIABLE	PUNCH PRESSES FIXED	PUNCH PRESSES VARIABLE	FINISHING FIXED	FINISHING VARIABLE
Molding presses	Direct	$ 48,151			$ 48,151	$ 48,151					
Punch presses	Direct		$ 48,965		48,965			$ 48,965			
Finishing	Direct			$ 31,444	31,444					$ 31,444	$ 31,444
Total Indirect Labor—Production Departments		48,151	48,965	31,444	128,560	48,151		48,965		31,444	31,444
General manager's staff	1/3 each	16,977	16,977	16,978	50,932	16,977		16,977		16,978	
Personnel	Total empl.	13,680	8,550	11,970	34,200	13,680		8,550		11,970	
Cost accounting	Total empl.	15,748	9,843	13,779	39,370	15,748		9,843		13,779	
Material control	No. of items	26,004	17,335	43,340	86,679	13,002	$ 13,002	8,668	$ 8,667	21,670	$ 21,670
Engineering	No. of items	13,607	9,071	22,678	45,356	13,607		9,071		22,678	
Quality assurance	No. of items	21,985	14,657	36,643	73,285	17,588	4,397	11,726	2,931	29,314	7,329
Purchasing	No. of items	8,183	5,456	13,639	27,278	8,183		5,456		13,639	
Maintenance	Analysis	71,970	35,985	11,995	119,950	35,985	35,985	17,992	17,993	5,998	5,997
Receiving and shipping	No. of items	18,467	12,311	30,779	61,557	5,540	12,927	3,693	8,618	9,234	21,545
Total Indirect Labor—Service Departments		206,621	130,185	201,801	538,607	140,310	66,311	91,976	38,209	145,260	56,541
Labor connected expenses (except O/T)	Total payroll	108,576	77,952	91,871	278,399	38,002	70,574	27,283	50,669	33,992	57,879
Overtime premium	Analysis	23,460	10,330	9,100	42,890		23,460		10,330		9,100
Total Labor-Connected Expenses		132,036	88,282	100,971	321,289	38,002	94,034	27,283	60,999	33,992	66,979
Electricity	Analysis	23,450	14,070	9,380	46,900	7,816	15,634	4,690	9,380	3,126	6,254
Telephone	Purch. & GM	2,736	1,824	4,560	9,120	2,736		1,824		4,560	
All other utilities	Analysis	3,769	2,931	1,675	8,375	3,769		2,931		1,675	
Total Utilities		29,955	18,825	15,615	64,395	14,321	15,634	9,445	9,380	9,361	6,254
Depreciation	Analysis	110,100	78,200	6,800	195,100	110,100		78,200		6,800	
All other facilities costs	Floor space	13,489	8,710	30,908	53,107	13,489		8,710		30,908	
Total Facilities Cost		123,589	86,910	37,708	248,207	123,589		86,910		37,708	
Maintenance materials	Analysis	39,420	19,710	6,570	65,700	19,710	19,710	9,855	9,855	3,285	3,285
Mold maintenance and amortization	Analysis	46,918	11,730		58,648		46,918		11,730		
All other supplies	D. L. empl.	14,665	12,570	14,665	41,900		14,665		12,570		14,665
Total Supplies and Mold Costs		101,003	44,010	21,235	166,248	19,710	81,293	9,855	34,155	3,285	17,950
Computer services	Analysis	1,050	1,050	1,400	3,500	1,050		1,050		1,400	
Rental of (computer) equipment	Analysis	3,180	3,180	4,240	10,600	3,180		3,180		4,240	
Travel expenses	Analysis	4,190	4,190	4,320	12,700	4,190		4,190		4,320	
All other office expenses	1/3 each	1,917	1,917	1,916	5,750	1,917		1,917		1,916	
Total Office Expenses		10,337	10,337	11,876	32,550	10,337		10,337		11,876	
Total Overhead		$651,692	$427,514	$420,650	$1,499,856	$394,420	$257,272	$284,771	$142,743	$272,926	$147,724
Production hours		60,800	49,900	65,100		60,800	60,800	49,900	49,900	65,100	65,100
Overhead costing rates		10.72	8.56	6.46		6.49	4.23	5.70	2.86	4.19	2.27

EXHIBIT 9-6:
BREAKING DOWN THE FULL COSTING OVERHEAD RATES INTO FIXED AND VARIABLE RATES

1. Using arbitrary methods for allocation of the expenses to the production cost centers. An example would be the use of direct labor as the basis for determining the amount of the expense to be allocated to each cost center. There are some exceptions, but these are relatively few.

2. Improper analysis when arbitrary methods are not used.

1. Using Arbitrary Methods

Direct labor is the most often applied arbitrary method for allocating indirect expenses (overhead) to the production cost centers. Obviously, there are some expenses that may properly be allocated by use of direct labor. Examples are indirect labor in the personnel department and factory supplies. Exhibit 9–7 (TVE company)* illustrates a case in which the correct breakdown of indirect labor for five service departments by cost centers is compared with the breakdown made with direct labor as the base. The percentages under each of the five service departments show the breakdown based on an analysis of the services rendered to each of the cost centers. The column headed "Direct Labor" shows the percentage that the direct labor in each of the production cost centers is to total direct labor. A comparison of the percentages actually used with the percentages if direct labor were used highlight the following deficiencies:

Production Control. The bulb washing machine requires 21 percent of the production control department's effort. Because the equipment is automated and uses very little direct labor, only 4 percent would have been allocated if a direct labor base had been used for the allocation.

Electrical Maintenance. Test sets require 54 percent of the effort of this service cost center—five times as much as use of the direct labor basis would have allocated.

Mechanical Maintenance. Here, the stem and flare machines require 23 percent of the time of this service department and rotary exhausts need 49 percent. The direct labor method would have allocated 3 percent for the former and 8 percent for the latter. In total, the percentage of mechanical maintenance required for these two production cost centers is 72 percent while direct labor would have allocated only 11 percent with the balance being allocated to the remaining production cost centers.

Production Engineering. This service department expends 21 percent of its effort in bulb processing, 20 percent to test sets, and 26 percent to rotary exhausts. This compares with 12, 11, and 8 percent, respectively. In total, actual services rendered to these three production centers adds up to 67 percent of the total. The amount that would have been allocated through use of direct labor is 31 percent with the balance of 69 percent being allocated to the remaining cost centers.

Quality. The major effort of this service department (60 percent) is expended to the five test sets. This figure would be only 11 percent if direct labor had been used.

---

*The TVE Company is a manufacturer of television picture tubes.

COST CENTER	PRODUCTION CONTROL LABOR	ELECTRICAL MAINTENANCE LABOR	MECHANICAL MAINTENANCE LABOR	PRODUCT ENGINEERING	QUALITY	DIRECT LABOR
16″ Bulb assembly	5.0%	1.0%	7.0%	4.0%	3.0%	6%
1 Bulb washing machine	21.0	1.0	6.0	1.0	5.0	4
2 RCA settling conveyors	2.0	1.0	3.0	9.0	5.0	3
Bulb processing	7.0	4.0	2.0	21.0	7.0	12
3 Lehrs	4.0	3.0	2.0	3.0	4.0	6
2 Stem & 1 flare machine	2.0	1.0	23.0	2.0	2.0	3
Mounting	13.0	2.0	1.0	8.0	3.0	32
4 Sealing machines	1.0	2.0	4.0	3.0	8.0	2
2 Basing wheels & base fill	1.0	1.0	1.0	2.0	1.0	3
5 Test sets (incl. pack.)	21.0	54.0	1.0	20.0	60.0	11
7 Rotary exhausts	8.0	28.0	49.0	26.0	*	8
Finishing	15.0	2.0	1.0	1.0	2.0	10
TOTAL PLANT	100%	100%	100%	100%	100%	100%

* Quality checks made at testing. These costs allocated to product when it reaches test sets.

Note: Production control in this company includes purchasing, receiving, and shipping. Personnel and accounting are allocated to production cost centers on the basis of direct labor.

EXHIBIT 9–7:
PERCENTAGE BREAKDOWN OF INDIRECT LABOR OF SERVICE DEPARTMENTS
(DIRECT LABOR BREAKDOWN SHOWN FOR COMPARATIVE PURPOSES)

Some accountants prefer to use direct labor (or machine hours) as a basis for making many of the allocations because of the simplicity. Some justify this with the argument that, no matter how arbitrary, the overhead is completely absorbed by the products.

An obvious fallacy of this argument is that products that are sold or transferred to another plant midway in the production process can be greatly over or understated in cost. Note that the mounting production department is heaviest in the percentage of direct labor—32 percent of the total. The average percentage of effort expended by the five service departments to mounting is 5.4 percent. Since the components made in the mounting cost center were being transferred to two other plants (as well as being used in this plant) at standard cost plus an 8 percent markup, use of direct labor would overstate the transfer price and understate the cost of the finished TV picture tubes sold to outside customers.

2. Improper Analysis When Arbitrary Methods Are Not the Problem

What is proper analysis in one company can be highly improper in another. The degree of sophistication followed in making the analysis must be gauged by the magnitude of the item. Energy costs provide a good illustration.

When Energy Costs Are Relatively Small

A company that is essentially an assembly operation with small equipment that does not require much energy does not warrant sophisticated analysis for making allocations to production centers. It might be perfectly adequate to allocate the electricity, for example, on the basis of the number of employees who use electrical energy.

When Energy Costs Are Relatively Large

In the TVE Company, electricity, gas, and oxygen were found to be larger in the aggregate than the indirect labor of seven of the nine service departments. The high cost is due largely to the great amount of heat required in the operation to process the glass bulb and the electricity required in the testing, as well as in heating a number of the ovens (Lehr department, for example). Note in Exhibit 9–8 that ovens using electricity are identified with an asterisk in the hours per month column. Exhibit 9–8 breaks down the monthly consumption of electricity by individual machine.

The steps in arriving at the monthly consumption of electricity are first to collect the following data by machine:

- Line amperes
- Line voltage
- Power factor
- One or three phases
- KW for single phase
- KW for three phase
- Hours per month
- KW per month

	LINE AMPS	LINE VOLTAGE	POWER FACTOR	PHASE-INDICATE WHETHER 1 OR 3 PHASE	KW SINGLE PHASE	KW THREE PHASE	HOURS PER MONTH	KWH PER MONTH
16″ Bulb Assembly								
1 Sand Blaster	18	220	.9	3		6.2	492	3050
2 Rotary Face Plate Sealers	200	220	.9	3		68.6	492*	16875
1 Rotary Neck Sealer	5	220	.9	3		1.7	492	836
Ovens	138	220	.9	3		473.3	328	77621
Total 16″ Bulb Assembly								98382
Bulb Washing								
1 Bulb Washing Machine	15	220	.9	3		5.1	492	2509
Other Equipment	8	220	.9	3		2.7	492	1326
Other Equipment	15	110	.9	1	1.5		492	752
Total Bulb Washing								4589
Settling Conveyors and Dispensers	6	110	.9	1	.6		492	310
	3	220	.9	3		1.0	492	492
Total								802
Bulb Processing								
2 Hand Dispensers	4	110	.9	1	.4		328	118
5 Aquadag Chucks	18	220	.9	3		6.2	410	2542
13 Drying Tables	260	110	.9	1	25.7		410	10553
Total Bulb Preparation								13213
Lehr								
1 Surface Combustion	50	220	.9	3		17.1	492	6413
1 Ross	1200	220	.9	3		411.5	492*	101229
1 Steiner Ives	600	220	.9	3		205.8	205*	21095
Total Lehr								128737
Mounting Department (Include Amonia Dissociator)	197	220	.9	1 & 3	42.2	1.7	720	31608
	20	100	.9	1	2.0		720	1426
Total Mounting Department								33034
Stem Department								
2 Stem Machine	8	220	.9	3		2.7	164	443
1 Flare Machine	3	220	.9	3		1.0	164	164
2 Annealing Ovens	60	220	.9	1	11.9		205*	2439
Total Stem Department								3046

EXHIBIT 9–8:
MONTHLY CONSUMPTION OF ELECTRICITY

	Number	Volts	Factor	Phase	KW (1φ)	KW (3φ)	Hours	Total
Sealing								
4 Sealing Machines	12	220	.9	3		4.1	369	1513
4 Preheaters	80	220	.9	1	15.8		369	5845
Repair Oven	20	220	.9	1	4.0		369	1462
Total Sealing								8820
2 Basing Wheels and 2 Base Filling Machines	50	220	.9	3		17.1	492	8413
Testing and Packing								
5 Test Sets	40	110	.9	1	4.0		328	1299
5 Gas Checkers	5	110	.9	1	.5		328	177
4 Sparkers	8	110	.9	1	.8		328	265
7 Aging Racks	14	110	.9	1	1.4		328	443
Life Test Equipment (100 Pos.)	120	110	.9	1	11.8		720	8554
Other Equipment	15	110	.9	1	1.5		720	1102
Total Testing & Packing								11840
Finishing								
2 Spray Booths	14	110	.9	1	1.3		164	221
2 Gas Checkers	2	110	.9	1	.2		164	30
1 Test Set	8	110	.9	1	.8		164	133
Other	13	110	.9	1	1.2		164	192
Total Finishing								576
Rotary (Including Bombarders)								
3 16 Head	480	220	.9	3		164.6	492*	40491
4 24 Head	2400	220	.9	3		823.1	492*	202482
Total Rotary								242973
Trolleys (Including Bombarders)	1490	220	.9	3		511.0	492*	125706
Air Conditioning	300	220	.9	3		102.9	492	50627
Compressor Room	196	220	.9	3		67.2	492	33062
Lighting	500	220	.1	1	110.0		492	54120
All Other (110)	200	110	.9	1	19.8		492	9742
All Other (220—3 Phase)	232	220	.9	3		79.6	492	39163
All Other (220—1 Phase)	227	220	.9	1	44.9		492	22096
Total Monthly Consumption Of Electricity								888941

*Indicates number of hours equipment will be in operation. Total KW per month based on number of hours equipment is expected to draw current. (Electric ovens assumed to draw current 50 percent of the time in operation)

EXHIBIT 9–8, continued

The calculation multiplies the line amps by voltage by power factor by the square root of the phase to arrive at the number of kilowatts. This number is then multiplied by the hours of usage of the machine per month to determine the KWH per month. This figure, multiplied by the cost per KWH, supplies the cost.

Applying this formula to the sand blaster in the 16-inch bulb assembly cost center, we get the following figures:

LINE AMPS		VOLTAGE		POWER FACTOR		SQUARE ROOT OF PHASE		KILO-WATTS		HOURS PER MONTH		KWH PER MONTH
18	×	220	×	.9	×	1.73	=	6.2	×	492	=	3,050

The information contained in Exhibit 9–8 was obtained from the plant electrician.

Exhibit 9–9, showing a similar breakdown by cost centers, lists the equipment that uses gas and equipment that uses oxygen, together with the total consumption per month. These items were measured by determining the rate of flow of the gases through the equipment with a flow meter and extending the rate of flow by the hours per month that the equipment is anticipated to be running.

	CU. FT. PER HOUR	HOURS PER MONTH	TOTAL CU. FT. PER MONTH
1 Surface combustion oven	2000	700	1,400,000
4 Sealing machines @ 180 cu. ft. per hr.	720	246	177,120
1 Base baking machine	35	492	17,220
2 Stem machines	300	164	49,200
2 Rotary face plate sealing machines	540	492	265,680
1 Rotary neck sealing machine	180	492	88,560
5 Glass lathes @ 50 cu. ft. per hr.	250	492	123,000
Total			2,120,780

	CU. FT. PER HOUR	HOURS PER MONTH	TOTAL CU. FT. PER MONTH
4 Sealing machines @ 125 cu. ft. per hr.	475	246	116,850
2 Stem machines	200	164	32,800
2 Rotary face plate sealing machines	350	492	172,200
1 Rotary neck sealing machine	120	492	59,040
5 Glass lathes	165	492	81,180
Total			462,070

EXHIBIT 9–9:
COMPARISON OF MONTHLY GAS AND OXYGEN CONSUMPTION

GUIDELINES TO DEVELOPING OVERHEAD COSTING RATES

The key elements in developing costing rates are summarized below:

**GUIDELINES TO DEVELOPING
OVERHEAD COSTING RATES**

Number of Overhead Costing Rates

The first step is to identify the major processes. Example of types of major processes for which costing rates should be developed:

    Plastics molding
    Punch presses
    Die casting
    Plating
    Assembly

Identify any variations within these processes that might warrant a separate rate. Example: If the plastics molding cost center consists of 4-, 8-, and 12-oz. automatic injection molding presses and a 96-oz. press is added, this would warrant a separate rate because the operating costs of a press that is so much larger would be much greater than the smaller presses.

Vehicle for Applying the Overhead Costing Rate

Direct labor hours would be used for operations that are highly labor-paced. Examples are hand assembly and assembly operations using nonautomatic machinery.

Machine hours are used when the operations are paced by the machine rather than by direct labor. Using machine hours rather than direct labor would eliminate the distortion that results when the crew size varies from one product to another.

Material dollars, weight or length (whichever is the most appropriate) is used as the vehicle for applying the overhead cost to the product when it results in a more equitable allocation of the overhead. *Example:* In a contract with a manufacturer, when the government supplies the material, the manufacturer must recover his material handling costs such as receiving, inspecting, and storing. Material is the most appropriate base particularly when there is a contract cancellation with very little or no actual manufacturing having been completed.

Level of Activity

Time span: Should include an annual cycle so the troughs and peaks are both considered.

Volume: Should be based on a sufficient sales volume to permit a normal turnover of investment.

Allocating Overhead Expenses to Production Cost Centers

Major effort on accuracy of allocations should be expended on major expenses. The one-step method of allocation should be used rather than the two-step except in unusual cases.

DEVELOPING THE FLEXIBLE BUDGET

As mentioned earlier, the general manager made the decision to use the actual figures incurred in the prior year for developing the standard hourly overhead costing rates developed in Exhibit 9–6. It was his feeling that the level of activity and the costs incurred in the prior year head been well-controlled and would provide a good basis for establishing the costing rates. The information contained in this exhibit also provides the basis for data needed in the development of the budget formula used in flexible budgeting.

The Budget Formula

The budget formula consists of two components:

1. Variable overhead cost per production hour
2. Fixed cost per unit of time

Variable Cost per Production Hour

The portion of Exhibit 9–6 that shows the fixed and variable breakdown of the expenses in the three production costs centers has been reproduced in Exhibit 9–10. The variable costs for each of the expenses in the three production cost centers that fall in the variable category have been divided by the total hours shown at the bottom of the exhibit, to show the variable cost per production hour. This calculation is shown for receiving and shipping as well as for total overhead in each of the three production cost centers (see Table 9–1).

	Molding Presses		Punch Presses		Finishing	
	Variable Cost	Cost/ hour	Variable Cost	Cost/ hour	Variable Cost	Cost/ hour
Receiving & shipping	$ 12,927	.21	8,618	.17	21,545	.33
Total overhead	257,272	4.23	142,743	2.86	147,724	2.27
Production hours	60,800		49,900		65,100	

TABLE 9–1

Fixed Costs per Unit of Time

Since all figures shown in Exhibit 9–10 are annual costs, the fixed items must be broken down into the fixed cost per month for use in preparing monthly flexible budgets. This segmenting of annual costs on a monthly basis is shown in Table 9–2 for the same items illustrated above:

	Molding Presses		Punch Presses		Finishing	
	Annual Fixed Cost	Fixed Cost/ Month	Annual Fixed Cost	Fixed Cost/ Month	Annual Fixed Cost	Fixed Cost/ Month
Receiving and shipping	$ 5,540	462	3,693	308	9,234	769
Total overhead	394,420	32,868	284,771	23,731	272,926	22,744

TABLE 9–2

BREAKDOWN OF OVERHEAD BY:
1. PRODUCTION COST CENTER
2. FIXED AND VARIABLE WITHIN THE COST CENTER
3. VARIABLE COST PER HOUR

	ALLOCATION BASIS	TOTAL OVERHEAD	BY FIXED & VARIABLE	
			TOTAL OVERHEAD FIXED	VARIABLE
Molding presses	Direct	$ 48,151	$ 48,151	
Punch presses	Direct	48,965	48,965	
Finishing	Direct	31,444	31,444	
Total Indirect Labor—Production Departments		128,560	128,560	
General manager's staff	1/3 each	50,932	50,932	
Personnel	Total empl.	34,200	34,200	
Cost accounting	Total empl.	39,370	39,370	
Material control	No. of items	86,679	43,340	$ 43,339
Engineering	No. of items	45,356	45,356	
Quality assurance	No. of items	73,285	58,628	14,657
Purchasing	No. of items	27,278	27,278	
Maintenance	Analysis	119,950	59,975	59,975
Receiving and shipping	No. of items	61,557	18,467	43,090
Total Indirect Labor—Service Departments		538,607	377,546	161,061
Labor connected expenses (except O/T)	Total payroll	278,399	99,277	179,122
Overtime premium	Analysis	42,890		42,890
Total Labor-Connected Expenses		321,289	99,277	222,012
Electricity	Analysis	46,900	15,632	31,268
Telephone	Purch & GM	9,120	9,120	
All other utilities	Analysis	8,375	8,375	
Total Utilities		64,395	33,127	31,268
Depreciation	Anlaysis	195,100	195,100	
All other facilities costs	Floor space	53,107	53,107	
Total Facilities Cost		248,207	248,207	
Maintenance materials	Analysis	65,700	32,850	32,850
Mold maintenance and amortization	Analysis	58,648		58,648
All other supplies	D. L. empl.	41,900		41,900
Total Supplies and Mold Costs		166,248	32,850	133,398
Computer services	Analysis	3,500	3,500	
Rental of (computer) equipment	Analysis	10,600	10,600	
Travel expenses	Analysis	12,700	12,700	
All other office expenses	1/3 each	5,750	5,750	
Total Office Expenses		32,500	32,550	
Total Overhead		$1,499,856	$952,117	$547,739
Total Hours				
Hourly Overhead Costing Rate				

EXHIBIT 9–10:
CALCULATION OF VARIABLE COST PER HOUR

EXHIBIT 9–10
CALCULATION OF VARIABLE COST PER HOUR

BREAKDOWN OF FIXED & VARIABLE BY PRODUCTION COST CENTER						VARIABLE COST/HOUR		
Molding Presses		Punch Presses		Finishing		Molding Presses	Punch Presses	Finishing
Fixed	Variable	Fixed	Variable	Fixed	Variable			
$ 48,151								
		$ 48,965						
				$ 31,444				
48,151		48,965		31,444				
16,977		16,977		16,978				
13,680		8,550		11,970				
15,748		9,843		13,779				
13,002	$ 13,002	8,668	$ 8,667	21,670	$ 21,670	$ .22	$ .18	$ .34
13,607		9,071		22,678				
17,588	4,397	11,726	2,931	29,314	7,329	.07	.06	.11
8,183		5,456		13,639				
35,985	35,985	17,992	17,993	5,998	5,997	.59	.36	.09
5,540	12,927	3,693	8,618	9,234	21,545	21	.17	.33
140,310	66,311	91,976	38,209	145,260	56,541	1.09	.77	.87
38,002	70,574	27,283	50,669	33,992	57,879	1.16	1.02	89
	23,460		10,300		9,100	.39	.20	.14
38,002	94,034	27,283	60,999	33,992	66,979	1.55	1.22	1.03
7,816	15,634	4,690	9,380	3,126	6,254	.26	.19	.10
2,736		1,824		4,560				
3,769		2,931		1,675				
14,321	15,634	9,445	9,380	9,361	6,254	.26	.19	.10
110,100		78,200		6,800				
13,489		8,710		30,908				
123,589		86,910		37,708				
19,710	19,710	9,855	9,855	3,285	3,285	.32	.20	.05
	46,918		11,730			.77	.23	
	14,665		12,570		14,665	.24	.25	.22
19,710	81,293	9,855	34,155	3,285	17,950	1.33	.68	.27
1,050		1,050		1,400				
3,180		3,180		4,240				
4,190		4,190		4,320				
1,917		1,917		1,916				
10,337		10,337		11,876				
$394,420	$257,272	$284,771	$142,743	$272,926	$147,724	$4.23	2.86	2.27
60,800	60,800	49,900	49,900	65,100	65,100			
6.49	4.23	5.70	2.86	4.19	2.27			

USING THE FLEXIBLE BUDGET FORMULA

This formula is a combination of variable costs per hour multiplied by the number of hours of activity plus the fixed cost per month. For expenses that are completely variable, only the first part of this formula would be used—that is, the variable cost per hour multiplied by the number of production hours. If an item is considered to be entirely fixed, only the fixed cost per month will be considered to be the budget allowance. The illustrative example shown in Exhibit 9–11 illustrates the application of the flexible budget formula to receiving and shipping as well as to total overhead. This would be done for each expense item. The actual expense would then be compared with the flexible budget allowance.

This chapter completes Section I, which deals with cost systems to fit management needs for control. The next section demonstrates how these cost systems are applicable to costing and pricing products for maximization of profits.

	VARIABLE COST/ HOUR	HOURS PER × MONTH =	TOTAL VARIABLE +	FIXED COST/ MONTH =	BUDGET ALLOW- ANCE
Molding Presses					
Receiving and shipping	$ .21	5,200	$1,092	$ 462	$ 1,554
Total overhead	4.23	5,200	21,996	32,868	54,864
Punch Presses					
Receiving and presses	.17	4,100	697	308	1,005
Total overhead	2.86	4,100	11,726	23,721	35,447
Finishing (Assembly)					
Receiving and shipping	.33	6,800	2,244	769	3,013
Total overhead	2.27	6,800	15,436	22,744	38,180

EXHIBIT 9–11:
CALCULATING THE FLEXIBLE BUDGET ALLOWANCES

SECTION II

Costing and Pricing Products
to Maximize Profits

10

Estimating Product Cost Problems and Requirements

The degree of cost estimating sophistication required by a company varies with the number and type of products as well as the nature of the manufacturing operations. If a company makes a single basic product with minor variations, it does not need a complex costing system. This was the case with the Ford Motor Company in its early years when the Model T reigned supreme. However, when more products were added, particularly the tractor line, the situation changed. The company realized that it must distinguish automobile costs from tractor costs. It also realized that now there were product differences within both categories that must also be recognized. In recognition of these needs, the company took steps to establish a costing and control system that would correct this deficiency—to wit, the well-publicized McNamara Whiz Kids. Although the forces of supply and demand determine the selling price for standard products, product cost estimates are needed to determine product profitability.

There are also companies making products that might be classified as "nonstandard" whose prices are based on cost plus a negotiated markup factor. These products are the research and development types for which no standard market price exists. Also included in this "nonstandard" category is the repair and overhaul of equipment. One company that was overhauling a number of machines of the same type was asked why it could not establish a standard price since the machines were so similar. The response was: "for the same reason that two cars of the same make and model year require different work to put them in running condition. A cost estimate isn't reliable until the unit in disrepair is dismantled to find the trouble." These nonstandard jobs call for a job cost system that determines the cost of doing the work.

COST ESTIMATES FOR NEW PRODUCTS AND VARIATIONS OF EXISTING PRODUCTS

Most companies of any size receive a continuous stream of requests for quotation. These are usually received from the marketing department. They should be screened upon receipt for several reasons. The reasons are embodied in the following questions that must be answered:

- Does the quotation request relate to a product that fits into the company's line of products? If not, the requestor should be promptly advised. The reply to the customer presents an opportunity to familiarize him with the company's line of products and to encourage future contacts.

- If the product does fit the line, a determination must be made as to the best way to manufacture it. The question must be raised as to whether or not there is a tricky feature to this product. If there is, and special tooling is needed to overcome a potential manufacturing problem, the cost of such tooling must be included in the price. The next question is to determine if the order is large enough to amortize the cost of the tooling. If the customer usually buys this product from another supplier, it is probable that the supplier has already amortized the tooling. This makes it more difficult for another company to compete. The decision as to whether or not to accept this request for quotation must be made in conjunction with the marketing department.

- Do competitors make this product on fully automated equipment? If so, it may be advisable for the company to concentrate on special products that are more suitable to the less automated facilities.

- Does the product fulfill the company's objectives and strategy? Is the product in a desirable stage of the life cycle? The early growth stage may be the most favorable for a volume producer who can produce the product at low cost and benefit by the higher prices that a relatively new product can command.

- Does the company have a large backlog of orders? If so, it may choose to quote a higher price. If the company has a low backlog, it may quote a lower price to keep its facilities busy.

- Is the company requesting the quotation on a "fishing expedition"? The plant manager of the TL Company noted, when he was approving finished quotations, that one of these was from a competitor with whom he was quite familiar. This competitor made the particular product in very large quantities for use within his own company. In addition, he made sales to other companies using this item. The plant manager recalled that this company's accounting department periodically sent out requests for quotations to check its interplant billing prices. A review was made of previous quotation requests by this company. Sure enough, price requests had been made for thirty-eight different items during the past two years with no purchases. The plant manager called this to the attention of the sales manager with the suggestion that these requests be followed through in the future by a phone call to the other company's purchasing manager or a personal visit to discuss the quotation and reasons that none of the thirty-eight had resulted in orders. The fishing expeditions by this company suddenly ceased.

These six questions (and there are others) point out that the cost estimating procedure must be more than a clerical function. The cost estimator must be more than a clerk; he (or she) must know the product line and be familiar with the manufacturing operations of the company. There must also be some understanding of the market and the nature of the competition.

ANALYSIS OF COST/SELLING PRICE RELATIONSHIP NOT THE ONLY USE FOR COST ESTIMATING

Product cost estimates serve more than one purpose. The procedures discussed in the preceding section will assure sound estimates that will be useful in:

1. Making product profitability analyses
2. Monitoring manufacturing efficiency
3. Making make-or-buy decisions
4. Providing basis for financial planning

1. Making Product Profitability Analyses (See Also Exhibit 7–1)

This type of analysis is a useful extension of cost estimating because it highlights the three major elements of manufacturing cost. This analysis has been prepared in two formats:

- Full costing
- Direct costing

Full Costing Format

The Product Line Profitability Report (Exhibit 10–1) breaks down the standard manufacturing costs into the major elements:

- Material as a percent of sales
- Direct labor as a percent of sales
- Overhead as a percent of sales

The total of these three (total standard manufacturing cost) is then subtracted from total sales to arrive at the percentage that total standard manufacturing costs are of total sales. The balance, as a percentage of standard gross profit to sales, is shown in the last column. Standard rather than actual costs are used because this company makes a standard product that is built to stock rather than to order. The difference between the standard cost and the actual cost would be reported as variances. These are identified by department for the three elements of cost. A company making a custom product would prepare this report at actual cost rather than standard as was illustrated in Exhibit 2–7. The actual costs, however, were compared with the originally estimated costs.

The product lines listed in Exhibit 10–1 are listed in order of profitability—the standard gross profit ranging from a high of 40 percent to a low of 14 percent. The last two products showing gross profits of 18 percent and 14 percent, respectively, indicate direct labor to be a substantially higher percentage of total manufacturing cost than for any of the other products. These direct labor percentages, 17 percent and 18 percent, are double the 9 percent shown for the average of all eight products.

Date _____

PRODUCT LINE NUMBER	SALES** $	%	STANDARD MATERIAL $	%	STANDARD DIRECT LABOR $	%	STANDARD* OVERHEAD $	%	TOTAL STD. MFG. COSTS $	%	STANDARD GROSS PROFIT $	%
P660	296	100		43		7		10		60		40
J200	1,380	100		33		10		19		62		38
2020	1,847	100		44		7		12		63		37
6100	499	100		51		5		10		66		34
F011	1,649	100		50		6		11		67		33
7007	867	100		53		8		15		76		24
8100	1,132	100		36		17		29		82		18
D166	130	100		32		18		36		86		14
TOTAL	7,800	100		43		9		16		68		32

*Under full costing, fixed overhead costs are included.
**$000 omitted.

EXHIBIT 10–1:
PRODUCT LINE PROFITABILITY REPORT—FULL COSTING BASIS*

Date _____

PRODUCT NUMBER	SALES* $	%	STANDARD MATERIAL $	%	STANDARD DIRECT LABOR $	%	STANDARD VARIABLE MFG. OVHD. $	%	TOTAL STD. VARIABLE COSTS $	%	MARGINAL CONTRIBUTION $	%	STANDARD FIXED MFG. OVERHEAD $	%	TOTAL STD. MFG. COST $	%	STANDARD GROSS PROFIT $	%
P660	296	100		43		7		8		58		42		2		60		40
J200	1,380	100		33		10		15		58		42		4		62		38
2020	1,847	100		44		7		10		61		39		2		63		37
6100	499	100		51		5		8		64		36		2		66		34
F011	1,649	100		50		6		9		65		35		2		67		33
7007	867	100		53		8		12		73		27		3		76		24
8100	1,132	100		36		17		23		76		24		6		82		18
D166	130	100		32		18		29		79		21		7		86		14
Total	7,800	100		43		9		13		65		35		3		68		32

* $000 omitted.

EXHIBIT 10–2:
PRODUCT LINE PROFITABILITY—DIRECT COSTING BASIS

When this report was being reviewed with the general manager and the plant manager, the plant manager acknowledged that these two products were more highly labor-paced than he had realized. Since these two (8100 and D166) were fabricated on the same equipment and volume was expected to grow rapidly in the near future, he saw justification for automating the operations to the extent that was economically feasible. He instructed his industrial engineer to prepare a feasibility study to review the economics.

Products 6100, F011, and 7007 showed the highest percentages of material. The percentages are 51, 50, and 53 percent, respectively, compared with the average of 43 percent for all products. The plant manager advised that he would have the engineering department look into the possibility of reducing the material content by possible simplification of the design. The study showed a potential reduction of 2 percent for products F011 and 7007. Product 6100 was not studied because it would soon be supplanted by a new product.

Overhead, like direct labor, was highest for the two products with the lowest profitability. There appeared to be two reasons for this:

- The labor-paced nature of the operation resulted in use of a large volume of factory supplies and material handling labor.

- The method of fabrication required a long firing cycle in an expensive heat-treating furnace.

The decision to automate the manufacture of these two products would result in a reduction of the overhead as well.

Direct Costing Format

The difference between this format (Exhibit 10–2) and the previous one is:

- The standard overhead is broken down into the variable and fixed segments.

- Total variable costs (material plus direct labor plus variable overhead) are subtracted from total sales to arrive at the marginal contribution percentage. This is the percentage left to cover fixed overhead and profit.

The analyses for material, direct labor, and overhead were already made under the full costing format. These same explanations apply to the direct costing format. The additional information contained in the latter is the marginal contribution percentage—the profit before manufacturing fixed costs are taken into account. Those who consider the fixed costs as a pool of costs that are not properly assignable to specific products look at the contribution margin rather than the gross profit. There will be a difference in the results depending on whether the contribution margin approach or gross profit measurement are used. This is demonstrated in Table 10–1.

Although the foregoing figures show differences in profitability of the two measures presented, they are not expressed in the same common denominator. To convert the marginal contribution and the gross profit percentages to a comparable basis, the marginal contribution percentages for each of the eight products were divided by the 35 percent shown as the average (total) for the eight product lines.

Likewise, the individual gross margin percentages were divided by the total, 32 percent. The result is shown in Table 10–2.

Product Line Number	Marginal Contribution %	Gross Profit %
P660	42%	40%
J200	42	38
2020	39	37
6100	36	34
F011	35	33
7007	27	24
8100	24	18
D166	21	14
Total	35%	32%

TABLE 10–1

Product Line Number	Marginal Contribution %	Gross Profit %
P660	120%	125%
J200	120	119
2020	111	116
6100	103	106
F011	100	103
7007	77	75
8100	69	56
D166	60	44
Total	100%	100%

TABLE 10–2

The spread of profitability for the marginal contribution percentages ranges from 60 to 120 percent while the range for the gross profit percentages is 44 to 125 percent. Using the above figures for determining the relative profitability of the various products, we find that under the marginal contribution calculation, D166, the least profitable of the eight, shows a contribution to profit of 60 percent. The comparable figure for gross profit is only 44 percent. Product P660, on the other hand, shows greater profitability under the gross profit method—125 percent of the average compared with 120 percent when the marginal contribution method is used. The difference between the two methods varies by the amount of fixed cost that has been allocated to the product lines. Which of the two methods is used for measuring product profitability is based on management philosophy in the treatment of fixed costs. This subject is dealt with further in other chapters.

2. Monitoring Manufacturing Efficiency

The steps followed in the development of cost estimates are quite similar to those followed in establishing standards for monitoring manufacturing efficiency. This applies to job costing as well as process costing.

Job Costing

Exhibit 2–7 on page 34 illustrates how one company measures performance by comparing the actual costs incurred with the original estimate that was used to establish the price for the product. Ideally, the original estimate should be broken down in sufficient detail to monitor individual materials and labor operations. This is not always done, however. There are cases when an estimate used for pricing is based on total costs of a similar product made previously. Differences are accounted for by adjusting segments of the previous product through use of adjusting percentages. In such cases, when pressure for time does not permit a detailed estimate to be prepared, such detail should be reconstructed when the order is received and put into production.

Process Costing

Companies making standardized products can utilize more sophisticated measurements of efficiency. The high volume and repetitive nature of the operations justifies this sophistication. See Exhibits 6–4 (page 114), 6–5 (page 116), 6–8 (page 119), and 6–9 (page 120).

3. Making Make-or-Buy Decisions

During the period that products with low gross profit were being reviewed, a make-or-buy study was also being made for product line D166—the line with the lowest gross profit. This was being done by the marketing manager who was interested in seeing product costs reduced because his function was measured by volume of gross profit. The marketing manager, working with the purchasing department, found a year's volume of D166 could be purchased from a competitor for $105,000 compared with a total manufacturing cost of $112,000. A strong argument for purchasing this product line was raised in view of this price difference which was presented to the general manager and plant manager in the form of Table 10–3.

(Figures in thousand dollars)

Product Line Number	Sales		Standard Material		Standard Direct Labor		Standard Overhead		Total Std. Mfg. Cost		Standard Gross Profit	
	$	%	$	%	$	%	$	%	$	%	$	%
D166 (Make)	130	100	42	32	23	18	47	36	112	86	18	14
D166 (Buy)	130	100	105	81	—	—	—	—	105	81	25	19

TABLE 10–3

MAKE-OR-BUY STUDY

PRODUCT NUMBER	(1) SALES $	%	STANDARD MATERIAL $	%	STANDARD DIRECT LABOR $	%	STANDARD VARIABLE MFG. OVHD. $	%	TOTAL STD. VARIABLE COSTS $	%	MARGINAL CONTRIBUTION $	%	STANDARD FIXED MFG. OVERHEAD $	%	TOTAL STD. MFG. COST $	%	STANDARD GROSS PROFIT $	%
Total[1]	7,800	100	3,354	43	702	9	1,014	13	5,070	65	2,730	35	234	3	5,304	68	2,496	32
D166[2] (Make)	130	100	42	32	23	18	38	7	103	57	27	43	9	29	112	86	18	14
Net[3]	7,670	100	3,312	43.2	679	8.9	976	12.7	4,967	64.8	2,703	35.2	225	2.9	5,192	67.7	2,478	32.3
D166[4] (Buy)	130	100	105	80.8	—	—	—	—	105	80.8	25	19.2	9	7.0	114	87.7	16	12.3
Total[5]	7,800	100	3,417	43.8	679	8.7	976	12.5	5,072	65.0	2,728	35.0	234	3.0	5,306	68.0	2,494	32.0

[1]Total line from Exhibit 10–2 with standard manufacturing cost dollars added. All products fall under "make."
[2]This product line subtracted because of proposal to buy product line D166 rather than make it.
[3] "Net" is the adjusted total after excluding product line D166.
[4]Product line D166 added back based on "buy" rather than "make."
[5]Total all product lines based on D166 bought rather than manufactured.

EXHIBIT 10–3:
PRODUCT LINE PROFITABILITY—DIRECT COSTING BASIS

The marketing manager pointed out that the cost of manufacturing D166 was $112,000 or 86 percent of the sales value. The cost of purchasing the same product from a competitor was shown to be only $105,000 or $7000 less. The comparison of gross profit showed that the product being manufactured had a gross profit of $18,000 or 14 percent of sales value compared with $25,000 or 19 percent of sales value.

The plant manager, whose staff had already completed a similar make-or-buy study in the direct costing format, came up with a comparison that took into consideration the fixed overhead costs that would not be eliminated if the D166 product line were purchased rather than manufactured. The results of this study are shown in Exhibit 10–3 using the direct costing format. This study, in addition to comparing the make-and-buy costs for D166, also compares the total of the eight product lines under the "make" and under the "buy" costs for D166.

In the marketing department's study, the "make" costs included the $9000 of standard fixed overhead when compared with the buy price of $105,000. Since these fixed costs would not be eliminated, the plant manager added them to the $105,000 purchase cost to arrive at $114,000, an increase of $2000 over the make cost. The resulting comparison of gross profit shows that the marketing department's estimate of $25,000 drops by $9000 to $16,000. The "buy" alternative therefore reduces gross profits by $2000. (See lines 2 and 4 in Exhibit 10–3.)

The plant manager's decision, in which the general manager concurred, was to continue to make D166. The feasibility study which the industrial engineer had completed, justified the purchase of automated equipment. This would reduce the costs of making the D166 and 8100, both of which could be processed on the same equipment.

4. Providing Basis for Financial Planning

Cost estimates that are used for pricing, for performance measurements and for make or buy studies can also provide the "bricks and mortar" for financial planning. The direct costing and full costing operating statement formats, break-even analyses, and variations in profits resulting from changes in product mix are examples. These are discussed in Chapter 7.

PROBLEMS IN COST ESTIMATING

The purpose of cost estimating is to develop product costs that are realistic. In the case of customized products, these estimates are an important factor in establishing prices. In the case of standard products in which the marketplace sets the price, a realistic cost estimate provides management with a means of determining the product's profitability.

The problems associated with cost estimating, although numerous, have been boiled down to six. These are:

1. Insufficient Lead Time

One of the salesmen in the DOT Company frequently brought requests for quotations to the cost estimating section with a request for speedy processing. He wanted to deliver the quotations to the customers personally the next morning.

While this type of personal follow-up—which is practiced in different variations—is commendable, it presents problems because of lack of time to do an adequate job and the possibility of errors. The cost estimate must often be based on certain assumptions. If these assumptions are incorrect, the cost estimate will not meet the requirements of realism.

It is important to spell out assumptions that are made when cost estimates are prepared with insufficient support data. These assumptions should also be spelled out in the quotation presented to the customer to avoid the possibility of the customer agreeing to the price but requesting a product which is more sophisticated in its requirements. Some buyers have been known to follow the practice of requesting quotations with very short lead time and sketchy details, then ordering a product with tight specifications. A study of past orders placed by this buyer led to the suspicion that he followed this practice regularly in order to obtain cheaper prices. From that point on, his requests were carefully scrutinized and additional information was requested when necessary.

2. Cost Estimates Either Too High or Too Low

There are several reasons that cost estimates may be high or low. One of these could be caused by contingencies that are provided for the unexpected. A study of cost estimating practices at several companies revealed wide differences in the logic of applying contingencies. Most of the cost estimates in this sample showed contingency percentages ranging from 5 to 10 percent. Two showed 15 percent and one showed 20 percent. When contingency percentages exceed 10 percent, this could be an indication of sloppy estimating. It should be possible to break down the cost elements making up a cost estimate to a point that the contingency factor does not exceed 10 percent (5 percent would be more desirable.)

Standardized products that are built to stock rather than to order are usually highly competitive. Unless the manufacturer is one of the leaders in the field, cost estimates will frequently be found to be too high in relation to the competitive price, with the result that profits will be lower. In such a circumstance, it will be found that the leader in the field has highly automated facilities justified by a high volume of production. Because of this higher volume, material costs may also be lower because of larger purchases. A high cost estimate would have to be adjusted downward to avoid overvaluing inventory.

Cost estimates for individual products may be flawed if differences in the manufacturing process are not properly taken into account. The most common deficiency in cost estimating occurs when a single plantwide overhead rate is used for costing products. Such a rate would average out the various overhead costs so that products using more of the high cost facilities would be undercosted and those using more of the lower cost facilities would be overcosted. The solution is to establish overhead rates by cost center. Availability of cost center rates will permit products to be costed in proportion to their usage of the various facilities.

3. Costing Procedure Not Correlated with Current Production Facilities

The study of cost estimating practices, referred to earlier, revealed several instances in which companies had purchased automated equipment for key operations. However, overhead rates had not been adjusted to reflect this. Cost estimates, therefore, were still reflecting costs based on the old methods. Some companies do not keep their overhead costing rates used for cost estimating current. Cost estimates will therefore be inaccurate.

4. Operating Personnel Not Consulted

The previously referred to study also revealed that the cost estimating function in some of the companies became too mechanical. As a result, operating personnel were not consulted as often as they should have been. One foreman, with whom several cost estimates were reviewed, had this complaint: "See that 96-ounce injection molding press? Instead of using a machine hour overhead rate, the accounting department bases the overhead on a labor hour basis. Some products, after molding, have to be placed on a shrink frame to assure that cooling does not distort the dimensional requirements. This means that an extra operator will be on that machine. The cost estimator applies the same overhead rate on two operators as he does on one. That means that the depreciation, maintenance, utility, and other machine-related costs are doubled when two operators are used. What kind of costing is that? No wonder our profits are falling. The products that are overcosted are overpriced so we can't sell as many. Those that are undercosted lose money because we underprice them." This example illustrates the importance of keeping in touch with operating personnel.

5. Size of Order Not Definite

One of the marketing managers interviewed in this study related his experience with the buyer of one of his customers. This buyer would submit a request for quotation for a given number of units of a product. A week or so after this price quotation was received, he would send in a purchase order requesting a much smaller quantity. The purchase order would show the price quoted for the larger quantity. When this ploy was discovered, a review of past orders revealed that three out of the past four orders received had been accepted without challenge. From that point on, all quotations specified a setup charge plus a cost per 100 pieces. This assured recovery of the setup charges for the small orders.

6. Poor Feedback

Feedback procedures are important in customized products since the price is related to the cost estimate. An ideal method for instituting such feedback is to monitor performance using the basic figures making up the cost estimate. Only four of the eight companies studied monitored performance on this basis. Two of these four established standards when the orders went into production. Performance was monitored by these standards and variances were reported for material, direct labor, and overhead. However, no comparison was made between the actual figures (standard plus variance) and the original cost estimate. This would provide a test of the accuracy of the original estimate with the opportunity of making better estimates in the future.

Although there are more than six problems in estimating, the six outlined above were cited by those being interviewed as being the most important. In fact, one of the interviewees consulted in the wrap-up discussion, estimated that these six probably accounted for 80 percent of all problems.

COST ESTIMATING REQUIREMENTS

As in "Problems in Cost Estimating," which enumerated six problems, this section will enumerate six requirements. These are:

1. Overhead rates should identify the variable and fixed segments to facilitate profit volume analyses. Availability of this kind of information can be helpful in establishing prices for a private brand based on the assumption that with the brand name absorbing its full measure of fixed overhead, the private brand need not be charged an equivalent amount.

   Availability of variable and fixed overhead rates also facilitates studies showing changes in profitability when product mix changes. See Exhibit 7–3 on page 132 for illustration of the effect of "two different sales (product) mixes on pretax profits."

2. Nonmanufacturing (corporate) costs such as selling, general administration, and research and development must also be included in cost estimates for cost/price comparisons. See section entitled: "Importance of allocating corporate costs to segments of the company" (Chapter 7).

3. Cost estimates should include a provision for production losses. The study of cost estimates for eight companies, referred to earlier, showed that some of the companies used an across-the-board provision for production losses. An across-the-board measure is acceptable for products that are homogeneous. But when they are not homogeneous, which is more frequently the case, the provision should take into account any differences in losses by individual products and processes.

4. Costs used in estimating should be current. They should reflect current prices, current labor rates, and current manufacturing procedures.

5. If cost estimates are being prepared for pricing an order to be delivered, say, six months hence, they should reflect the anticipated costs at that time.

6. Cost estimates should provide sufficient information, such as setup costs, to facilitate the determination of unit costs for various quantities to be priced. The same applies to tooling that must be amortized over the quantities ordered.

These six requirements list the predominant types of omissions that reduce the effectiveness of cost estimating in many companies.

Conflicting Demands of Cost Estimating

The preceding two sections, "Problems in Cost Estimating" and "Cost Estimating Requirements," appear to be in conflict with each other. In the first section, one of the critical problems identified is the insufficient lead time available for making cost estimates. In the second section, emphasis was placed on the need for timeliness and sufficient detail.

Commenting on this, one general manager cited the high cost of preparing cost estimates, since his experienced yield had been about ten orders for each 100 requests for quotation received. The discussion then turned to the question of screening out some of the quotations. This discussion bore fruit because the general manager acknowledged that effective screening could eliminate about 20 percent of the requests without reducing the number of orders. In fact, the 10 percent yield would then become 12.5 percent because the base would now be 80 rather than 100. This discussion resulted in a meeting with the marketing manager, controller, and general manager to establish procedures for screening incoming requests for quotations and departmental responsibilities for furnishing information needed in the cost estimating process.

The next chapter on Cost Estimating Procedures will include further discussion of the subject of screening requests for quotation.

11

Cost Estimating Procedures

This chapter, in outlining proper cost estimating procedures, covers two general areas:

- Screening the incoming requests for quotation
- Sources of information

SCREENING THE INCOMING REQUESTS FOR QUOTATION

The process of screening includes not only the determination of which requests will be accepted for quoting—it also includes the assignment of priorities and the degree of detail in which each of the quotations will be prepared.

Considerations in Accepting an Order

There are two important considerations in determining whether a request for quotation should be accepted.

The first consideration concerns itself with the backlog of business on hand. If the backlog is very high—so that acceptance of additional orders would affect efficiency—the company should consider turning down the request for quotation. The request would then be returned to the customer advising that because of lack of capacity, the order could not be filled within the time requested. An invitation should be extended to the customer to resubmit the request if a later date (which should be specified) might be acceptable.

During periods of short capacity it might be well to take advantage of the sellers' market by increasing the markup on the product being quoted. The argument in favor is that during buyers' markets prices are forced downward because of competitive forces, so why not raise them during sellers' markets.

The key is not to arbitrarily increase the price during a sellers' market. Since the marketplace influences prices during buyers' markets, it also influences them when sellers have the "upper hand." To increase the markup substantially without considering the marketplace could be self-defeating in the long run.

The second consideration concerns itself with the ability of the company to make the product competitively. The point can be illustrated by citing a case example relating to the Rodwin Corporation.

> This company, which makes electronic measurement equipment, also manufactures many of the small metal parts used in the equipment. The sales manager, finding that there was some extra machine capacity, made the offer to find outside customers interested in purchasing small parts. When the sales manager's proposal was explored further, it was noted that the metal parts manufacturing department was geared up to meeting the tight specifications required by a government agency to whom the measuring equipment was being sold. Since this sales manager dealt with the commercial side of the business only, he was advised that the present extra capacity was limited to making the high-cost parts used for the measurement equipment sold to the government. Thus, it would not be feasible to solicit sales of these parts to the commercial customers whose emphasis was on price rather than quality.

> The Abel Foundry manufactured castings for valve manufacturing companies. These were the type of valves discussed in Chapter 2. The foundry made these in small quantities because the valves were highly customized to suit the various uses. Although the company was efficient, it could not compete with the highly automated foundries that made the more standardized products that were sold in high volume. In view of this, there was no point in the company accepting requests for quotation for the standard high volume castings.

The assignment of priorities to requests for quotation and the degree of detail in which the quotations should be prepared will be discussed later.

SOURCES OF INFORMATION

Requests for quotation are usually received through the marketing (sales) department. These requests may be received by salesmen in the field or they may be mailed directly to the company.

Before any cost estimating can be started, the request for quotation must be edited by the engineering department to identify the product in terms of the company's bill of materials (referred to as parts lists by some companies). This editing function sometimes provides the engineer with an opportunity to suggest product improvements to the customer. One engineer, in editing a customer's order found a subassembly that required eleven individual plastic and metal parts. By a suggested redesign of this subassembly, in which a die casting was substituted for some of the parts the cost could be cut by 18 percent. When this was discussed with the customer, he agreed to the change. At a later date he advised that the redesigned product resulted in fewer production rejects and therefore less rework. This is an example of good innovative thinking that can result in good customer service.

Once the editing has been completed, the cost estimating process can be started. Exhibit 11–1 summarizes the data requirements and the sources of this information.

	ENGINEERING	QUALITY CONTROL	INDUSTRIAL ENG'G	PURCHASING	PERSONNEL	COST ACCOUNTING
Material specifications	X					
Quantity of material per unit	X					
Material purchase price				X		
Provision for production losses		X	X			X
Tooling requirements			X			
Manufacturing operations	X		X			
Sequence of operations	X		X			
Operation time required			X			
Hourly labor rates					X	
Overhead costing rates						X

EXHIBIT 11–1:
COST ESTIMATING DATA REQUIREMENTS AND SOURCES OF INFORMATION

Breakdown of Sources of Information

Exhibit 11–1 lists six sources of information: engineering, quality control, industrial engineering (manufacturing engineering), purchasing, personnel, and cost accounting. It also lists the ten key information requirements needed for cost estimating. The association of information and sources from which it is obtained is analyzed below.

Material Specifications. This has to do with the characteristics and makeup of the material. Using for illustrative purposes the brass stem illustrated at level 04 in Exhibit 8–2 on page 146, the brass used in making the stem consists of a combination of copper, zinc, lead, nickel, tin, and other metallic elements. The combination in which these are melted makes up the specifications for the material. Establishing material specifications is the responsibility of the engineering department.

Quantity of Material per Unit. This, also, is determined by the engineering department. In the case of the brass stem referred to above, the gross amount of material used per 1000 stems is 37.8 pounds less 17.0 pounds of unavoidable scrap due to turnings. Exhibit 3–5 on page 67, uses these figures in calculating the material cost of product 01-02608-5036.

Material Purchase Price. This information is furnished by the purchasing department. The costs used in Exhibit 3–6 represent the standard prices. If the company were making up a request for quotation for a new product (or variation thereof), the purchasing department would furnish the current prices. It must be noted that if the request for quotation is for products to be delivered at a future time, say, six months later, the anticipated prices at that time would be used.

PROVISION FOR PRODUCTION LOSSES

The earlier section, "Quantity of Material per Unit," referred to unavoidable scrap due to turnings. This section considers three categories of production losses:

- Spoiled production
- Production losses that are uneconomical to recover
- Production losses that can be reworked

Spoiled Production

This refers to a part or product that has not been made according to the required specifications. In short, it must be scrapped or reworked. Spoilage can occur at startup when a sample run is made to assure that the machines are in proper adjustment and tools are in good condition. It could also occur in the course of a run when the operator is not attentive. Some of the startup spoilage could be considered as unavoidable. The amount that can be considered to be allowable would be determined by the quality control and the industrial engineering departments. This allowance would be included in the cost estimate as a provision. (Some might refer to this as a contingency.) Some companies have been found to use an across-the-board percentage allowance for such spoilage even though the percentage can vary widely depending on the nature of the process. It is important that differences in spoilage by process be taken into account unless it has been found that the rate does not vary greatly from one process to another.

Production Losses That Are Uneconomical to Recover

Such losses are those in which high-speed equipment "spits out" small parts at such a high volume that some of the parts are thrown out of the machine and scattered on the floor. When these parts are of a low unit value, it is normally uneconomical to salvage them. Some provision must, likewise, be made for this category of losses since it is a cost of doing business. The industrial engineering department is usually the appropriate department to establish the factor that should be used to provide for such losses in the cost estimates.

Production Losses That Can Be Reworked

Many products are of a type that will not be considered as production losses because they can be reworked to eliminate the defect. The cost accounting department usually identifies such costs in a separate account so the amount will be known. When a job costing system is in effect, the rework cost for the individual jobs will be known. In a process costing system, rework costs will be known only in total. In the first instance, past experience of rework can therefore be estimated by job. In process costing, rework will become part of the overhead rate.

Tooling Requirements

The industrial engineering department is normally responsible for the monitoring of tooling requirements. In some companies, the tools are purchased on the outside; in others, they may be made on site. When made on site, the tool department comes under the jurisdiction of the industrial engineering department.

Manufacturing Operations

The engineering department establishes the operations that are required to make the product. Frequently, factory floor experience will dictate the need for changes in some of the operations. This possibility should be recognized when cost estimates are being prepared. It is also important that the engineering records note these changes. The industrial engineering department frequently collaborates with the engineering department in establishing and revising the operations.

Sequence of Operations

The engineering department and the industrial engineering departments establish the sequence of operations in the manufacture of a product. Generally, the engineering department lists the operations and their sequence on new products. The industrial engineering department will make changes as new equipment and new processes are introduced.

Operation Time Required

The operation time required for the various operations is based on estimates or standards based on time studies. See Exhibit 5–2, Illustrative Time Study, on page 95. Note that allowances must be made for time required just as is done for quantity of material required. This is the responsibility of the industrial engineering department.

Hourly Labor Rates

Hourly labor rates are usually established by the personnel department. These rates are based on various factors such as mental effort, skill, physical effort, and the like. See Exhibit 5–3 on page 96.

Overhead Costing Rates

Development of overhead costing rates is covered elsewhere at greater length. This is the responsibility of the cost accounting department.

HOW INFORMATION SOURCES CAN ENHANCE PROFITABILITY

Much of the literature on product costing and pricing discusses information sources and responsibilities of various departments in furnishing such information, but fails to point out how these disciplines can be used to enhance product profitability. Some examples of how profitability can be increased are listed below.

Marketing

Sales personnel working in the field have direct contact with the customers. They have the opportunity of knowing a good deal about the customers' product line and the applications that are made of these products. They also know the customers' problems and needs. One innovative salesman sold his company's plastic parts to a TV picture tube manufacturer that was having problems with bent pins in the picture tube base. In the process of shipping this product, many of the pins that plug into the socket in the TV set were bent. When the salesman returned to his office, he mentioned this problem to one of the engineers. The engineer designed a plastic plug that could be placed over the pins during shipment and storage. This product could be made cheaply because it could be molded from the "regrind" plastic material. The regrind material was obtained from the runners that were cut off after plastic parts were formed in the molds. It was also obtained from finished defective parts. The reground plastic could be reused in normal production by mixing it with virgin material. But since there was a limit to the amount of such reground material that could be used, there was an excess that was frequently built up in the warehouse. The reground material could be used in making the protective plugs at minimal material cost. The company made some samples that were given to the salesman. The customer immediately placed an order for a large quantity. Not only did his company benefit from reuse of the large stock of regrind material, it could run this product almost continuously on an automatic machine that required only minimal operator supervision. Availability of such a product also provided an entree into other picture tube manufacturers.

Engineering

The engineer who edits incoming requests for quotation can be helpful to the customer by making recommendations for design changes to avoid certain "bugs" that he may be able to anticipate. He can familiarize the customer with certain new material that could be substituted for assuring better performance or reducing costs. Suggestions such as these are helpful in cementing relations with customers and assuring more business.

The engineer of one company, in editing a customer request, noted that the request specifications called for use of numerous screws in the chassis of a new type of electronic measuring equipment. He made a suggestion that screws be used in only certain key points and that spot welding be substituted in those areas in which fastening of two pieces of sheet metal was to be the only function served by the screws. As simple as this suggestion was, the customer hadn't thought of it. The suggestion was adopted and the prospective customer submitting the quotation request increased the volume of business he did with this engineer's company by over 50 percent.

Quality Control

One of the major responsibilities of the quality control department is to assure that the product being manufactured meets the requirements called for in the specifications. Quality monitoring starts with receipt of key materials in the receiving department, includes first-piece checks of machined parts, subassembly inspection at various stages of production and final inspection.

Most quality control departments accumulate statistics on defects. These are distributed to the department heads and the plant manager to alert them to problem areas. Unfortunately, many such reports are overly detailed. This is particularly true of the reports that have been computerized. In the ETT Company, the new quality control manager described his philosophy in reporting defects in a simpler but more effective manner.

A Case Example

In spite of the availability of highly detailed reports listing production defects, the ETT Company was being plagued with a high percentage of customer returns because of product defects. Because the quality control manager did not have the management's confidence, a replacement was hired. The new quality control manager advised that the basic information that was available on the computer was of value but, because of excessive detail, none of the department heads could make effective use of the figures. The new man described his philosophy of reporting and control as follows:

"Department heads are too busy to pore over page after page of lists of defects. This data must be presented in a digest that points out the key items that can be handled promptly. My approach is to select the key items that need immediate attention and to present these as a daily spoilage report for each area. The report is issued each morning for the previous day. Each of these reports, by area, is summarized on a weekly basis by type of unit and defect causing the rejection. Dollar values are then assigned, and a listing is made in order of dollar magnitude of spoilage with the highest cost items appearing at the top of the list. The part number rejected is shown as well as the final product in which the part appears. The week's scheduled production is shown in order that a relationship (see Exhibit 11–2) might be made as to the magnitude of the rejects. While a 'Percent Rejects to Week's Scheduled Production' might be useful for this purpose, it was decided that every additional column adds to the cost of the report and to the preparation time. The next to the last column shows the reject code, while the last column shows the dollar cost of the rejects that have been selected for emphasis. The total value of the items selected for presentation (representing 75 to 80 percent of the total reject value) is shown in the exhibit as $2477.26. This figure is also shown on an annualized basis to emphasize the magnitude. This year's annualized total is compared with the same figure for the previous year.

"The report is closed out at the close of business on Tuesday and issued Wednesday morning, at which time a meeting of the quality control representative and production foremen discuss the causes of spoilage and remedies to correct the problems. When appropriate, representatives of the other disciplines are called in. If a machine is suspect, the maintenance head would be a party to the discussion. If the quality of the material is being questioned, the purchasing agent would be asked to sit in."

This type of reporting was adopted for all production areas in the ETT Company. The weekly meetings, which were attended by the plant manager as well as the regular participants, proved to be highly effective. In the first three months, the annualized total value of rejects was reduced by more than one-third.

PART #	USED ON PRODUCT NO.	WEEK'S SCHEDULED PRODUCTION	NO. OF REJECTS	TYPE OF DEFECT	TOTAL COST
603	78396	300	19	116	$ 625.38
301	69842	150	9	43	531.52
673	39461	75	8	52	503.61
498	21312	890	150	14	342.16
306	14398	250	14	16	221.03
403	31982	600	32	6	114.32
106	21699	300	25	55	98.14
198	4443	250	8	62	41.10
					$2,477.26

This week's annualized total $123,863.00
Prior week's annualized total $114,132.75

**EXHIBIT 11–2:
SAMPLE WEEKLY SPOILAGE REPORT**

Industrial Engineering (Manufacturing Engineering)

Industrial engineers, in their work in establishing the operational sequences through which a product passes, are in a position to make changes to accommodate the introduction of a new process or a new machine. Through such changes, savings can often be made. In one company in which there were no changes in the method of manufacture, an industrial engineer noticed that a steel product went through a heading machine, then degreasing, threading, and another degreasing operation before drilling a hole to complete the part: Although this had been a standard procedure for years, the industrial engineer could see no reason for degreasing between the heading and threading operations. His recommendation for eliminating the first degreasing operation was adopted.

This department is usually responsible for making recommendations with regard to the tooling design. If the quantity of production justifies it, the company can save money in metal stamping through use of a sectional die. This permits replacement of individual parts of the die with a minimum of maintenance time.

In the case of molding, volume of production of a particular part will determine the optimum number of cavities.

Purchasing

The responsibility of the purchasing department to obtain the lowest possible prices can be affected by the lead time allowed in fulfilling the customer's order. If the allowed lead time is too short, it may be necessary to obtain the required material by expensive air freight. In providing prices on the request for quotation, the purchasing department should point out whether the lead time provided by the quotation request is sufficient for making economical purchases. If not, the quotation should indicate the extra cost due to air freight.

The various buyers are in a position to suggest which parts might be standardized to reduce the number of similar items in stock. This must be done in concert with the engineering department. The purchasing department head in one company discovered that different engineers making up the parts lists for various products favored certain brands of components, small motors for example. A check with the stockroom showed that there were four different brands of motors in stock. When this was pointed out to the plant manager, he asked the stockroom supervisor to make up a list of the various products that were stocked in more than one brand. When the list was completed, a review was made with the engineering department with the recommendation that the number of different brands be reduced to a minimum. When the work was completed, the stockroom supervisor estimated that sixty-five feet of shelf space would be made available by elimination of multibrand stocking.

Personnel

Although the personnel department establishes the rate of pay to be paid for the various labor grades in the GJ Company, there was a practice of moving employees around in a manner that resulted in higher rated employees being assigned to lower rated jobs. When the personnel manager became aware of this, he calculated the amount of excess labor payments resulting from these violations of labor rate schedules. The total excess dollars paid was approximately $100 on the day the test was made. At this rate, the total excess cost could reach $25,000 for a year or one-fourth of the total profit in the preceding year.

Cost Accounting

The manner in which overhead rates are established can be quite important in product costing (cost estimating). Chapter 9 discusses the development of such rates, and the effect on the rates of arbitrariness in allocating overhead to the various production centers.

The same principle applies in the provision for production losses. The percentage allowance for such losses cannot be made on an arbitrary, across-the-board basis. Actual departmental differences must be taken into account to avoid undercosting one product and overcosting another.

ASSIGNMENT OF PRIORITIES AND DEGREE OF DETAIL IN QUOTING

The assignment of priorities may sometimes be influenced by the amount of detail required in preparing the cost estimate, but this is not always the case.

Assignment of Priorities

The sequence in which requests for quotation are received is not necessarily the sequence in which machine time becomes available. If the company has a large amount of available capacity in one particular area, it would make sense to assign a high priority to those quotations that would fill up this capacity. When this recommendation was made, the plant manager's response was a loud "amen." He then went on to explain that at his previous company, requests for quotation were prepared on a "first-come-first-served" basis because this was the policy established and followed by the cost estimators.

High priority should also be given to those quotations that are relatively simple and do not require much time to prepare. These would not require much detailed analysis because they are similar to another product or can be slotted into an existing family of products.

Degree of Detail Required in Quoting Will Also Influence Priorities

Reference was made above to quotations that do not require much time and would therefore be disposed of quickly. Quotations of this type would fall under the following two categories:

• Those that change in cost because of a predominant cost ingredient.

• Those that can be slotted into an existing family of similar products.

Quotations That Change in Cost Because of Changes in Magnitude of a Major Cost Ingredient. Material is an example of a major cost ingredient that could change because of such factors as length or weight. The brass used in making the tire valve stem, referred to in Exhibit 8–2 (page 146), is a good example. Two of these stems are shown in Exhibit 11–3. The brass required in making these two is heavier for the one shown on the right. However, the cut off and head, thread rolling, heading and degreasing take exactly the same time for both sizes.

The costing of the new stem would be quite simple because the material cost will be related to its weight while the other manufacturing costs would be the same as the other stem. Obviously, the costs used for the quotation must consider the material costs per pound and the manufacturing costs at the time that the order is to be produced.

Because of the relatively simple process involved in costing this product, the quotation can be disposed of quickly—it should not be placed at the bottom of a pile

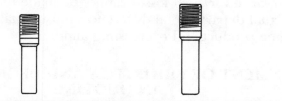

MATERIAL REQUIREMENTS ARE DIFFERENT BUT FABRICATING TIME IS THE SAME
FOR BOTH BECAUSE THE SAME SET-UP IS USED

EXHIBIT 11–3:
TWO TIRE VALVE STEMS

of other quotations that will require a substantial amount of detailed calculations and consultation with the various department heads.

In other products, material could be a constant cost because of similarity in size while such operations as drilling and tapping could vary because a different number of holes are required.

Those That Can Be Slotted into an Existing Family of Similar Products.

Exhibit 11–4 illustrates how three new products have been slotted into an existing family of products.

This exhibit shows the costs of seven battery sockets of a "family." Four types have been in the line for some time, but three types, 43-2424, 43-2425, and 45-2507, are variations of the existing types for which selling prices must be established.

MATERIAL	2 CONTACTS		3 CONTACTS		4 CONTACTS		5 CONTACTS
Top Plate	42-2511	42-2440	43-2424	43-2425	44-2467	44-2447	45-2507
12-2524 1/32 XP	3.60						
12-2466 1/16 XP		3.74					
12-2448 1/16 XP			5.62				
12-2460 1/32 XP				5.62			
12-2440 1/32 XP					7.50		
12-2423 1/32 XP						7.50	
12-2412 1/32 XP							9.37
Bottom Plate							
13-2524 1/16 XP	4.00						
13-2466 3/64 XP		4.24					
13-2448 3/64 XP			6.37				
13-2460 3/64 XP				6.37			
13-2440 3/64 XP					8.50		
13-2423 3/64 XP						8.50	
13-2412 3/64 XP							10.62
Contacts							
10-431	2.00	2.00					
10-562			3.00				
10-567				3.00			
10-632					4.00	4.00	
10-626							5.00
Eyelets							
46	.60	.60	.60	.60			
48					.70	.70	.70
Total component cost	$10.20	$10.58	$15.59	$15.59	$20.70	$20.70	$25.69
Assembly labor and overhead	2.00	2.00	2.20	2.20	2.40	2.40	2.40
Spoilage allowance	.24	.25	.36	.36	.46	.46	.56
Total cost	$12.44	$12.83	$18.15	$18.15	$23.56	$23.56	$28.65
Selling price	15.75	16.00	24.00*	24.00*	31.00	31.00	38.75*
% cost to selling price	79%	80%	76%*	76%*	76%	76%	74%*

*New types

NOTE: Selling prices rounded off to nearest $0.25

EXHIBIT 11–4:
SLOTTING NEW PRODUCTS INTO A FAMILY OF SIMILAR PRODUCTS

All costs are based on optimum volume and optimum efficiencies, therefore they represent costs which are competitive. To arrive at selling prices for the three new types, the percentage of cost to selling price was first calculated for the existing types. This percentage showed that the high volume sellers which were in great demand had a 79% and 80% ratio of cost to selling price while the lower volume 4-contact socket, which required a large investment in equipment and inventories per unit, had a 76% ratio.

This indicated that the market would allow only 79% to 80% of the selling price to cover manufacturing costs when the item was in general demand and sold in large volume. However, in the case of the 4-contact socket, which is not manufactured in large volume runs, as are the other types, the price recognizes that the higher investment per unit must be repaid through a higher selling price, as evidenced by the fact that costs consume only 76% of the sales dollar in the two 4-contact sockets compared with 79% and 80% for the 2-contact sockets.

In determining the selling prices for the three new types, an evaluation would first be made of investment requirements and potential volume of these types.

In the case of 43-2424 and 43-2425 it was felt that the 76% ratio which applies to the 44-2467 and 44-2447 should apply to these; the potential volume and investment requirements being about the same. The 76% was then divided into the cost of $18.15 to arrive at a selling price of $24.00 per thousand. For the 45-2507 the anticipated industry volume was somewhat lower than any of the other sockets because the number of applications for this socket were fewer. Volume would be lower and investment would therefore be higher per unit than for any of the others. While a 72% or 73% ratio would have been desirable, this would have resulted in a selling price which would have exceeded the selling price of a 2-contact plus a 3-contact socket. Therefore, a 74% ratio was chosen.

Exhibit 11–5 illustrates how another company adjusted the costs of one product to a related product without rebuilding the new cost estimate from the ground up. Column 1 shows the costs of a seven-contact molded socket of the type used in electronic equipment. Column 2 shows no change in material costs because the same molded socket used for a seven-contact socket is used for the five-contact version. In the five-contact socket, two of the seven holes are left intact. The assembly costs and purchased components in column 2 are adjusted to subtract the costs relating to the two contacts that are omitted. Column 3 makes the adjustments for cost changes due to material and other price changes. Column 4 shows the estimated cost of the five-contact exclusive of the saddle which was also omitted.

This chapter discussed the broad procedures in cost estimating to assure that proper procedures and responsibilities have been enumerated. It also discussed the importance of a pragmatic approach toward cost estimating in which requests for quotation were properly screened and the simplified types of estimates were properly expedited rather than piling up a large reservoir of quotations to be handled in the same sequence as they were received.

We will discuss next the more detailed types of cost estimates.

Components	ESTIMATED COST OF 7-CONTACT MOLDED SOCKET (1)	ADJUSTMENT TO ARRIVE AT COST OF 5-CONTACT MOLDED SOCKET W/O SADDLE (2)	ADJUSTMENTS FOR PRICE CHANGES (3)	TOTAL ESTIMATED COST OF 5-CONTACT SOCKET W/O SADDLE (4)
Material	$ 2.42	$ 0	$ .12	$ 2.54
Processing	13.52	0	0	13.52
Spoilage allowance	.32	0	0	.32
	$16.26	$ 0	$ .12	$16.38
Assembly Costs Plus Purchased Components				
Purchased contacts	14.00	(4.00)	.50	10.50
Purchased saddle	3.00	(3.00)	0	0
Assembly operation	5.35	(.62)	0	4.73
Spoilage in assembly	.39	(.10)	.02	.31
	22.74	(7.72)	.52	15.54
MANUFACTURING COST	$39.00	$(7.72)	$ .64	$31.92
CUMULATIVE COST	$39.00	$31.28	$31.92	$31.92

EXHIBIT 11–5:
ADJUSTING THE COST OF A SEVEN-CONTACT SOCKET TO DETERMINE THE COST OF A FIVE-CONTACT SOCKET

12

Detailed Methods of Cost Estimating

In the discussion of priority assignment to incoming quotation requests in the preceding chapter, a recommendation was made to assign a high priority to those requests that could be prepared expeditiously by making a comparison with a closely related product. It is only natural for a customer to expect faster action when the quotation request covers a product within an existing family.

This chapter will discuss the more detailed methods of product costing and pricing that cannot readily be prepared by making comparisons with other similar products. These include:

- Conventional methods of product costing and pricing
- The return-on-investment method
- The marginal contribution method
- Allocating corporate expenses

CONVENTIONAL METHODS OF PRODUCT COST ESTIMATING AND PRICING

The tire valve stem, one of the products discussed in Chapter 3, is illustrative of the conventional build-up of costs by operation to arrive at total manufacturing cost. Exhibit 3–3 (page 63) illustrates this product build-up graphically. Exhibit 3–4 (page 65) traces the manufacturing processes on the factory floor layout. Exhibits 3–5 and 3–6 (pages 67 and 68) illustrate the cost build-up in an indented bill of material format. Exhibit 12–1 summarizes the cost build-up in the same format as the physical product build-up is shown in Exhibit 3–3.

The manufacturing cost shown at the top of Exhibit 12–1 (see arrow) shows the total material cost, total direct labor, and total overhead cost required per 1000 brass stems used for completed tire valve stems. Each of these three elements of cost is "pure." This means that the material represents only the pure material (and purchased components) entering into the product. The direct labor and overhead are likewise pure, without combining the three elements at one level and carrying them forward as material in the next level (see Exhibit 12–2).

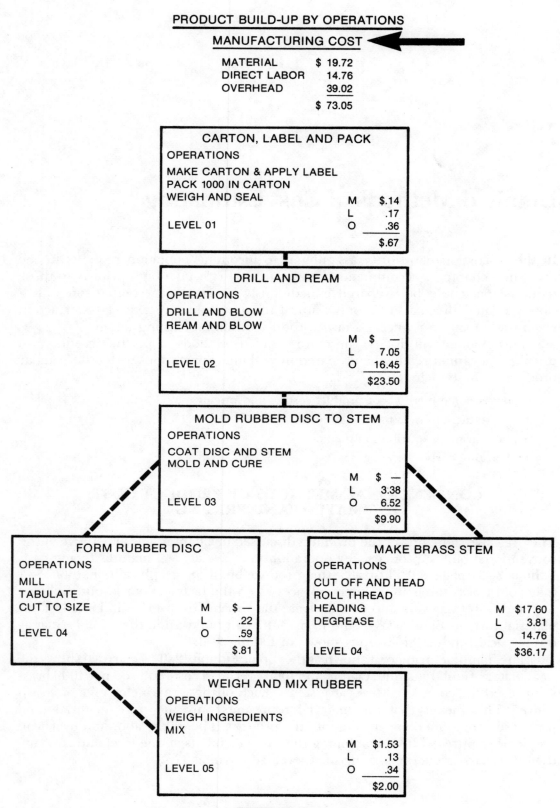

PRODUCT BUILD-UP BY OPERATIONS

MANUFACTURING COST

MATERIAL	$ 19.72
DIRECT LABOR	14.76
OVERHEAD	39.02
	$ 73.05

CARTON, LABEL AND PACK

OPERATIONS

MAKE CARTON & APPLY LABEL
PACK 1000 IN CARTON
WEIGH AND SEAL

LEVEL 01

M	$.14
L	.17
O	.36
	$.67

DRILL AND REAM

OPERATIONS

DRILL AND BLOW
REAM AND BLOW

LEVEL 02

M	$ —
L	7.05
O	16.45
	$23.50

MOLD RUBBER DISC TO STEM

OPERATIONS

COAT DISC AND STEM
MOLD AND CURE

LEVEL 03

M	$ —
L	3.38
O	6.52
	$9.90

FORM RUBBER DISC

OPERATIONS

MILL
TABULATE
CUT TO SIZE

LEVEL 04

M	$ —
L	.22
O	.59
	$.81

MAKE BRASS STEM

OPERATIONS

CUT OFF AND HEAD
ROLL THREAD
HEADING
DEGREASE

LEVEL 04

M	$17.60
L	3.81
O	14.76
	$36.17

WEIGH AND MIX RUBBER

OPERATIONS

WEIGH INGREDIENTS
MIX

LEVEL 05

M	$1.53
L	.13
O	.34
	$2.00

**EXHIBIT 12–1:
PRODUCT BUILD-UP BY OPERATIONS**

LEVEL	PROCESS	MATERIAL	DIRECT LABOR	OVERHEAD	TOTAL
05	Weigh and mix rubber	$ 1.53	.13	.34	2.00
04	Form rubber disc	–	.22	.59	.81
04	Make brass stem	17.60	3.81	14.76	36.17
03	Mold rubber disc to stem	–	3.38	6.52	9.90
02	Drill and ream	–	7.05	16.45	23.50
01	Carton, label, and pack	.14	.17	.36	.67
	TOTAL	$19.27	14.76	39.02	73.05

EXHIBIT 12–2:
MAINTAINING PURITY OF THE THREE ELEMENTS OF COST THROUGHOUT THE MANUFACTURING PROCESS—Cost per 1000

LEVEL	COST ELEMENT	COST	MANUFACTURING OPERATIONS
05	Material	$ 1.53	Ingredients for rubber
	Direct labor	.13	
	Overhead	.34	Weigh and mix ingredients
		$ 2.00	Completed Rubber Cost
04	Material	$ 2.00	Rubber transferred from level 5
	Direct labor	.22	Mill, tubulate and cut to size
	Overhead	.59	
		$ 2.81	Completed Rubber Disc
04	Material	$17.60	Brass rod
	Direct labor	3.81	Cut off and head, roll thread heading, and degreasing
	Overhead	14.76	
		$36.17	Completed Brass Stem
03	Material	$38.98	Rubber disc and brass stem from level 04
	Direct labor	3.38	
	Overhead	6.52	Coat disc and stem; mold and cure
		$48.88	Rubber Disc Molded to Brass Stem
02	Material	$48.88	Rubber disc molded to brass stem from level 03
	Direct labor	7.05	
	Overhead	16.45	Drill and blow: ream and blow
		$72.38	Completed Stem
01	Material	$72.52*	Completed stem plus carton plus label
	Direct labor	.17	Pack 1000 in carton, weigh, and seal
	Overhead	.36	
		$73.05	MANUFACTURING COST PER 1000

*$72.52 made up of $72.38 (total cost of completed stem plus $.14 for the carton and label)

EXHIBIT 12–3:
COMBINING THE THREE ELEMENTS OF MANUFACTURING COST AT EACH LEVEL AND CARRYING THEM FORWARD AS MATERIAL AT THE SUCCEEDING LEVELS—Cost per 1000

	MAINTAINING PURITY OF THE THREE ELEMENTS OF COST THROUGHOUT THE OPERATIONS	COMBINING THE THREE ELEMENTS AT EACH LEVEL AND CARRYING TOTAL TO NEXT LEVEL AS MATERIAL COST
Cost Estimating	Mechanics of cost estimating simplified, particularly when attempting to fit a new product into an existing family.	Material classification at each succeeding level is a mixture of material, direct labor, and overhead.
Inventory	Total material, direct labor, and overhead content of the inventory readily available. When overhead rates are broken down by variable and fixed portions, further analysis is facilitated.	Cumulative costing at each level simplifies the valuation of the various components and subassemblies in the work-in-process inventory.
Product Profitability Analysis	Facilitates product profitability analyses because magnitude of each element of cost can be readily associated with the individual products.	Requires "unbundling" of cost accumulations classified as material to identify the various cost elements.

EXHIBIT 12–3(A)
COMPARISON OF TWO METHODS OF ACCUMULATING MANUFACTURING COSTS THROUGH THE MANUFACTURING OPERATIONS

Exhibit 12–3 illustrates how the figures in Exhibit 12–2 are often recast to build up the cost cumulatively by combining the three elements of cost transferred to each succeeding level. The material, direct labor, and overhead for mixing the rubber ingredients, for example, is combined into a single figure and classified as material at the next level. This procedure is followed successively through all the levels.

A comparison of the methods illustrated in Exhibits 12–2 and 12–3 and their impact on cost estimating, updating of cost files, inventory valuation, and product profitability analyses is seen in Exhibit 12–3(A).

Cost estimates rarely follow either one or the other formats exclusively; variations of both are used. The next two examples will deal with two levels, fabrication and assembly. The first will relate to a seven-contact molded socket with metal saddle which is used in electronic applications. The second will deal with the manufacture of a plastic cosmetic case.

Seven-Contact Molded Socket with Metal Saddle

Column 1 in Exhibit 11–5 showed the various costs of the seven-contact molded socket. These costs were used to make adjustments for arriving at an estimated cost of a five-contact molded socket without the metal saddle. The original cost estimate from which the figures in column 1 were taken is shown in Exhibit 12–4. This exhibit shows the manufacturing detail which was used as the basis for costing. Under the material category, the number of pounds per 1000 sockets and material cost are shown. Such other factors as cycle time, number of cavities in the mold and assembly rates are also included. Note that the elements of manufacturing cost for molding and for assembly are shown separately. Labor and overhead, however, are combined in a single figure because molding is an automated operation with labor and overhead built into a common rate that is applied to machine hours. The same cost element separation is followed for the assembly operation. The completed cost of the molded socket bodies is then transferred to the next level of manufacturing—the principle followed in Exhibit 12–3.

Material required	5.5#
Material cost	$0.44 per pound
Curing cycle	90 seconds
Number of cavities	30

Cost of Molded Body

	COST PER 1000
Material	
5.5# powder @ $0.44	$ 2.42
Labor and Overhead	
Cycle time of 90 sec. = 40 cycles/hr.	
40 cycles x 30 cavities =	
1200 socket bodies per hour	
1200 socket bodies @ press rate of $16.22/hr.	13.52
Other	
2% allowance for spoilage	.32
Total cost per 1000 socket bodies	$16.26

Cost of the Assembled Socket

	COST PER 1000
Material	
1 Molded body	$16.26
1 Saddle	3.00
7 Contacts	14.00
Labor and Overhead	
2000 assembled per hour @ 10.71/hr.	5.35
Other	
1% allowance for spoilage	.39
Total cost per 1000 completed sockets	$39.00

EXHIBIT 12–4:
MANUFACTURING COST OF SEVEN-CONTACT MOLDED SOCKET WITH SADDLE

Plastic Cosmetic Case

Exhibit 12–5 illustrates a cost estimate for manufacture of plastic cosmetic cases. Note that this format combines the features shown in Exhibit 12–2 as well as in Exhibit 12–3. The costs of the molded top and bottom are transferred to assembly individually. The horizontal columns show the breakdown of the three elements of cost for each of the components and assembly operations. Note, however, that labor and burden (overhead) are combined in those operations in which machine hours are used (molding) as a base for allocating labor and overhead. The last line shows the total cost by element. Also shown at the lower right is the calculation of the selling price per 500. (Costs are calculated on a per 1000 basis.)

Many Cost Estimate Format Variations

There are probably as many variations in the formats used for cost estimating as there are companies. Exhibits 12–6, 12–7, and 12–8 are blank forms showing three more formats.

Use of a single percentage markup divider

The conventional method of marking up products to arrive at desired selling prices is to divide the manufacturing cost by a percentage divider which provides for the Selling, G&A and profit allowance. There are two potential deficiencies in the use of this single percentage divider.

- The single divider percentage assumes that Sales, G&A and profit allowances maintain a constant ratio to manufacturing costs in all products.
- The single divider percentage does not recognize the differences in amount of investment required for the products in the line.

The deficiencies inherent in the single markup percentage can be illustrated by the experience of Apex, Inc. (name disguised).

CASE EXAMPLE

Selling Expenses

This company manufactured copying machines and the sensitized paper used in these machines. In discussing sales expenses with the sales manager, it was learned that the copiers were sold by a different group of salesmen than the paper and other supplies. Since the average order for the copiers is substantially greater in dollar value than the average order for paper and supplies, the percentage of sales expense for copiers will be substantially smaller than the percentage applicable to the paper and supplies. The use of a single average percentage would overstate the sales expense applicable to copiers and understate the amount applicable to paper and supplies.

General & Administrative Expenses

The study of G&A revealed that it contained a fairly large amount of Research and Development cost. Since this could be identified by the two product categories, separate percentages should be developed for the two categories based on a study of past R&D project costs. This recommendation was adopted and implemented.

After removing the R&D expenses from the G&A, the smaller balance that was left proved to be allocable to the two products at the same ratio as the sales expenses.

Profit Allowance

Since the investment required in the manufacture of copiers was different from the investment required for sensitizing paper, an analysis was made of the level of investment required for both products. Net fixed assets and inventory represented about 90 percent of the investment directly related to manufacturing. These two items were used in the analysis (Table 12–1).

	Total (in Millions)	Copiers (in Millions)	Sensitized Papers (in Millions)
Net fixed assets	$70	$45	$25
Inventory	35	20	15
Total	$105	$65	$40
Desired return*	13%	15%	10%
Desired profit (in millions)	$13.8	$9.8	$4

*Desired return based on competitive market factors. Figures and percentages have been rounded.

TABLE 12–1

Apex is illustrative of a company in which a single markup percentage divider would distort the resulting selling price because of the disparate nature of the two categories of products. This may not be the case in all companies. If there is any question, a test similar to the foregoing should be made.

RETURN-ON-INVESTMENT PRICING

Many small companies have for years determined the selling prices of their products by doubling the prime cost (material plus direct labor). This practice started early in the industrial revolution when investment in equipment and inventory was inconsequential. A retired entrepreneur, now serving on the board of directors of one of the companies being surveyed, recounted his experience as the owner of a fountain pen factory in the 1930s.

> The fountain pens of those days were made of hard rubber with a rubber sac which held the ink. We purchased the parts from fabricators and assembled them. The operation was quite simple—principally bench work and the necessary fixtures used in assembly. Our major costs were material (all purchased parts) and direct labor. Overhead was minor because the operations were simple and the products were quite homogeneous. We didn't need departmental overhead rates—just one rate for the whole plant. Our pricing was equally simple. We simply doubled the cost of the finished pen. This took care of manufacturing costs, selling, administrative office expenses, and profit.

In modern-day manufacturing the investment in manufacturing facilities is more substantial, the two major items being fixed assets and inventory.

Effective Jan. 1, XX

Quantity—1,000
(500 per case)

MATERIALS OR OPERATION DESCRIPTION	CODE NUMBER	QUANTITY SPECIFIED	% WASTE	STANDARD	UNIT OF MEASURE	MATERIAL RATE	MATERIAL COST	LABOR RATE	LABOR COST	BURDEN RATE	BURDEN COST	TOTAL COST
Top: Plastic	771	20.0	5	21.0000	Lb.	.134	2.81					2.81
Molding	38			.3768	Hr.					12.70	4.79	4.79
							2.81				4.79	7.60
Bottom: Plastic	771	21.0	5	22.0500	Lb.	.134	2.95					2.95
Molding	38			.4072	Hr.					12.70	5.17	5.17
							2.95				5.17	8.12
Issue to Assembly Floor:												
Molded plastic top	151	1,000	4	1,040	M	7.600	7.90*					7.90
Molded plastic bottom	152	1,000	4	1,040	M	8.120	8.44**					8.44
Carton (holds 500)	6	2	5	2.1000	Ea.	.268	.56					.56
Bag	18	50	5	52.5000	Ea.	.031	1.63					1.63
Crate	6	2	5	2.1000	Ea.	.162	.34					.34
Assemble and pack	64			1.0000	Hr.			2.58	2.58	6.32	6.32	8.90
							18.87		2.58		6.32	27.77
Transfer Value to Finished Goods	2131	1,000	1	1,010	M	27.77	28.06					28.06
							28.06					28.06
				Total Cost by Element			8.61		2.61		16.84	28.06

	$ PER CASE	%
Sales Price	17.35	100.0
Standard Cost	14.03	80.8
Gross Profit	3.32	19.2

*Molded top $7.60 plus 4% waste = $7.90
**Molded bottom $8.12 plus 4% waste = $8.44

**EXHIBIT 12–5:
PLASTIC COSMETIC CASES**

Standard Cost Data Sheet

	$/M	%
S/Price		100.0
Std. Cost		
G/P		

Product No. _____

Prepared By _____

Date _____

DESCRIPTION OF PRODUCT _____

$ — PER — M _____

MOLDING						MATERIAL	LABOR	BURDEN	TOTAL
RAW MATERIAL			COST	¢LB	REJECTS%				
PART WT.		SPRUE		TOTAL WT.					
MACHINE SIZE			CYCLES PER HR.		CAVITIES				
BURDEN RATE PER HR.			REJECT%		NET YIELD				
MOLD AMORTIZATION			MOLD #						
LABOR OPERATION #			# OF OPER.		NET YIELD				
LABOR RATE PER HR.			BURDEN RATE PER HR.						
TOTAL COST — PART NO.									

						MATERIAL	LABOR	BURDEN	TOTAL
RAW MATERIAL			COST	¢LB	REJECTS%				
PART WT.		SPRUE		TOTAL WT.					
MACHINE SIZE			CYCLES PER HR.		CAVITIES				
BURDEN RATE PER HR.			REJECT%		NET YIELD				
MOLD AMORTIZATION			MOLD #						
LABOR OPERATION #			# OF OPER.		NET YIELD				
LABOR RATE PER HR.			BURDEN RATE PER HR.						
TOTAL COST — PART NO.									

ASSEMBLY

OPER. NO.	LABOR RATE	BURDEN RATE	STD. PCS PER HR.	OFF STD. %	NET YIELD PER HR.	OTHER				
TOTAL LABOR & BURDEN IN ASSEMBLY										

OTHER – MATERIAL REQUIREMENTS

TYPE OF MATERIAL	DESC.	INV. A/C	PIECES PER UNIT	UNIT COST	ALLOW. %				
CARTON									
LINER									
UNIT PACK									
TOTAL OTHER MATERIAL									

TOTAL COST				

EXHIBIT 12–6:
STANDARD COST DATA SHEET (Format #1)

COMPRESSION MOLDING
ANALYSIS & STANDARD CARD

CUSTOMER

CUSTOMER NO.

QUANTITY QUOTE | EST. NO. | DATE

USED ON

PART DESCRIPTION

I. B. M. PART NO.

MATR. NO.

DRAWING SERIES

REV.

MATERIAL DATA

MATERIAL TYPE

MACHINE & MOLDING DATA

PILL WT. | PILLS LB. | CYCLE SEC. | MOLD TOP | TEMP. BOTTOM | PILL DIA.

PRODUCTION DATA

LBS/M POWDER | LBS/HR POWDER | PCS/ LB. | PCS/ HR. | ACTUAL PER.HR.

OTHER INFORMATION

NO. OF SETS / SET | CAV. / SET | PRESS TYPE | LAND AREA SQ. IN.

PACKAGING DATA

MISCELLANEOUS

CARTON NO. | NO/M

DIVIDER NO. | NO/M

PCS/BOX | NO/M

NET WT. | GROSS WT.

CRIB LOCATION

SECTION | SHELF

SPARE PART LOCATION

REMARKS

MISC. INFORMATION

INSPECTION PROCESS NO.

WT. FACTOR PAGE NO.

OTHER PARTS MADE

COST DATA

MATERIAL COST   # / M x $ _____ /M

PACKING

COMPONENT PARTS

DESCRIPTION | NO/M | PRICE/M

TOTAL MAT'L. COST

MACHINE COST _____ / HR. @ $ _____ / HR.

SECONDARY OPERATIONS

OPERATION | HRS/M | RATE

BURDEN ON SECONDARY OPERATIONS

MOLD MAINTENANCE

SHRINKAGE _____ %

TOTAL MANUFACTURING COST

MOLD AMORTIZATION

ACTUAL | EST.

SELLING PRICE _____ % DIVIDER

QUANTITY | PRICE/M

SETUP CHARGE

MINIMUM ORDER WITHOUT SETUP

TOOLING COST

DESIGN

MECHANICAL

OTHER

TOTAL

TOOL DELIVERY

ESTIMATED MOLD LIFE

1

2a | 2b

3a | 3b

REMARKS & OPERATIONAL SEQUENCE

PREPARED BY:

APPROVED BY:

EXHIBIT 12–7:
STANDARD COST DATA SHEET (Format #2)

PLASTICS ASSEMBLY STANDARDS

SHOP NO.		AMT. TO SCHELD.		CUSTOMER PART NO.		
	ORDER NO.			ISSUED BY:	APPROVED BY:	ESTIMATE NO.
DESCRIPTION OF PRODUCT			CUSTOMER		EFF. DATE	SUP. REV.

QUANTITY	STD. AMT.	PART NUMBER	AVAILABLE	STD. SHEET NO.	OPERATION	JOB CODE NO.	HRS/M ITEMS	HRS/M UNITS QUOTA	# OF OPR	MACH. HRS/M UNITS

SUB-ASSEMB.

MATERIAL COST

DESCRIPTION	PART NUMBER	NO/M	PRICE/M

SHRINKAGE_____%

TOTAL MATERIAL COST

LABOR AND/OR BURDEN

MACHINE BURDEN _____HRS. @ $_____/HRS.

_____HRS. @ $_____/HRS.

DIRECT LABOR _____HRS. @ $_____/HRS.

DIRECT LABOR BURDEN _____HRS. @ $_____/HRS.

SHRINKAGE_____%

TOTAL MANUFACTURING COST

AMORTIZATION/M

	ACTUAL	EST.
	$	$
	$	$
	$	$
	$	$

SELLING PRICE_____% DIVIDER

QUANTITY	PRICE/M

SETUP CHARGE $_____
MINIMUM ORDER WITHOUT SETUP

TOOLING COST

MOLDS	
DIES	
ASSEMBLY TOOLS	
TOTAL	$

TOOL DELIVERY _____

PACKAGING DATA

CARTON NO.	NO/M
DIVIDER NO.	NO/M
MISC. NO.	NO/M
PCS/BOX	
NET LBS.	GROSS WT.

REMARKS

EXHIBIT 12–8:
STANDARD COST DATA SHEET (Format #3)

241

In addition to representing the predominant segment of invested capital in the factory, these two asset groups can be fairly well pinpointed to the product line for which the investment was incurred. These are generally controllable by the factory manager since he is responsible for effective utilization of his facilities and proper turnover of inventory.

Calculating the Desired Return-on-Investment Markup on Manufacturing Cost

The controller of Tico company felt that the return-on-investment to be used in calculating the markup percentage should reflect the markup percentage at the gross profit level. (See Exhibit 12–9), Projected Income Statement. The selling prices, then, would not include marketing and administrative expenses—these would have to be added separately.

Step 1: Manufacturing-Related Investment

The two major investment items are shown in Exhibit 12–9(A). These were based on adjusted balance sheet figures—$1,100,000 for inventory and $1,210,000 for net fixed assets—adding up to $2,310,000. At a 40 percent return, this would yield a gross profit of $924,000. (See Projected Income Statement in Exhibit 12–9.)

Step 2: Breaking Down the Manufacturing-Related Investment

Since the markup percentage on material will be calculated separately for material and conversion cost, the investment must be broken down into these two parts. The inventory investment of $1,100,000 contains $860,000 of material and $240,000 in conversion costs. (Direct labor plus overhead.) The fixed assets, being part of overhead, are classified as conversion cost-related. The total investment of $2,310,000 then breaks down into a total of $860,000 as material-related and $1,450,000 as conversion-cost related. Applying the 40 percent to these two figures shows a gross profit of $344,000 on the material-related investment and $580,000 on the conversion-cost related—adding up to the $924,000 in the first column of Exhibit 12–9(A).

Step 3: Calculating the Return-on-Investment Markup

This calculation is shown in Exhibit 12–9(B). The markup percentage must take investment turns into account. This is accomplished as follows:

The estimated cost (column 1) of material and conversion cost are divided by the related investment for these two items (column 2). The estimated cost was taken from the cost of sales figures shown in Exhibit 12–9. The related investment for material and for conversion cost was taken from the investment breakdown columns in Exhibit 12–9(A). The division of column 1 by column 2 shows the number of turns of these items per year. The material turns are shown to be 4.0 times per year while the conversion cost turns amount to 1.6 turns per year. When the 4.0 turns are divided into the 40.0 percent desired return (shown in column 4), the markup percentage to be applied to the material content of the product is 10 percent (column 5). When the conversion cost turns per year of 1.6 times (column 3) is divided into the 40.0 percent, the indicated markup percentage for conversion costs is 25.0 percent. Column 6 might be called the "proof" column; it multiplies the material and conversion costs in column 1 by the markup percentages in column 5. When the two dollar figures are added, they show a total gross profit of $924,000, which is indicated in Exhibit 12–9.

Step 4: Calculating the Selling Price for Product B Using the Single Percentage Markup on Manufacturing Cost

This calculation is shown in the upper part of Exhibit 12–9(D). Conversion cost for product B is calculated by multiplying the hourly cost rates (shown in Exhibit 12–9C) by the hours per 1000 pieces required in the molding and finishing (assembly) departments. For molding, the hourly costing rate of $13.47 is multiplied by 0.45 hours to arrive at a manufacturing cost in that center of $6.06. The same is done for the finishing operation. The conversion costs add up to $15.16. When the material cost of $9.19 is added to the $15.16, the total manufacturing cost becomes $24.35. The $24.35 is then multiplied by the single markup percentage of 16 percent to arrive at a selling price of $28.25 (before addition of marketing and administrative expense).

Step 5: Calculating the Selling Price for Product B Using the Multiple Percentage Markup on Manufacturing Cost

The multiple percentage markup is shown in the lower portion of Exhibit 12–9(D). The manufacturing cost is shown in column 1. This figure ($24.35) is the same as used in calculating the manufacturing cost for the single percentage markup. In applying the markup, however, the 25 percent markup is applied to the conversion cost while 10 percent is applied to the material cost of $9.19. The selling price, shown in column 4, is now indicated as $29.06 (exclusive of marketing and administrative expenses). The $29.06 is $.81 more than the calculation made with a single percentage markup. The reason is that when the multiple percentage method is used, the higher conversion cost is multiplied by 25 percent while the smaller material cost is multiplied by 10 percent.

Step 6: Multiple versus Single Percentage Markup—Comparison of Three Products

The difference between the results when multiple percentage markups are used in lieu of the single percentage markup is demonstrated for three products in Exhibit 12–9(E). All three products have the same manufacturing cost—$24.35. However, the relationship of conversion cost to material cost is different for the three. In product A, conversion cost is 42 percent of manufacturing cost. In product B, it is 62 percent while in product C, the percentage drops to 28 percent. Since under the multiple percentage markup 25 percent is the factor applied to conversion cost, the larger the percentage of conversion cost in the product, the higher the selling price. This exhibit shows that under the single percentage markup all three products show the same selling price (exclusive of marketing and administrative expenses). Under the multiple markup method, the selling prices vary as shown on the last line of the exhibit.

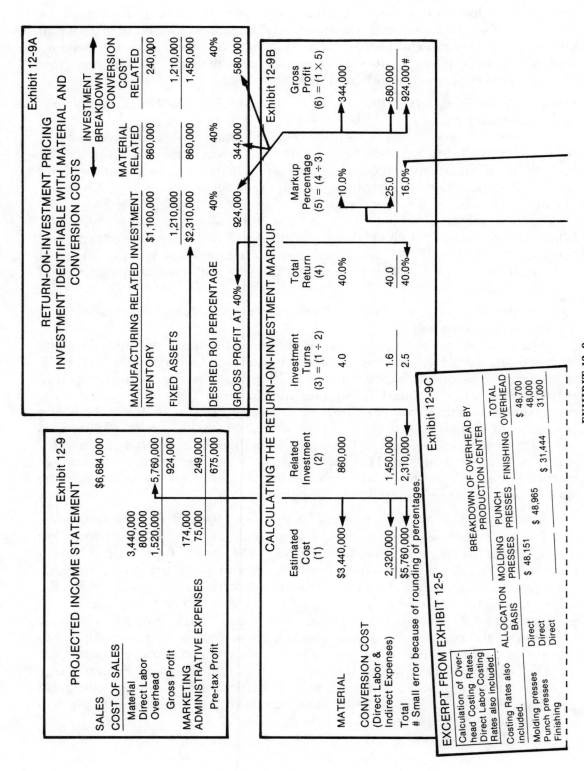

EXHIBIT 12–9:
STEPS IN DEVELOPMENT OF RETURN-ON-INVESTMENT PRICING

Exhibit 12-9D

RETURN-ON-INVESTMENT PRICING
SINGLE PERCENTAGE MARKUP ON TOTAL MANUFACTURING COST
PRODUCT B

	HOURLY COSTING RATE	HOURS PER 1000 PIECES	MFG. COST PER 1000 PIECES
Conversion cost:			
Molding	$13.47	.45	$ 6.06
Finishing (Assembly)	10.71	.85	9.10
Total Conversion Cost	—		$15.16
Total Material Cost	—	—	9.19
TOTAL MANUFACTURING COST			$24.35
Markup percentage	16%		
Markup amount			3.90
SELLING PRICE (PRODUCT B)			$28.25

RETURN-ON-INVESTMENT PRICING
MULTIPLE PERCENTAGE MARKUP
PRODUCT B

	MANUFAC-TURING COST (1)	MARKUP % (2)	MARKUP DOLLARS (3) = (1 × 2)	SELLING PRICE (4) = (1 + 3)
Conversion cost	$15.16	25%	$ 3.79	$ 18.95
Material	9.19	10%	.92	10.11
TOTAL	$24.35			$ 29.06

MARKETING AND ADMINISTRATIVE EXPENSES MUST BE ADDED TO SELLING PRICES SHOWN IN EXHIBITS 12-9D and 12-9E

Total Indirect Labor—Production Departments		48,151	48,965	31,444	128,00
General manager's staff	1/3 each	16,977	16,977	16,978	50,0
Personnel	Total xxxx	13,600	9,550	11,070	00,0
Computer services	Analysis	1,050	1,050	1,400	
Rental of (computer) equipment	Analysis	3,180	3,180	4,240	
Travel expenses	Analysis	4,190	4,190	4,320	
All other office expenses	1/3 each	1,917	1,917	1,916	
Total Office Expenses		10,337	10,337	11,876	
		$651,692	$427,514	$420,650	$100,
Total Overhead		60,800	49,900	65,100	
Total Hours					
Overhead costing rates		10.72	8.56	6.46	
Direct labor costing rate		2.75	3.14	4.25	
TOTAL COSTING RATE PER HOUR		$13.47	$11.70	$10.71	

Exhibit 12-9E

RETURN-ON-INVESTMENT PRICING
MULTIPLE VERSUS SINGLE PERCENTAGE MARKUP
COMPARISON OF THREE PRODUCTS

	PRODUCT A	PRODUCT B	PRODUCT C
SINGLE PERCENTAGE MARKUP			
Total Manufacturing Cost	$24.35	24.35	24.35
Single Percentage markup @ 16%	3.90	3.90	3.90
SELLING PRICE	$28.25	28.25	28.25
MULTIPLE PERCENTAGE MARKUP			
Conversion Cost	10.25	15.16	6.75
Material Cost	14.10	9.19	17.60
Total Manufacturing Cost	$24.35	24.35	24.35
Material markup @ 10%	1.41	.92	1.76
Conversion Cost markup @ 25%	2.56	3.79	1.69
SELLING PRICE	$28.32	29.06	27.80

EXHIBIT 12-9, continued

Conventional versus Return-on-Investment Pricing

Probably the vast majority of companies use the conventional method of marking up manufacturing costs with a single percentage divider applied to cost. This method will give reasonable results (1) when the products and manufacturing processes are reasonably homogeneous (2) if all products require approximately the same fabricating time on similar equipment and (3) the type of material used is reasonably similar for all products. The test, boiled down, is how consistent a relationship is maintained between conversion costs and material. If the relationship between these two categories of costs for all products is reasonably similar, the use of a single markup percentage will provide reasonably good results.

If, however, some products require a small amount of material cost and a large conversion cost and others require a great deal of material cost and relatively little conversion effort, the return-on-investment method, which distinguishes between conversion cost markup and material markup, is mandatory. In using this method, the material costs must remain pure as illustrated in Exhibit 12–2. Material, labor, and overhead on one level of manufacture cannot be considered as material at the next higher level as illustrated in Exhibit 12–3.

Note in Exhibit 12–10 the three porcelain lampholders bearing catalog numbers 8693, 9882, and 9726C. The porcelain, which makes up the major portion of each of these three items is made of clay—an inexpensive material. The firing of this clay in the kiln, however, is a very high cost operation. The range of cost differences in converting the clay is fairly wide. Catalog number 8693 is a one-piece keyless base mounted fixture. Catalog number 9882 is only slightly larger, but there are two pieces that must be fired rather than one—thus adding additional kiln cost. Catalog number 9726C is substantially larger than either of the other two. In addition, there are two pieces, the smaller piece being roughly the same size as either of the other two. The greater amount of clay that must be fired adds substantially to the conversion cost, as compared with the other two. The use of the return-on-investment method of marking up the products will provide greater accuracy than the conventional method of using a single percentage markup on total manufacturing costs.

MARGINAL CONTRIBUTION PRICING

Up to this point, our discussion of product costing has been based on the full costing concept. The marginal contribution method is based on the direct costing concept (see Chapter 7). This method evaluates products not on the basis of their full cost but rather on the basis of how much each product contributes to fixed costs and profits. The cost computation is made by calculating the balance after deducting variable costs from the selling price to determine the contribution to fixed costs and profits.

NO. 8693

ONE-PIECE KEYLESS BASE MOUNTED

Unglazed porcelain body. Two threaded bushings for 8-32 screws spaced on 1-1/2 inch centers are assembled to base. Screw terminals set in deep well for ample wiring room. Mounting screws not furnished.

DIMENSIONS: Base 2-1/16″ O.D. x 1-7/8″ overall height.

660W — 250V

CAT. NO.	DESCRIPTION	STD. CTN./PKG.	WT. LBS.
8693	One-piece — Base mounted Lampholder	10/50	15

NO. 9882

TWO-PIECE KEYLESS SURFACE MOUNTED

White glazed porcelain base and ring. Well in bottom is 3/8 inch deep. Wire from rear or through side wire ways on side of base. Mounting holes spaced on 1-3/8 inch centers, through body. Can be mounted directly on metal surface. Two screws furnished.

DIMENSIONS: Base 2-5/16″ O.D. x 1-1/8″ H. Glazed Ring 3/4″ H.

660W — 250V

CAT. NO.	DESCRIPTION	STD. CTN./PKG.	WT. LBS.
9882	Surface mounted Lampholder	10/100	36

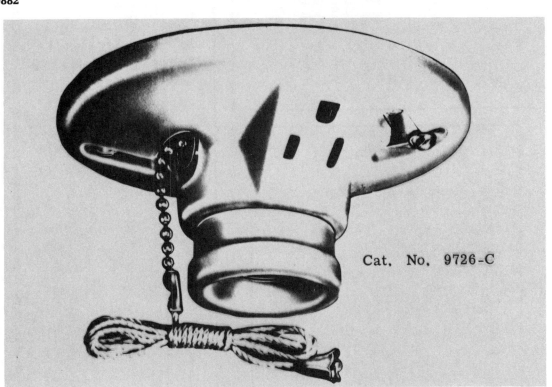

Cat. No. 9726-C

EXHIBIT 12–10:
THREE TYPES OF LAMPHOLDERS
Used with permission of Leviton Manufacturing Co., Little Neck, N.Y.

247

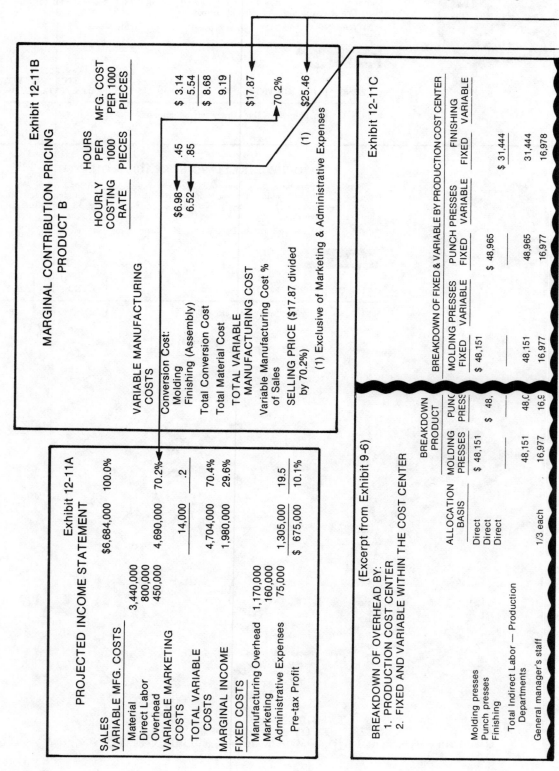

Exhibit 12-11A

PROJECTED INCOME STATEMENT

SALES		$6,684,000	100.0%
VARIABLE MFG. COSTS			
Material	3,440,000		
Direct Labor	800,000		
Overhead	450,000	4,690,000	70.2%
VARIABLE MARKETING			
COSTS		14,000	.2
TOTAL VARIABLE			
COSTS		4,704,000	70.4%
MARGINAL INCOME		1,980,000	29.6%
FIXED COSTS			
Manufacturing Overhead	1,170,000		
Marketing	160,000		
Administrative Expenses	75,000	1,305,000	19.5
Pre-tax Profit		$ 675,000	10.1%

Exhibit 12-11B

MARGINAL CONTRIBUTION PRICING
PRODUCT B

	HOURLY COSTING RATE	HOURS PER 1000 PIECES	MFG. COST PER 1000 PIECES
VARIABLE MANUFACTURING COSTS			
Conversion Cost:			
Molding	$6.98	.45	$ 3.14
Finishing (Assembly)	6.52	.85	5.54
Total Conversion Cost			$ 8.68
Total Material Cost			9.19
TOTAL VARIABLE MANUFACTURING COST			$17.87
Variable Manufacturing Cost % of Sales			70.2%
SELLING PRICE ($17.87 divided by 70.2%) (1)			$25.46

(1) Exclusive of Marketing & Administrative Expenses

Exhibit 12-11C

BREAKDOWN OF FIXED & VARIABLE BY PRODUCTION COST CENTER

	MOLDING PRESSES FIXED	MOLDING PRESSES VARIABLE	PUNCH PRESSES FIXED	PUNCH PRESSES VARIABLE	FINISHING FIXED	FINISHING VARIABLE
	$ 48,151		$ 48,965		$ 31,444	
	48,151		48,965		31,444	
	16,977		16,977		16,978	

BREAKDOWN OF OVERHEAD BY:
1. PRODUCTION COST CENTER
2. FIXED AND VARIABLE WITHIN THE COST CENTER

(Excerpt from Exhibit 9-6)

	ALLOCATION BASIS	MOLDING PRESSES	PUNCH PRESSES
		BREAKDOWN PRODUCT	
Molding presses	Direct	$ 48,151	$ 48,
Punch presses	Direct		48,0
Finishing	Direct		16,9
Total Indirect Labor — Production Departments		48,151	
General manager's staff	1/3 each	16,977	

EXHIBIT 12–11:

STEPS IN DEVELOPING MARGINAL CONTRIBUTING PRICING

	D. L. empl.						
All other supplies		14,665	12,0	14,665	9,855	12,570	14,665
Total Supplies And Mold Costs		101,003	44,0	81,293		34,155	17,950
Computer services	Analysis	1,050	1,0	1,050	1,050	1,050	1,400
Rental of (computer) equipment	Analysis	3,180	3,1	3,180	3,180	3,180	4,240
Travel expenses	Analysis	4,190	4,1	4,190	4,190	4,190	4,320
All other office expenses	1/3 each	1,917	1,9	1,917	1,917	1,917	1,916
Total Office Expenses		10,337	10,3	10,337	10,337		11,876
Total Overhead		$651,692	$427,5	$257,272	$284,771	$142,743	$272,926	$147,724
Total Hours		60,800	49,9	60,800	49,900	49,900	65,100	65,100
Overhead Costing Rates		10.72	8.0	4.23	5.70	2.86	4.19	2.27
Direct Labor Costing Rates		2.75	3.0	2.75	5.70	3.14	—	4.25
TOTAL COSTING RATE PER HOUR		$13.47	11.0	$6.98	5.70	6.00	4.19	6.52

Exhibit 12-11D

USING MARGINAL CONTRIBUTION
FOR PRICING VARIOUS ORDER SIZES

	------------------ORDER SIZES------------------		
	10,000	25,000	50,000
SELLING PRICE PER 1000 (1)	$39.71	29.78	25.46
VARIABLE MANUFACTURING COSTS PER 1000			
Conversion Cost:			
Molding	$ 3.14		
Finishing (Assembly)	5.54		
Total Conversion Cost	$ 8.68		
Total Material Cost	9.19		
TOTAL VARIABLE MANUFACTURING COSTS	$17.87	17.87	17.87
PROFIT CONTRIBUTION PER 1000	21.84	11.91	7.59
PROFIT CONTRIBUTION %	55.0%	40.0%	30.0% (2)

(1) Selling Prices exclude Marketing & Administrative Expenses
(2) Rounded

EXHIBIT 12–11, continued

Exhibits 12–11(A) through 12–11(C) show the steps in developing marginal contribution pricing. Exhibit 12–11(A) provides, through the same projected income statement as was used in Exhibit 12–9, the variable manufacturing costs. These amount to $4,690,000 for the year or 70.2 percent of projected sales. Although marketing expenses are included in the income statement, these were excluded for consistency in comparing marginal contribution pricing with return-on-investment pricing.

Step 1: Costing Product B (same product as used in ROI illustration)

The conversion cost includes molding and finishing (assembly). The hourly costing rate for molding is $6.98 per hour. This is made up of $4.23 per hour for variable overhead and $2.75 per hour for direct labor. One direct-labor operator operates two molding presses. His $5.50 rate of pay per hour therefore becomes $2.75 per machine hour.

The hourly costing rate for finishing is $6.52. This is made up of $2.27 per hour (labor hour) for variable overhead and $4.25 per hour for direct labor. The costing rates are shown in Exhibit 12–11(C). This exhibit has been excerpted from Chapter 9.

Multiplying the molding hourly costing rate of $6.98 by 0.45 hours indicates that the molding cost per 1000 pieces is $3.14. Multiplying the finishing hourly costing rate of $6.52 by 0.85 hours shows a finishing cost of $5.54. These two add up to a total of $8.68 conversion cost per 1000. Adding to this total, the $9.19 cost for material shows a total variable manufacturing cost of $17.87. To determine the selling price, (exclusive of marketing and administrative expenses) the total variable manufacturing cost of $17.87 is divided by the variable percentage of 70.2 percent referred to earlier. The resulting selling price is $25.46 per 1000 pieces. These figures are shown in Exhibit 12–11(B).

Step 2: Using Marginal Contribution for Pricing Various Order Sizes

Exhibit 12–11(C) shows how this company adjusts its selling prices for various order sizes. For product B, 50,000 and above represents the optimum-size order. Any quantity less than this would represent a loss because of set-up and start-up expenses. The price is increased to $29.78 for 25,000 and to $39.71 for quantities of 10,000. The profit contribution percentage for the 50,000 quantity is shown as 30 percent (actually 29.6 percent rounded). For the 25,000 quantity the contribution percentage rises to 40 percent and for 10,000 it rises to 55.0 percent. *Although these percentages appear to increase at a high rate, it must be remembered that set-up and start-up costs remain the same and must be absorbed over smaller quantities as the order size decreases.*

As in the case of the return-on-investment method, the three elements of manufacturing cost must remain pure throughout all levels of production, as demonstrated in Exhibit 12–2. The reason is the need to identify the expenses by their fixed and variable characteristics.

COMPARISON OF RETURN-ON-INVESTMENT WITH MARGINAL CONTRIBUTION PRICING

Comparisons of different methods of pricing are not necessarily conclusive because of differences in the assumptions that have been made. Although the same projected income statement figures were used, showing a pretax profit of 10.1 percent, the return-on-investment approach assumed a return that was not necessarily consistent with a pretax profit of 10.1 percent. This should be kept in mind when reviewing the comparisons shown in Exhibit 12–12 for product B.

Return-on-Investment

Selling price—Single percentage markup	$ 28.25
Selling price—Multiple percentage markup	$ 29.06

Marginal Contribution

Selling price	$ 25.46

Note: Selling Prices exclude Marketing & Administrative Expenses

EXHIBIT 12–12:
COMPARISON OF RETURN-ON-INVESTMENT WITH MARGINAL CONTRIBUTION PRICING

Although the two methods are not comparable in the amount of profit built into the price, the two figures in the Return-on-Investment section are based on similar profit assumptions. However, the prices for the single and multiple percentage markup application will differ from product to product depending on the relationship between the material and conversion cost content of the products. The return-on-investment (ROI) method should be seriously considered when there is a large variation in the material and conversion cost elements. The controller of one of the companies surveyed had the following comment to make regarding the ROI method.

"Even though the marketplace dictates the selling price, I like to know which of my products is more or less profitable than the competitive price. Then, I can make recommendations as to whether we should delete some of the unprofitable items from the line. If there is resistance by the marketing department, we can put pressure on Engineering to review the design or find some substitute materials that will lower the cost."

The executive vice-president of a candy manufacturing company had this to say about his controller's new marginal pricing system: "We recently purchased an automatic chocolate molding machine for making the Easter bunnies and Santa Clauses. This eliminated a large number of hand operations and, overall, reduced the cost of these products. I recall that my chief accountant came to me one day pointing out through his marginal pricing system that because variable costs of these products had dropped from 65 percent to only 15 percent of the selling price, we could drop our prices and increase volume because the marginal income (contribution to profit) had increased from 35 percent to 85 percent. He was quite embarrassed when I reminded him that the new molding equipment had required an investment of over $350,000. This is the point where I changed the pricing policy to the ROI method."

The president of another company making a brand product leaned toward the marginal contribution to profit method. The reason given was: "We recover all our fixed costs through sales of the brand product. It occurred to me that if we marketed the same product under a private brand, we would not expect to recover the same amount of fixed costs per unit as we do for our brand product. Naturally, our price would be lower for the private brand."

COST ESTIMATING METHODS	ADVANTAGES	DISADVANTAGES
Conventional Method (See Exhibits 12–4 and 12–5.) Exhibit 12–4 shows total manufacturing cost, as does Exhibit 12–5. However, the latter applies a markup percentage to total manufacturing cost to arrive at the selling price which includes selling and administrative expenses.	Cost buildup follows steps in the same sequence in which the product is manufactured. It shows the types of material, quantity required, and cost. Also shown are the manufacturing operations, cost of labor, and overhead and allowances for production losses.	Most companies apply the same markup percentage to material and conversion cost.
Return-on-Investment See Exhibits 12–9 through 12–9E. (These do not include selling and administrative expenses which are added separately.)	Manufacturing-related investments are identified as to those that relate to material and those that relate to conversion costs. Separate markup percentages are then applied to material and to conversion costs.	If some operations require high investment in equipment and others require a small investment, it may be necessary to develop a number of markup percentages to accommodate various combinations of operations on different products.
Marginal Contribution See Exhibits 12–11A through 12–11D. (These do not include selling and administrative expenses which are added separately.)	Availability of profit contribution percentages by products identifies individual product profitability. This can be useful in lowering the price of private brands when the brand products absorb their full measure of fixed costs.	Tends to depress selling prices because many companies use this method for the purpose of "shaving" fixed costs.

EXHIBIT 12–13:
KEY FEATURES OF THREE DETAILED METHODS OF COST ESTIMATING

Key Features of the Three Detailed Methods of Cost Estimating

The key features of the conventional method, return-on-investment and marginal contribution methods of cost estimating are summarized in Exhibit 12–13. The key features have been listed under "Advantages" and "Disadvantages."

ALLOCATING SELLING, ADMINISTRATIVE, AND OTHER CORPORATE EXPENSES

In estimating their costs and selling prices, many (probably most) companies provide for the corporate (and divisional) expenses in the markup factor applied to the product manufacturing cost. This approach, in which an all-encompassing markup percentage is applied, can result in inaccuracies. The reason is that there is a built-in assumption that these nonmanufacturing expenses are incurred in each product in direct proportion to the manufacturing cost.

During the years when the United States was the major producer of television sets, the executive vice-president of the television set division of a large electronics company cited the following case example in which corporate office allocations caused distortions in reported profits.

Case Example

Our company is made up of several divisions. My division produces television sets which contain purchased material amounting to 78 percent of total manufacturing cost. Our semiconductor division's proportion of material in its manufacturing costs is 43 percent. The metal parts division has a material content of 48 percent and the plastics molding division's portion of material is 36 percent. The controller of our corporate office insists on allocating the corporate expenses such as selling, G&A, and R&D to the various divisions on the basis of sales. With the high percentage of purchased material in the television set—cabinets and TV picture tubes, for example—we are being clobbered by this method of allocation. If material were excluded from the allocation base, we would be achieving our required return on investment. This would be a more realistic method which I plan to discuss at our next management committee meeting.

Case Example

The controller of this company related the following story. "Our company has made plastic eyeglass frames for years. It occurred to us one day that we had some extra capacity during part of the year. To utilize this capacity, we decided to get into the manufacture of combs because this product used the same material, and would provide long runs. In addition, the same salesmen who sold the parts for the glasses could sell the combs with little additional effort—no additional salesmen would be required. Nor would commissions increase because salesmen are paid a fixed salary. The president of the company wanted the sales expense to be apportioned between the two products on the basis of sales. The question that this raised was that the plastic eyeglass frames and other parts such as temples and nose pieces were the reason for this company being in business. Since the combs were sold only incidentally to absorb some excess capacity, the benefits of which would be reflected in reduced unit costs for both products, any sales and G&A allocations made to the combs would understate the true cost of selling the eyeglass items. Also, fluctuations in sales between the two products would result in profit fluctuations which would be confusing." The controller was searching for a suitable remedy that would satisfy the president and also present profits that would not fluctuate because of an arbitrary allocation of corporate expenses. The suggestion that was made was that since combs accounted for only 10 percent of the total volume of sales, a fixed allocation should be developed to reflect the estimated time required to service the comb business. This fixed amount would be charged against the combs each month and the balance would be charged to the eyeglass products. This recommendation was accepted.

ALLOCATING CORPORATE EXPENSES ON A RETURN-ON-INVESTMENT INTEREST RATE METHOD

The treasurer of one company who was highly return-on-investment oriented established an interest rate method for allocation of such corporate expenses as marketing, administration, and research and development. The interest rate is calculated once a year by dividing the budgeted corporate expenses by the budgeted investment in the manufacturing operations. These include raw material, work-in-process, finished goods, net fixed assets, and receivables.

At the end of each accounting period, the average investment for each division is calculated by averaging the investment at the beginning and the end of the period. The interest rate is then applied to each division's investment for the period. This assessment is totaled for the company and compared with the actual selling and administrative expenses. The assessment for the total company is then looked upon as the budget for corporate expenses. In turn, the divisions have some control in lowering the amount of their assessment by keeping down their investment.

ALLOCATING CORPORATE (AND/OR) DIVISION EXPENSES BY CLASS OF SALES

The Consumer Products Corporation had sales that came to $15,377,000, resulting in a profit of 4.9 percent on sales, as shown in Exhibit 12–14(A). The controller complained that the various methods for allocating corporate expenses such as selling, product service, warehousing, advertising, bad debts, and product design did not work in his company because the Consumer Products Corporation was made up of only two divisions, which were more like plants than divisions. During peak demand periods some of the products are manufactured in both plants, making clear-cut allocations between the two locations difficult. A study of the product line revealed that the company's products could be identified by several classes of sales. These appeared to have varying requirements of corporate services, therefore allocation by class of sales was studied.

Sales made through independent distributors (jobbers) who purchase products at reduced prices and stock them in their own warehouses. These distributors are usually located in locations not serviced by the company's sales force.

Income Statement for
Year Ended December 31, 19___

Gross Sales		$15,377,000
Less:		
Discounts and Allowances	$676,000	
Royalties	176,000	852,000
Net Sales		14,525,000
Cost of Sales		11,610,000
Gross Profit		2,915,000
Selling Expenses		676,000
Product Service Expenses		220,000
Warehouse Expenses		144,000
Advertising		801,000
Bad Debts		74,000
Engineering and Product Design		242,000
Total Expense		2,157,000
Pretax Profit		758,000
% Profit on Sales		4.9%

(A)

Breakdown of Income Statement
by Three Major Sales Categories

	Total	Export Sales	Distributors	Direct Selling
Gross Sales	$15,377,000	5,126,000	5,126,000	5,125,000
Less:				
Discounts and Allowances	676,000	163,000	513,000	—
Royalties	176,000	59,000	59,000	58,000
Net Sales	14,525,000	4,904,000	4,554,000	5,067,000
Cost of Sales	11,610,000	3,870,000	3,870,000	3,870,000
Gross Profit	2,915,000	1,034,000	684,000	1,197,000
Selling Expenses	676,000	101,400	101,400	473,200
Product Service Expenses	220,000	110,000	—	110,000
Warehouse Expenses	144,000	24,000	24,000	96,000
Advertising	801,000	—	400,500	400,500
Bad Debts	74,000	—	37,000	37,000
Engineering and Product Design	242,000	81,000	81,000	80,000
Total Expense	2,157,000	316,400	643,900	1,196,700
Pretax Profit	758,000	717,600	40,100	300
% Profit on Sales	4.9%	14.0	.8	—

Note: Total sales assumed to be equally divided to facilitate analysis of expense allocations.

(B)

	Total Direct Selling	One Large Customer	Special Custom Line	All Other
		Breakdown of Direct Selling		
Gross Sales	$5,125,000	1,708,300	1,708,300	1,708,400
Less:				
Discounts and Allowances	—	—	—	—
Royalties	58,000	19,300	19,300	19,400
Net Sales	5,067,000	1,689,000	1,689,000	1,689,000
Cost of Sales	3,870,000	1,290,000	1,290,000	1,290,000
Gross Profit	1,197,000	399,000	399,000	399,000
Selling Expenses	473,200	71,000	201,100	201,100
Product Service Expenses	110,000	36,700	36,700	36,600
Warehouse Expenses	96,000	48,000	—	48,000
Advertising	400,500	133,500	133,500	133,500
Bad Debts	37,000	—	18,500	18,500
Engineering and Product Design	80,000	26,700	26,700	26,600
Total Expense	1,196,700	315,900	416,500	464,300
Pretax Profit	300	83,100	(17,500)	(65,300)
% Profit on Sales	—	4.9%	(1.0%)	(3.8%)

Note: Total direct selling assumed to be equally divided to facilitate analysis of expense allocations.

(C)

EXHIBIT 12–14:
BREAKDOWN OF INCOME STATEMENT BY SALES CATEGORIES

Classes of Sales

This company has three major classes of sales, one of which is broken down further into three classes. The listing of these classes is:

- Export sales
- Distributor
- Direct selling
- One large customer (house account)
- Special custom line
- All other direct selling

Export Sales. These are sales that are made to the export affiliate. Although the sales to the export group are included as part of the sales of $15,377,000 made by the Consumer Products Corporation, they do not show the sales made by the export affiliate. The export group incurs its own expenses and maintains a separate set of books. However, it receives the same types of corporate services as those received by the other segments in the company.

Direct Selling. Sales made by salesmen who are on the company payroll. They are not in direct competition with the distributors because their selling areas are different.

One Large Customer

This represents sales made to a large customer through a company executive other than one whose function is selling. In this case, the large customer is related to one of the top company officers.

Special Custom Line

This sales class represents products that require special treatment. They are usually not standard specifications that are stocked in advance, unless a special commitment is made by the customer.

All Other

These are usually newly launched products that were recently developed. In some instances, this class of sales includes items manufactured by another company and purchased for resale for the purpose of maintaining a rounded line.

The income statement in Exhibit 12–14 was first broken down into the three major sales classes—export sales, sales to distributors, and direct selling (see Exhibit 12–14B). The six corporate expenses were then estimated for the three classes of sales under the assumption that each had the same annual sales ($5,126,000). The actual breakdown was 30, 34, and 36 percent.

Direct selling, which contained its own three classes of sales, was likewise broken down into equal sales segments (see Exhibit 12–14C). The actual breakdown was 29, 38, and 33 percent. The six corporate services required for each of the three classes was ascertained through estimates made by the heads of the departments rendering the corporate services.

Considerations in Making the Estimates by Class of Sales

The department heads of each of the six corporate service departments were asked to estimate the magnitude of effort required for the various classes. The results for each of the six departments are shown below:

Selling Expenses. In reviewing Exhibit 12–14, the sales manager estimated that the effort of his department was broken down as follows: export sales, 15 percent; distributors, 15 percent; and direct selling, 70 percent. Direct selling (Exhibit 12–14C) was estimated to be 15 percent for the one large customer, 42 percent for the special custom line, and 43 percent for all other types of direct selling. Export and distributor sales did not require the costs related to salesmen, although customer service effort was required.

Services to one large customer (the house account) were low, with most of the effort going to the special custom line and all other direct selling.

Product Service Expenses. This service relates to assisting the customer in adapting his product to his particular need. None of this service was required for distributor or export sales. Because the distributor rendered such assistance to his customers through his own network, he received larger discounts than were given to the other classes of sales. The breakdown for export sales was 50 percent, and for direct selling, 50 percent. The breakdown for the three types of direct selling is one-third each.

Warehouse Expenses. The demands for warehousing were low for export sales and distributor sales but high for direct selling. The percentages are ⅙, ⅙, and ⅔, respectively. Within direct selling, the breakdown is 50 percent for the house account and 50 percent for all other products. No warehousing is required for the special custom line because these items are not built to stock.

Advertising. Export sales are not charged for advertising because no advertising is required to sell to the export affiliate. The total advertising expense is broken down into 50 percent for distributor sales and 50 percent for direct selling. Within direct selling, the allocation of such services was broken down into thirds for each of the three classes of direct sales.

Bad Debts. The controller felt that no charge for this item was warranted for export sales so the total amount was broken down equally to distributor and direct sales. Within direct selling, no charge was made to the house account because this was a large company that was not likely to default. However, 50 percent of the direct selling allocation was charged to the special custom line and 50 percent to all other products.

Engineering and Product Design. This includes the initial design of new products, changes in design, and analysis of manufacturing problems that may be encountered. The chief engineer estimated that export sales, distributors, and direct selling should all be allocated one-third of this type of expense. Within direct selling, the same one-third allocation would apply.

The general philosophy followed by the department heads was that their services included "readiness to serve." Therefore, using the example of engineering and product design, the chief engineer felt that each of the classes of products that was assigned one-third of the cost of his services were really paying for this readiness. Also taken into consideration was the fact that there was some relationship among the various products that were sold by this company. Therefore, a new benefit derived in products sold in one class of sale frequently benefited products in other classes.

As can be seen in Exhibits 12–14(B) and (C), the breakdown of the income statement into sales classes shows entirely different profit results. Note in Exhibit 12–14(B) that export sales shows a 14 percent profit while direct selling shows a breakeven situation. Distributor sales show a minor amount of profitability. When direct selling is broken down into its three sales classes in Exhibit 12–14(C), the one large customer shows a profit of 4.9 percent while the other two classes show losses.

Although there could be some difference of opinion in the manner in which some of the allocations for the six expenses were derived, consistent use and analysis of the results of these figures will provide a better focus on changes that may be required. This points out that there is no one right way to allocate corporate (and division) expenses to products. Exhibit 12–15 summarizes the advantages and disadvantages of three methods for allocating nonmanufacturing costs such as selling, administration, research, and other corporate- or divisional-level expenses.

ALLOCATION METHOD	ADVANTAGES	DISADVANTAGES
Include nonmanufacturing costs in markup percentage applied to manufacturing costs.	Simplifies allocation.	Assumes that nonmanufacturing costs vary directly with manufacturing costs.
Include nonmanufacturing costs in markup percentage applied to direct labor and overhead only (conversion cost).	Excludes the influence of variations in material content of the various products.	Assumes that nonmanufacturing costs will always vary with conversion costs.
Allocate nonmanufacturing costs to products on the basis of sales volume; minor products charged a small fixed fee representing a "readiness-to-serve" cost.	Avoids penalizing small volume products that permit the company to utilize idle time of the equipment during off-peak periods.	Allocation on basis of sales may not reflect nonmanufacturing costs incurred on individual products.
"Interest rate" method applied to each plant on the basis of the plant's investment in inventory and net fixed assets. Interest rate calculated by dividing total nonmanufacturing costs by total factory investment.	Provides incentive to individual factories to maintain minimal investments consistent with production requirements.	Incurrence of nonmanufacturing costs may not always be directly related to factory investment.
Allocate nonmanufacturing costs to categories of sales on the basis of services rendered.	Recognizes incurrence of certain nonmanufacturing costs, such as those required for export sales, sales to distributors, and selling direct to customers through company sales force.	Not useful in companies that fabricate parts and sub-assemblies in some plants and assemble the finished product in others.

EXHIBIT 12–15:
ALLOCATING NON MANUFACTURING COSTS BY SALES CATEGORIES

13

External Factors and Internal Strategies Affecting Costs and Prices

The objective of pricing products for sale is to maximize the return on investment. Some of the factors that affect costs and prices are:

EXTERNAL FACTORS

- Stage of the product life cycle
- Competition within the industry
- Substitute material
- Special features of the product
- Services and assistance to customers
- Government controls
- Impact of inflation

Stage of the Product Life Cycle

Newly launched products with an innovative feature, with the advantage of "being there first," can be priced higher to recover the development costs. As demand for a new product grows, competitors will seek a share of this market. Since the competitors did not incur the initial development expense, their selling prices will be lower—forcing the innovator to lower his price. In addition, the innovator who does not provide sufficient production capacity to fill orders for his new product invites competition.

Market acceptance of an innovative product is difficult to predict with accuracy. Automobiles and airplanes, in their first twenty years, had quite different degrees of acceptance by the public. The first acceptable auto was made in 1903, and it was recognized as the standard road vehicle of the twentieth century in 1910. The airplane, on the other hand, had a great deal of difficulty with acceptance by the public. Even those responsible for designing and building of airplanes were found to be reluctant to fly.

The low unit cost products also have had their problems. Westclox was established in the late 1800s by a highly skilled clockmaker who had a good reputation for making a quality product. The greed of the company's stockholders, who wanted quick profits, resulted in downgrading of quality. The result was disastrous for the company. In 1889, five years after the establishment of the company, the assets and controlling interest were purchased by a smart businessman. He simplified the operations as well as the number of styles and varieties of watch and clock products, with the result that the company prospered.

H. H. Timken recognized the need for a new type of bearing when he observed that trains in the 1880s made horrible noises in rounding curves and riding on rough roadbeds. This resulted in a high degree of wear and tear to axles and other train parts. The existing ball bearings and straight bearings did not solve the problem. Continued experimentation resulted in the tapered bearing. Since the tapered bearing had good application in the manufacture of carriages, Timken, in addition to expanding the bearing manufacturing facilities, also built a plant for the manufacture of carriages.

The four products discussed above have long since passed their development stage and have enjoyed a long period of growth and maturity. This does not mean that further improvements in these products has stopped. It was not too long ago that the piston-type airplane engine was replaced by the jet engine. Windup watches are being replaced by the battery-operated types, resulting in a new surge of growth. During the growth period, as demand increased, the then existing prices produced more profitable operations. However, as the number of competitors grew, prices were forced downward. We need only look at the computer market for examples of the downward pressure on prices as product maturity comes closer and closer.

During the declining stage in the life cycle, volume drops and the number of producers declines. Depending on the product and the number of competitors that remain, profitability drops and will level off at a relatively low level. Buggy whips are sometimes given as an example of a product that is obsolete; yet there are five manufacturers who still have buggy whips in their product line.

Competition Within the Industry

Market price is the price that satisfies the largest number of buyers and sellers. Each purchase made by a company has a maximum price that will be paid. Each sale made by the supplier company has its minimum sale price that it considers acceptable. The market price at any moment is the price that is acceptable to the largest number of buyers and the largest number of sellers. The stock market is an excellent example of how the price of stock is established by interaction of buyers and sellers. Exhibit 13–1 illustrates graphically how the market price is established by such interaction.

During times of business recessions/depressions, buyers become more aggressive in their insistence on buying at lower prices. With the reduced demand

HOW THE MARKET PRICE IS ESTABLISHED

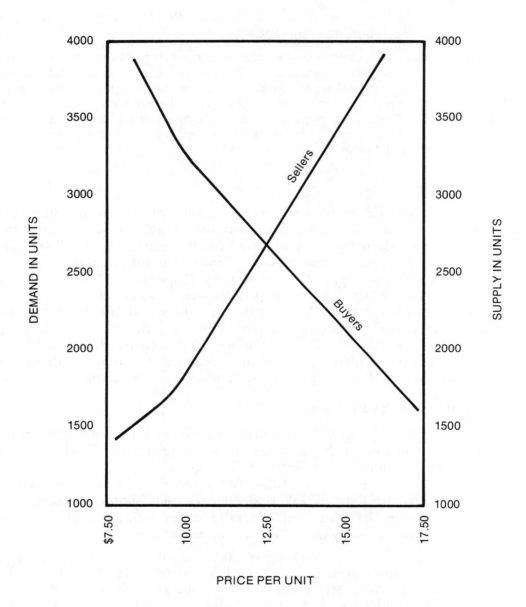

EXHIBIT 13–1:
EFFECT OF INTERACTION BETWEEN BUYERS AND SELLERS ON MARKET PRICE

because of poor economic conditions, sellers are more willing to reduce their prices. During periods of recovery and booms, sellers are in a more favorable position—with prices rising.

Amax, Inc., in a leaflet dated April 1, 1982, entitled "Meeting the Economic Challenge," made the following comment:

> In most business cycles, the rebound in demand for metals and minerals comes some months after the general economy turns up. The rebound is usually sudden and vigorous. Prices move up sharply. The strong demand at the upturn comes mainly from the need to increase inventories at all levels in the producer-to-end-customer chain. The odds favor the present recession in the minerals business ending in the same way, with faster recovery in areas where our customers are carrying bare minimum working inventories.

Substitute Materials

Competition and desire for lower costs on the part of the manufacturer frequently results in the use of substitute materials. Exhibit 13–2 illustrates the reduction in the manufacturer's sales price for cable from $0.239 to $0.112 per foot. The illustration of garbage cans, however, shows that substitution of plastics increases the manufacturer's price from $4.81 per garbage can to $7.31 each for the plastics version. The higher price of the plastic garbage cans does not necessarily mean that buyers will avoid the higher priced product. The plastic version has certain advantages over its metal counterpart. These include greater resistance to denting, reduction of noise in handling, and less weight. Generally, it is not likely that the manufacturer of plastic garbage cans would also manufacture those that are made of galvanized sheet, and vice versa. The same could be true of the cable.

Special Features of the Product

The manufacturer of special products has greater latitude in setting prices because of the uniqueness of the products he makes. Examples of such products were described in Chapter 2 (Job Costing Systems).

The June 7, 1982, issue of the *Wall Street Journal* (page 23), in an article entitled: "How an Entrepreneur Revived Faltering Firm Despite Slump," reports on a company that increased its production of a product line with a special feature to improve profits. The following are excerpts from the article:

> In 1978, Frank Taylor bought Rockford Headed Products, Inc., Rockford, Illinois, a small, privately owned maker of screws, bolts, and other fasteners that was losing sales to cheap imports. After Mr. Taylor took over, the economy soured, industrial production fell, and fastener demand shrank. Yet the company has done well under his direction. First Quarter sales set a record, and the 56-year-old entrepreneur predicts sales for the year will be $4.4 million, 10 percent ahead of last year.
>
> Mr. Taylor's research showed that special-purpose fasteners were a way out of the price-cutting competition that sapped many small bolt and screw companies. Rockford Headed Products' former owner had invented some special items, including a self-threading screw, that speed assembly time or hold better than ordinary fasteners in

	RAW MATERIAL	MFR'S. SALES PRICE	ADDED VALUE RAW MATERIAL TO MANUFAC-TURER'S SALES PRICE	RETAIL PRICE	ADDED VALUE RAW MATERIAL TO RETAIL PRICE	% RAW MATERIAL TO MFR'S SALES PRICE
Cable per Foot						
6 strand wire, ½"	$ .076	.239	214%	.284	273%	31.7%
Plastic, ½"	.030	.112	273	.136	353	26.8
Garbage Cans						
Galvanized sheet	1.03	4.81	366%	7.99	676	21.4
Plastic	3.01	7.31	143	16.35	443	41.2

*This material has been adapted from Elizabeth Marting, Editor, CREATIVE PRICING (New York: American Management Association, Inc., 1968) p. 36.

EXHIBIT 13–2:

PRICE CHARACTERISTICS OF TWO COMPETING MATERIALS

This material has been adapted from Elizabeth Marting, Editor, *Creative Pricing* (New York: American Management Association, Inc., 1968) p. 36.

certain materials. But these items accounted for a small part of the company's sales. Common screws sell for as little as $5 a thousand—half a cent each—versus $55 to $100 a thousand for special items.

Services and Assistance to Customers

A company can benefit by higher prices, even in a highly competitive industry, by rendering good service to its customers. Good service means more than delivery of orders on time. It also includes assistance in helping the customer solve problems in manufacture. One of the companies discussed in an earlier chapter received a request for quotation for parts making up a subassembly. The engineer of the supplier company, in reviewing the print accompanying the request for quotation noted that several parts making up the subassembly could be formed in one piece. He advised the sales department of his company which, in turn, contacted the prospective customer. The prospect was pleased to receive the suggestion. The request for quotation was made up on the suggested method and the prospect became a steady customer. In making up the quotation, this item was treated as if it were a special product at a higher price. This was a valid approach inasmuch as no competitor was quoting on this suggested change of design.

Government Controls

Prices charged by monopolies such as utility companies are controlled by government agencies who review planned price increases. Once the costs are accepted, a rate is applied to assure that the utility will recover an adequate return on its investment. This might be likened to the cost/plus type of work done by contractors doing work for the government. The "plus" added to cost is frequently a fixed fee.

When government controls are relaxed as they were in freight and the airlines, then a period of readjustment sets in while competition takes over. The December 31, 1981, issue of the *Wall Street Journal* cites the case of the Illinois Bell Telephone Company and its relationship to AT&T in the article, "Illinois Bell Faces New Environment as Era of Competitive Pricing Nears."

> "Pricing in the past has always been very easy," says John A. Koten, vice president for corporate communications. "All we had to do was determine our costs, and then we'd go to the commission—and they'd give us the allowable rate of return." Much of that is changing. In October, the Senate passed a bill that would split American Telephone & Telegraph Co., Illinois Bell's parent, into two supposedly independent parts, one for regulated services, the other for competitive ones. The subsidiary competing in the market would sell and lease telephone equipment and provide services not supplied by the regulated unit. It would perform its own research and development and do its own manufacturing. 'Baby Bell,' as the free-market unit has come to be called, would set prices on its own, the way any unregulated business does.

The AT&T split-up is, of course, now history.

Government controls can also influence prices on commodities that it stockpiles. This has been done at times when the price of particular commodities has risen to a level considered to be too high, by reducing the stockpile through selling off certain amounts. This happened to copper in the 1960s and frequently to gold to bring down prices.

Impact of Inflation on Costs and Prices

Inflation is one facet of the economy that touches everyone. The greater the amount of "fiat" money in circulation, the higher the rate of inflation. The rate of inflation affects the frequency and magnitude of price increases.

This can be demonstrated by the price increases in first class postage during the fifty years from July 6, 1932, to November 1, 1981. The first increase from three to four cents took approximately twenty-six years. The next two increases took five years each; the following two took three years. The next one took one year and the following one took three years. The move from fifteen to twenty cents was actually all part of the same rate case. The Postal Rate Commission would only grant a three cent increase which was put into effect in March 1981. At the same time, the governors of the Postal Service asked the commission to reconsider the case for the full five cents. They did make the review but held with their original recommendation of eighteen cents—at which point the governors modified the PRC decision (which they can do under law) and put in effect a twenty-cent rate in November 1981. Table 13–1 illustrates the impact of inflation on the above price increases.

Date of Increase	First Class Postage	CPI Index*	Adj. Factor	Price Adjusted for Inflation
July 6, 1932	3¢	40.8	6.87	20.6¢
August 1, 1958	4¢	86.8	3.23	12.9¢
January 7, 1963	5¢	91.1	3.08	15.4¢
January 7, 1968	6¢	102.0	2.75	16.5¢
May 16, 1971	8¢	120.8	2.32	18.6¢
March 2, 1974	10¢	143.1	1.96	19.6¢
December 31, 1975	13¢	166.3	1.69	22.0¢
May 29, 1978	15¢	193.3	1.45	21.8¢
March 22, 1981	18¢	265.2	1.06	19.1¢
November 1, 1981	20¢	280.4	1.00	20.0¢

*1967 = 100%

TABLE 13–1

The foregoing table adjusts the postage stamp prices for each of the years from 1932 through November 1, 1981, to the inflation level as of the latter date. This is done in the following steps:

1. The Consumer Price Index (CPI) was determined for each one of the dates on which increases were made.

2. This figure for each date was divided into the CPI on the date of the last increase to arrive at the adjusting factor.

3. The adjustment factor for each of the dates is multiplied by the actual price for that date. This adjusts the actual price to the November 1, 1981, level of inflation.

These steps are shown in the following example for the year of 1932.

$$\frac{\text{November 1981 CPI Index}}{\text{July 1932 CPI Index}} = \frac{280.4}{40.8} = 6.87 \text{ (adjusting factor)}$$

1932 price × adjusting factor = 1932 price adjusted to November 1981 price level. 3¢ × 6.87 = 20.6¢

A review of the prices after adjustment shows that seven of the adjusted prices are lower while two are higher. The 1981 price increase to twenty cents is approximately a half-cent lower than the adjusted 1932 price.

This type of analysis, which can be applied to manufactured products as well as postal rates, makes it possible to monitor the extent to which the product prices include recovery of higher costs due to inflationary pressures. When adjusted prices are lower than the inflationary rate, this is not always an indication that pricing is incorrect; it could mean that greater efficiency has been achieved through better production flow, increased efficiency, or automation.

Inflation must be taken into account in any comparisons that are made of figures during periods of volatility. Distortions that occur when this is not done will be discussed later.

INTERNAL FACTORS

It is sometimes difficult to segregate the external and internal factors that affect prices. The product life cycle, for example, has been discussed as an external factor and internal factor as well. In the discussion of this factor as an external influence, it is assumed that the manufacturing company is subject to trends in the industry—market acceptance, for example. As an internal strategy, on the other hand, the company must recognize that its pricing cannot be based on a consistent relationship between cost and selling price.

Changing Cost/Selling Price Ratios

A study of product life cycles, made by the A. C. Nielson Company in 1968, revealed that the average life span of a new household product is 2.9 years. This includes the period of development, growth, maturity, and decline. During the development period, costs are high and profits low; in the growth period profits rise because of increasing demand and higher volume. As the product reaches maturity and competition is at its peak, there is usually high pressure on profits—during which period they decline. In the last stage of life when sales are declining, profits become low or they turn to losses. During these four periods of the life cycle, it is only natural that the relationship of cost to selling price will vary depending on the stage of the cycle. The percentage of cost to selling price is high in the development stage; it drops during the growth stage as the volume increases because the fixed costs are spread over a broader base. During maturity, when competition has reached its peak, costs usually increase as a percentage of sales. In the decline stage, the percentage of costs to selling price increases further.

A company that expects the cost relationship to sales price to remain at a fixed ratio is following the wrong strategy if its pricing strategy presupposes this constant relationship.

STATUS OF BACKLOG OF NEW ORDERS

With competition as fierce as it is, modern industry must constantly have its finger on the pulse of customer requirements. A clue to these requirements is available through a study of the trend of new orders. The company which can move quickly, and ship these orders promptly is the company which will be remembered by the customer when subsequent new orders are placed. Utilization of this technique for customer good will is equivalent to having an invisible sales force. Many companies prepare a daily or weekly report showing the new orders received, shipments, and the resulting backlog. The backlog is a residue figure which can be used for an indicator as to whether incoming orders are on the increase or decrease. Exhibit 13–3 illustrates such a report. A new week is added to the preceding weeks so that prior reports need not be filed or consulted. Exhibit 13–4 plots the figures contained in Exhibit 13–3 to show pictorially the trend of new orders as reflected in the backlog. The graph could be used to the exclusion of the statistical report where the emphasis is on watching trends.

The line showing the backlog is calculated by adding new orders and subtracting shipments from the prior week's backlog. This line shown in Exhibit 13–4 indicates a steady downward trend. This is an important trend to watch because some companies use it as a precursor to changes in selling price. A falling backlog could be an indication of a faltering economy which might result in falling prices. A rising backlog, on the other hand, could be an indicator of business recovery and rising prices. A highly sophisticated controller of one company carried the analysis of backlog a step further. His approach and reasoning was stated as follows.

After we calculate our overall backlog each week, we break it down by work centers. This tells us which cost centers will be overloaded and which will be underutilized. This allows us to take the following steps:

Overloaded work centers

We extend the lead times to permit longer runs. The longer lead times permit us to schedule the runs on a more logical basis. We not only gain by scheduling longer runs; we are able to schedule in a manner in which the changeovers from one machine to another are sequenced to avoid having a radical changeover for one run and then immediately tear down the entire setup for the next run. Another saving is that we have fewer changeovers and less time spent in setting up the equipment.

Week	New Orders	Shipments	Backlog
1	$26,310	$11,415	$120,065
2	15,960	16,205	119,820
3	12,100	12,402	119,518
4	12,350	12,075	119,793
5	21,100	10,779	130,714
6	13,965	11,905	132,774
7	17,014	9,642	140,146
8	22,212	18,060	144,298
9	16,126	13,782	146,642
10	17,130	18,392	145,380
11	21,324	23,062	143,642
12	19,134	26,436	136,340
13	16,031	37,345	115,026
14	11,213	13,619	112,620
15	11,962	19,947	104,635
16	13,402	14,696	103,341
17	12,111	13,390	102,062
18	10,320	12,165	100,217
19	10,721	20,736	90,202
20	11,420	23,580	78,042
21	11,306	15,046	74,302
22	11,904	13,225	72,981
23	13,416	17,731	68,666
24	13,333	15,738	66,261
25	12,620	14,781	64,100
26	11,220	12,270	63,050
27	11,350	12,300	62,100
28	11,441	11,561	61,980
29	16,688	15,643	63,025
30	15,843	14,878	63,990
31	14,400	14,328	64,062
32	13,926	15,946	62,042
33	14,667	13,062	63,647
34	16,660	16,591	63,716
35	18,899	18,417	64,198
36	25,554	14,360	75,392
37	20,002	18,349	77,045
38	18,309	14,738	80,616
39	14,445	14,023	81,038
40	13,212	12,053	82,197
41	13,196	12,057	83,336
42	11,778	16,198	78,916
43	11,662	10,470	80,108
44	15,925	18,261	77,772
45	20,669	27,403	71,038
46	12,210	13,031	70,217
47	13,312	18,030	65,499
48	14,121	18,503	61,117
49	14,365	17,426	58,061
50	20,259	30,103	48,217

EXHIBIT 13–3:
ORDER INTAKE VERSUS SHIPMENTS AND BACKLOG

Thousand Dollars

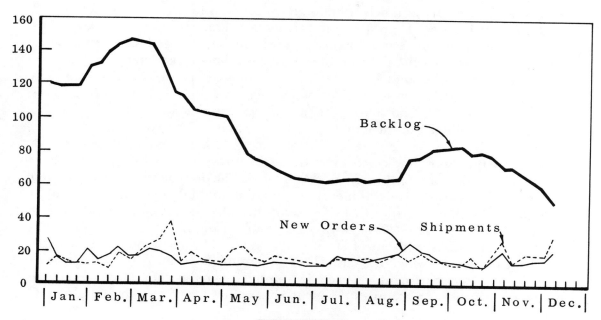

EXHIBIT 13–4:
ORDER INTAKE VERSUS SHIPMENTS AND BACKLOG—GRAPH

Underutilized work centers

When we find that some work centers will be underutilized, we determine which items in our product line will bring back additional volume for that center. This information is communicated to the marketing department. We also look into the possibility of soliciting work from other manufacturers whose facilities might not be adequate for their needs. We recently purchased some computer controlled equipment which is not fully loaded. Our marketing department contacted two companies in our area who were only too anxious to buy part of our unused time on these machines.

IMPACT OF CUSTOMER PROFIT STRATEGIES

In one of the management meetings of key executives that one company held each month, it was the purchasing manager's turn to make a presentation on profit improvement ideas—not only by his department's efforts but by contributions that other departments in the company could make. He started by pointing out that practically all of the companies he was familiar with identified their inventory by A, B, and C items. The A and B items accounted for the bulk of the dollars (65 to 85 percent) but only 15 to 20 percent of the items. The C items, on the other hand, represented the minor portion of the dollars that were left (15 to 35 percent) but the bulk of the items (60 to 80 percent).

Because of the lower dollars tied up in the C items, the buyers for these companies did not pay as much attention to prices paid for the C items as they did for the A and B types. Therefore, the pricing of C items need not be "shaved" as closely as pricing for the A and B items. The sales manager raised the question as to how one could tell which of the items sold to customers constituted C items. The materials manager responded by pointing out that the nature of the customer's product was a good indicator of the items that constituted A, B, and C. This information could be shown on the incoming requests for quotation by the engineer who edited the incoming quotation requests. The controller, who was responsible for the cost estimating group, argued that companies sending in requests for quotation, indicated by so doing, that they were seeking competitive bids regardless of whether the item was A, B, or C. The division manager reminded the controller that there were numerous standard items built for stock and listed in the catalog. He stated further that these items were frequently discounted further by the sales department: "Here is where the purchasing manager's recommendation regarding items sold out of stock might apply. The recommendation might bear fruit in cases in which the customer's C item might be an A production item for us. Our sales department has been discounting from the standard list price. We should review these procedures, particularly as they pertain to the customer C items."

ESTIMATING MANUFACTURING COSTS OF COMPETITORS

It is not unusual for companies to disassemble competitors' products to estimate the competitor's manufacturing costs. This was common practice with television sets during the early 1950s. The practice of disassembling competitive products was not only helpful in checking out costs but the competitor's engineering design as well.

NEW PRODUCT INNOVATIVENESS

In Chapter 11, the section, "How information sources can enhance profitability," cited the case in which a salesman noted a problem that a customer who manufactured television picture tubes was having. The problem was bent pins in the base of the picture tube during shipment. He related this problem to the engineering department of his company. As a result a protective plug was developed. This product not only added a new profitable product to the company's line; it had other benefits as well:

- It permitted an increase in utilization of a machine that was being operated below capacity.
- Reground plastic, which can only be used by mixing with virgin material, tends to build up in the stockroom. The new product will be a means for working off the excess reground material.
- This product will not be reused because it will be shipped to the end user as part of the picture tube. The cost of collecting these protective plugs and reshipping to the manufacturers of the tubes would not pay.

MONITORING THE COST ESTIMATING AND PRICING FUNCTION

The cost estimating and pricing function includes the determination of product costs, establishment of selling prices (subject to approval), and monitoring the results of feedback on costs and selling prices. It is in the monitoring of results of feedback that many cost estimating and pricing functions fall down.

Qualifications of Cost Estimators

The cost estimator must be factory-wise; he must feel comfortable in a factory atmosphere and must be able to associate factory processes with the costs of performing the various operations making up the processes. In addition to these technical qualifications, he must have good personality traits. The latter is important because of the need to deal with different individuals within the company and the need to challenge information diplomatically. The various functional heads with whom the cost estimator must deal and the problems that are encountered in cost estimating and pricing are dealt with in Chapters 11 and 12.

To Whom Should the Cost Estimating and Pricing Function Report?

The lines of organization, insofar as the cost estimating and pricing function is concerned, varies from company to company. The advantages and disadvantages of three different reporting relationships are shown below:

REPORTING RELATIONSHIP	ADVANTAGES	DISADVANTAGES
Reporting to sales manager	The sales department exerts pressure to reduce manufacturing costs	Pressure may be exerted on estimator to understate estimated costs
		Pressure to get out the quotations might result in shortcuts. This would eliminate the detail required for effective feedback analysis
Reporting to plant manager	Cost estimator more likely to be up-to-date on changes in the manufacturing process	Sense of urgency in getting out the quotation may not be as great as it would be if under the direction of the sales manager
Reporting to accounting department	Cost estimates will be more complete and accurate	Approach to estimating could become too mechanical. Emphasis on clerical accuracy and detail, rather than production considerations, could lead to unrealistic estimates.

The determination as to whom the cost estimating and pricing function should report cannot be dogmatically stated through a judgment based on the advantages and disadvantages stated above. The sales department is closest to the marketplace and is therefore the most knowledgeable of competitive selling prices. Although these selling prices must be met to retain share of market, each company is likely to make a different rate of profit—some more, some less than their competitors—depending on the product. Ideally, sales commissions of salesmen should be based on the profitability of the products that have been sold rather than on the selling price. This approach will have two advantages: (1) the salesmen will "push" the more profitable items, and (2) they will exert pressure to reduce costs in order to increase profitability.

However, this procedure should not be automatically instituted unless the manufacturing executive approves the cost estimates to make certain that there is no unauthorized "shaving" of costs to create a "phantom" profit. This should also preclude the use of an overly mechanical approach in which the computer "spews out" the figures without taking into account judgmental factors that cannot be programmed into the computer. A logical system of "checks and balances" is more important than to whom the cost estimating section reports.

NEED FOR COST HISTORY

Good historical information is important to an effective costing and pricing function. This file of information would contain records of products that have been previously estimated. Even though the products are different, it is probable that historical data would provide basic data for components that may be common to a number of products. Availability of such information can save hours of estimating time, particularly when the estimating relates to new products (or variations thereof) that will fit within an existing family of products.

Exhibit 2–7 on page 34 illustrates one type of cost history that can be very useful. This format provides a comparison of the actual with the estimated costs. There is a breakdown of material by major components making up the product. Labor and overhead costs (both actual and estimated) are also broken down by work centers. Selling prices and gross profit are shown. This exhibit also shows, in the lower portion, similar costs for each product on an individual sheet. In addition to the foregoing history, the following data should also be maintained:

- Production losses
- Excess rework
- Unplanned secondary operations
- Equipment problems
- Tooling problems

In the maintenance of the above data, it is important to identify unusual problems with specific products or components being manufactured at the time. This will facilitate the identification of unusual conditions for which adjustments must be made.

IMPORTANCE OF FEEDBACK

When a request for quotation materializes into an order, some companies establish standards for the job with little or no reference to the estimates used in the quotation. Performance is monitored against the standards rather than against the estimates used in arriving at the product costs. The argument for using the standards rather than the estimates is that the estimates were considered to be "guesstimates" and that more realistic measures could now be used. It is unfortunate that the original estimates cannot always be used as standards for measuring performance, because of lumping of costs representing several operations. This is no excuse, however, for not comparing the difference between the standards and the original estimates. Unless such a comparison is made, the accuracy of the cost estimating procedure will never be known.

Monitoring the Markup

It is just as important to monitor the markup as it is to monitor the accuracy of the cost estimates. The success ratio in requests for quotation are a means of monitoring the markup. Such an evaluation made in one company is shown in Table 13–2.

SUCCESS RATIO IN REQUESTS FOR QUOTATIONS

Markup %	Number of Quotations	Number of Successful Bids	% of Successful Bids
40% and higher	38	0	0%
35 to 39%	96	3	3
30 to 34%	84	7	8
25 to 29%	42	9	21
5 to 24%	21	8	38
	281	27	10%

TABLE 13–2

The key to developing information on the success ratio in bidding requires the logging of all requests for quotation as they come in as well as logging those that have been accepted by the customer. Note in the above table that of a total of 281 quotations received, only twenty-seven were accepted by customers, approximately 10 percent. A 10 percent success ratio must be judged in two ways:

- Whether the 10 percent is an adequate return of orders for quotations that were made
- Whether the breakdown by markup percent represents a normal distribution

Whether a 10 percent success ratio for quotations that materialize in firm orders is an acceptable figure depends upon the competitiveness and nature of the industry. Another factor is the quality of screening of incoming requests for quotation. As mentioned in an earlier chapter, quotations are sometimes sent in by companies who are merely "fishing" to determine what competitors are charging.

In other cases, quotation requests cover products that are not made by the recipient company. If these are included in the number of quotations column, the success ratio percentage would be understated. Therefore, such quotation requests should be excluded in the calculations through good screening.

Note also in the above table that the 10 percent shows the greatest success ratio in the lowest markup percentage range—5 to 24 percent gross profit; the next largest is in the 25 to 29 percent range—both figures being relatively small for recovery of gross profit. The success ratio analysis can also be helpful to management in determining whether its markup policy is adequate to yield an acceptable profit.

Monitoring Product Profitability

A recommended format for monitoring product profitability is illustrated in Exhibit 13–5. The first column shows the total sales for the various products that were sold in the month. Since the sales figures in this column reflect the net amount after all allowances, the percentages of the cost elements (shown at standard) will be more realistic than if they had been measured from the anticipated selling price. The costs in this exhibit provides two types of analyses:

- Marginal contribution
- Gross profit

These two measurements will show the profitability difference between direct costing and full costing. (See Chapter 7 for discussion of direct versus full costing.) The first two products, P660 and J200, show the largest marginal contribution (contribution to profit before fixed costs) of the eight products listed. The marginal contribution for these two is 48 and 53 percent of sales, respectively. The same two items show a gross profit of 40 and 38 percent of sales, respectively—just the reverse. (These eight products are also discussed in Chapter 10 in a different context.) The reason for J200 being less profitable under full costing than under direct costing is that the fixed overhead is so much greater (15 percent of sales compared with 8 percent for P660). In analyzing these figures, the perceptive management will raise questions such as the following:

- By looking at the marginal contribution before fixed costs, are we ignoring the higher cost of the 96-ounce molding press used in making the J200 versus the 8-ounce press for the P660?

- What was the rationale used in separating fixed and variable costs for the large pool of overhead costs? If this was done on an arbitrary basis, as many companies unfortunately do, the fixed costs could be excessively high and the variable costs correspondingly low; thus distorting the marginal contribution percentage. (Chapter 10 uses this same report but shows a different breakdown between fixed and variable costs.)

- What is the level of activity used for developing the fixed overhead rate? If it is substantially lower than practical capacity, particularly for the 96-ounce press, then the 15 percent figure for fixed costs as a percentage of sales might be overstated.

PERIOD _____

PRODUCT NUMBER	SALES $	SALES %	STANDARD MATERIAL $	STANDARD MATERIAL %	STANDARD DIRECT LABOR $	STANDARD DIRECT LABOR %	STANDARD VARIABLE MFG. OVHD. $	STANDARD VARIABLE MFG. OVHD. %	TOTAL STD. VARIABLE COSTS $	TOTAL STD. VARIABLE COSTS %	MARGINAL CONTRIBUTION $	MARGINAL CONTRIBUTION %	STANDARD FIXED MFG. OVERHEAD $	STANDARD FIXED MFG. OVERHEAD %	TOTAL STD. MFG. COST $	TOTAL STD. MFG. COST %	STANDARD GROSS PROFIT $	STANDARD GROSS PROFIT %
P660	296	100	127	43	21	7	6	2	154	52	142	48	24	8	178	60	118	40
J200	1,380	100	456	33	138	10	55	4	649	47	731	53	207	15	856	62	524	38
2020	1,847	100	813	44	129	7	37	2	979	53	868	47	185	10	1164	63	683	37
6100	499	100	254	51	25	5	10	2	289	58	210	42	40	8	329	66	170	34
F011	1,649	100	824	50	99	6	33	2	956	58	693	42	149	9	1105	67	544	33
7007	867	100	460	53	69	8	26	3	555	64	312	36	104	12	659	76	208	24
8100	1,132	100	408	36	192	17	68	6	668	59	464	41	260	23	928	82	204	18
D166	130	100	42	32	23	18	9	7	74	57	56	43	38	29	112	86	18	14
TOTAL	7,800	100	3384	43	696	9	244	3	4324	55	3476	45	1007	13	5331	68	2469	32

EXHIBIT 13–5:
MONTHLY PROFITABILITY REPORT WITH VARIABLE COSTING ELEMENTS
Figures in $(000)

Before any final conclusions can be drawn and final decisions made, questions such as the above must be answered. Clues to potential cost reduction possibilities as was pointed out in an earlier chapter on cost estimating, can be determined from an analysis of the material and direct labor content of the various products. Note that products 6100, F011, and 7007 contain material that is 50 percent of the selling price or higher. While this may be perfectly acceptable, this high percentage does warrant a review to determine if less material would be needed with a different design or through use of a substitute material. The last two products, 8100 and D166, indicate a 17 and 18 percent direct labor content—the highest of the products listed. The question here, is whether there is a potential for automation that might reduce the labor cost. Although cost reduction possibilities are not immediately pertinent to the feedback process for cost estimating and pricing, they should, nonetheless, be given high priority.

Practical Problems in Monitoring Product Profitability

The preceding example, although theoretically sound, cannot be implemented on an ad hoc basis in the real world of business. This becomes obvious when one realizes that the inventory of many medium- and large-size companies can include hundreds of individual products. In some companies this figure can number in the thousands. Monitoring product profitability can be difficult in nonmanufacturing businesses even if the number of product lines is relatively small for another reason—material is a minor cost as compared to a manufactured product in which material content can average in excess of 40 percent of sales. Thus, if one attempted to use the format shown in Exhibit 13–5, the column showing material costs would be blank (or very small), leaving direct labor as the only element of cost that can be associated with the product with any reasonable degree of accuracy. The overhead (referred to as operating cost in some nonmanufacturing businesses) presents the same type of problems of allocation to product lines as it does in manufacturing.

Monitoring the Overall Picture

Exhibit 13–6, "Analysis of Operations," demonstrates a pictorial method for monitoring the various components making up the selling price. This is actually a line of closely related products. The bar charts show, month by month, the breakdown per thousand units of manufacturing costs. The breakdown shows the material, direct labor, and overhead—the latter being broken down by the fixed and variable segments. The line depicting the sales value per thousand shows the selling prices month by month. The line above sales value reflects the markup divider—the percentage that is divided into total manufacturing cost to arrive at the sales value. The units per machine hour could be looked upon as a measure of productivity. Note that as the productivity increases, the manufacturing cost per thousand decreases—and vice versa.

The importance of feedback on the effectiveness of the cost estimating and pricing procedures cannot be limited to this function alone. The principle of feedback must encompass every facet of the company's operations. The remaining chapters will deal with this.

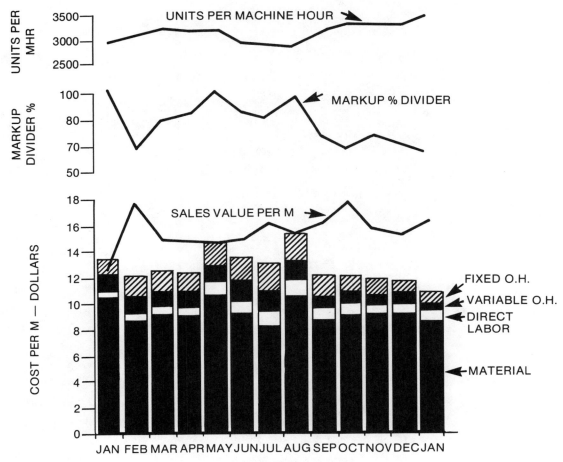

EXHIBIT 13–6:
ANALYSIS OF OPERATIONS

SECTION III

Assuring Effective Performance

14

Analyzing Financial Results

When businesses were highly labor-paced, profits were measured as a percentage of return on sales. As labor costs soared, more and more companies found it difficult to remain in business. As a result, many businesses failed or were absorbed into the stronger companies. This left fewer companies to share the same volume of production and facilitated more product standardization and the introduction of automation.

Product Standardization. This permitted the design of basic products whose components could be produced on automated equipment using standardized processes. Addition of various options to the basic products permits the expansion of the product line. The automobile is a prime example of this.

Automation. Standardization of components making up the product line facilitates longer runs with the resulting economies through fewer setups and changeovers. The lower unit costs permit building components to stock for later assembly.

Although automation lowers labor costs, it does require increased investment in equipment, tooling, utility services, and building costs necessary to accommodate the equipment. As a result of such increases in investment percentage of return on equity (investment) becomes as important as the percentage of return on sales for measuring profitability.

VARIATIONS IN PROFITABILITY MEASUREMENTS FOR FOUR LINES OF BUSINESS

The return on sales and return on equity (investment) varies by line of business. The Dun and Bradstreet selected key business ratios for thirty-one manufacturing lines of business reflects these variations. Four of these lines of business have been selected for illustrative purposes (Table 14–1).

Line of Business	No. of Companies	% Return on Sales	% Return on Equity	Annual Turns of Equity
Dairy products	125	1.2	11.1	9.3
Meat products	113	1.5	13.9	9.3
Paperboard containers and boxes	115	3.4	12.5	3.7
Paints, varnishes, lacquers, enamels, and allied products	104	3.4	12.4	3.6

TABLE 14–1

Note that dairy products and meat products have a low return on sales—1.2 and 1.5 percent, respectively. The percentage of return on equity for these two lines of business is 11.1 and 13.9 percent, respectively.

The other two lines of business, paperboard containers and paints, each show a return on sales of 3.4 percent. The return on equity is 12.5 and 12.4 percent, respectively.

Note that the percentage of return on equity for all four lines of business is approximately the same, roughly 12.5 percent. However, in order for all four lines of business to attain approximately the same percentage of return on equity, the annual turns of equity must be 9.3, 9.3, 3.7, and 3.6. The annual turns of equity, using dairy products as an example, can be determined by dividing the return on sales of 1.2% into the return on equity of 11.1%. Therefore, $\underline{11.1\%} = 9.3$ turns. If 1.2% the sales volume had been large enough to result in 10 turns, rather than 9.3 turns, the return on equity would have been 12.0 rather than 11.1 percent.

Although the four lines of business illustrated above show a return on equity of about 12.5 percent, this is not the case for all thirty-one lines of business listed under manufacturing. The amount of return will vary with the industry. Manufacture of aircraft parts and engines, for example, will show a return on sales of 6.9 percent and return on equity of 26 percent with turns of 3.8 per year for 1980.

VARIATIONS IN PROFITABILITY MEASURES FOR FOUR INDUSTRIES

The preceding section dealt with lines of business as they are categorized by Dun and Bradstreet. This section makes the same type of analysis for two companies in each of four industries. The breakdown of profitability measures for these eight companies is shown in Table 14–2. The year 1980, rather than more recent years, was used to avoid distortions due to the serious deterioration that occurred in our domestic steel industry. The figures for 1980, in Table 14–2A, were calculated for Polaroid, as illustrated in Table 14–2B.

VARIATIONS IN PROFITABILITY FOR FOUR INDUSTRIES OVER A TEN-YEAR PERIOD

The same profitability measures that were summarized for two companies in each of four industries for the year of 1980 will now be shown for the ten-year period 1971 through 1980. This period of time was taken because it started with a rising economy, it included the institution of price controls, the energy shortage, recovery, increasing foreign competition, and the start of a downtrend in the economy.

Photographic Industry. The two companies chosen in this industry were Polaroid and Eastman Kodak. Polaroid considers itself to be in a single line of business—instant photography. Eastman Kodak, on the other hand, in addition to photography, is in the chemical, fiber, and plastics business. Because of these differences, Polaroid's profitability will be greatly influenced by the fortunes of its

	% Return on Sales	Year of 1980 % Return on Equity	Annual Turns of Equity
Photographic Industry:			
Polaroid	5.9	8.8	1.5
Eastman Kodak	11.9	20.2	1.7
Chemical Industry:			
Dow Chemical	7.6	18.1	2.4
Allied Corporation	6.8	16.8	2.5
Steel Industry:			
Republic	1.4	3.4	2.4
Bethlehem	1.8	4.7	2.6
Tire Industry:			
Firestone	2.2	7.9	3.6
Goodyear	2.7	10.0	3.7

TABLE 14–2(A)

$$\text{Return on sales} = \frac{\$ 85,406 \text{ (Net income)}}{\$1,450,785 \text{ (Total sales)}} = 5.9\%$$

$$\text{Return on shareholder equity} = \frac{\$ 85,406 \text{ (Net income)}}{\$ 970,854 \text{ (Shareholder income)}} = 8.8\%$$

$$\text{Annual turns of equity} = \frac{\$1,450,785 \text{ (Total sales)}}{\$ 970,854 \text{ (Shareholder equity)}} = 1.5 \text{ turns}$$

TABLE 14–2(B)

single line of business while Eastman Kodak will have the benefit of diversity. Exhibit 14–1 shows, graphically, the return on sales, return on equity, and turns per year for both companies.

Although Polaroid's sales were attaining record heights during most of this ten-year period, profits were adversely affected by high development and marketing expenses for the SX-70 system. The return on sales and return on equity improved steadily during the four-year period of 1975 through 1978—after the SX-70 problems of development and marketing were overcome. The year 1979 was one of retrogression, with profits down to $36.1 million from $118.4 million in 1978, although sales were down only slightly. This was probably due to a decrease in number of cameras sold, as well as additional development costs. The year 1980 improved to approximately the level of 1975 because of healthy SX-70 film sales and introduction of Time-Zero film.

Eastman Kodak experienced a higher level of profitability during the first three and last three years of the decade. During the middle four years, the trend of profitability was down. This was just the reverse of Polaroid which had its best years during the middle four years.

$$*\text{TURNS PER YEAR} = \frac{\text{SALES}}{\text{SHAREHOLDER EQUITY}}$$

POLAROID CORPORATION

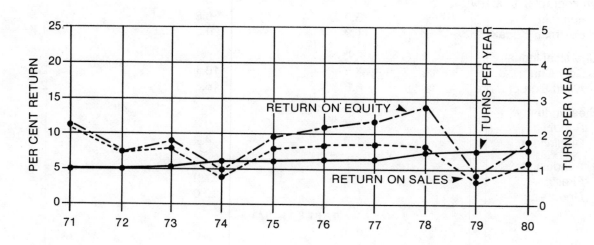

EASTMAN KODAK COMPANY

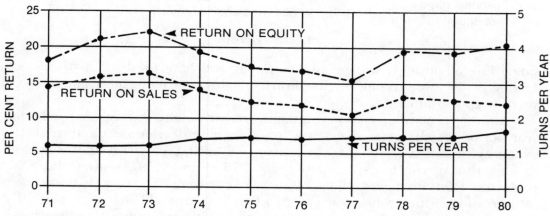

Polaroid considers itself to be in only one line of business — Instant photography.
Eastman Kodak, in addition to photography, is in the chemical, fiber, and plastics business.

EXHIBIT 14–1:
TEN-YEAR TREND OF RETURN ON SALES, RETURN ON SHAREHOLDER EQUITY, AND
TURNS OF SHAREHOLDER EQUITY PER YEAR*
(POLAROID CORPORATION AND EASTMAN KODAK COMPANY)

During this ten-year period the turns per year of equity ranged from 1 to 1.5 turns for Polaroid and from 1.3 to 1.7 for Kodak, a relatively narrow range.

Chemical Industry. Although the pattern of return on equity and return on sales is approximately the same, the return for Dow Chemical is higher (see Exhibit 14–2). The annual turns of equity for Dow range for 1.7 to 2.4 while the turns for Allied Corporation range from 1.7 to 2.5.

Steel Industry. The pattern of return on equity and return on sales is quite similar for both Republic Steel and Bethlehem Steel, except that the latter company suffered a large loss in 1977 (see Exhibit 14–3). This loss position was due to the lag in construction, bleak capital goods markets, and foreign competition. Although Republic Steel's reduction in profits did not result in a loss, it too, was affected by foreign competition. However, because Republic is a major flat-rolled steel producer, it benefited by the all-time high in production of lightweight trucks and vans. Its dip in profits did not, therefore, result in a loss. The range of turns of equity started at 1.3 in 1971 and ended at 2.4 turns in 1980, while Bethlehem started at 1.5 turns and ended with 2.6 turns in 1980. In both instances, there were years within the ten-year period in which the turns went above the 1980 turns. Republic exceeded the 1980 turns in 1974 (2.5), 1978 (2.6), and 1979 (2.9). Bethlehem's turns exceeded its 1980 turns of equity in 1978 (2.9) and in 1979 (3.0).

Tire Industry. The pattern of return on equity and return on sales is approximately the same for both Goodyear and Firestone except for the year of 1978 in which Firestone's profits suffered from a recall of several million steel-belted radial tires (see Exhibit 14–4). The range of annual turns of equity for Goodyear was 2.5 in 1971 and 3.7 turns in 1980. For Firestone, 1971 showed 2.1 turns and 1980 showed 3.6.

This examination of eight companies in four industries indicates that return on sales and return on equity can vary widely within an industry, while still maintaining a relatively similar pattern of profitability trends. This similarity in directional trend could be the result of such external factors as the direction of the economy and foreign competition, factors that would affect all companies in the particular industry. There appears to be a greater stability in annual turns of equity however.

USE OF PROFITABILITY MEASUREMENTS IN MONITORING PROFIT PERFORMANCE

The Barget Company introduced a variation of the concept of profit measurement discussed above. This concept is presented graphically in Exhibit 14–5. A comparison is made of the percentage of return on sales with the investment turns per year by quarters over a five year period. Note that a loss, or a near-loss situation exists when the investment turns are below twice per year. This is true in the third quarter of year 2 and in the period covering the third quarter of year 3 through the third quarter of year 4. The early quarters of year 1 show a high percentage of return on sales and high investment turns, in spite of low sales.

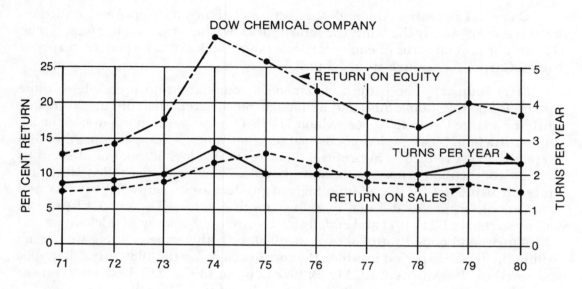

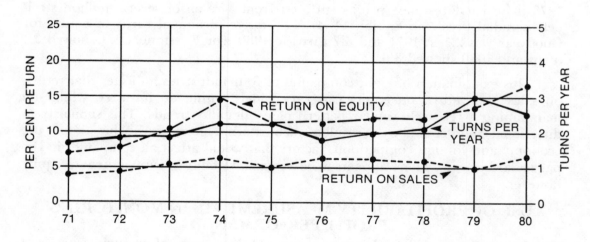

EXHIBIT 14–2:
TEN-YEAR TREND
(DOW CHEMICAL COMPANY AND ALLIED CORPORATION)

$$\text{*TURNS PER YEAR} = \frac{\text{SALES}}{\text{SHAREHOLDER EQUITY}}$$

REPUBLIC STEEL CORPORATION

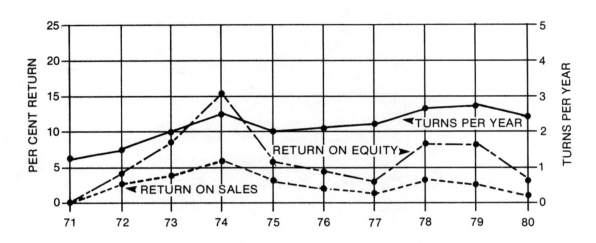

BETHLEHEM STEEL CORPORATION

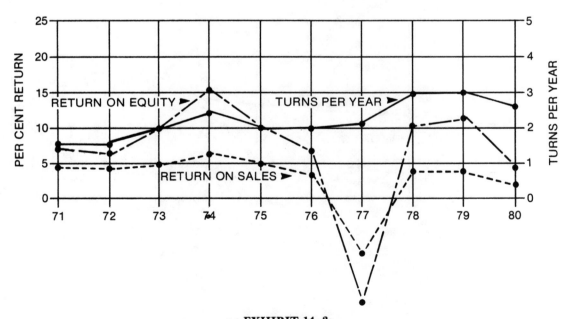

EXHIBIT 14–3:
TEN-YEAR TREND
(REPUBLIC STEEL CORPORATION AND BETHLEHEM STEEL CORPORATION)

$$*\text{TURNS PER YEAR} = \frac{\text{SALES}}{\text{SHAREHOLDER EQUITY}}$$

GOODYEAR TIRE & RUBBER COMPANY

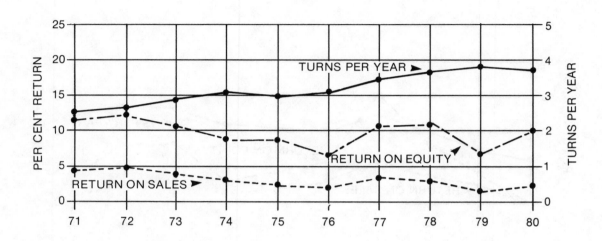

FIRESTONE TIRE & RUBBER COMPANY

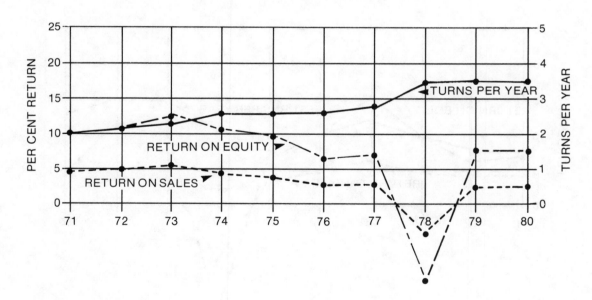

EXHIBIT 14–4:
TEN-YEAR TREND
(GOODYEAR TIRE & RUBBER COMPANY AND FIRESTONE TIRE & RUBBER
COMPANY)

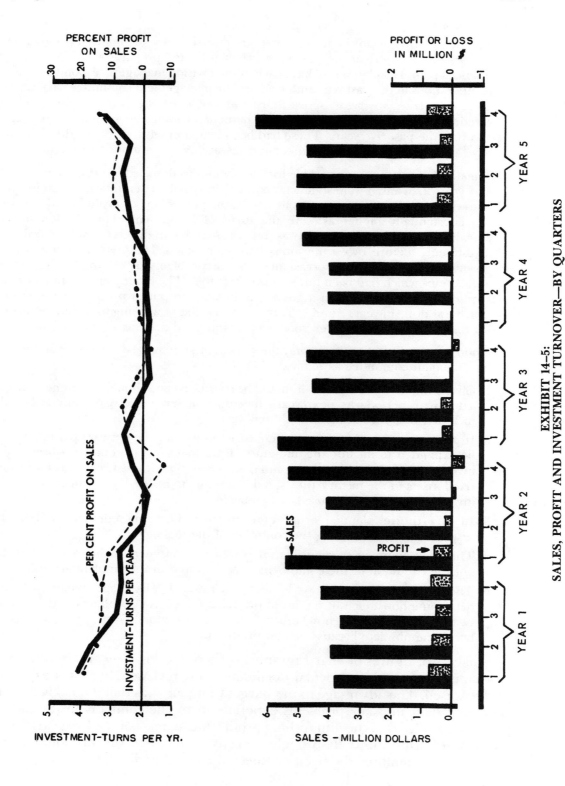

EXHIBIT 14–5:

SALES, PROFIT AND INVESTMENT TURNOVER—BY QUARTERS

Case Example

The new company president instituted an annual review of financial progress in the various divisions just prior to issuing instructions for preparation of the new year's financial plan. His plan was to have each of the division managers respond to questions on operations in the past year and to advise the management committee what would be done to correct any weak spots. Since this would be the first year in which such meetings would be held, the president had charts similar to Exhibit 14–5 prepared covering the past five years. These had been issued in advance so the divisions would have an opportunity to review them and research any questions that might be asked.

The division manager responsible for the operations depicted in the exhibit was asked why years 2, 3, and 4 were so much poorer than year 1. He emphasized that in spite of sales that were about the same as in year 4, the percentage of profit on sales in year 1 was substantially higher as were the turns of investment. The division manager explained that the first year was represented by a different mix of sales and investment—before two acquisitions had been made. He advised further that the downtrend in profits was occasioned by the problems of absorbing the two new acquisitions which had been timed closely together. The tooling and equipment of the acquired companies needed a good deal of work to put in proper operating order, which was done in years 2 and 3. Year 4 was a period of working to regain lost business because of inability to render good service and good product to the customers.

Upon completion of the meeting, the president summarized his observations to the management committee as follows:

1. Charts similar to Exhibit 14–5 should be continued and should be extended to cover a ten-year period. At next year's meeting the same five-year period should be included plus the results of each new year.

2. In redrawing the chart or equivalent to accommodate the ten-year period, it should be expanded to include the amount of investment in each quarter—breaking the investment down into inventory and fixed assets. Since these two items are the major fixed assets in the factory, they should continue to be used to calculate the turns of investment as they were used in Exhibit 14–5.

3. In any future planned acquisition the manufacturing engineer will be held responsible for overseeing the condition of the tooling.

4. The plant engineer (responsible for plant and equipment maintenance) will check out the condition of the equipment to be acquired in future plant acquisitions.

5. The materials manager would also be involved. His responsibility will be to determine how much of the inventory relates to current products of the company being acquired—and how much is excess inventory from products that are becoming obsolete because of new products.

Analysis of figures or charts (graphs) such as Exhibit 14–5 are useful, not just for what is shown in the particular document being reviewed, but for the questions that are raised. The advantage to the Barget Company was that it quickly launched a new president into key problems experienced by the company in the past five years. These related to the diminishing profits during most of the five years because of two hasty acquisitions. It brought forcibly to mind to the president and his management committee the need to "check the merchandise before paying for it."

It also resulted in a better overview of the need to exercise good controls over investment—whether the investment is acquired or already in place.

Case Example

Apex, Inc. manufactures office copying equipment and is illustrative of a company that was enjoying a rapid demand for its products. Seeing no immediate limitation to demand, the company built a second plant to broaden its line.

After several years of rapid expansion of facilities and sales, sales increased 10 times (from $3,000,000 to $30,000,000 annually), while cost of facilities and inventories increased 11½ times over the same period. Sales, instead of continuing the upward climb, suddenly turned downward to less than $14,000,000, and profits quickly reverted to losses. The reason for this was the success of a large competitor in developing a copier that used ordinary unsensitized paper. This cut sharply into the sales of all manufacturers of the then conventional copying machines.

Apex, in a belated review of the basic factors, realized how badly inventories and fixed assets had outstripped the growth of sales. Exhibit 14–6 shows sales, inventories, and fixed assets plotted on a semi-logarithmic scale—emphasizing percentage rather than absolute dollar relationships, and thus facilitating comparison of the rate of growth.

The chart shows dramatically how the increase in inventories and fixed assets outstripped the growth of sales. As soon as sales turned down in the seventh year, profits quickly reverted to losses.

The company acknowledged that it had overextended itself through too rapid expansion of facilities and turned its attention to a program of retrenchment. The marketing department had been asked for a realistic appraisal of the company's share of the market. After considering the various competitive factors, an estimate was made that sales would stabilize at $10 to $12 million per year.

Since the sales volume was about evenly split between the eastern and midwestern plant—and since both were about the same size—the decision was made to move all facilities to the midwestern location. Either plant could provide room for further expansion to about $15,000,000 per year. In the event that even further expansion beyond this level was required, both plants had ample area for additional construction.

The decision to consolidate at the midwestern facilities was based on the observation that this had always been the more profitable of the two locations. The company felt it would gain because the less profitable of the two plants would then be disposed of— further narrowing down the losses.

Selection of the midwestern location proved to be erroneous. What the company had failed to recognize was that the greater profitability of the midwestern plant was due to its being favored with the longer runs. The eastern plant had the bulk of the technical know-how and it ran the less profitable, more difficult, short runs—which were eventually transferred to the other plant when demand increased and the "bugs" were worked out. Most of the employees with the know-how would not move out of the East—this meant that the company lost many of its experienced employees with the resulting detrimental effect on the profitability of the products produced in the East.

The move to the Midwest was carried out—with the result that quality on many of the more difficult products deteriorated badly and customer rejections increased. Development of new products almost ceased. Sales, instead of stabilizing at $10 to $12 million, dropped to $7 million.

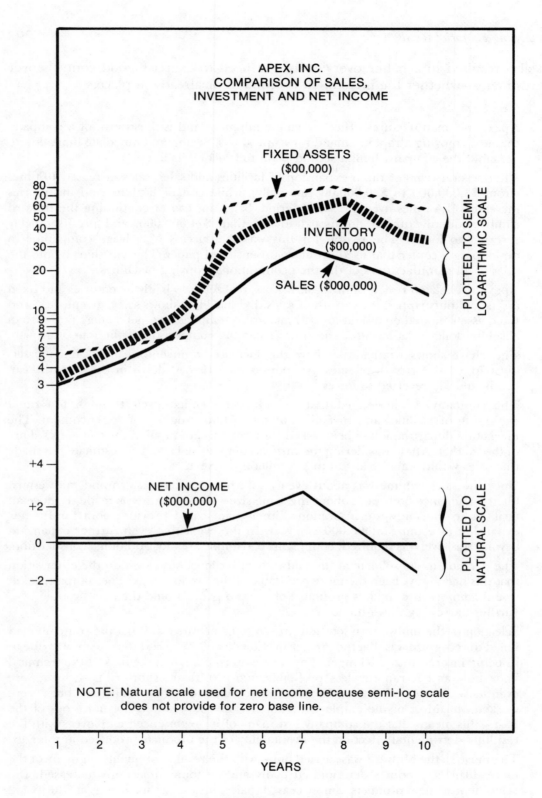

EXHIBIT 14–6:
COMPARISON OF SALES, INVESTMENT AND NET INCOME

The entry of the new copier and its effect on the existing types being manufactured could not have accurately been predicted. Apex, along with many of its competitors, could not have avoided a serious deterioration in its sales volume. However, had Apex confined its expansion within the existing facilities in the East, it would not have found retrenchment so painful. Additionally, and even more important, it would not have lost the technical personnel so necessary in this age of high technology.

Case Example

The group vice-president of Lang Division, following a period of decline in his division's return-on-investment, began to study the recent uptrend of inventory levels in one of the division's plants that he considered to be out of control. The figures that caused his concern were based on a comparison of inventory levels and sales for the three past years and comparing these figures with the number of employees (Table 14–3).

Year	Direct Labor Employees	Inventory Total $	Inventory $ per employee	Sales Total $	Sales $ per employee
19X2	665	$3,227,000	$4853	$20,268,000	$30,478
19X3	553	4,311,000	7796	20,049,000	36,255
19X4	568	4,852,000	8542	18,500,000	32,570

TABLE 14–3

The vice-president was disturbed because inventories were growing while the number of employees and the annual sales were declining. He was pleased that the sales per employee increased from $30,478 per employee to $32,570. Because it now required fewer employees to attain higher sales per employee, it was obvious that this would have a more favorable effect on profits. But the increase in inventory per employee from $4853 to $8542 meant that the inventory investment increased 76 percent. In terms of inventory turns, the decrease was from 6.3 turns per year to 3.8 turns.

The Lang Division manufactured decorative kitchen and bathroom hardware. Like many modern-day products, the design of these products changed with the tastes of homeowners and builders. The excess inventory was due to failure to phase out manufacture of a design that was being replaced by a new one. This oversight was due to poor communications between the material control manager and the engineering design group. To assure that this would not recur, the vice-president instituted a policy in which the engineering design group would notify the material control manager of any changes in writing rather than through the informal verbal communications that were used in the past.

Case Example

The old cliche "There are liars, damn liars and statisticians" can be applied to incomplete financial analyses as much as it can be applied to statistical reports.

Many acquisitions have been made with insufficient analysis of the basic informaton. The Artego Company, anxious to get into a new line of business, made a decision over a weekend to purchase a company with annual sales of $3 million. The purchase was authorized by the management committee on the recommendation of the vice-president of development and the president. The financial figures used as a basis for approval covered the previous four years' sales and gross margin. Nonmanfacturing costs were excluded because the selling and administrative expenses would be provided by the parent's existing selling and central office organization. The financial figures presented to the management committee were:

($000 Omitted)	Year 1	Year 2	Year 3	Year 4
Net sales	$1,304	1,902	2,755	2,742
Gross margin	362	450	572	563

After the company had been acquired for a year, the management committee was shocked to find that the gross margin was now only 10 percent of sales. If selling and administrative expense allocations were considered, the newly acquired company would show a loss.

The management committee and the president now realized that something had gone wrong and sought out more information. A more complete financial statement for the four years shown above was prepared. A fifth year, representing the financial results after acquisition, was added. Exhibit 14–7 shows the picture for the five years. The statement is abbreviated, but it contains the essential elements.

	YEAR 1		YEAR 2		YEAR 3		YEAR 4		YEAR 5	
	$	%	$	%	$	%	$	%	$	%
Gross Sales	1,309	100	1,908	100	2,763	100	2,793	100	3,014	100
Less: Returns and Allowances	5	1	6	1	8	—	51	2	71	2
Net Sales	1,304	99	1,902	99	2,755	100	2,742	98	2,943	98
Actual Cost of Sales	942	72	1,452	74	2,183	79	2,179	78	2,642	88
Actual Gross Margin	362	27	450	25	572	21	563	20	301	10
Inventories	517		726		934		1,296		958	

EXHIBIT 14–7:
INCOME STATEMENT—FIVE-YEAR ANALYSIS ($000 omitted)

The full financial statement showing the major elements makes obvious several trends that should have been considered when acquisition of the new company was being discussed.

1. The cost of sales as a percentage of sales had risen from 72 percent in year 1 to 78 percent in year 4. In year 5 under the new management, the percentage rose to 88 percent.
2. Gross margin dropped from 27 percent in year 1 to 20 percent in year 4. Year 5 showed a severe drop to 10 percent.
3. Inventories increased from $517,000 in year 1 to $1,296,000 in year 4. In year 5, they dropped to $958,000.
4. Year 4 showed $51,000 in returns and allowances. Year 5 showed $71,000.

Cost of Sales Percentage

The company that was acquired, being privately owned, did not keep sophisticated records in which costs by job were accumulated. The owner considered record keeping to be expensive, therefore insufficient detail existed to make a meaningful analysis of product costs. It was also possible that sales prices did not keep up with inflation; this could be a factor in causing the rising cost of sales percentage.

Gross Margin

Since the gross margin is the complement of the cost of sales plus the returns and allowances percentages, the answer to the cost of sales question will furnish the answer to the gross margin downtrend.

Inventories

As a rule, the profitability of a company increases when the rate of inventory accumulation rises and it drops as the rate inventory accumulation declines. The reason is that when inventory increases more of the nonvariable costs are deferred in inventory.

When inventory is decreased, the costs previously deferred are now relieved. They reflect an increased cost of sales percentage—thus reducing profits. In year 1, inventory is 39 percent of sales while in year 4 the percentage rose to 46 percent. During these four years, since the gross margin is in a downtrend and inventory on the increase, it is probable that if inventories had not risen, profits would have been even lower.

Financial Results in the First Year after Acquisition of the Company

The Artego Company management estimated that the company it had acquired had almost double the inventory that it required. The financial statement for year 5 reflected the results after a reduction of over 25 percent of the inventory. This meant that the nonvariable costs which had been deferred in prior periods were now being reflected in cost of sales along with current nonvariable costs. The result was a reduction of the gross margin from year 4. Another factor that affected profitability adversely was the high level of product rejects—quality standards were tightened and training programs instituted to increase the level of quality. In addition to reduction of inventory and improvement of quality, a study was made of the method of establishing selling prices. The company had some flexibility because the products did have some unique features. This project would take some time—at least six months—because the company was working off backlogs in which it had commitments to selling prices that had been established prior to acquisition.

The management committee acknowledged that year 6 would be another year of correction of inventory levels, production rejects, and study of selling prices. All members of the committee agreed that any future acquisitions that are made must provide assurance that all problems be investigated before rather than after the new company is acquired.

This chapter might well have been titled "The many faces of analysis." Each of the examples is sufficiently different to support the need for the various perspectives applicable in the different situations.

The first of these emphasized the interrelationship of return on sales, return on equity (investment), and annual turns of equity for the decade of the seventies. The figures were taken from the annual reports for two companies in each of four industries.

The case example of the Barget Company is illustrative of a variation of the method referred to above and illustrated in Exhibits 14–1, 14–2, 14–3, and 14–4. The Barget Company's method monitors the figures by quarter. In addition to return on sales, return on investment, and turns of investment per year, the dollar sales and profits are also shown for the same periods.

Apex, Inc.—a fast-growing company in the copier industry—analyzed its investment, sales, and net income over a ten-year period. The analysis reflected that growth of fixed assets and inventory outpaced the growth of sales. When sales started downward in year 7, the investment moved downward but at a slower rate. Profits moved downward in the seventh year at a faster rate than they rose prior to year 7. In the ninth year, profits became losses. This study, illustrated graphically in Exhibit 14–6, was helpful in making the decision to close one of the two plants and to combine the operations under a single roof.

The Lang Division of the Cortex Company, concerned with increasing inventories during the latest three-year period, found that the inventories had increased 50 percent while sales dropped 9 percent. The number of employees had dropped from 665 to 568, a reduction of 15 percent. The analysis denominated inventories and sales in terms of so much per employee provided a different approach to the investigation of the problems depicted by excess inventories. These figures raised a number of interesting questions that were subsequently useful in resolving the approach to be taken in reducing the investment. This analysis in terms of "per employee" was also helpful in establishing broad standards to be used in the future to monitor inventories and sales until more sophisticated controls were being developed.

15

Reporting Financial Results

The complexities of modern business and the dynamic nature of our economy have made it necessary for management to develop special techniques for reporting, coordinating, and controlling the operation of a business. Decisions must be made quickly to adjust courses of action as external and internal forces change direction.

OBJECTIVES OF REPORTING

Reporting procedures must be sufficiently detailed to provide the flexibility to "home in" and make corrections in problem areas yet not to be so detailed that reporting becomes burdensome and expensive. The owner and president of a medium-size company, in seeking suggestions for improving his reporting procedures, complained that his controller had developed a "bookkeeping factory" in which he analyzed accounting-related costs with microscopic precision but avoided the more important big picture. As a case in point, three of the functions for which standards were prepared are shown below:

Function	Standards developed
Maintaining accounts receivable records	Cost per customer account
	Cost per sales order
	Cost per sales transaction
Billing	Cost per invoice line
	Cost per item
	Cost per invoice
	Cost per order line
	Cost per order
Credits and collections	Cost per sales order
	Cost per account
	Cost per credit sales transaction

After relating these examples, the president stated: "I could care less what it costs per order line or per sales order to bill a customer. We have only a few people in accounting, so there's not much in the way of potential savings in the accounting department through use of these kinds of standards. I would rather see the time spent on calculating the profitability of the various products I manufacture. I would also want to know how I can change my sales mix to increase overall profits. As far as standards are concerned, sure, I expect the accounting department to measure itself against budgets and standards, but I also expect the controller to institute budgeting procedures for the rest of the manufacturing operations, not just for his own department."

VARIANCES MUST BE ADEQUATELY EXPLAINED

The executive vice-president of another company that had budgets by departmental responsibility complained that variances from budget were not being properly explained. His accounting department merely recapped the variances in a separate section of the report with such comments as:

- Unfavorable material variance $19,890
- Direct labor unfavorable variance   7,496

This executive went on to explain that he had one of the members of his manufacturing staff investigate the reasons behind the variances. The findings for material were:

- Parts were being run on presses that were too light with the result that the upper and lower parts of the die mismatched at the point of impact. Because of this many parts had to be scrapped. In addition, the dies were being damaged—resulting in high die maintenance costs.

The findings for direct labor were:

- A metal stamping die for part number 4526AO was damaged while being transported to the machine. This caused labor delays while temporary repairs were made. In addition, overtime was incurred on this order to meet customer delivery requirements.

The explanation that parts were being run on presses that were too light provided the general manager with information on which he could take action. His investigations revealed: (1) that the foreman of the press department was not sufficiently familiar with press equipment (he was therefore transferred to the assembly department, where an opening had just occurred and a more experienced foreman replaced him); and (2) shop scheduling was also found to be deficient because the scheduling of work to the various machines was left entirely to the foremen. Too much reliance was being placed on "hot sheets" to meet shipping commitments to customers. To monitor future performance in scheduling, the general manager issued instructions that he be placed on distribution for every "hot sheet." The mere issuing of such instructions reduced the number of these sheets by 50 percent in the first month.

The labor problem was an accident that would probably not recur very often. Giving the accident visibility would undoubtedly result in more careful procedures in handling tools during transport.

Reporting must not only give visibility to the more important information, it must also identify the causes of deviations from budget (standard) in terms that can be translated to corrective action. Availability of reports that identify problem areas by responsibility and by cause provide the means for better coordination and cooperation among the different disciplines who would know that if they were inefficient "they would be found out."

Several of the reports that were presented in Sections I and II are repeated in this chapter to reiterate the importance of using them properly.

THE MANUFACTURING COST REPORT (EXHIBIT 15–1)

This report, titled "Overview Report for Manufacturing Cost," is intended to familiarize the reader with manufacturing cost content. These figures were used in Chapter 9 to illustrate the development of overhead costing rates. The purpose for including the report in this chapter is to call attention to the budget (allowance) column, which provides the plant manager with an overview of performance of his manufacturing plant. The manufacturing cost report shown here is a recap of the previous year's actual manufacturing costs. In the monthly reports for the coming year, budget figures would be included in the columns provided. Note that both the individual month's actual and budget columns, as well as the year-to-date actual and budget columns, are provided for.

Monitoring Procedures

Material Usage. In this plant, the three major materials are steel, resins, and packing material. The budget figure for each of these will be based on the volume of production. The standard cost of each of these is multiplied by the standard cost content in each of the products manufactured during the month. Although the breakdown is shown by material, the underlying analyses identify the production centers that use the material.

Direct Labor. These figures are broken down by the three production centers. The budget figure (standard) is developed in the same manner as the budget figures for material; units produced multiplied by the standard cost per unit.

Indirect Labor. The budget for indirect labor for each of the three production centers is developed as part of the flexible budget for overhead items. See Indirect Labor–Service Departments for explanation of flexible budget allowance determination.

Indirect Labor–Service Centers

This section of the manufacturing cost report shows the payroll costs of all indirect labor in the service departments. The budget is based on the flexible budget allowance which takes into account the level of activity—as in the case of all other overhead items. The determination of the budget for receiving and shipping is demonstrated on an annual basis in Table 15–1 from figures taken from Exhibit 9–10 on page 198.

MANUFACTURING COST REPORT

Plant _____   Year of 19 _____

Summary	Year to Date		Month	
	Actual	Budget	Actual	Budget
Sales Value of Production	7,800,000			
Material	3,711,540			
Direct Labor	746,823			
Total Prime Cost	4,458,363			
Indirect Labor-Prod'n. Depts.	128,560			
Indirect Labor-Service Depts.	538,607			
Labor Connected Expenses	321,289			
Non-Payroll Expenses	511,400			
TOTAL OVERHEAD	1,499,856			
TOTAL COST OF PRODUCTION	5,958,219			

OPERATING STATISTICS	ACTUAL % OF COST	BUDGET % OF COST	ACTUAL % OF SALES VALUE	BUDGET % OF SALES VALUE
Sales Value of Production			100.0	
Material	62.3		47.5	
Direct Labor	12.5		9.6	
Indirect Labor-Prod'n. Depts.	2.2		1.7	
Indirect Labor-Service Depts.	9.0		7.0	
Labor Connected Expenses	5.4		4.1	
Non-Payroll Expenses	8.6		6.5	
TOTAL COST	100.0		76.4	

MATERIAL

Plant _____   Year of 19 _____

	Year to Date		Month	
	Actual	Budget	Actual	Budget
Steel	2,094,416			
Resins	1,242,062			
Packing Material	375,062			
TOTAL MATERIAL COST	3,711,540			

DIRECT LABOR

Department	Year to Date		Month	
	Actual	Budget	Actual	Budget
Molding Presses	283,151			
Punch Presses	225,646			
Finishing	238,026			
TOTAL DIRECT LABOR	746,823			

INDIRECT LABOR-PRODUCTION DEPARTMENTS

Department	Year to Date		Month	
	Actual	Budget	Actual	Budget
Molding Presses	48,151			
Punch Presses	48,965			
Finishing	31,444			
TOTAL INDIRECT LABOR-PROD'N.	128,560			

EXHIBIT 15–1:
OVERVIEW REPORT FOR MANUFACTURING COST

INDIRECT LABOR-SERVICE DEPARTMENTS

Plant _____   Year of 19 _____

Department	Year to Date		Month	
	Actual	Budget	Actual	Budget
General Manager's Staff	50,932			
Personnel	34,200			
Cost Accounting	39,370			
Material Control	86,679			
Engineering	45,356			
Quality Assurance	73,285			
Purchasing	27,278			
Maintenance	119,950			
Receiving and Shipping	61,557			
TOTAL INDIRECT LABOR-SV.	538,607			

LABOR CONNECTED EXPENSES

Account Name	Year to Date		Month	
	Actual	Budget	Actual	Budget
Overtime Premium	42,890			
Shift Premium	10,154			
Vacation Expense	27,166			
Unemployment Insurance	29,778			
Group Life Insurance	12,430			
Hospitalization	35,595			
Pension Expense	43,505			
Compensation & Liability Ins.	25,990			
Payroll Taxes	93,781			
TOTAL LABOR CONNECTED	321,289			

NON-PAYROLL EXPENSES

Plant _____   Year of 19 _____

Account Name	Year to Date		Month	
	Actual	Budget	Actual	Budget
UTILITIES				
Water	4,000			
Gas	4,100			
Electricity	46,900			
Telephone	9,120			
Acetylene	275			
FACILITIES COST				
Rent	2,000			
Property Taxes	8,290			
Purchased Services	5,400			
Depreciation	195,100			
Insurance	2,817			
Fuel Oil	34,600			
SUPPLIES				
Stationery	5,900			
Postage	3,100			
Expendable Tools	20,700			
Maintenance Materials	65,700			
Lubricants and Chemicals	8,000			
Factory Supplies	4,200			
Tool Maintenance & Amortization	58,648			
OFFICE EXPENSES				
Employment Expenses	4,750			
Subscriptions	500			
Dues & Memberships	500			
Computer Services	3,500			
Rental of Equipment	10,600			
Auto Expense	12,700			
TOTAL NON-PAYROLL EXPENSES	511,400			

EXHIBIT 15–1, continued

	Annual Figures*			Variable Cost per
			Production	Production
Molding Presses	Fixed	Variable	Hours	Hour
Receiving & Shipping	$ 5,540	12,927	60,800	$.21
Punch Presses				
Receiving & Shipping	3,693	8,618	49,900	.17
Finishing				
Receiving & Shipping	9,234	21,545	65,100	.33
Total Plant	$18,467	43,090		

*The application of the budget formula is also demonstrated for use in monthly reporting in Exhibit 9–11 on page 200.

TABLE 15–1

Because the above figures represent the actual figures the budget for receiving and shipping will total $61,557—the same as the figure shown as "actual." See Exhibit 9–10.

On a month by month budget, the fixed costs would be adjusted to a monthly basis. The variable percentage of production hours would be the same for the month as for the year, except that the appropriate production level would be used to calculate the variable allowance.

Labor-Connected Expenses and Nonpayroll Expenses

The same procedure would be applied to these expenses as demonstrated above for the indirect labor in the service departments.

OPERATING STATISTICS

The actual percentage of sales value of production could provide the plant manager with an advance look at the profitability of his operation—at gross margin level—before the corporate operating statements are issued. The gross margin shown on the income statement will usually be at variance with the figure determined from the manufacturing cost report because of increases and decreases in inventory. In spite of variations in gross margin figures between the cost report and the income statement, the plant manager will have a greater measure of control because he can more readily determine where costs went astray if the actual gross margin falls short of budget.

Monitoring "Phantom" Inventory Buildup

Many companies experience periodic phantom inventory buildups when the year-end physical inventory values fall short of the inventory value carried on the books. This can be caused by under-reporting of defective production, inconsistent costing of input versus output, incomplete paperwork, and over-reporting of production. Many controllers who have experienced the nightmare of explaining what happened to several hundred thousand dollars or more of inventory are continually on the lookout for a simple early warning signal for monitoring phantom buildups.

One such simple early warning signal would be to compare the year-to-date cost of production (manufacturing cost) with the year-to-date cost of sales. In any one month or even two months, there could be a divergence between the two figures because of valid inventory changes. However, the further into the year the year-to-date comparison is made, the closer the cost of production and cost of sales should come together. If the divergence between the two continues to spread in the year-to-date comparison, the probabilities are that phantom inventories are building up. This could be the signal to take an inventory and make a comparison with the book values rather than waiting until year-end. Obviously, this is not an accurate type of control but it should be helpful during the period that more sophisticated controls are being implemented.

A summary of the information sources and key features of the manufacturing cost report follows:

MANUFACTURING COST REPORT FEATURES

SECTION	INFORMATION SOURCES	KEY FEATURES
Summary section	Summarizes the material, direct labor, and overhead in a concise manner.	Many companies concentrate on direct labor reports and overhead reports as two separate documents. Most companies do not provide a sufficient amount of information on material usage. The manufacturing cost report summary provides the complete overview of all elements in a single report.
Operating statistics	Actual costs as a percentage of the sales value of production are arrived at by dividing each of the major cost elements by the estimated sales value of production. The sales value of production in this company is determined by applying an experienced markup factor to total manufacturing costs.	Provides a means for the plant manager of a factory to evaluate the profitability of his operation in denominators that are familiar to him and over which he feels that he has some measure of control.
Material	The input of material into production is based on issues out of and returns into the stockrooms.	When production rejects are inaccurately reported, the material usage figure would be incorrect.

Direct labor	Payroll identifies the portion of the payroll applicable to factory direct labor.	Failure to correctly identify rework on spoiled production could result in over-reporting of production. This, like unreported production rejects, would result in a buildup of "phantom inventory."
Indirect labor–production departments	Payroll identifies portion applicable to nondirect labor personnel working in the production departments.	Identification by production cost centers (departments) provides more accurate product costing and better control of a fairly sizable portion of the payroll.
Indirect labor–service departments	Payroll identifies portion applicable to nondirect labor personnel working in the service departments.	The service department payroll represents from 85 percent to 95 percent of the total cost of service departments. Many companies that report service department costs clutter up such reports by including numerous small nonlabor items.
Labor connected expenses	These growing expenses are shown in a separate section because of their growing magnitude.	This section provides constant visibility to these expenses and is a constant reminder to management that inefficiency of labor includes more cost than only wages and salaries.
Nonpayroll expenses	The source of these expenses, in many companies, is referred to as the expense analysis.	Although many companies attempt to break down these expenses by departmental responsibility, they are more economically controlled on an overall basis without the need for "splintering" by department.

The column entitled "Key Features" also points up potential areas in which inaccuracies can occur. Material usage, for example, can be incorrectly reported if the production losses of material are not correctly accounted for or if components and products are relieved at values that are not consistent with the costs of input.

The same applies when labor expended in rework is classified as direct rather than indirect labor (overhead). Nonsalvageable production losses that are under-reported can also contribute to the build-up of phantom inventories that cannot be accounted for until a physical inventory is taken. These inaccuracies will reflect in the operating statements.

PRODUCT COSTS

The Manufacturing Cost Report will provide the plant manager with a simplified overview of factory costs. This report also provides a breakdown of the major costs by responsibility. The next logical type of information that the plant manager, as well as others, need is information on the costs of the products that are being manufactured. There are numerous formats in which product costs can be presented; however, three will be presented.

Standard Products Built to Stock

The first of these, previously shown as Exhibit 12–5, is again shown in this chapter as Exhibit 15–2. Standard products built in large quantities are normally costed at standard. For cost estimating purposes in establishing selling prices, allowances can be added to allow for contingencies, especially if the product is new. Under standard costing, product costs are not calculated at actual, because of the impracticality of identifying actual costs, particularly when the component parts are interchangeable. The plant manager would exercise control by monitoring the departmental (cost center) variances. Zero variances (an unlikely circumstance) would mean that the products made that month were made at standard. The point of control would not be the individual products but the variances and their reason for occurrence. If the maintenance department's cost is high because of overtime incurred to do maintenance on the generator equipment furnishing the electicity, no attempt would be made to charge the individual products for such excess costs; the standard overhead rate which includes maintenance would be used in developing the product costs. In the same way, material and labor would be assigned to the various products at standard and the point of control would be the variance.

Customized Products

These are the products for which anticipated actual costs are determined in arriving at product cost, as in the case of the gate valves (discussed in Chapter 2) which are made to different specifications for different customers. The selling price of the product is based on these anticipated actual costs, taking into account such items as setup and rework when these costs are an unavoidable part of the process. Setup and rework in customized products, unlike standard costing, would be considered as a direct labor charge to the product rather than overhead. Exhibit 15–3, "Job Cost History," is the same exhibit which appeared in Chapter 2 as Exhibit 2–7 to demonstrate job costing. The exhibit shows the key cost elements incurred in the manufacture of the valves. These provide the plant manager with a

Standard Product Cost Sheet

Quantity—1,000
(500 per case)

Effective Jan. 1, XX

MATERIALS OR OPERATION DESCRIPTION	CODE NUMBER	QUANTITY SPECIFIED	% WASTE	STANDARD	UNIT OF MEASURE	MATERIAL		LABOR		BURDEN		TOTAL COST
						RATE	COST	RATE	COST	RATE	COST	
Top: Plastic	771	20.0	5	21.0000	lb.	.134	2.81					2.81
Molding	38			.3768	hr.					12.70	4.79	4.79
							2.81					7.60
Bottom: Plastic	771	21.0	5	22.0500	lb.	.134	2.95					2.95
Molding	38			.4072	hr.					12.70	5.17	5.17
							2.95					8.12
Issue to Assembly Floor:												
Molded plastic top	151	1,000	4	1,040	M	7.600	7.90 *					7.90
Molded plastic bottom	152	1,000	4	1,040	M	8.120	8.44 **					8.44
Carton (holds 500)	6	2	5	2.1000	Ea.	.268	.56					.56
Bag	18	50	5	52.5000	Ea.	.031	1.63					1.63
Crate	6	2	5	2.1000	Ea.	.162	.34					.34
Assemble and Pack	64			1.0000	Hr.			2.58	2.58	6.32	6.32	8.90
							18.87		2.58		6.32	27.77
Transfer Value to Finished Goods	2131	1,000	1	1,010	M	27.77	28.06					28.06
							28.06					28.06
Total Cost by Element							8.61		2.61		16.84	28.06

	$ per Case	%
Sales Price	17.35	100.0
Standard Cost	14.03	80.8
Gross Profit	3.32	19.2

*Molded top $7.60 plus 4% waste = $7.90.
**Molded bottom $8.12 plus 4% waste = $8.44.

EXHIBIT 15–2:
STANDARD PRODUCT COST SHEET—PLASTIC COSMETIC CASES

308

UNIT COSTS OF ORDERS SHIPPED

		TOTAL MATERIAL COST						TOOLING AND PATTERNS	TOTAL LABOR AND OVERHEAD				TOTAL MFG. COST	SELLING PRICE	GROSS PROFIT %	NON-MFG. DIRECT CHARGES
ORDER NO.	QUAN.	BODY	BONNET	DISC.	OPERATOR	OTHER	TOTAL		MACHINING	WELDING	ASSEMBLY AND TEST	TOTAL				
4" 300# S.S.																
Actual 22113-11	2	$327	$268	$54	$966	$235	$1,850	$24	$617	$318	$299	$1,234	$3,108	$5,044	38.4%	$410
Estimate	2	620	460	35	834	213	2,162	—	721	350	371	1,442	3,604	5,044	28.5	580
12" 900# Ca. St.																
Actual 26126-12	1	3,123	991	165	3,904	1,341	9,524	2,140	3,174	1,597	1,578	6,349	18,013	16,602	(8.5)	1,040
Estimate	1	2,138	874	126	2,004	1,027	6,169	2,515	2,056	1,019	1,037	4,112	12,796	16,602	22.9	796
20" 150# Ca. St.																
Actual 23957-15	2	1,288	154	229	—	376	2,047	15	682	362	320	1,364	3,426	5,910	42.0	804
Estimate	5	1,015	148	297	—	260	1,720	—	607	365	342	1,314	3,034	5,910	48.7	760
30" 150# Ca. St.																
Actual 24628-16	2	2,943	349	441	—	688	4,421	—	1,474	716	757	2,947	7,368	20,200	63.5	1,149
Estimate	2	4,984	300	501	—	861	6,646	5,028	2,215	1,097	1,119	4,431	16,105	20,200	20.3	1,296

COST HISTORY RECORD
UNIT COST

Product 20" 150# GATE VALVE

		MATERIAL COST						HOURS					TOTAL MFG. COST	SALES PRICE	GROSS PROFIT	NON-MFG. DIRECT CHARGES
SHOP ORDER #	QUAN.	BODY	BONNET	DISC.	OPERATOR	OTHER	TOTAL MATERIAL	UPGRADE*	MACHINE SHOP	WELD	ASSEMBLY	TOTAL HOURS				
21428-16	3	$1,285	$163	$246	—	$346	$2,040	3	57	14	21	95	$3,521	$5,910	$2,389	$1,519
21585-17	2	1,273	162	241	—	345	2,021	4	58	12	18	92	3,502	5,910	2,408	1,307
23561-14	2	1,311	189	220	—	298	2,018	5	71	29	22	127	3,982	5,910	1,928	1,275
23957-15	5	1,288	154	229	—	376	2,047	4	63	16	21	104	3,426	5,910	2,484	804

*Upgrade refers to Rework

EXHIBIT 15–3:
JOB COST HISTORY

cost picture for the major material costs, the labor and overhead costs in the various production centers as well as the selling price, gross profit percentage and nonmanufacturing charges. The actual costs incurred can be compared with the original cost estimates used in the establishment of the selling price. The lower portion of the exhibit summarizes the key data for one of the product types—showing a running record of past costs of making this product.

As might be expected, there is no one way in which to maintain a record of product costs. Exhibit 15–4 illustrates the format in which another company making the same type of valve keeps its job cost history. In this case, the breakdown by cost elements is shown by material, direct labor and burden (overhead), for each component. The total manufacturing cost of the components is then totaled on a summary card. This company accumulates the actual costs but has not yet provided for comparing these costs with a "standard" or "estimate," although the column for this figure is provided for on the summary card.

A TOUCH OF RIVALRY

Developing a competitive spirit among the operating units can be effective in boosting profits, as was demonstrated in the LeBlanc Corporation.

Case Example

The LeBlanc Corporation has twelve operating divisions. Each month, the year-to-date profits are ranked from the highest to the lowest. The percentage of profit on sales is also shown and ranked from the highest to the lowest. The format of this statement is shown as Exhibit 15–5. The division names are disguised as is the name of the company. The dollar profit and percentage of return on sales are actual figures, however, to provide a real world insight as to the range in which profitability within a company can fluctuate.

This comparative statement shows in a glance who the "winners" and "losers" are. It shows that one-half of the divisions have profits and one-half have losses. The number one division in the ranking of profit dollars is number three in ranking on percentage of profit on sales. The building products, transformers, small appliances, and industrial electronic tubes are hovering at breakeven. This type of comparative statement is likely to excite divisions such as these that are running "neck-and-neck." Since they appear to be in the same league as far as profitability is concerned, a small improvement would push them over the top. Although the new products division shows a 17.4 percent loss, the company is not too concerned because these products were just released into production. As production kinks are ironed out for the individual products, the products will be transferred to the appropriate division in which they fit. The company does not expect this new products division ever to be in a profitable position, since it is actually a "preproduction" operation.

As far as the semiconductor products are concerned, the company is seriously studying the market and its position in that market to determine whether it should remain in this business. If it decides to continue with this product line, it must consider the high cost of withstanding the ravages of the periodic shakeouts.

SUMMARY — COST HISTORY RECORD

DESCRIPTION: 20" GATE VALVE

DATE MO	YEAR	ORDER NO	CUSTOMER	UNIT COST STANDARD	UNIT COST ACTUAL	SELLING PRICE
9	7X	27327-18	J.C.P.E.		49,600 00	56,718.00
9	7X	27327-19	"		51,241 80	56,718.00
10	7X	26499-31	"		44,369 67	56,718.00
12	7X	29320-32	"		50,394 92	56,718.00
12	7X	29320-33	"		51,271 31	56,718.00

BODY ASSEMBLIES — COST HISTORY RECORD

DATE	ORDER NO.	QUAN. MADE	ALLOY	MATERIAL	DIRECT LABOR	BURDEN	TOTAL COST
9-7X	27327-18	1	CP	22,702 97	853 79	2,625 72	26,182 48
9-7X	27327-19	1	CP	22,721 04	1,018 53	3,045 35	26,784 92
10-7X	28699.31	1	CP	21,991 74	1,562 40	5,374 07	28,928 21
12-7X	29320-32	1	CP	22,001 64	1,616 66	5,639 88	29,258 18
12-7X	29320-33	1	CP	24,918 06	821 59	2,827 44	28,567 09

BONNETS — COST HISTORY RECORD

DATE	ORDER NO.	QUAN. MADE	ALLOY	MATERIAL	DIRECT LABOR	BURDEN	TOTAL COST
	27327-18	1	CP	6,255 06	391 74	1,235 20	7,882 00
	27327-19	1	CP	6,262 43	446 53	1,418 73	8,127 69
							7,539 08

DISCS — COST HISTORY RECORD

DATE	ORDER NO.	QUAN. MADE	ALLOY	MATERIAL	DIRECT LABOR	BURDEN	TOTAL COST
9-7X	27327-18	1	CP	2,354 16	656 03	2,133 10	5,143 29
9-7X	27327-19	1	CP	2,324 75	345 75	1,138 61	3,808 41

STEMS — COST HISTORY RECORD

DATE	ORDER NO.	QUAN.	ALLOY	MATERIAL	DIRECT LABOR	BURDEN	TOTAL COST
			CP	302 80	150 83	504 37	958 00

ALL OTHER — COST HISTORY RECORD

DATE	ORDER NO.	QUAN. MADE	ALLOY	MATERIAL	DIRECT LABOR	BURDEN	TOTAL COST
						1,142 62	9,434 23

EXHIBIT 15–4:
JOB COST HISTORY: BROKEN DOWN BY MATERIAL, DIRECT LABOR AND BURDEN,
BY COMPONENT

311

MONTH OF JANUARY 19X2

DIVISION	AFTER-TAX PROFITS*		RANKING	
	$	%	$	%
Aerospace	$1,109	3.0%	1	3
Electronic Systems	180	3.8	2	2
Electrical Equipment	130	1.7	3	4
Molded Products	28	6.5	4	1
Lighting Products	10	1.6	5	5
Building Products	7	.6	6	6
Transformers	(9)	(.5)	7	8
Small Appliances	(11)	(.3)	8	7
Industrial Electronic Tubes	(31)	(1.0)	9	9
New Products	(38)	(17.4)	10	11
Commercial Testing Eqipment	(83)	(4.7)	11	10
Semiconductors	(447)	(27.5)	12	12
TOTAL AFTER-TAX PROFITS	$ 845	1.5%		

*Figures in thousand dollars.

EXHIBIT 15–5
LEBLANC CORPORATION RANKING OF DIVISIONAL PROFITS

THE SUCCESSFUL REPORT MUST ATTRACT AND HOLD THE INTEREST OF THE READER

When Henry Ford's first attempt to form a manufacturing facility failed in 1899, he realized that he needed an event that would attract the public's attention, before he could expect to be successful in his planned venture. That event proved to be the race in which Ford entered a racing car driven by Barney Oldfield. By winning the race, Ford was approached by financiers, and the Ford Motor Car Company became a reality. The financiers were attracted because the race was won by Ford's racing car—even though the car Ford was to build had little in common with his racer.

Although the report must be factual, it must have features that provide key executives with new perspectives—such as a running breakeven point based on each month's operations. The ranking of the various divisional profits, as was demonstrated by the LeBlanc Corporation case, is another example of a method for attracting attention and holding the interest of the report reader, while still providing management with the basic information needed for control.

The value of cost controls breaks down when reports are "ground out" mechanically without the exercise of judgment. This brings us back to an earlier section in this chapter entitled, "Variance must be adequately explained." The next chapter will point out some frequently overlooked examples of weaknesses that result in variances. It will also illustrate how periodic operational reviews can be made to seek out potential weaknesses in the operations that could cause large unfavorable variances.

16

Finding the Weaknesses That Cause Unfavorable Variances

Top level executives are often frustrated because of their inability to come to grips with the reasons behind reduced profits—in spite of highly sophisticated financial reporting that shows variances from standards and explanations of the reasons for the deviations.

Some financial executives responsible for the design and preparation of the financial statements frequently cannot understand this frustration on the part of superiors; they feel that the figures in the statement reflect, by individual element of cost, the amount of variation of actual costs from the financial goals that were approved by the top level executives for the current year. These financial executives argue that the variances serve their purpose well by indicating the trouble spots and assigning a dollar value to the amount of excess costs. They point out, for example, that:

- Material variances identify excess prices paid for materials that have been purchased as well as identifying by type of material and department where excessive amounts of material have been used.

- Direct labor variances show the differences between the actual hourly rates of pay and the standard rates at which production is valued. Labor efficiency variances are shown by department.

- Overhead variances are broken down to show the deviations from budget for the individual expenses as well as the variances caused by changes in the production level.

In the mind of this financial executive, what better cost and operating controls could anyone ask for?

VARIANCES HIGHLIGHT THE SYMPTOMS RATHER THAN REVEALING THE TRUE CAUSES

There is no doubt that the variances serve a useful purpose in identifying areas of excess cost by cost element. However, these are only the symptoms. What is lacking is an explanation of the cause of the variances.

Examples of Weaknesses That Cause Variances

Following are some illustrative examples of deficiencies in the factory operations that result in variances:

- Poor scheduling of production that does not allow sufficient lead time for purchase of the required material. This can cause material price variances because (1) the purchasing department does not have sufficient lead time to obtain at least three bids to assure that the material has been purchased at the lowest price, and (2) shortage of lead time can require that the material be shipped by air freight rather than by less expensive means.

- Unbalanced inventories could result in use of more material than called for in the standard. Illustrative of this is the use of wider strip material than should have been used in a part formed on a punch press. As a specific example, one company forming a high volume part made of phosphor bronze did not have 2⅞″ strip stock in inventory. Therefore, a 3″ width was used. The ⅛″ excess width did not seem great. However, the production run was very large and phosphor bronze was very expensive, hence a large material usage variance, which was not explained in the variance report. This precluded appropriate corrective action from being taken.

- In another company, an unfavorable volume variance was explained as being due to reduction of production volume in the screw machine department. This was an inadequate explanation because management could not take immediate action without making a complete analysis of the situation. The reasons that should have been given for this variance are:

  - Many of the tools issued by the tool crib were in need of sharpening. When a machine is set up with tooling in marginal condition, an interruption in the run can be expected. In this case, stoppages for sharpening resulted in a great deal of idle machine time, as well as idle labor.

  - A check of several drawers of tools in the tool crib revealed obvious signs of wear. The corrective action recommended was that a program be instituted in which all tools be sharpened upon completion of a job and before return to the crib.

Thus, a properly explained reason for a variance can be helpful in taking corrective action to minimize recurrence.

REGULAR OPERATIONAL REVIEWS ARE NECESSARY

Deficiencies such as those discussed above, need not wait for signals sent out by unfavorable variances. Regular reviews, say, once a year, should be made to ferret out weaknesses.

These reviews should be formalized in the form of a written report circulated among the key executives. Illustrative of this is a consultant's report to a client. Although the company depicted is fictitious, the report is based on actual events revealed in many such reviews. This type of review of operations can serve any of the following three purposes:

1. The financial executive, considering retaining consultants to make such a review, will obtain a good picture of the approach followed by the consultant and the nature of the format in which the findings and recommendations will be presented.

2. The report can serve as a model for the executive who wishes to use his or her own staff to conduct a similar survey of operations.

3. The reader may find in this report a number of recommendations that are useful ideas to consider in approaching weaknesses in the reader's own company.

The consultant's report, which follows, outlines the approach and scope of the review, organization of the report, highlights of the study, overview and highlights of the findings, and recommendations. The more detailed findings and recommendations will be found in Chapter 37 of the *Controller's Handbook,* which was written by the author. The handbook was edited by Sam R. Goodman and James S. Reece (Dow Jones-Irwin, Homewood, IL 60430, 1978).

(Sample Report)

Ernst & Whinney

153 East 53rd Street
New York, New York 10022

Mr. Norton E. Pauls
President and CEO
Excelon, Incorporated
139 Broadway
New York, NY 10005

Dear Mr. Pauls:

We have completed our survey of cost and operating controls at the South Orange, N.J., plant and present herewith our findings and recommendations.

APPROACH AND SCOPE

The objective of our study was to examine the information systems and controls, both financial and operating, to assure that they conform to company policy and that they are responsive to the company management's current and future needs. We therefore approached this assignment through the following steps:

1. Familiarized ourselves with corporate policy.
2. Made a plant tour to familiarize ourselves with the manufacturing processes.
3. Interviewed key management personnel as well as other supervisory employees in the various departments.
4. Reviewed the various reports and source documents as well as the procedures followed in developing the reports.
5. Upon conclusion of our field work we met with the general manager, operations manager and the controller to review our findings and recommendations.

ORGANIZATION OF THE REPORT

This report is made up of the following sections:

Section I	Background
Section II	Cost Controls
Section III	Operating Controls

316

HIGHLIGHTS OF THE STUDY

We have capsulized below, the contents of this report which is presented in more detailed form in Sections II and III.

OVERVIEW

We found the personnel at this plant to be technically competent. Areas of weakness were: excessive rejects, weak controls over quality of purchased parts, loose inventory controls, and some erroneous costing practices.

COST CONTROLS

Findings	Recommendations

PRODUCT LINE INCOME STATEMENTS

This report, which shows gross profit by product line, is a useful report that has high acceptance by the Marketing Department.

The accuracy of this report would be improved if:

- Setup costs were identified by product line rather than being spread to all products through the conventional overhead rate application.
- Tooling costs, which vary widely from product to product, should, in similar fashion, be assigned by product rather than being "leveled out" through an overhead rate application.

PRODUCT PROFITABILITY

In testing the profitability of several products, we found that the percentage of the selling price for product line G required to cover prime cost (material plus direct labor) ranged from a low of 27 percent to a high of 49 percent. This means that in one case, 73 percent of the selling price is left to cover all other costs and profit; in the other case, only 51 percent of the selling price is left after prime costs.

We recommend that a report similar to that illustrated in Exhibit I of this report be maintained on a current basis for all products. The advantages of such a report are:

- It will indicate the relative profitability of the various items within each product line.
- It will highlight the products that have an unusually high material or direct labor cost and thus point up potential cost reduction areas.

317

| | | STANDARD COST | | %SELLING PRICE | | |
| | SALES | | DIRECT | | DIRECT | PRIME |
	PRICE	MATERIAL	LABOR	MATERIAL	LABOR	COST
PRODUCT LINE A						
Model 4A	$ 7.63	$2.90	$ .81	38.0%	10.6%	48.6%
Model 4H	9.79	2.80	1.00	28.6	10.2	38.8
Model 5A	6.99	2.52	.92	26.1	13.2	49.3
Model 5K	8.92	2.75	.99	30.8	11.1	41.9
PRODUCT LINE B						
#44589	12.99	4.41	1.37	33.9	10.5	44.5
#56894	13.99	4.92	1.51	35.2	10.7	45.9
#67875	15.65	5.16	1.70	33.0	10.8	43.8
PRODUCT LINE C						
A-657	19.05	7.36	1.61	38.6	8.5	47.1
A-789	12.99	7.05	.71	54.2	5.5	59.7
B-456	18.65	9.02	1.15	48.3	6.2	54.5
PRODUCT LINE D						
E-8981	14.40	3.18	1.21	22.1	8.4	30.5
E-9905	16.19	3.23	1.16	20.0	7.2	27.2
J-4450	16.70	3.65	1.31	21.9	7.8	29.7
L-5430	17.60	4.62	1.40	26.3	8.0	34.3
PRODUCT LINE E						
IL-67	16.95	4.18	1.34	24.6	7.9	32.5
LE-135	16.49	7.95	.68	48.2	4.1	52.3
MO-035	19.26	5.48	1.41	28.5	7.3	35.8
MO-046	13.64	3.91	1.35	28.7	9.9	38.6

EXHIBIT 1:
PRODUCT PROFITABILITY REPORT

Findings	Recommendations

COST ESTIMATING

In preparing cost estimates for arriving at desired selling prices, we found that the same percentage markup is applied when the product has a high material content as is applied when the material content is low. For that reason, the company finds that it cannot compete in products that have a high material content. Conversely, it is possible that products with low material content are undercosted.

Profits are normally based on converting. While some return should be expected for the investment and handling of material, the markup would normally be different for material than for the conversion cost. We recommend that a study be made to determine proper markup percentages.

OVERHEAD RATES

Although individual overhead rates are available for each of the thirty-two departments, this does not result in accurate costing. A number of these departments are a mixture of labor intensive and capital intensive operations which are not used in the same proportion by all products passing through the department.

Overhead rates should be developed for the process rather than for the department.

STANDARDS

In developing standards for labor, a blanket allowance is applied equally to all operations. This does not provide for certain differences in job difficulty such as heat and fumes.

Instead of overall blanket allowances, individual allowances should be assigned by the type of process. The operation of loading and unloading a furnace at over 100° temperatures warrants a higher allowance than an operation performed in a well ventilated room, for example.

CONTROL OF INVENTORIES

Because of certain weaknesses in the control of inventories, which are listed below, we feel there is danger of a physical to book discrepancy.

Findings	Recommendations
Paperwork Controls	
Documents on which issues and transfers are reported to Production Control are not being controlled.	All documents should be prenumbered and missing numbers accounted for. Submission of batches of documents should be controlled by numbering the batches sequentially.
Tie-in of Cost System to Production Control	
The cost system does not follow the same physical accountability for inventory that is used by Production Control. Instead of segregating inventories on the books into raw material, work-in-process, and finished goods, only one inventory account is maintained.	The single inventory account should be broken into three major segments. Transactions affecting Work-in-Process should recognize two separate inventories: • Components stockroom • Floor inventory Transfers into the stockroom should be based on good components accepted into stock. This will eliminate the dependency on accurate scrap reporting. Floor inventory should be valued by using the open balances of physical quantities shown on the shop orders maintained by the Production Control Department.
Physical Controls	
Shipping areas are not fenced in. This allows easy access to areas in which finished products are available.	The shipping area should be fenced in. The gate should be kept shut except when a truck is being loaded. The same rules of access and egress should be applied at this point as in the stockrooms.
Customer Returns	
Returns from customers are not being properly controlled. We found instances in which items returned by customers were disassembled and the salvaged parts moved into the components stockroom. However, the difference between the total value of the returned goods and the value of salvaged items was not removed from the finished value.	Returned goods should be accounted for in a separate inventory. When items are moved out for disassembly, the entire value should be taken out of the inventory. Then, if any components are salvaged, the salvage value should be added to the components stock.

Findings	Recommendations

DATA PROCESSING SUPPORT

We found instances in which reports that had been computerized caused more work rather than less. As examples:

- In five price lists that were computerized, three different formats were used.

Price lists should be prepared in a standardized format to facilitate speed in quoting prices. The standardized format also mimimizes errors.

- Certain discount calculations that appeared on the previous lists were eliminated in the computerized version.

In computerizing, there should be no loss of information.

Written procedures are not being updated when computerization takes place. Illustrative of this is a breakdown in communications between the payroll and personnel functions, when new and recalled employees are to be added to the payroll.

Procedures in all departments in which paperwork has been automated should be reviewed. The work of the data processing department should not be considered complete until this has been done.

Certain reports, particularly operator efficiencies, are so overly detailed that foremen ignore them.

Reports should be summarized on an exception basis to facilitate review through highlighting of unusual performance.

OPERATING CONTROLS

QUALITY CONTROL

Scrap and rejects are too high because:

- Inspectors are not catching rejects soon enough in the process.
- Vendor quality is poor.

The following steps must be taken to improve product quality through reduction of the number of rejects:

- Require inspectors to show an identifying mark on each item that has been inspected. This will pin down responsibility.
- Eliminate the present haphazard approach to inspection of incoming material. Establish definite procedures using statistical sampling techniques.

Findings	Recommendations

QUALITY CONTROL (continued)

Findings	Recommendations
Process controls are weak.	Hire a senior quality control engineer with the specific assignment of: • Writing procedures for controlling the processes. • Training personnel in the application of these procedures. • Monitoring compliance.

PURCHASING

Findings	Recommendations
One-third of the parts that we sampled were purchased more than three times a year, yet they were not being included in blanket orders.	Encourage the use of blanket orders for high-volume purchases.
Although many of the items purchased outside could also be made in-house, there is no make-versus-buy procedure to evaluate the economics of making purchases outside.	Establish a make-versus-buy committee headed by the manager of purchasing. Before buying on the outside, consideration should be given as to which items are best made within the plant and which are best purchased on the outside.
Material purchases are compared with the standard material prices only.	Buying performance should be measured against the previous prices paid as well as the standard purchase price.
Vendor performance on price and delivery not furnished to the vendor.	Vendor performance ratings should be continually monitored. This information should be reported to the vendors.

METHODS

Findings	Recommendations
The assembly processes are conveyorized. However, some of the products are hand loaded on carts and wheeled to the packaging area rather than being transported on the conveyorized line.	Extend the conveyor line to the packaging area to eliminate wasteful hand loading and carting.

LAYOUT

Findings	Recommendations
Present layout is inefficient because of overcrowding.	Part of the new addition presently being constructed for warehousing purposes and office space should be used for production to permit a more efficient layout.

Findings	Recommendations

MANUFACTURING ENGINEERING

There is no program to system-
atically review and update standards.

A program of review should be
implemented.

NEW PRODUCT DEVELOPMENT

The quality control department is
not furnished with operating specifications for new products. This leaves
the task of writing such specifications
to personnel in the quality control
department.

The new product development
group which designs new products
should be held responsible for writing operating specifications for all
products turned over to production.

   The foregoing represent the highlights of our findings and recommendations—the detail information is contained in Sections II and III of this
report.

Very truly yours,

ERNST & WHINNEY

[1] Sections I, II, and III can be found in *Controller's Handbook* edited by Sam R.
Goodman and James S. Reece. (Homewood, IL: Dow Jones-Irwin, 1978). See Chapter 37
authored by Thomas S. Dudick.

Index